VINCENT Van Gogh

A Life in Letters & Art

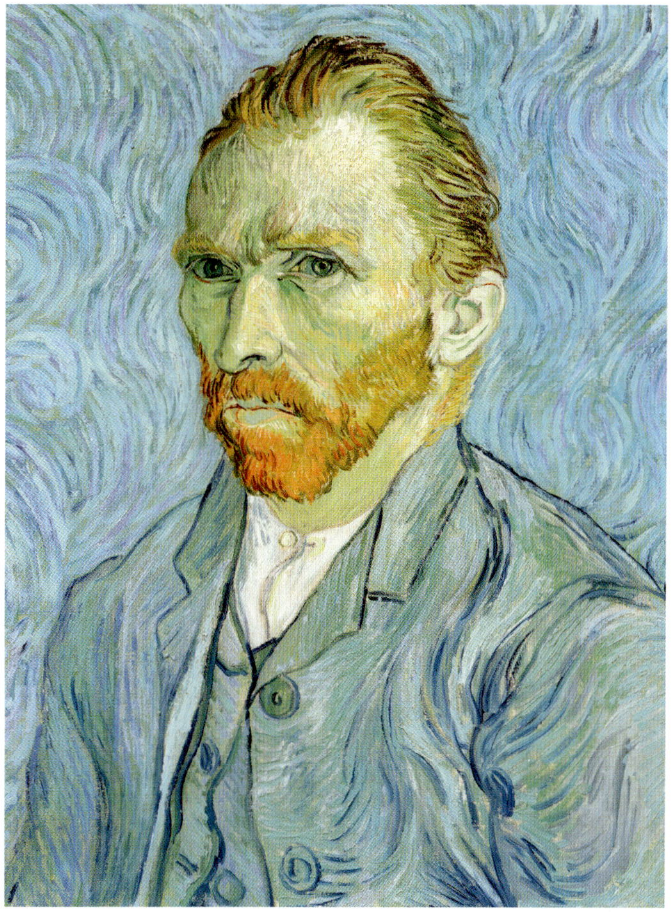

Publisher and Creative Director: Nick Wells
Project Editor and Picture Research: Chelsea Edwards
Art Director: Mike Spender
Digital Design and Production: Chris Herbert
Copy-editor: Anna Groves
Proofreader: Helen Tovey
Indexer: Penny Brown

Special thanks to: Stephen Feather, Digby Smith and Catherine Taylor

This edition first published 2011 by
FLAME TREE PUBLISHING
Crabtree Hall, Crabtree Lane
Fulham, London SW6 6TY
United Kingdom

www.flametreepublishing.com

11 13 15 14 12

1 3 5 7 9 10 8 6 4 2

Flame Tree is part of The Foundry Creative Media Company Limited

A CIP record for this book is available from the British Library.

ISBN: 978-1-84786-992-0
Special ISBN: 978-0-6815-4417-8

PUBLISHER'S NOTE

All illustrations are by Vincent van Gogh (1853–90), unless otherwise stated.
All letters are written from Vincent van Gogh to his brother, Theo van Gogh (1857–91), unless otherwise stated.

CREDITS

All letter illustrations are courtesy of the Van Gogh Museum Amsterdam (Vincent van Gogh Foundation).
Letter of 24 July 1875: 17; Letter of mid-September 1881: 3, 46; Letter of 5 or 6 August 1882: 64; Letter of 1 October 1882: 75; Letter of *c.* 20 May 1888: 127; Letter of 5 June 1890: 176.
The majority of the translations used in this book come from the work of Johanna van Gogh-Bonger. The remaining translations are the work of Robert Harrison, and are copyright © 2011 WebExhibits. All rights reserved.

ROSALIND ORMISTON (author)

Rosalind Ormiston is a lecturer at Kingston University, Surrey, where she teaches History of Art, Design and Architecture. Her specialist subjects include Classical Civilization, Renaissance Italy and Contemporary Architecture. She has lived in New York and Piedmont, Italy, and now divides her time between London, Cumbria and Italy. She writes features for both academic journals and consumer publications. She is currently researching Cumbrian architectural practice in the mid–late nineteenth century.

Printed in China

VINCENT Van Gogh

A Life in Letters & Art

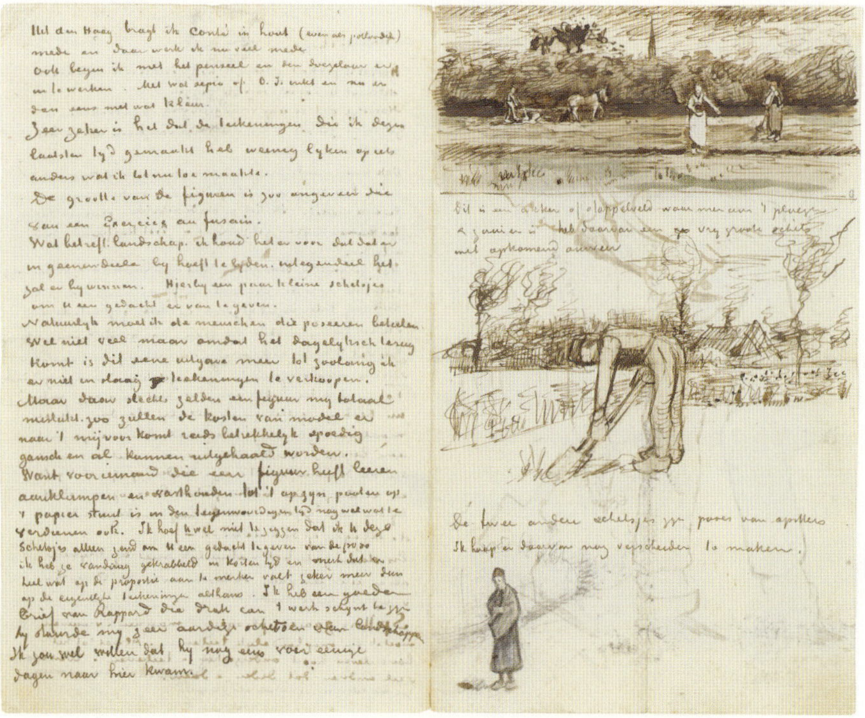

by Rosalind Ormiston

FLAME TREE
PUBLISHING

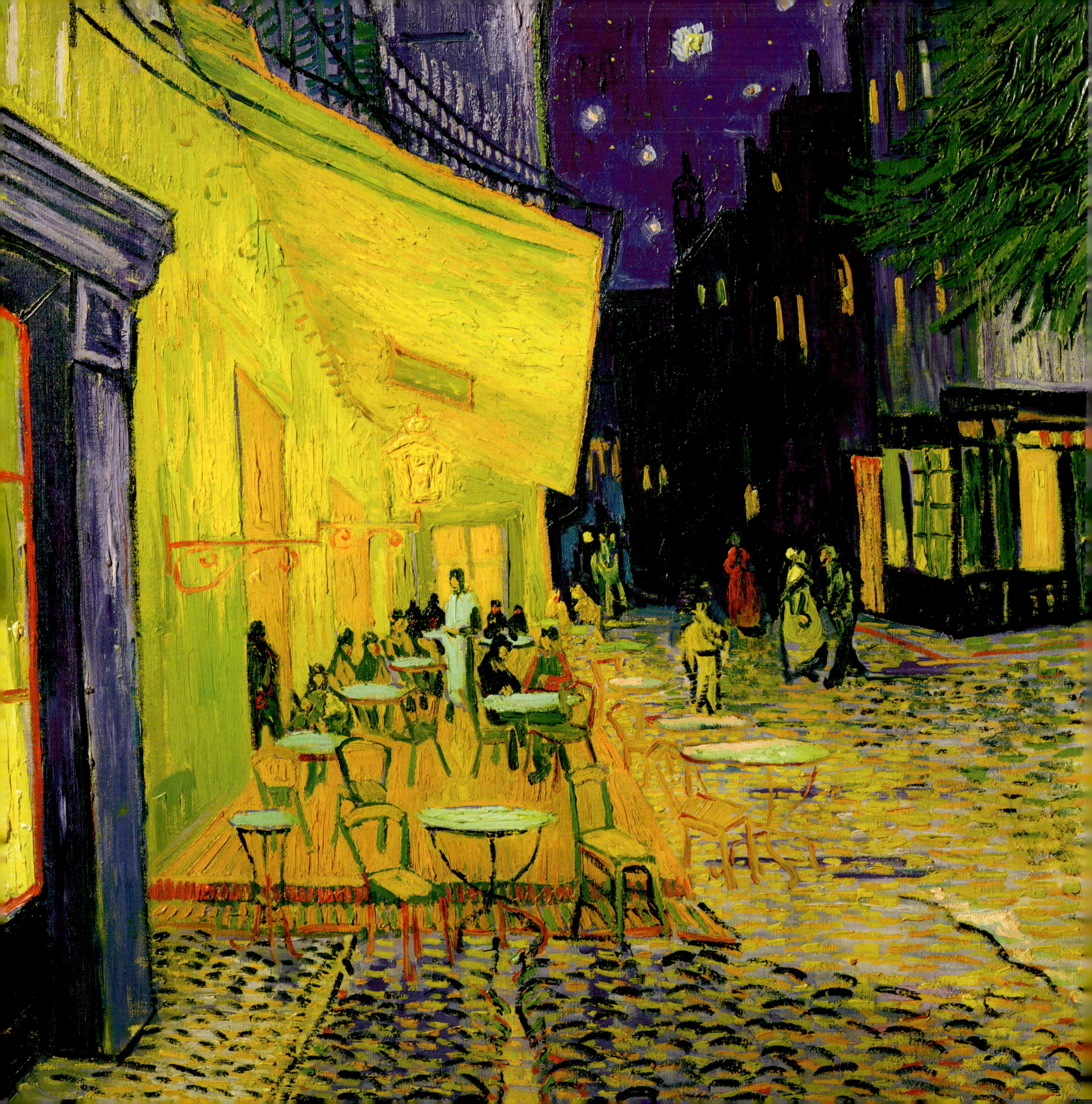

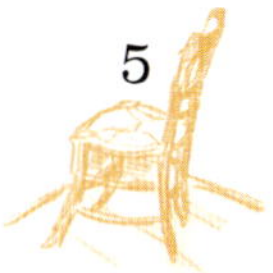

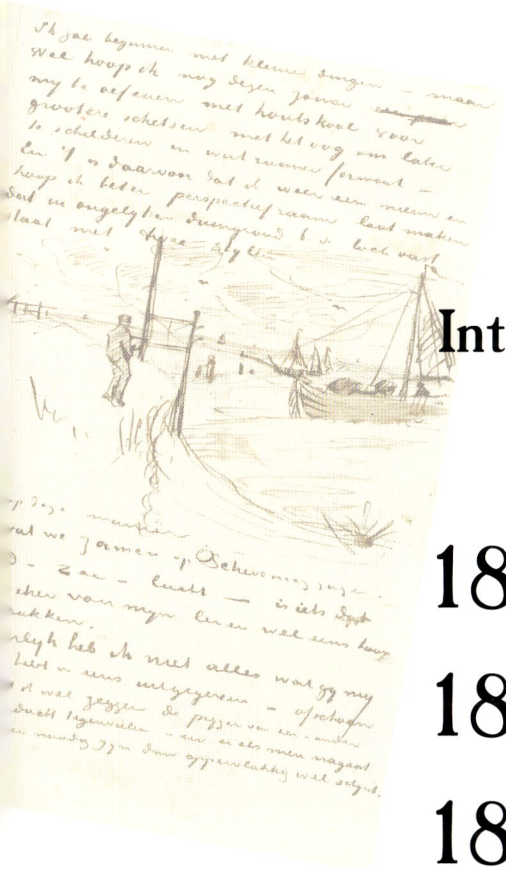

Contents

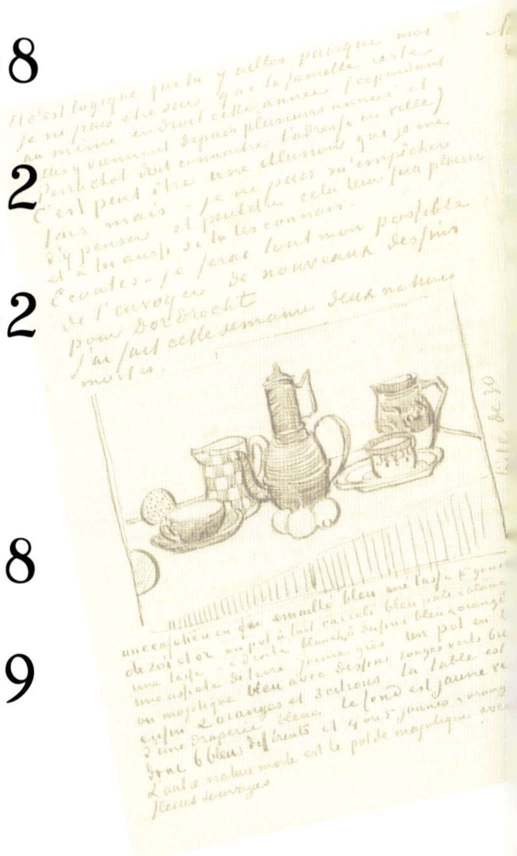

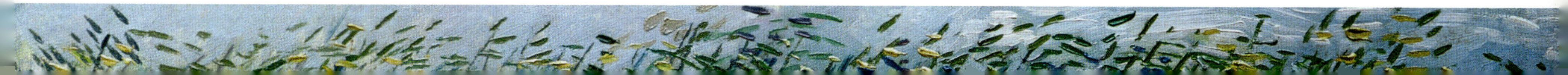

Introduction

'I am so glad that both of us are now to be in the same profession and in the same firm. We must be sure to write to each other regularly.' So begins Vincent van Gogh's letter to his brother Theo, written from The Hague, on 13 December 1872, one of hundreds upon hundreds of letters the pair would exchange over an 18-year period. Vincent was delighted that he would be in regular contact with his younger brother. The letter coincided with Theo's first job working for the art dealers Goupil & Cie, in The Hague, the same company that Vincent had joined in 1869.

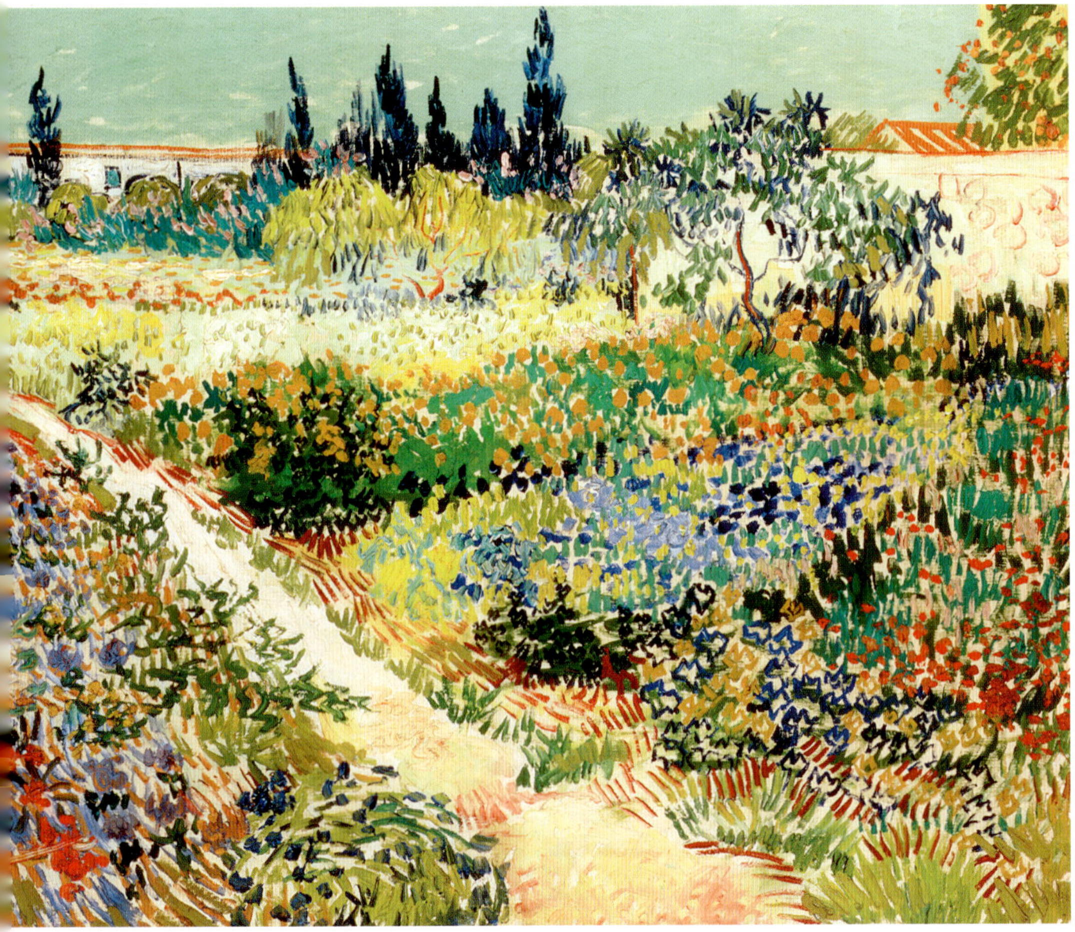

Vincent van Gogh (1853–90) was born on 30 March 1853, to Anna Cornelia van Gogh, née Carbentus (1819–1907), one year to the day after her first son was stillborn. Anna and her husband Theodorus van Gogh (1822–85) gave the new baby the name of his dead brother, Vincent Willem van Gogh. More children followed, two boys and three girls: Anna Cornelia (1855–1930) and Theo (1857–91), named after their parents, and Elisabeth (Lies) Huberta (1859–1936), Willemina (Wil) Jacoba (1862–1941) and Cornelis (Cor) Vincent (1867–1900). The family lived in Groot Zundert, a town in southern Holland, where Theodorus was a pastor of the Dutch Reformed Church. At school Vincent learnt English, French and German. As a boy he was sometimes singled out by fellow pupils for his unusual looks: bright red hair and greenish-blue eyes. He was known for his surly manner, which could become aggressive. Vincent recorded his own recollection of those years, 'my youth was gloomy and cold and sterile'.

Vincent had access to artworks from an early age. Three of his uncles were successful art dealers and one was a sculptor. Taking an interest in Vincent's prospective career, his Uncle Cent, an art collector and partner in the art house Goupil & Cie, arranged for him to work for the company. Vincent began working in The Hague, before moving to company branches in Paris and London. After a failed love affair in London he transferred to Paris. He was employed for nearly six years, a period that taught him much about art, artists and art techniques. A favourite artist was Rembrandt van Rijn (1606–69). Leaving the company in January 1876, for reasons never clearly explained, Vincent travelled to England in April the same year, becoming an assistant teacher at a school in Ramsgate. By July he had joined a Methodist church in Isleworth as a lay preacher. He returned to his family home in Etten and by July 1878 Vincent was working as an evangelical preacher, determined to succeed but failing to make it his vocation. Two years later he discovered his real ambition, to be an artist.

Vincent's life, particularly his aspiration to succeed as a painter, is laid out in his letters. A total of 819 letters written by Vincent van Gogh and 83 letters written to him have survived in collections. There may be as many as 2,000 if one takes into account his references to documentation and notes and letters sent by him. These are yet to be discovered, are lost or known to be destroyed. Letters from his parents have not survived. Of the letters sent to him many have perished due to Vincent having regular clear-outs of his possessions. For the reader, Vincent's letters add insight to the life he led before he became a professional artist and during his highly creative 10-year period of painting, reproducing his life in letters and art.

As a gifted letter-writer and erudite thinker, who tried to work out his problems on the page with the help of his brother, his letters reveal the very real and intimate details of Vincent's world: his aspirations, his elations, doubts, troubles and determination to overcome obstacles that threatened both his personal relationships and his ambitions as an artist. The letters that remain from his period as a painter are devoted to the discussion of painting techniques, particularly his colour palette and use of it. In letter after letter he describes not only the scene he is painting but the reasons for his choice of colours, enumerating colours such as 'sand red', 'violet', 'dark, dark, dark blue' and 'citrus yellow'. These were the vibrant colours that expressed his thoughts, the colours he could see in the landscape of gardens and parks in the city, in the countryside on train journeys, in the wheat fields around Auvers. Vincent came to life, in the best and worst of times, through his art. The tubes of paint, the pots of paint brushes and the steady supply of canvases were paid for out of Theo's salary, sent in small and large amounts during the 10-year development of Vincent's career as an artist in Antwerp, Arles, Saint-Rémy and Auvers-sur-Oise.

Vincent's output of artworks over 10 years was nearly as prolific as his letter writing, estimated at around 2,000 works – 1,100 drawings and sketches and close to 900 paintings. In the months spent in Auvers, Vincent produced 78 paintings and 30 drawings, a prodigious output for a man whose health was fragile. The canvases, apart from those painted for his family

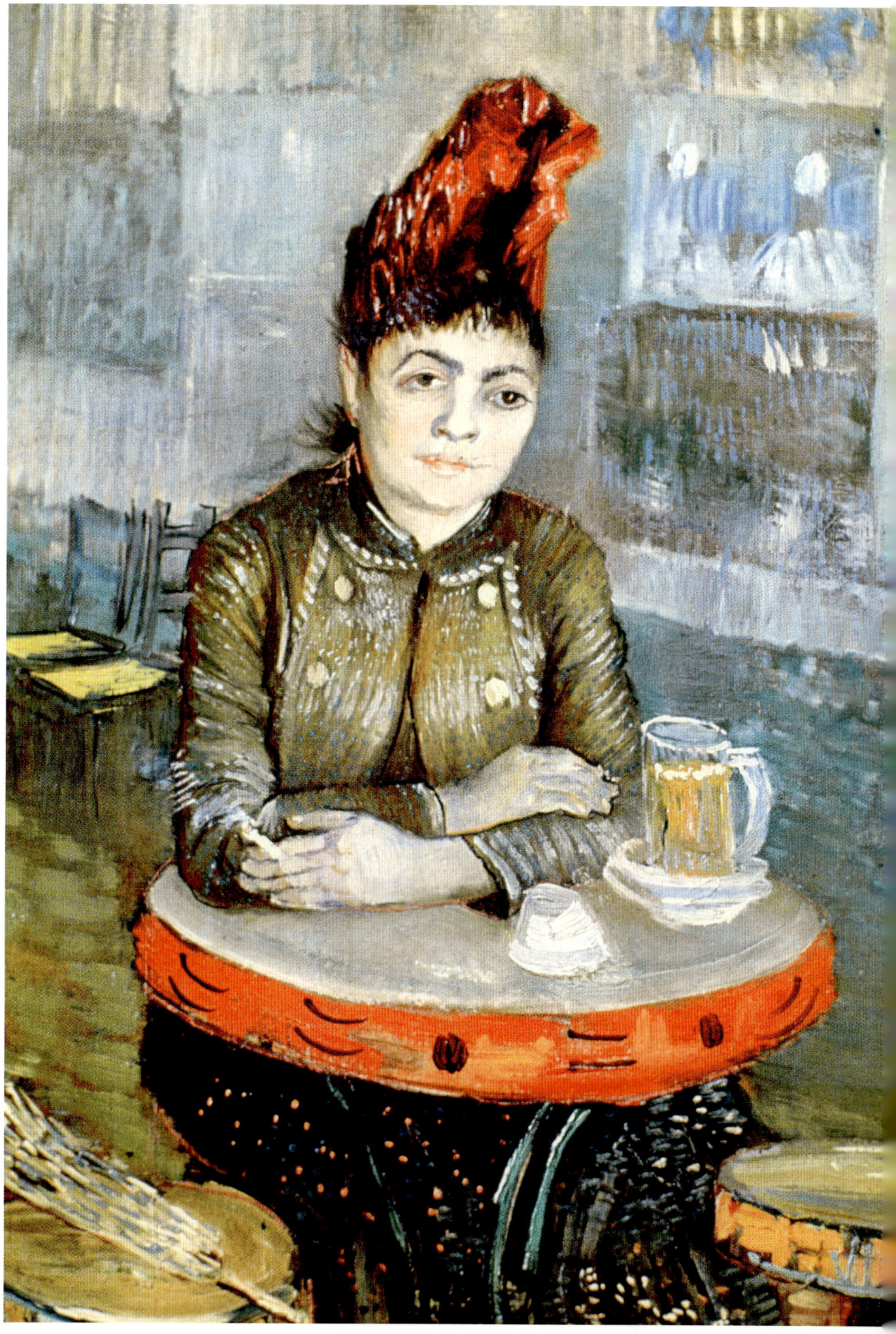

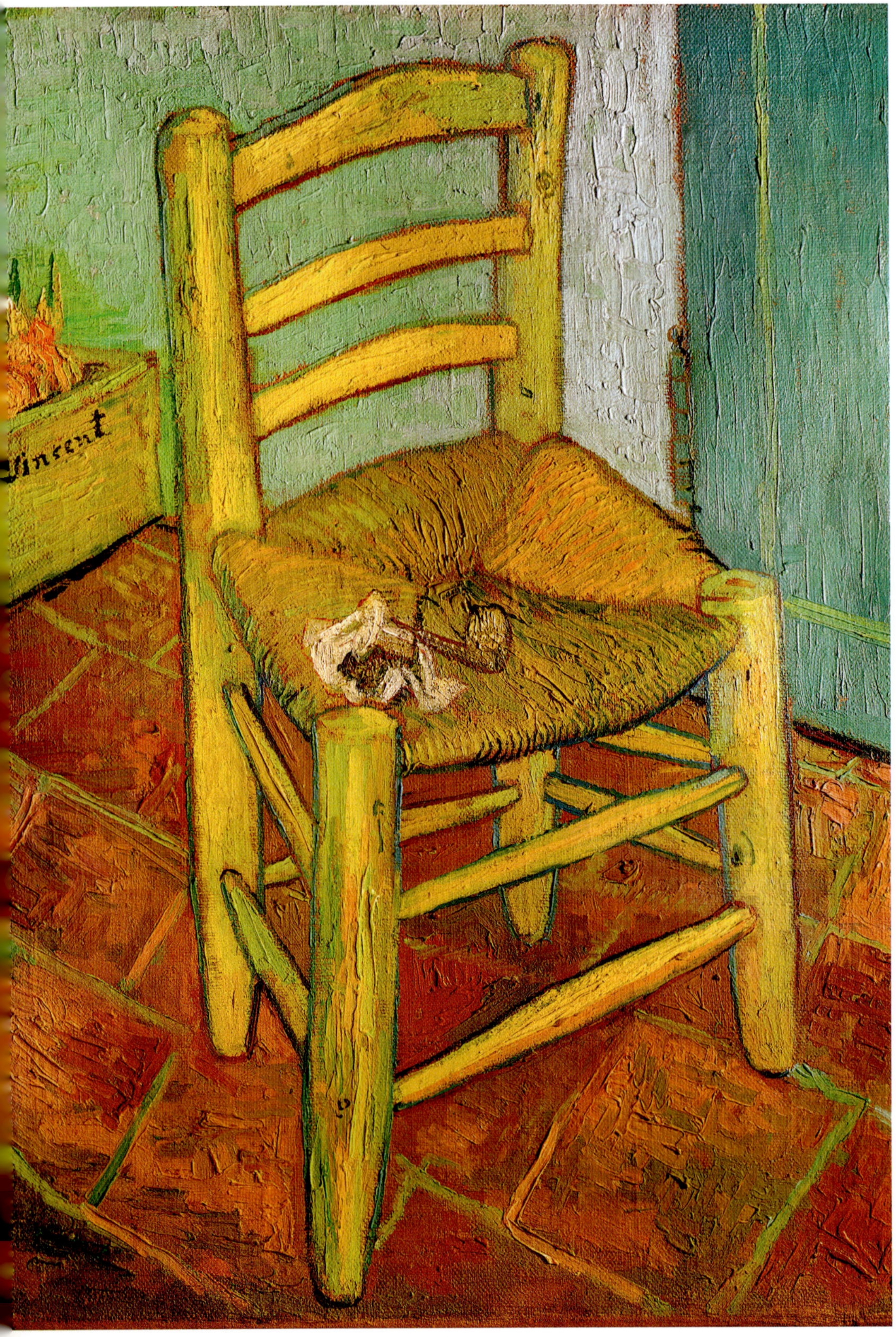

and friends or used to settle a bill, were sent to Theo, in trust that they would be exhibited and sold. Theo did his best. The sale of one painting is recorded. *The Red Vineyard*, 1888 exhibited at the annual *Les Vingtes* exhibition in Brussels and was bought by Anna Boch (1848–1936), a Belgian Impressionist painter, who purchased it for the sum of 400 francs.

Letters written in later years reveal Vincent's increasing reliance on Theo, not only for money but also to help see him through his debilitating illness. This was diagnosed in 1889 and today is thought to have been a form of epilepsy. Throughout, it was Theo who spoke to Vincent's doctors and made the plans for his move from the asylum in Arles to the asylum in Saint-Rémy, and on again into the care of Dr Gachet in Auvers-sur-Oise, north-west of Paris, moving Vincent closer to him. The constant support Theo gave his brother probably affected his own health. On a visit to Theo and his wife Jo (Johanna van Gogh Bonger, 1862–1925) in July 1890, Vincent noticed how ill his brother had become. Historians debate that it was this visit that led to Vincent's realization that he, after so many years of passing on his problems to Theo and using him to fund his life as a painter, had left his brother near dead. Soon after the visit Vincent took a gun and walked into the fields near his home in Auvers, shooting himself in the chest. He did not die but struggled back to his home. Theo was called and came immediately to stay with his brother during the last night and day of his life. Vincent died on 29 July 1890. Six months after Vincent's death Theo died after suffering a physical and mental collapse. It was left to Theo's wife Jo to gather up the brothers' correspondence and Vincent's artworks, and she devoted her life to keeping the names of Vincent and Theo van Gogh uppermost in the minds of the art world.

Readers unfamiliar with Vincent's letters can look forward to sharing his discoveries, learning about his reading habits, his views on Old Masters and the new Impressionists, and gleaning abundant observations on the techniques of painting and drawing. His letters follow his journeys to the places he visited, the houses he lived in and the people he met. Moreover, one can sit with him, sharing the intimate corners of shady gardens where he drew and painted on a daily basis. The letters add to our knowledge of his art, revealing the artist as much as embellishing the landscapes of his life. The contents of letters to Theo and to friends and family allow one to look beyond the canvas, to read the artist's thoughts, fears and aspirations. His letters give clearer understanding of his views on life and fill in the details such as the books he read and the painters he admired. The majority of his letters were written to his loving brother Theo, who responded in kind. Vincent's desire to engage the interest of the recipient of his letters is clear, particularly when writing to Theo; many of the letters are affectionately signed 'Your loving brother, Vincent'.

The sudden death of Vincent on 29 July 1890 and soon after his brother Theo on 25 January 1891 left Johanna van Gogh Bonger with Vincent's catalogue of canvases and the vast collection of his letters. From that moment she worked tirelessly to bring Vincent's art to a wider public, through exhibitions in Europe. She annotated his letters with the plan to publish them after Vincent's art gained recognition. In 1914 three volumes of letters were published, allowing readers a private glimpse into Vincent's life, in letters and art.

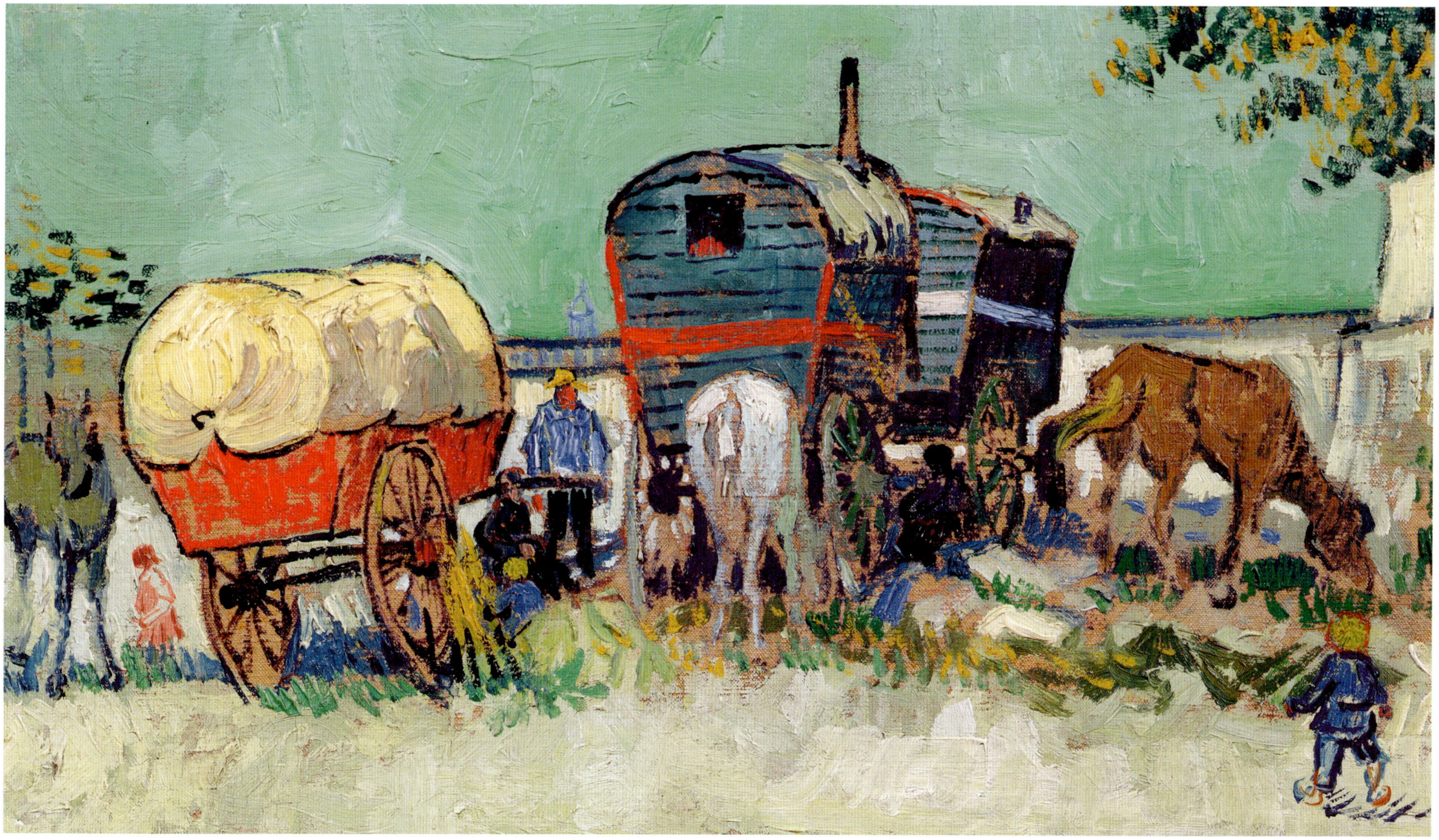

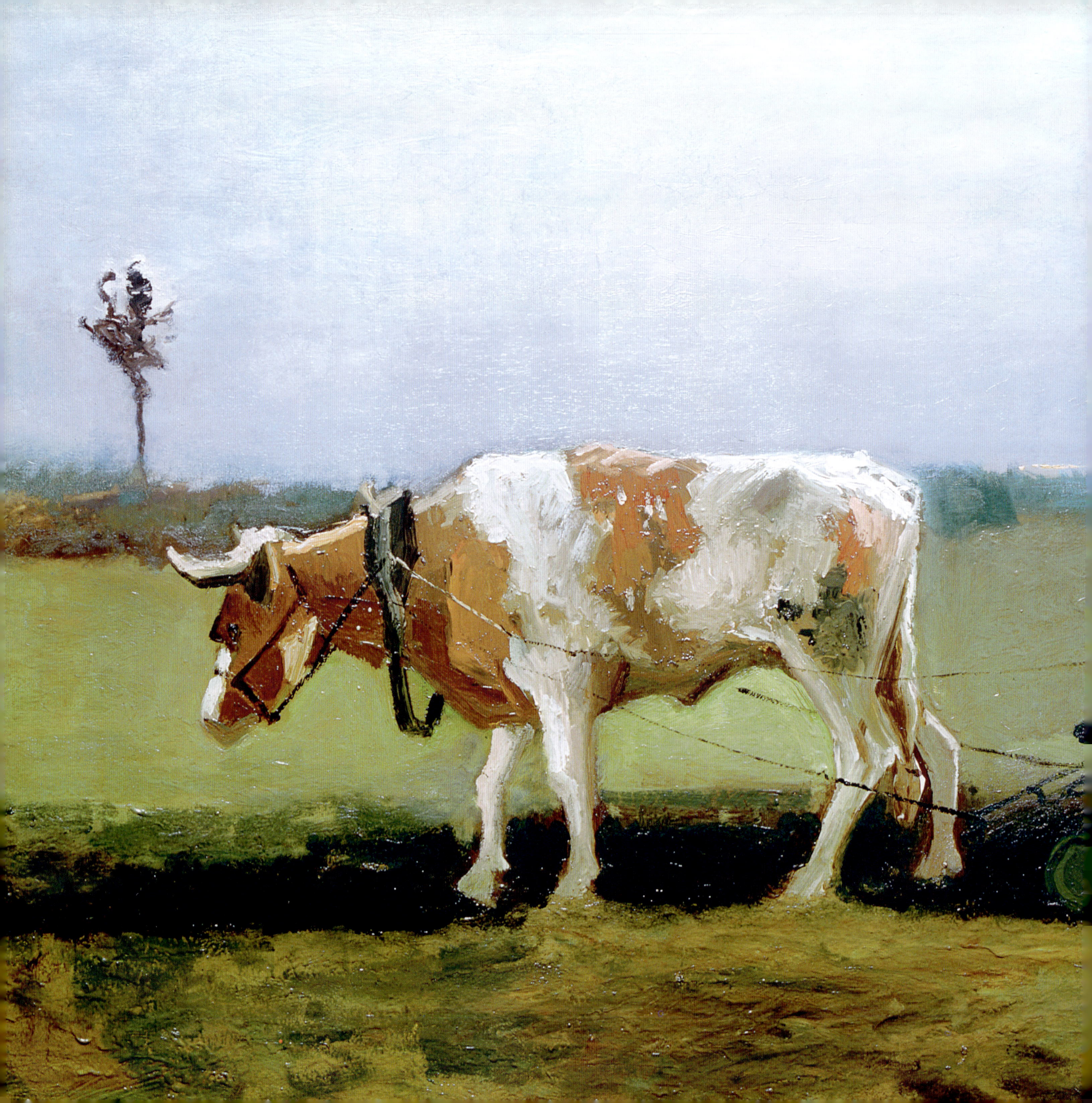

Vincent van Gogh: A Life in Letters & Art

1872–80

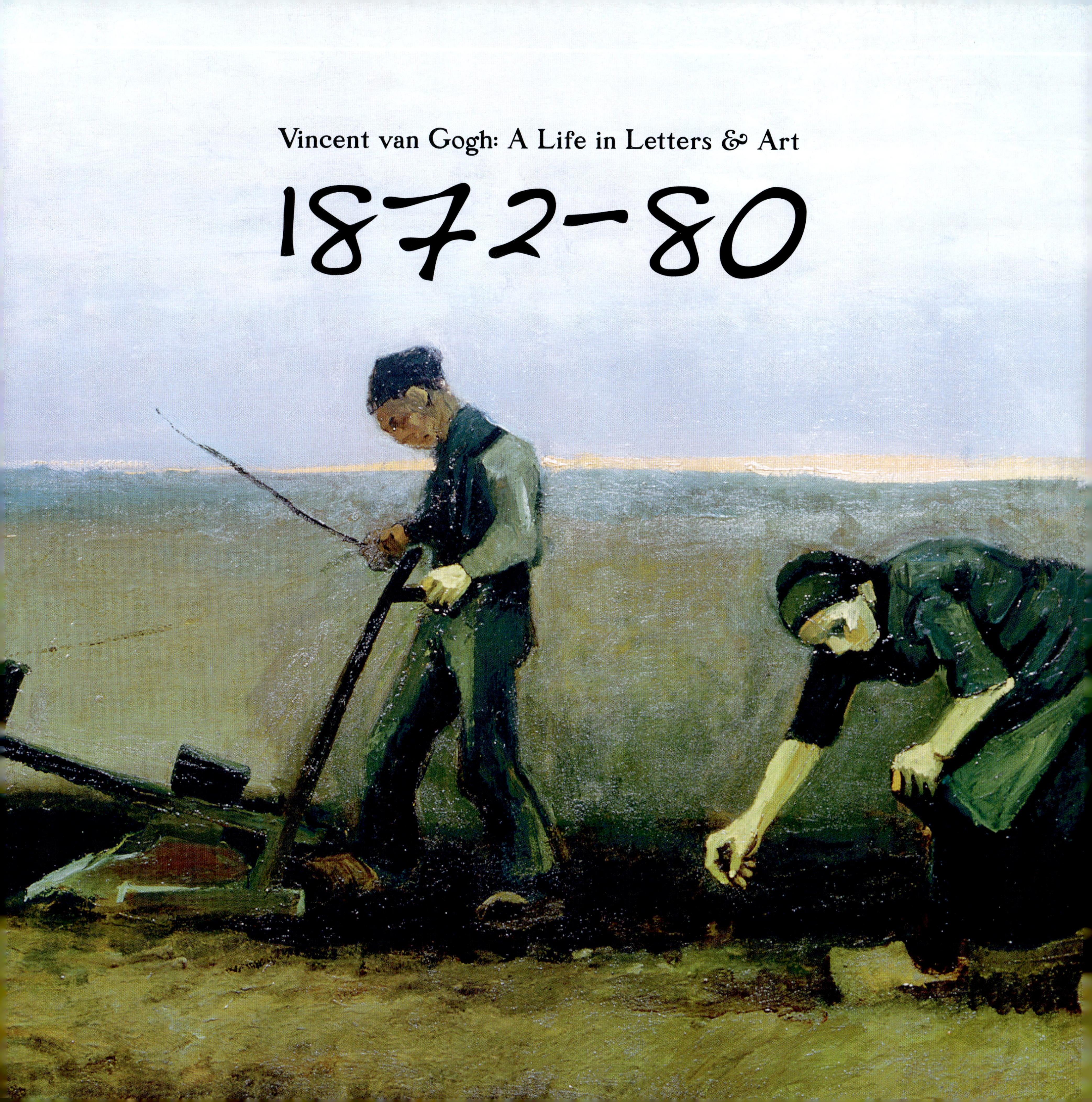

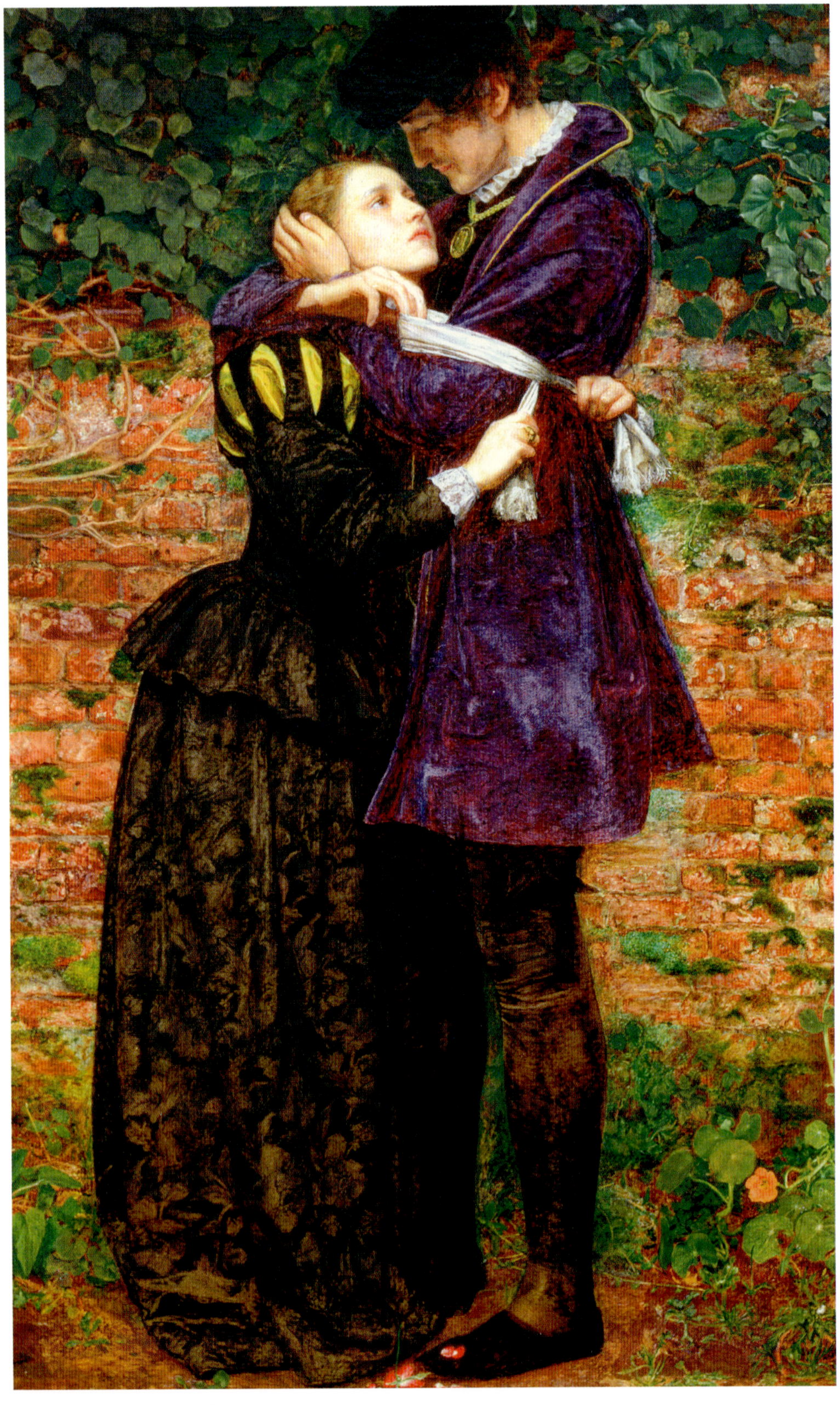

From Vincent van Gogh to
Theo van Gogh
Extract from
The Hague, *13 December 1872*

Dear Theo,

What good news I've just read in Father's letter. I wish you luck with all my heart. I'm sure you will like it there, it's such a fine firm. It will be quite a change for you.
I am so glad that both of us are now to be in the same profession and in the same firm.
We must be sure to write to each other regularly. [...]

Theo had just been employed by the art dealers Goupil & Cie, where Vincent also worked. They would now have new common interests, working in the same profession. It is from this time that Theo and Vincent became regular correspondents.

Extract from
London, *20 July 1873*

[...] At first English art did not appeal to me; one must get used to it. But there are clever painters here, among others, Millais, who has painted: 'The Huguenot', 'Ophelia', etc., of which I think you know the engravings; his things are beautiful. Then

The Huguenot, 1851–52, (detail)
by Sir John Everett Millais (1829–96)
MEDIUM: Oil on canvas
© The Makins Collection/
The Bridgeman Art Library

Ophelia, 1851–52
by Sir John Everett Millais (1829–96)
MEDIUM: Watercolour on paper
Courtesy of Private Collection/Photo
© Peter Nahum at The Leicester Galleries, London/The Bridgeman Art Library

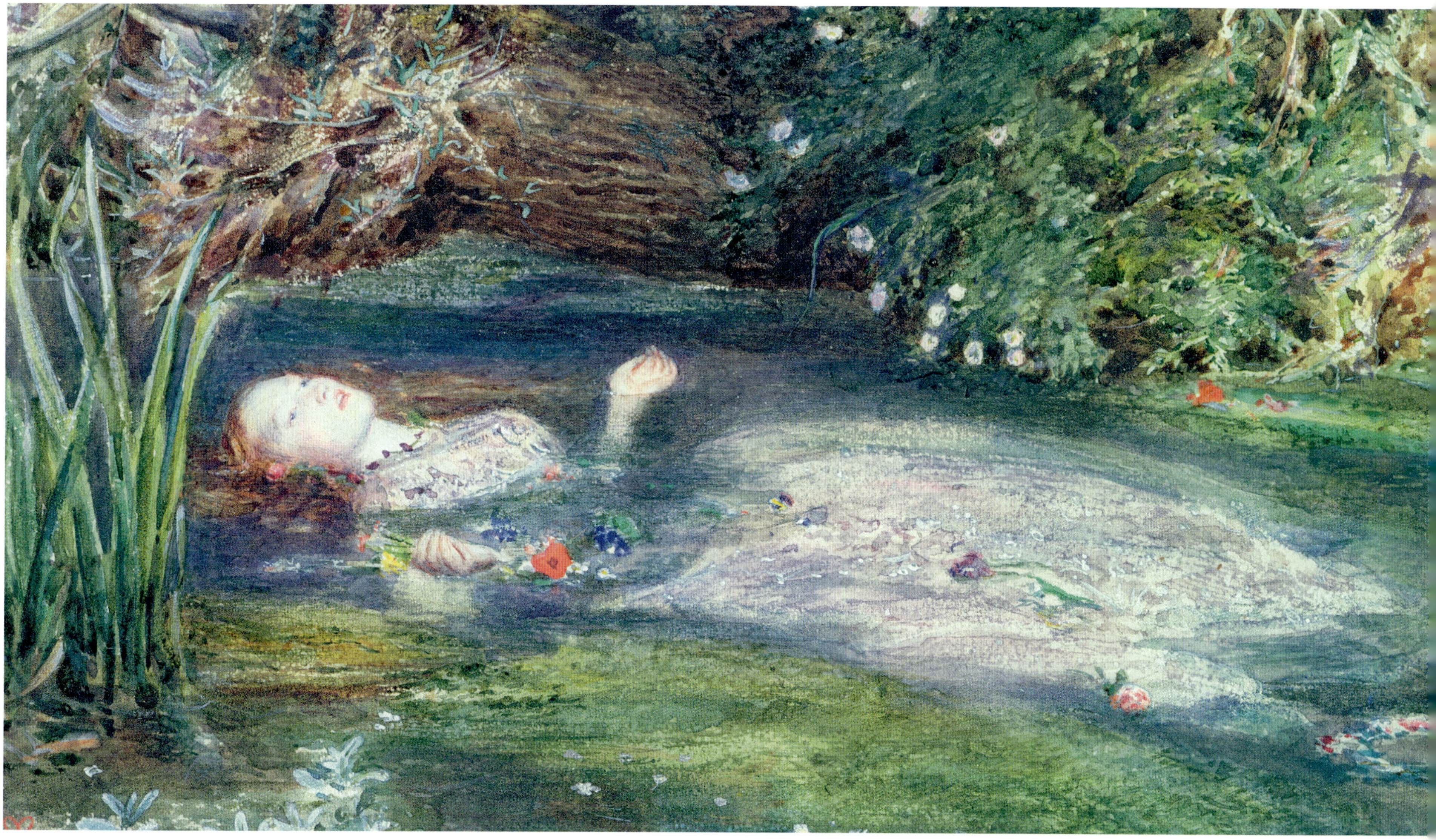

there is Boughton, whose 'Puritans Going to Church' is in our Galerie Photographique; I have seen wonderful things by him. Among the old painters, Constable was a landscape painter who lived about thirty years ago; he is splendid – his work reminds me of Diaz and Daubigny. Then there are Reynolds and Gainsborough, whose forte was very beautiful ladies' portraits, and Turner, whose engravings you must have seen. [...] "

Vincent writes to Theo, pleased that his brother has settled in to his new job and accommodation. He takes the opportunity to discuss English art, admitting that it does not appeal to him.

He gives praise to one of the founders of the Pre-Raphaelite Brotherhood, the English painter John Everett Millais (1829–96), describing his work as 'beautiful' and singling out his paintings *Ophelia* (1851–52) and *The Huguenot* (1851–52). Another special mention is given to the Norfolk-born, Anglo-American painter George Henry Boughton (1833–1905) and his *Pilgrims Going to Church* (1867). Vincent also admires the art of two recently deceased English landscape painters, John Constable (1776–1837) and J.M.W. Turner (1775–1851), and the eighteenth-century portrait painters Sir Joshua Reynolds (1723–92) and Thomas Gainsborough (1727–88).

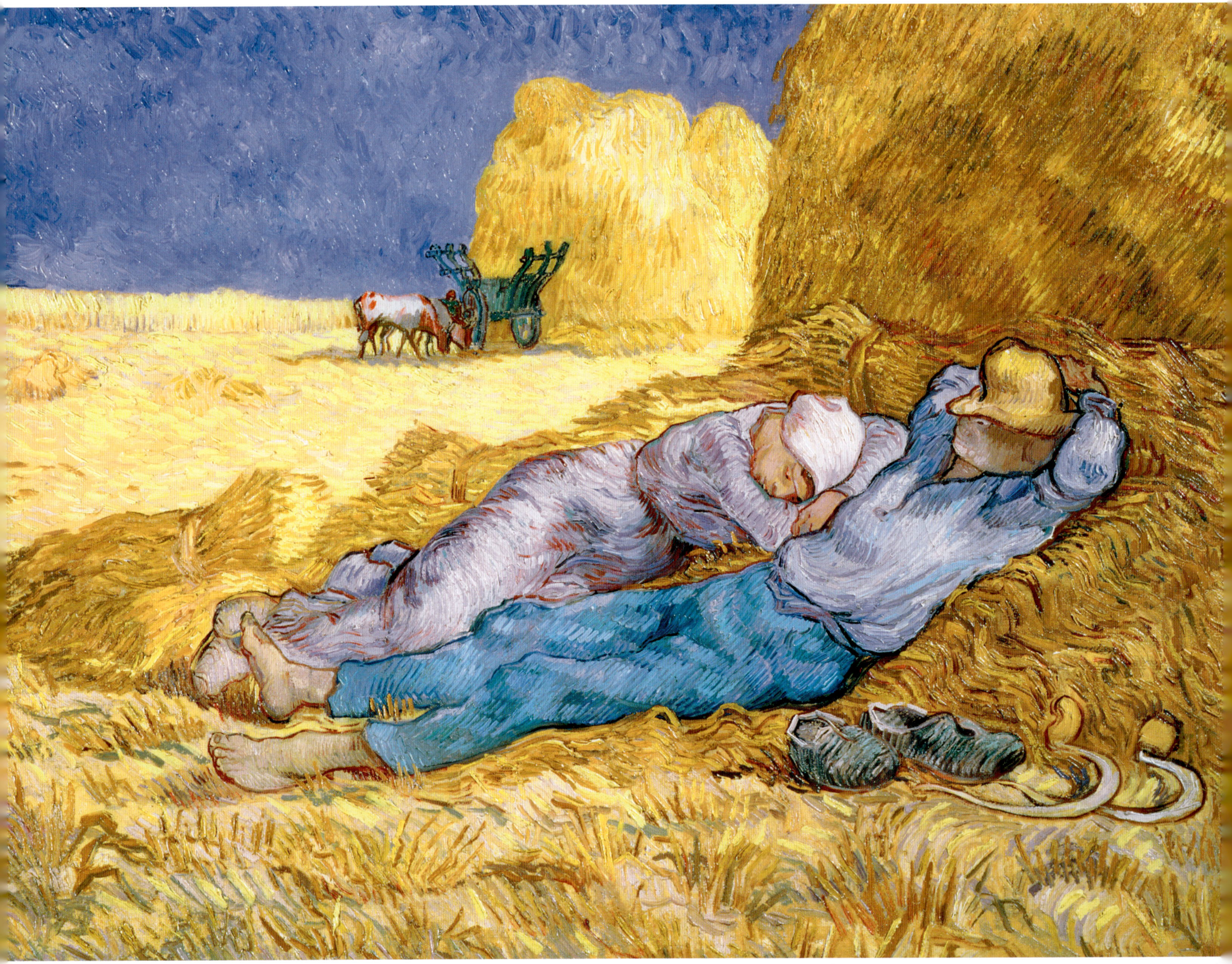

Extract from
London, *January 1874*

[…] I'm glad you like Millet, Jacque, Schreyer, Lambinet, Frans Hals, etc., for as Mauve says, 'That's it.' That painting by Millet, 'L'angélus du soir', 'that's it', indeed – that's magnificent, that's poetry. How I wish I could have another talk with you about art; but we'll just have to keep writing to each other about it. *Admire* as much as you can; most people *don't admire enough.*

Here are the names of a few of the painters I particularly like. Scheffer, Delaroche, Hébert, Hamon, Leys, Tissot, Lagye, Boughton, Millais, Thijs [Matthijs] Mans, De Groux, De Braekeleer Jr., Millet, Jules Breton, Feyen-Perrin, Eugène Feyen, Brion, Jundt, George Saal, Israëls, Anker, Knaus, Vautier, Jourdan, Jalabert, Antigna, Compte-Calix, Rochussen, Meissonier, Zamacois, Madrazo, Ziem, Boudin, Gérôme, Fromentin, de Tournemine, Pasini, Decamps, Bonington, Diaz, Th. Rousseau, Troyon, Dupré, Paul Huet, Corot, Jacque, Otto Weber, Daubigny, Wahlberg, Bernier, Émile Breton, Chenu, César de Cock, Mile. Collart, Bodmer, Koekkoek, Schelfhout, Weissenbruch, and last [but] not least, Maris and Mauve.

But I could carry on like that for I don't know how long, and then there are still all the old masters, and I am sure I have forgotten some of the best of the modern ones.
Do go on doing a lot of walking and keep up your love of nature, for that is the right way to understand art better and better. Painters understand nature and love her and *teach us to see.*

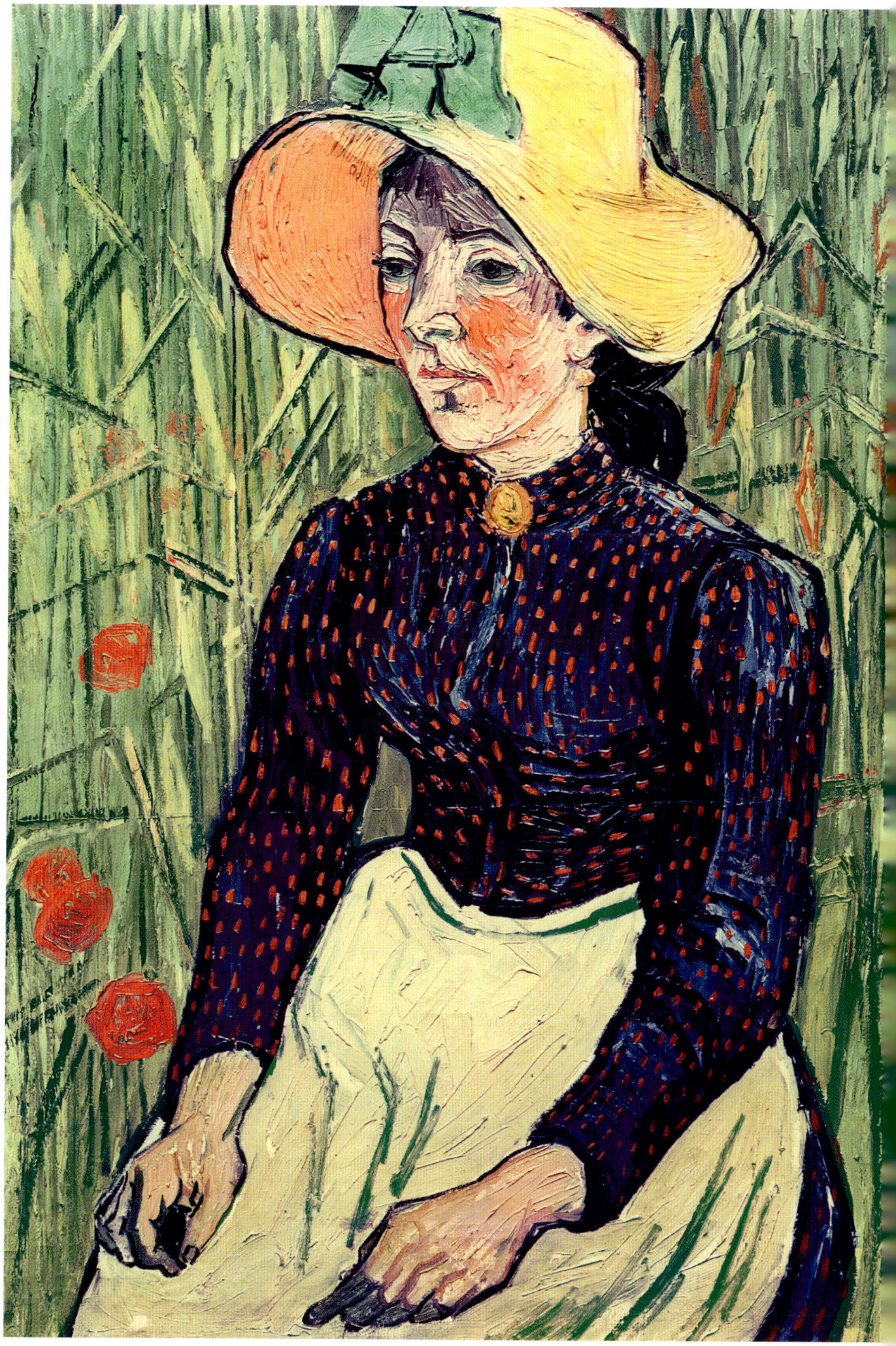

***The Siesta (after Millet)*, 1890, (detail)**
MEDIUM: Oil on canvas
Courtesy of Musée d'Orsay, Paris, France/Giraudon/The Bridgeman Art Library

***Young Peasant Girl in a Straw Hat Sitting in Front of a Wheatfield*, 1890**
MEDIUM: Oil on canvas
Courtesy of Private Collection/ The Bridgeman Art Library

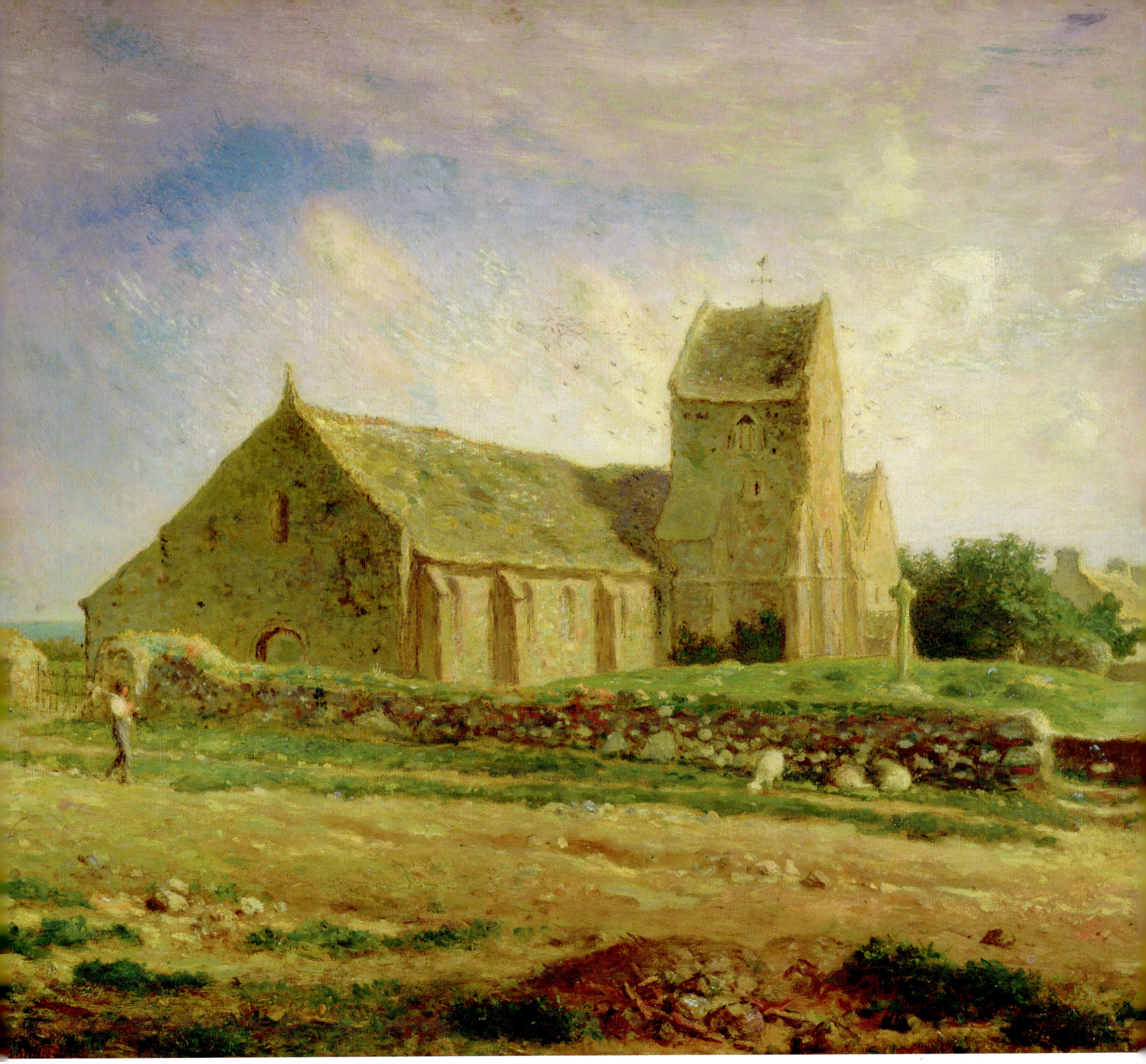

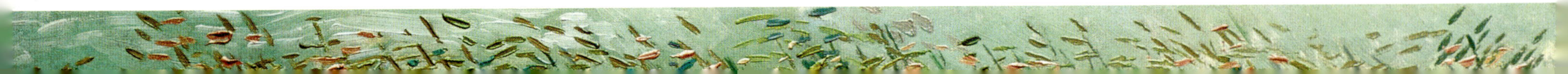

Vincent includes in his letter a long list of the artists he admires and is delighted that Theo responds positively to the works of '...Millet, Jacque, Schreyer, Lambinet, Frans Hals...'. Jean-François Millet's (1814–75) painting 'L'angélus du soir', or *The Angelus* (1857–59), was a painting that Vincent would use as a visual reference in his own drawings. The expression 'that's it' – in reference to a work of art that captures the essence of a portrayal – is made by their artist-cousin Anton Mauve (1838–88). The advice to Theo to do a lot of walking, to take in the surrounding landscape, 'to keep up your love of nature, for that is the right way to understand art better', was Vincent's own method by which he combined art and nature.

***The Church at Gréville*, c. 1871–74**
by Jean-François Millet (1814–75)
MEDIUM: Oil on canvas
Courtesy of Musée d'Orsay, Paris, France/Giraudon/The Bridgeman Art Library

Extract from
Paris, *29 June 1875*

I don't know whether I have already written to you about it or not, but there has been a sale here of drawings by Millet. When I entered the hall of the Hôtel Drouot, where they were exhibited, I felt like saying, 'Take off your shoes, for the place where you are standing is Holy Ground.'

You know that Millet lived at Gréville. Well, I do not know whether it was at Gréville or Granville that the man whom I told you of died. However this may be, I looked at Millet's drawings of 'The Rocks of Gréville' with extra care. There is now a picture of his at the Luxembourg, 'The Church at Gréville'. [...]

Vincent's deep admiration for the works of the French Realist painter Jean-Francois Millet, founder of the Barbizon School, is evident in this letter. Millet had died on 20 January 1875. It was from Millet's drawings and paintings that Vincent drew inspiration for his own art.

Extract from
Paris, *24 July 1875*

[...] A few days ago we [Goupil & Cie] received a picture by de Nittis, a view of London on a rainy day, Westminster bridge and the house of Parliament. I used to pass over Westminster bridge every morning and evening and know how it looks when the sun sets behind Westminster abbey and the house of Parliament, and how it looks early in the morning, and in winter in snow and fog.

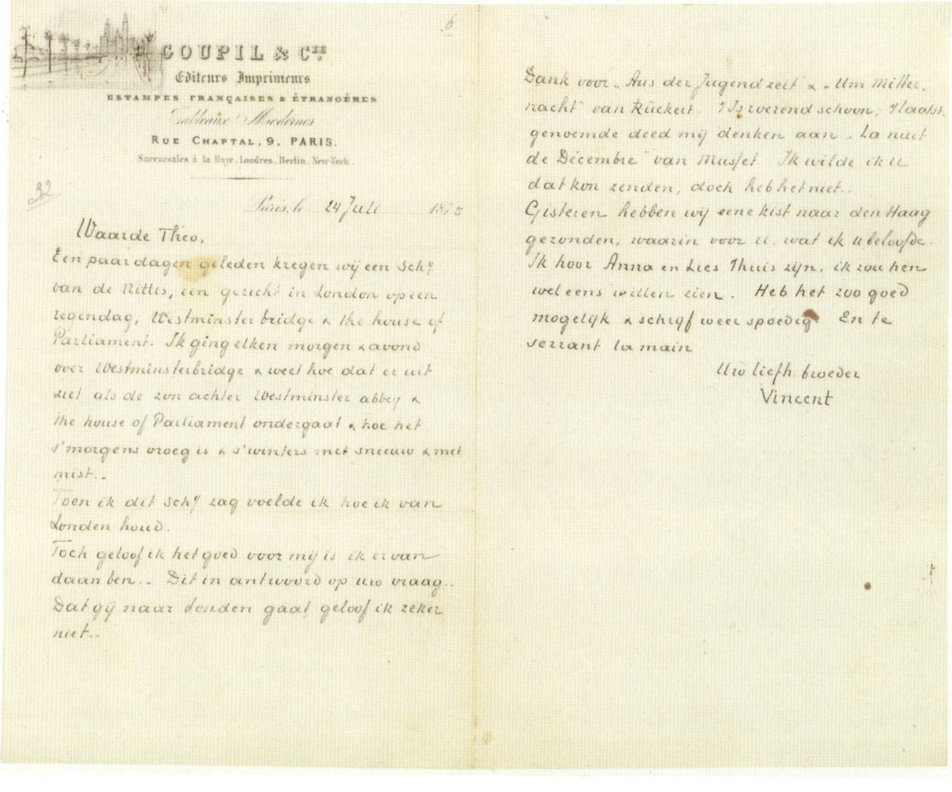

GOUPIL & Cie
Éditeurs Imprimeurs
ESTAMPES FRANÇAISES & ÉTRANGÈRES
Tableaux Modernes
RUE CHAPTAL, 9, PARIS.
Succursales à la Haye, Londres, Berlin, New-York.

Paris, le 24 Juli 1875

Waarde Theo,
Een paar dagen geleden kregen wij een Schy van de Nittis, een gezicht in London op een regendag, Westminster bridge & the house of Parliament. Ik ging elken morgen & avond over Westminsterbridge & weet hoe dat er uit ziet als de zon achter Westminster abbey & the house of Parliament ondergaat & hoe het s'morgens vroeg is & s'winters met sneeuw & met mist.
Toen ik dit Schy zag voelde ik hoe ik van Londen houd.
Toch geloof ik het goed voor mij is ik er vandaan ben.. Dit in antwoord op uw vraag.. Dat gij naar Londen gaat geloof ik zeker niet.

Dank voor „Aus der Jugendzeit" & „Um Mitternacht" van Rückert. 't Is zeer schoon, 't laatst genoemde deed mij denken aan „La nuit de Décembre" van Musset. Ik wilde ik u dat kon zenden, doch heb het niet.
Gisteren hebben wij eene kist naar den Haag gezonden, waarin voor u, wat ik u beloofde.
Ik hoor Anna en Lies thuis zijn, ik zou hen wel eens willen zien. Heb het zoo goed mogelijk & schrijf weer spoedig. En te serrant la main

Uw liefh. broeder
Vincent

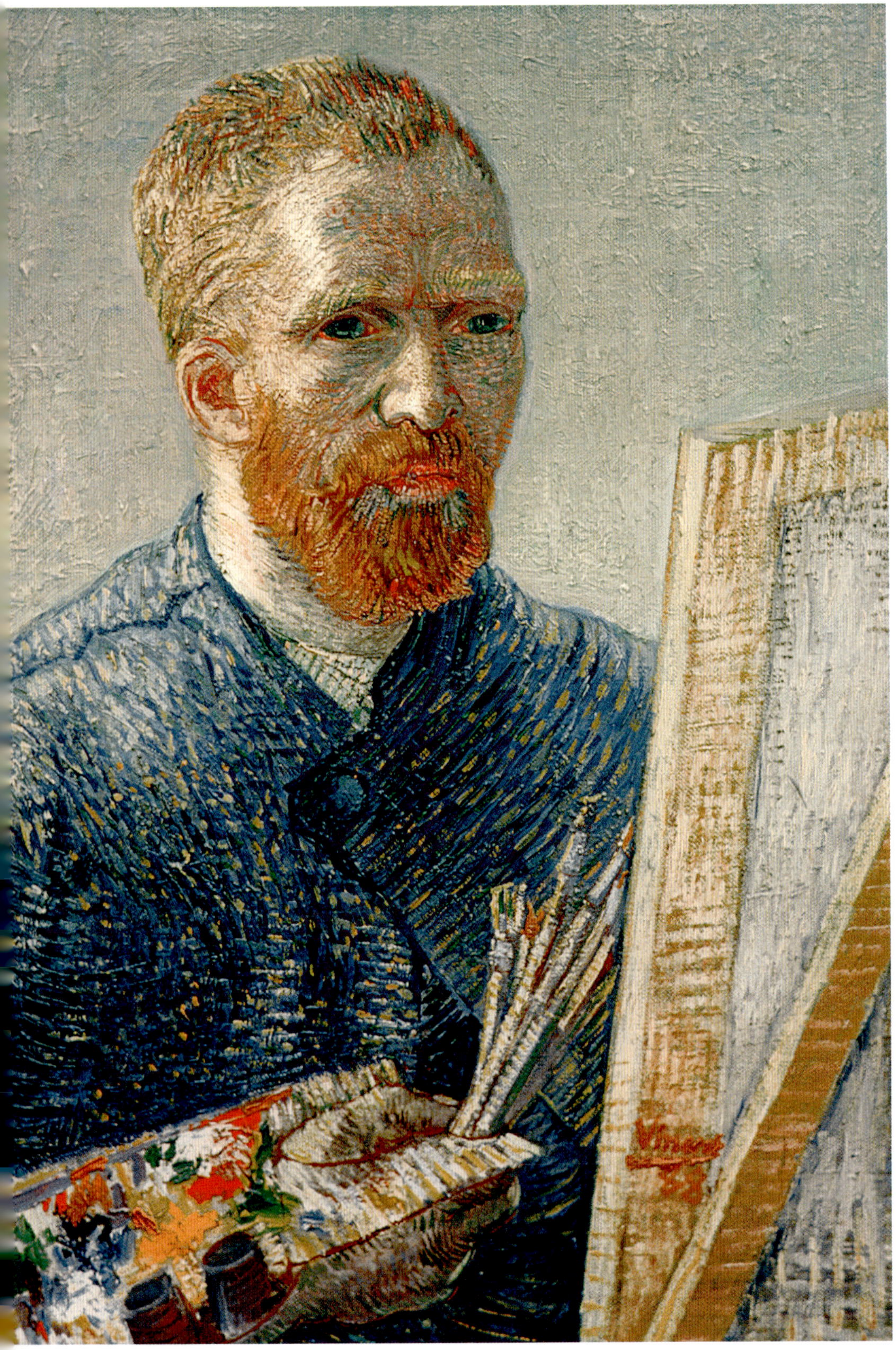

When I saw the picture I felt how much I loved London. Still I think that it is better for me that I left it. [...]

Vincent refers to the Italian Impressionist painter Giuseppe de Nittis (1846–84) who created several studies of London featuring Westminster Bridge. Viewing it made Vincent nostalgic for his own days spent in London.

From Theo van Gogh to Vincent van Gogh Extract from The Hague, *7 September 1875*

Dear Vincent,

Last spring Weehuizen died. I thought you knew. [...] He died very suddenly. [...] He had read Michelet's *L'Amour* and often talked about it to me, and he loved nature so much and sought the still sadness in it. Last Sunday I heard a beautiful sermon. Jesus wept. [...]

Recollecting the death of his friend, Theo mentioned that Weehuizen had read one of Vincent's favourite books, *L'Amour* (1858) by the French writer Jules Michelet (1798–1874). He includes reference to 'a beautiful sermon' he had heard and quotes 'Jesus wept' from the Bible, John 11:35. As sons of a pastor of the Dutch Reformed Church, the Bible was an integral part of life to Theo and Vincent.

***Self Portrait as an Artist*, 1888**
MEDIUM: Oil on canvas
Courtesy of Van Gogh Museum, Amsterdam, The Netherlands/ The Bridgeman Art Library

***Labourer and Peasant Planting Potatoes*, 1884**
MEDIUM: Oil on canvas
Courtesy of Van der Heydt Museum, Wuppertal, Germany/Giraudon/ The Bridgeman Art Library

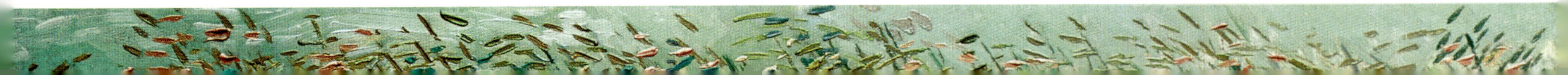

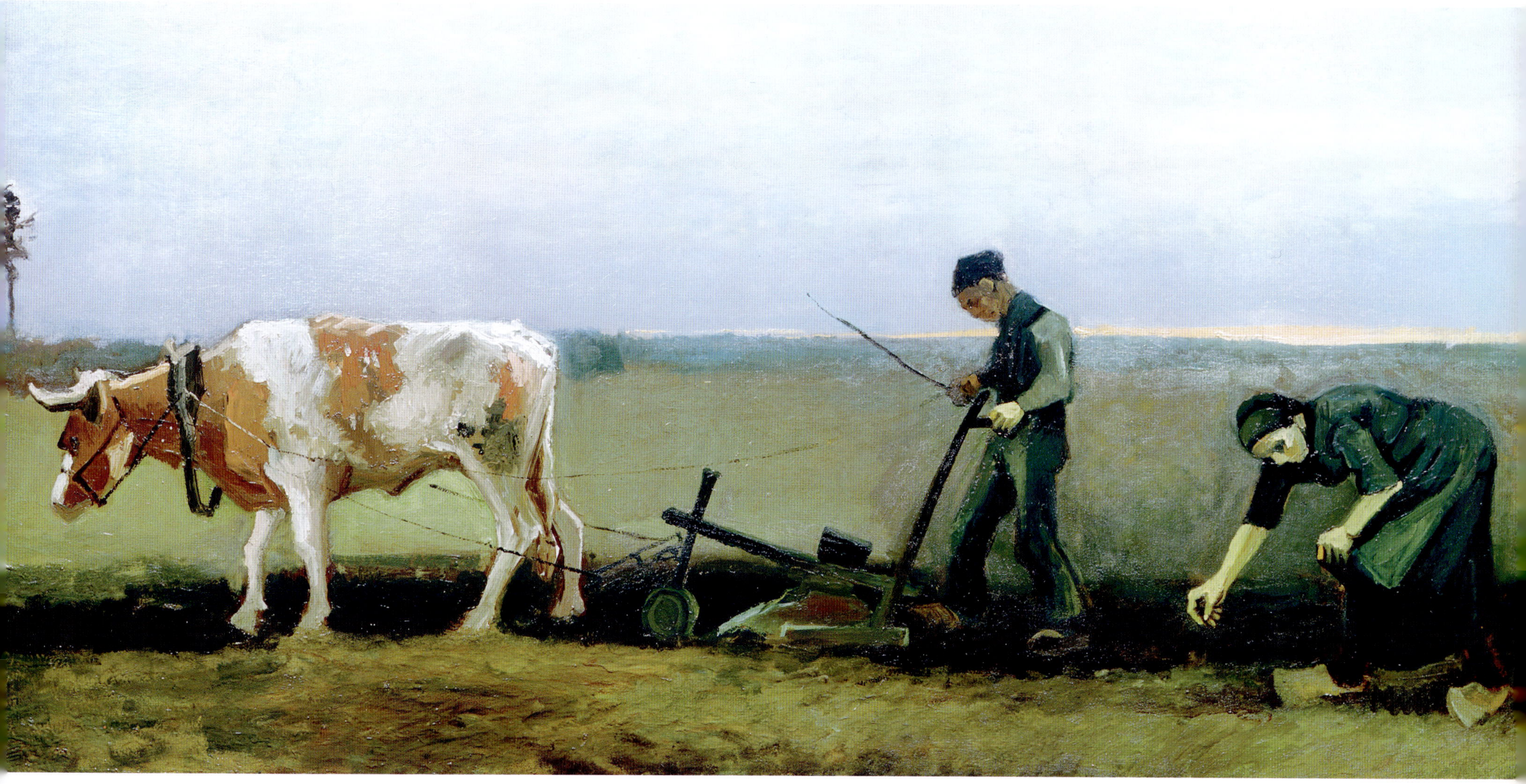

From Vincent van Gogh to
Theo van Gogh
Extract from
The Hague, *8 September 1875*

Dear Theo,

"[...] Theo, I want to make a suggestion that may perhaps surprise you. Do not read Michelet any longer or *any* other book but the Bible till we meet again at Christmas. [...]"

Vincent was an avid and passionate reader and he shared his passion for books in letters to Theo and to his friends. His letters contain over 800 references to literary sources. One of his favourite authors was the French writer Jules Michelet and so it is with surprise that he writes, in reply to Theo's letter of 7 September, to advise him to drop Michelet and any other author he may be reading and to read only the Bible for the next three months. Vincent's religious fervour was becoming evident in his letters. A follow-up letter to Theo, from Paris, dated 27 September 1875, is a long religious sermon beginning, 'The kingdom of God cometh not with observation: the kingdom of God is within you.'

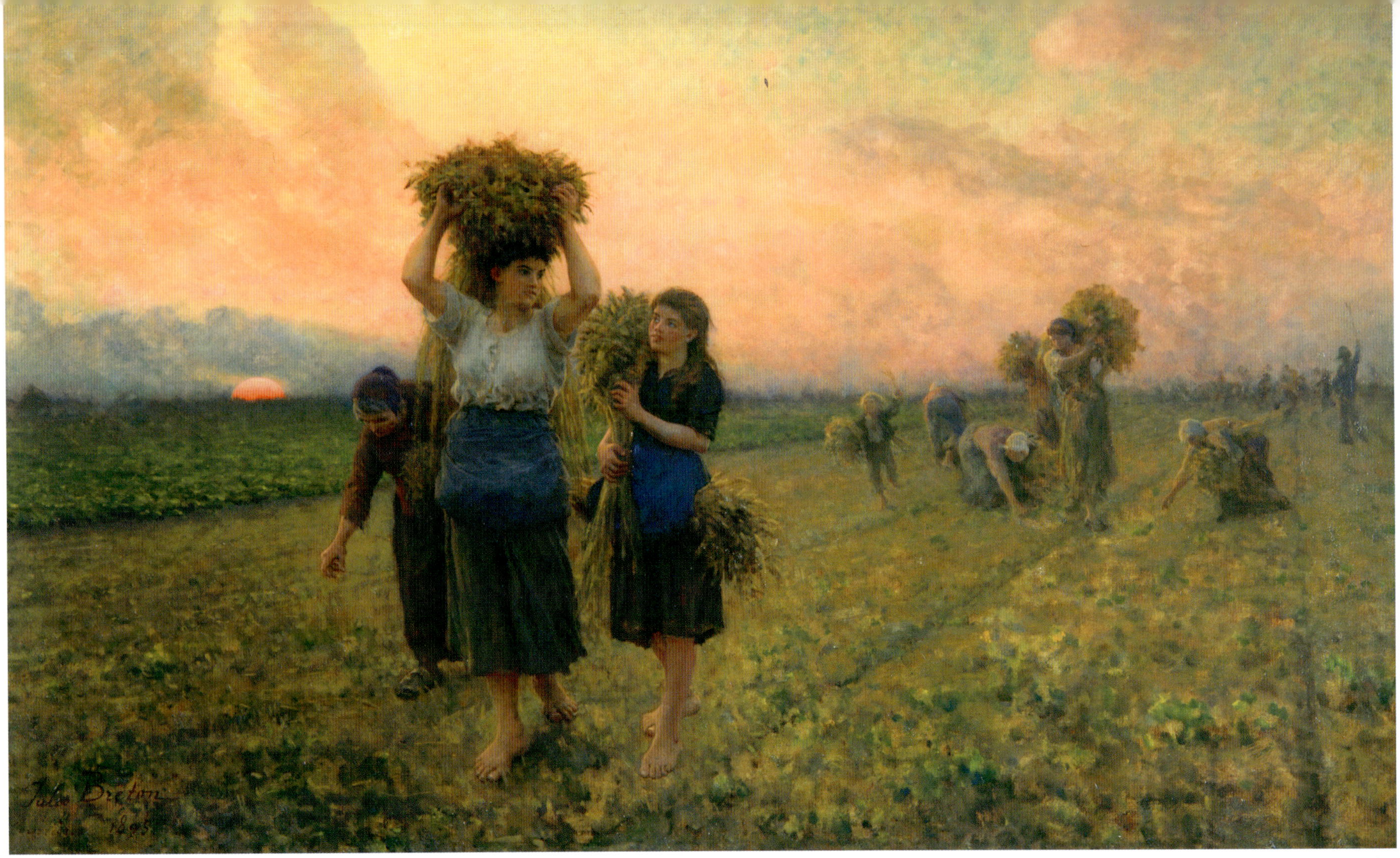

Extract from

Paris, *9 December 1875*

[...] This morning I heard from home what had happened to you, and I wanted to write you at once. I wish I could do something for you; one of these days a box will be sent to The Hague, I will put some chocolate in it for you. Gladwell calls that 'consolation'. I will also send you the book by Jules Breton – at least, if I can get it back, as I lent it to somebody. I am anxious to know how you are; write soon and please give me some details about how you spend your days. [...]

In December 1875 Vincent was working in Paris at Goupil & Cie. On 4 December, he wrote to Theo, excited that they would be soon spending Christmas together in Holland. His follow-up letter, sent a few days later, was reaction to the news that Theo had seriously injured his foot, falling down in a slippery street. That Vincent wrote as soon as he heard of the incident was typical of his concern for his younger sibling. The two young men had been close since childhood in spite of a four-year age-gap. One can read much into the status of their relationship during the early years of their correspondence, which was dominated by Vincent's concern for and advice to Theo. In the letter of 9 December, Vincent's anxiety is clear: '...I heard from home what had happened to you, and I wanted to write to you at once.' He offers consolation with the promise of chocolates and a book by Jules Breton (1827–1906), the French Realist painter and writer whom Vincent admired.

The Last Gleanings, 1895
by Jules Breton (1827–1906)
MEDIUM: Oil on canvas
Courtesy of Huntington Library and Art Gallery, San Marino, CA, USA/©The Huntington Library, Art Collections & Botanical Gardens/The Bridgeman Art Library

Approaching Storm, c.1820–25, (detail)
by Georges Michel (1763–1843)
MEDIUM: Oil on canvas
Courtesy of Indianapolis Museum of Art, USA/Delavan Smith Fund/The Bridgeman Art Library

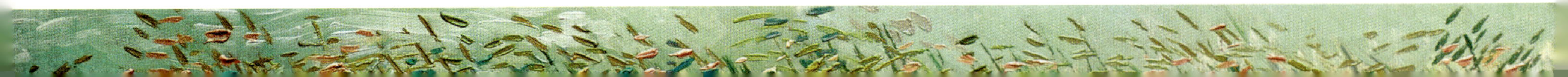

Extract from
Paris, *10 January 1876*

"[...] I have not again written to you since we saw each other. Meanwhile something happened to me that was not entirely unforeseen.

When I saw Mr. Boussod again, I asked him His Excellence if he approved of my being employed in the house for another year, and told His Excellence that I hoped that he had nothing serious to reproach me with?

But, alas, it was the case, and His Excellence has forced me, as it were, to say that I would leave on 1st April, after having thanked the gentlemen for all that I might have learned with them.

When the apple is ripe, a soft breeze will make it fall from the tree, and such was the case here. I have probably done things that in a certain sense have been very wrong, this is why I have never made a big thing to answer back.

Well, my boy, I am not at all clear what I should do next, but we shall try to maintain hope and courage.

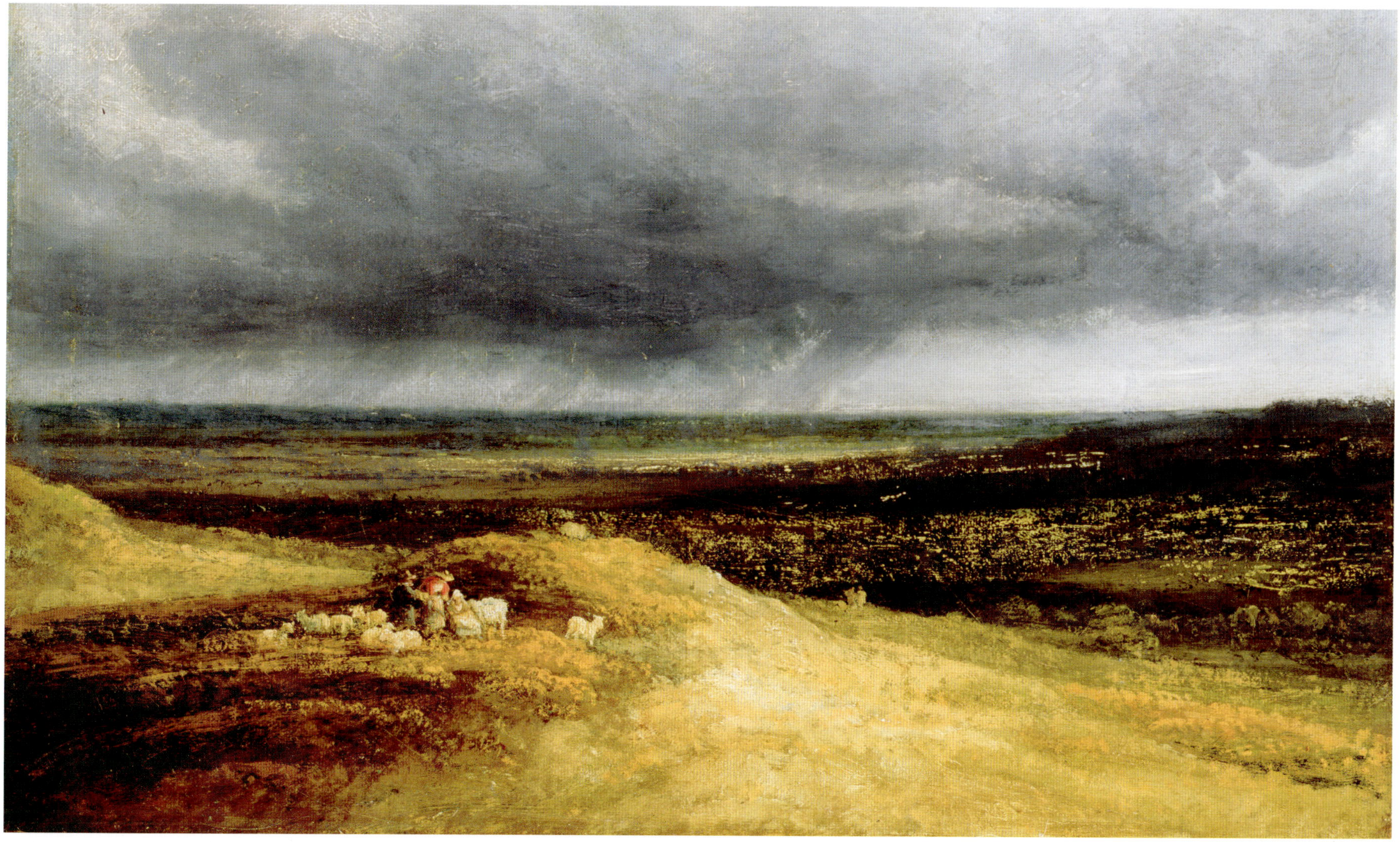

Oblige me by showing this to Mr Tersteeg, His Excellence may know what has happened, but I believe that it is better if you do not tell it to anyone else; and to act as if nothing has happened. Write to me soon and believe me.

Vincent had joined The Hague branch of the Parisian art dealers, Goupil & Cie, in 1869. His father's older brother, Vincent or 'Uncle Cent' (1820–88), was a partner in the company. His notable art collection was known to Theo and Vincent through regular visits to his home. To help his young nephew Uncle Cent had found him a placement, as the youngest employee in the company, under the guidance of his friend Mr Tersteeg. Six years later, the contents of this letter with news of his dismissal from the company must have shocked Theo and Uncle Cent particularly, who may have considered Vincent a likely successor of his partnership. After sending him to work in The Hague, London and Paris, Goupil & Cie no longer required Vincent's services. In the letter the reasons for his dismissal are not elaborated upon, but Vincent creates the analogy that 'when the apple is ripe, a soft breeze makes it fall from the tree'. He hints that the dismissal was not wholly unexpected on his part. He had been in a melancholy state in the last months of his job in London due to his persistent yet unrequited love for Ursula, the daughter of his landlady Mrs Loyer. To remove him from this delicate situation, it was arranged that he move to the Paris branch of the company in May 1875, at first for a few weeks and then until further notice. The enforced move had made Vincent deeply unhappy and from his letter it would seem that he acknowledges that he is mostly to blame for his dismissal. The sacking would obviously not have been well received by his family, particularly relations who had helped to promote his art-dealer career.

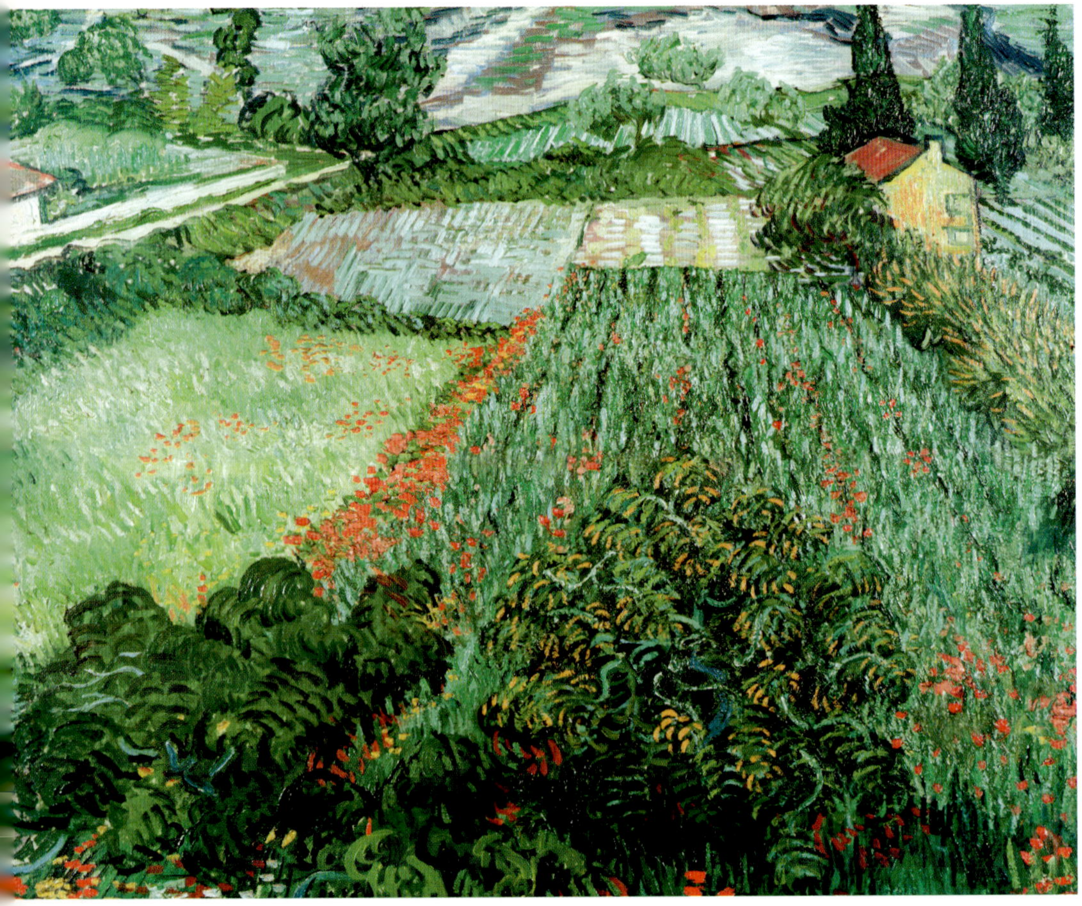

Extract from Paris, *28 March 1876*

Just one word more, probably the last I shall write from Paris. I leave here on Friday night and shall be home Saturday morning at the same time as at Christmas.

Yesterday I saw six pictures by Michel, how I wish you could have seen them too! Sunken paths through sandy fields leading to a mill, or a man going home across the heath with grey skies above – so simple and beautiful. I think the 'Men of Emmaus' saw nature in the same way as Michel and I always think of them when I see one of his pictures.

***Field with Poppies*, 1889**
MEDIUM: Oil on canvas
Courtesy of Kunsthalle, Bremen, Germany/The Bridgeman Art Library

***The Harvester*, date unknown, (detail)**
MEDIUM: Oil on canvas
Courtesy of Museum Folkwang, Essen, Germany/ Giraudon/The Bridgeman Art Library

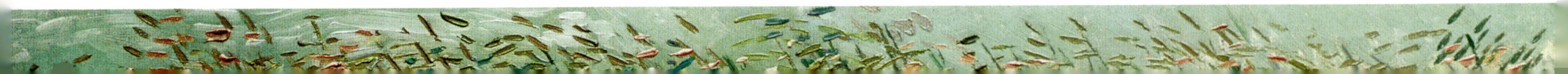

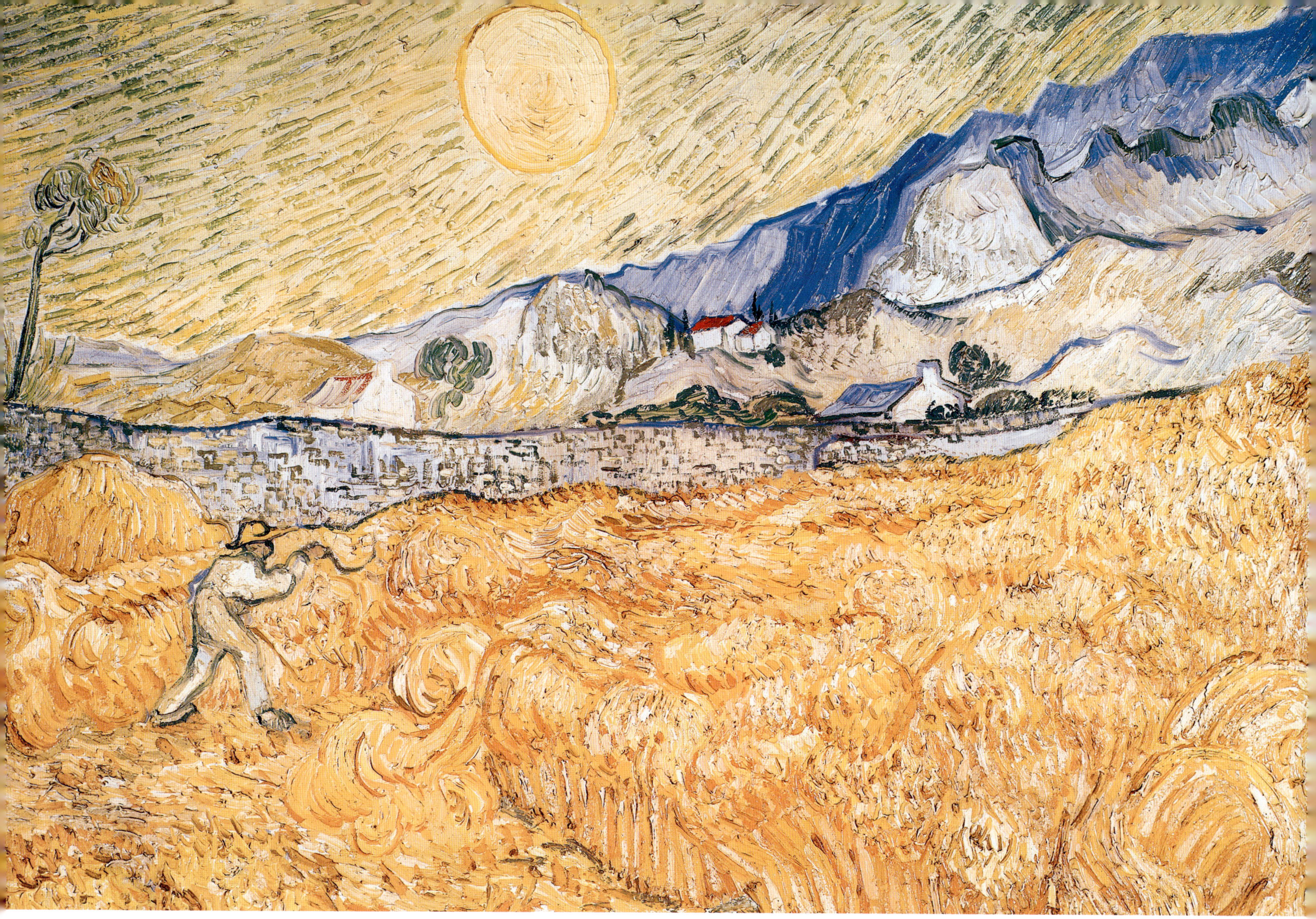

At the same time I saw a very large picture by Jules Dupré. There is black marshy soil as far as one can see, on the second plane is a river, and in the foreground, a pool with three horses. Both the river and the pool reflect a bank of white and grey clouds, behind which the sun has set. The sky is a soft blue, with some grey-red and purple at the horizon.

I saw these pictures at Durand Ruel's; more than twenty-five etchings after Millet, the same number after Michel and a great number after Dupré and Corot. All the other artists can be purchased there at 1 franc apiece; it was tempting. I could not resist the Millet and bought the last three that were to be had after 'The Angelus'; of course, my brother will get one of them at the first opportunity. ”

Vincent was about to leave Paris. He paid a final visit to the art dealers Durand Ruel, to view etchings, singling out works after Jules Dupré (1811–89) and Georges Michel (1763–1843), two of his favourite painters. He purchased three etchings of Millet's *The Angelus* (1857–59).

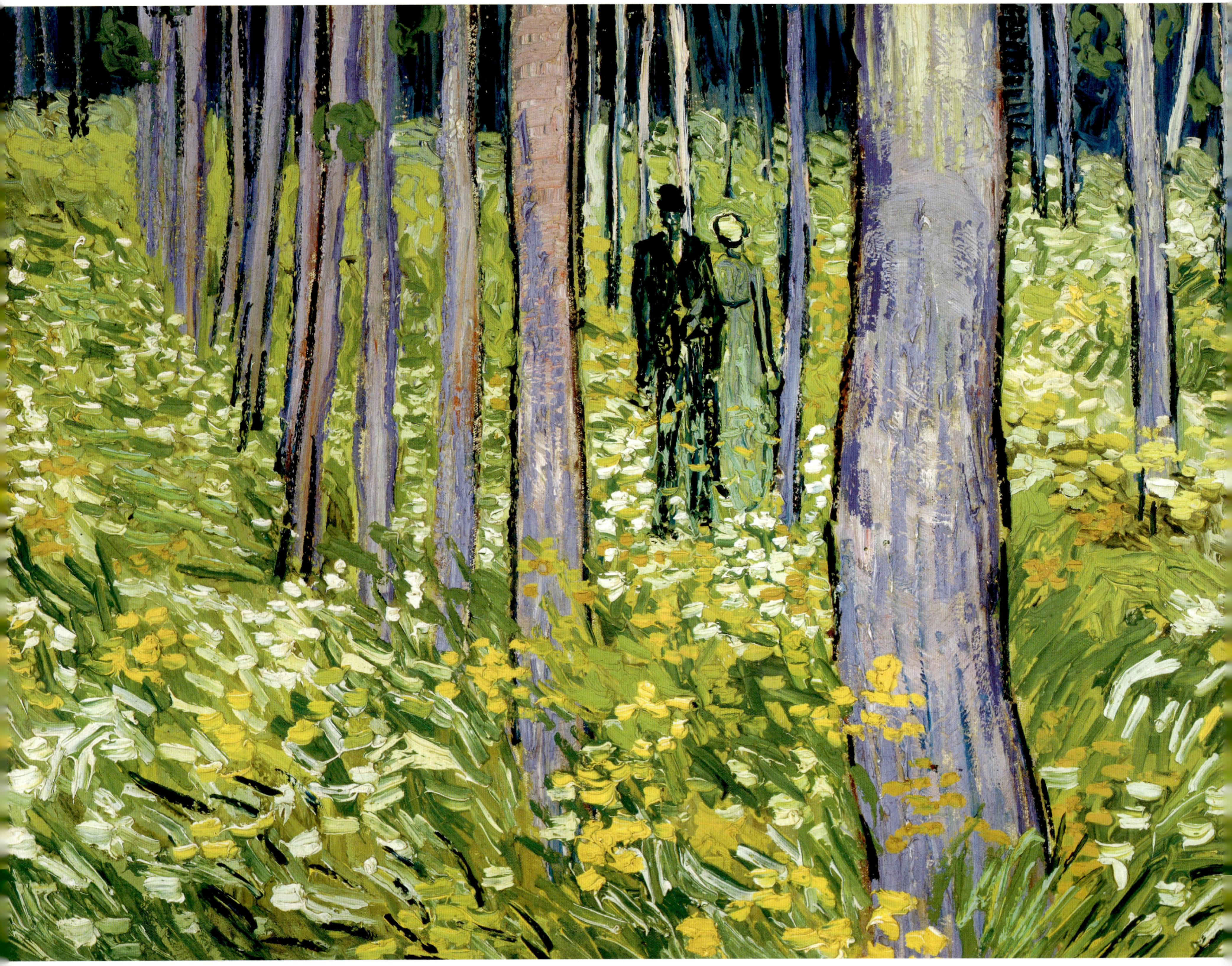

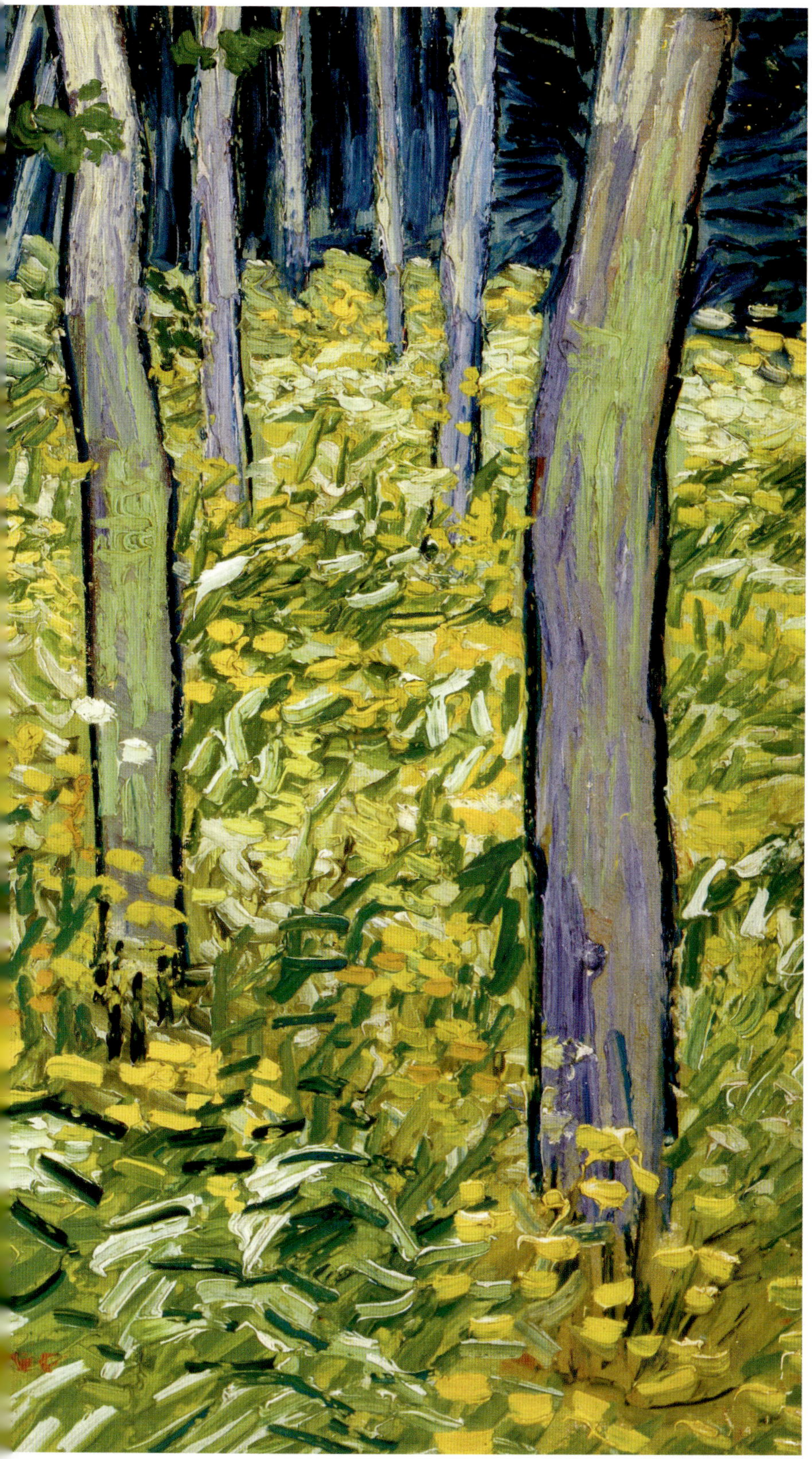

Extract from
Ramsgate, *28 April 1876*

[...] Mr. Stokes has told me that he intends to move after the holidays, of course with the whole school, to a little village on the Thames about three hours from London. There he will organize his school somewhat differently and perhaps enlarge it. Now I am going to tell you about a walk we took yesterday. It was to an inlet of the sea, and the road thither led through fields of young corn and along hedges of hawthorn, etc.

Arriving there, we saw to our left a high steep ridge of sand and stone as tall as a two-storey house. On the top of it were old, gnarled hawthorn bushes, whose black and grey moss-grown stems and branches were all bent to one side by the wind; there were also a few elder bushes.

The ground on which we walked was covered all over with big grey stones, chalk and shells.

To the right lay the sea, as calm as a pond and reflecting the light of the transparent grey sky where the sun was setting.

The tide was out and the water very low.

On 17 April 1876, Vincent left the family home to travel to England. A letter to his parents written on the same day highlights his sadness at leaving: 'These first few hours after our parting – which you are spending in church, and I at the station and on the train – how we are longing for each other...' From April until the end of June 1876, Vincent was

***Undergrowth with Two Figures*, 1890**
MEDIUM: Oil on canvas
Courtesy of Cincinnati Art Museum, Ohio, USA/Bequest of Mary E. Johnston/ The Bridgeman Art Library

employed as an assistant school teacher in Ramsgate, on the south-east coast of England, working for the headmaster, Mr Stokes without remuneration. He taught the boys elementary French, German and Mathematics. Since leaving Goupil & Cie, his reliance on religion had grown as he tried to work out what he wanted to do with his life. In his letter to Theo, Vincent steps away from the difficulties of his current situation to 'paint' a stunningly visual portrait of everything he had observed on a walk he had taken through fields of corn toward the sea, 'as calm as a pond and reflecting the light of the transparent grey sky...'. To be in touch with nature was his security during times of loneliness and anxiety.

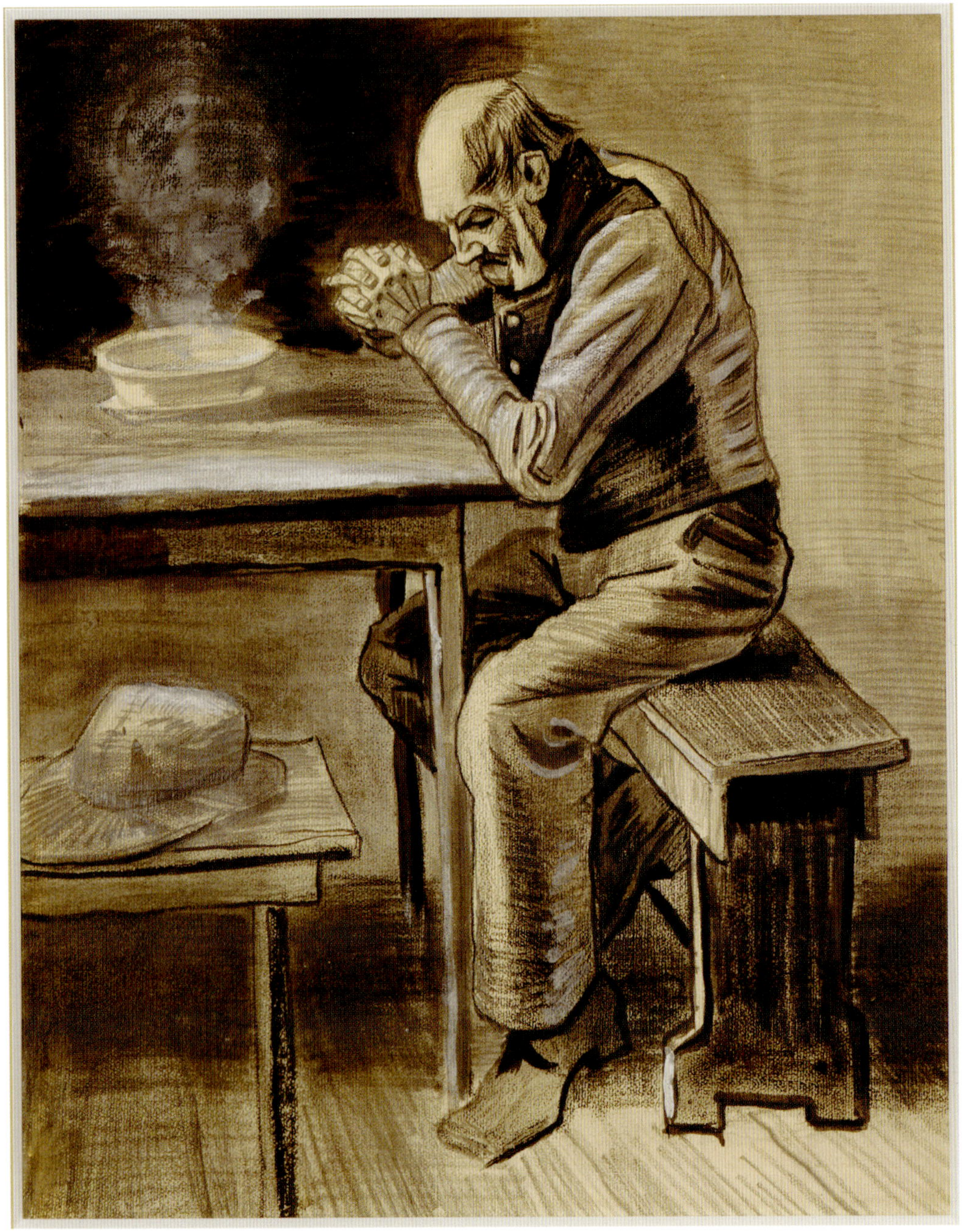

From Vincent van Gogh to
Reverend Jones
Extract from
Ramsgate, *17 June 1876*

Reverend Sir,

"A clergyman's son who, because he has to work for his living, has neither the time nor the money to keep up studies at King's College, and is in any case already a few years older than is usual for those who go there and has not yet even started the preliminary studies in Latin and Greek, would, all this notwithstanding, be very glad to find a position connected with the church, albeit the position of a university-educated clergyman is beyond his reach.

My father is a clergyman in a village in Holland. I went to school when I was 11, staying on until I was 16. I then had to choose a profession and did not know which to choose. Through the kind offices of one of my uncles, a partner in the firm of Goupil & Cie, art dealers and publishers of engravings, I obtained a position in his business in The Hague. I was employed in this business for 3 years. From there I went to London to learn English and, after 2 years, moved on to Paris. Various circumstances have, however, compelled me to leave Messrs G. & Cie, and for the past two months I have been teaching at Mr Stokes's school in Ramsgate. But since my aim is a position in connection with the church, I must look elsewhere.

Although I have not been trained for the church, perhaps my past experience of travels, of living in different countries, of associations with various people, poor and rich, religious and irreligious, of work of various kinds, days of manual labour followed by days of office work, &c., perhaps also my ability to speak various languages, may in part make up for my not having been to a university. […]

[…] when I think of my past life and of my father's house in the village in Holland, a sense of: 'Father, I have sinned against heaven, and before thee, and am no more worthy to be called thy Son: make me as one of thy hired servants. Be merciful to me a sinner.'

When I lived in London I often attended your church and have not forgotten you. Now I would ask for your recommendation as I look for a position, and also that you keep your fatherly eye on me should I find such a position. I have been left a good deal to myself, and I believe your fatherly eye will do me good. […]

Thanking you in anticipation for what you may feel able to do for me. […] ”

Vincent's aim was to secure a religious profession. On 1 July he joined a new school run by Mr Jones, a Methodist clergyman. In his new employment he would take on the role of novice curate.

From Vincent van Gogh to
Theo van Gogh
Extract from
Dordrecht, *21 January 1877*

Dear Theo,

“ You probably expected a letter from me sooner. I am getting along pretty well at the bookstore and am very busy; I go there at eight o'clock in the morning and I leave at one o'clock at night. But I like it that way.

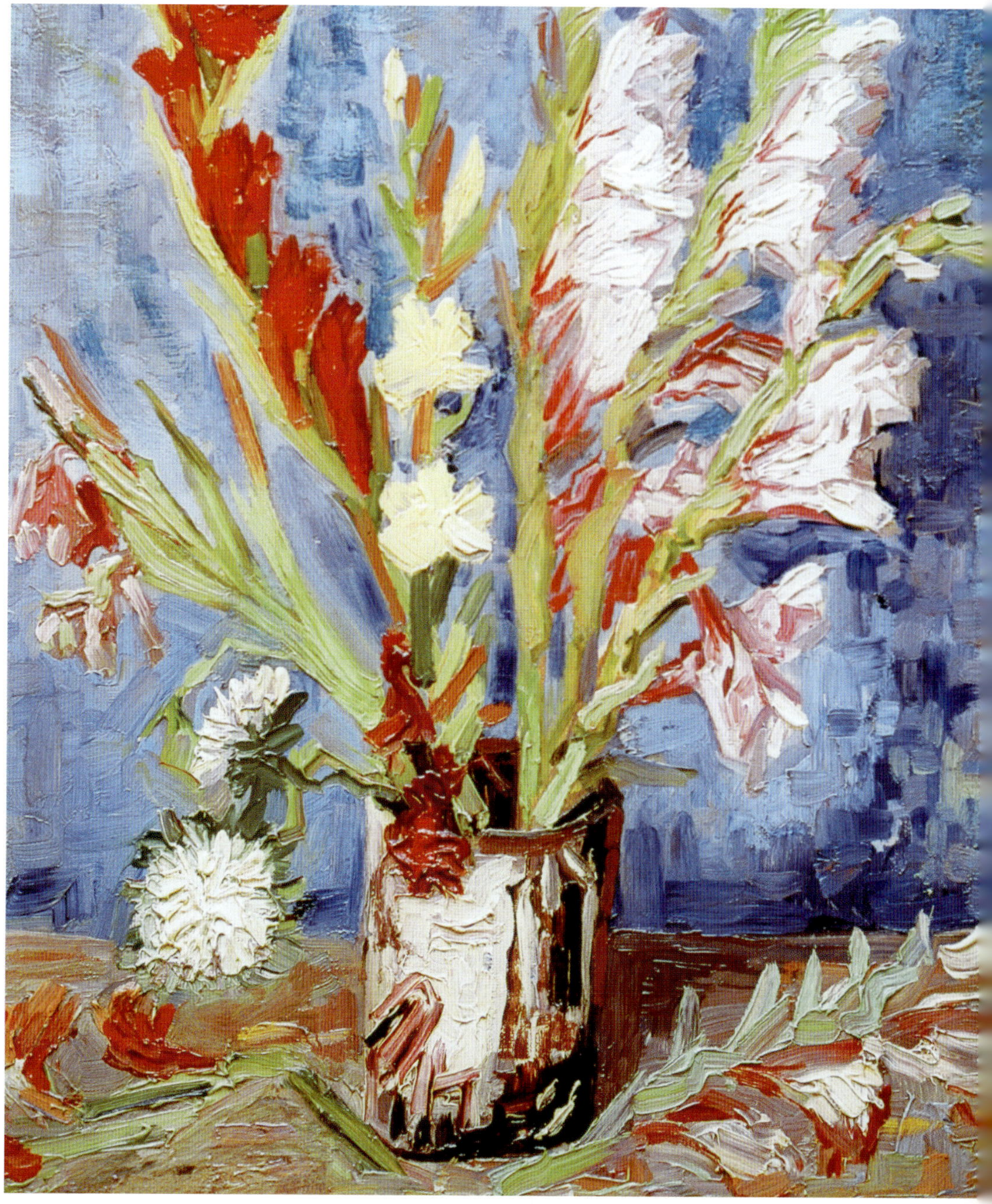

The Prayer, 1882
MEDIUM: Pencil, charcoal & ink heightened with white gouache on paper
Courtesy of Private Collection/Photo © Christie's Images/The Bridgeman Art Library

***Vase with Gladioli*, date unknown**
MEDIUM: Oil on canvas
Courtesy of Private Collection/The Bridgeman Art Library

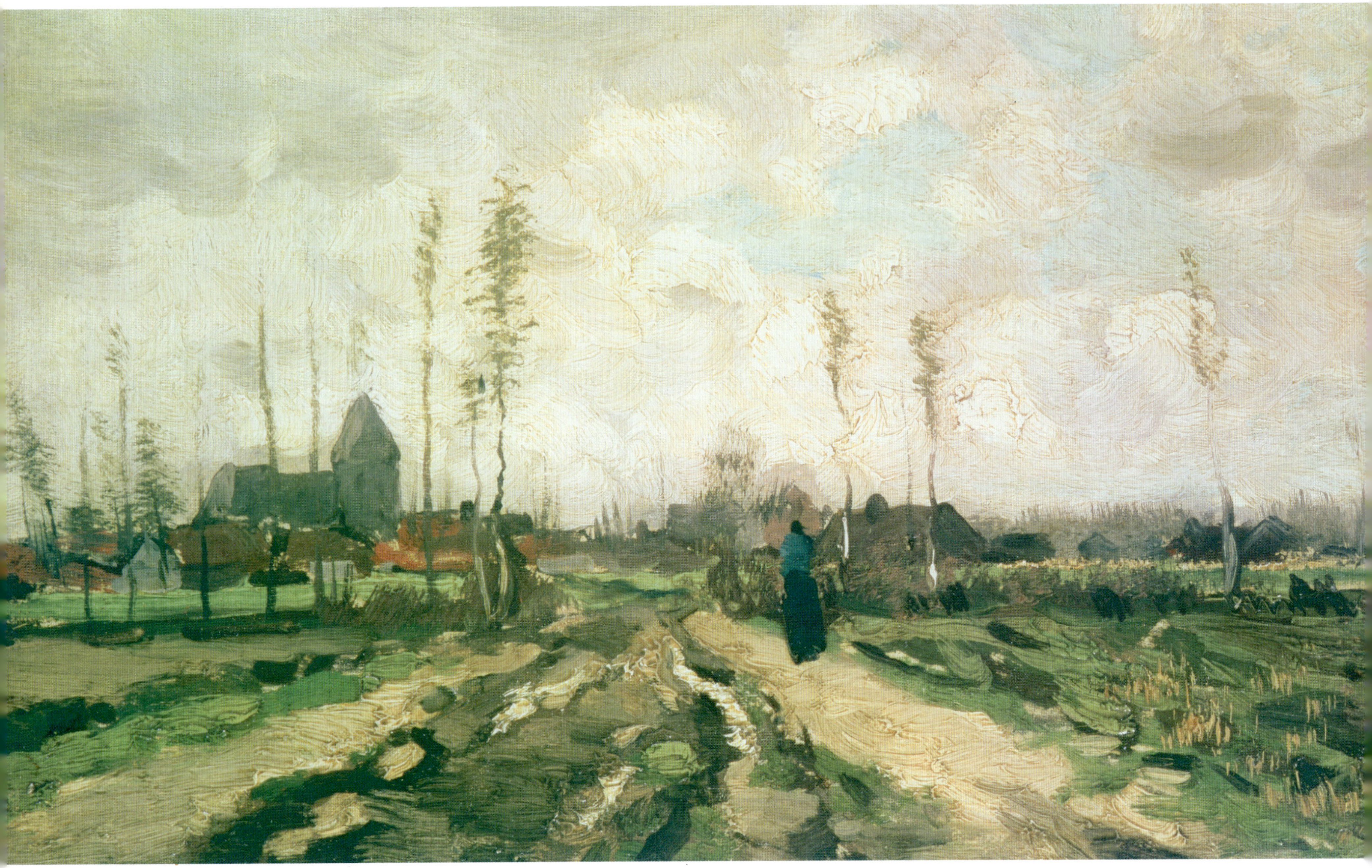

I hope to go to Etten on 11 February, as you know, we celebrate this day as father's birthday. Will you be there also? [...]

Last Sunday, I wrote to Mr & Mrs Jones to tell them that I was not coming back, and unintentionally the letter became rather long – out of the fullness of my heart. I wished them to remember me and asked them *to wrap my recollection in the cloak of charity*.

I have hung in my bedroom the two engravings Christus Consolator that you have given me. I saw the pictures at the museum, as well as Scheffer's 'Christ in Gethsemane,' which is unforgettable. Then there is a sketch of 'Les Douleurs de la Terre' and several drawings, a sketch of his studio, and, as you know, the portrait of his mother. [...]

The first Sunday I was here, I heard a sermon on 'Behold, I make all things new'. This morning I heard the Reverend Mr Beversen in a little old church. There was Communion, and his text was: 'If any man thirst, let him come unto me, and drink.' The window in my bedroom looks out on the gardens where I can see pine trees, poplars, and the backs of old houses etc., one of them has a gutter covered with ivy. Dickens said: 'A strange

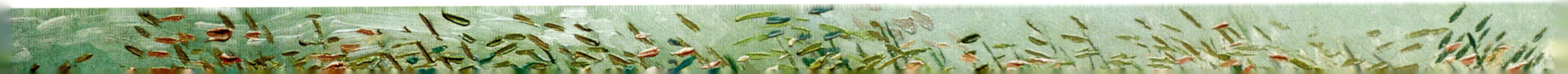

Landscape with a Church and Houses, Nuenen, 1885
MEDIUM: Oil on canvas
Courtesy of Private Collection/ Photo © Christie's Images/ The Bridgeman Art Library

The Ravine of the Peyroulets, 1889
MEDIUM: Oil on canvas
Courtesy of Rijksmuseum Kroller-Muller, Otterlo, Netherlands/Giraudon/ The Bridgeman Art Library

old plant is the ivy green.' This view from my window can be solemn and gloomy, but you should see it in the light of the morning sun. Then when I contemplate it, I imagine a letter of yours in which you talked to me of houses covered with ivy. Do you remember it? [...]

This evening when the setting sun was reflected in the water and in the windows and cast a bright golden glow over everything, it looked just like a picture by Cuyp. [...]"

Vincent had returned home for Christmas where a decision was made that he would not return to England. He wrote to his former employer Mr Jones, the Methodist clergyman, and his wife, apologizing for his decision to leave. To earn money he took a job in a bookstore, tackling the work with zeal. The content of the letter shows how his thoughts quickly turn from paintings, to literature, to the view from his window that reminds him of the paintings of the seventeenth-century Dutch landscape artist Albert Cuyp (1620–91).

Extract from Amsterdam, *31 May 1877*

"[...] If I one day have the joy to become a pastor and to acquit my task like our father, I will thank God.

I have strong hopes of success: once somebody who was more advanced in life than I and who was no stranger to Jerusalem – meaning he had sought after it and found it – said to me, 'I believe you are a Christian'. It did me so much good to hear this! Whatever you wish for yourself, too, hold firm to the thought of Christ and treasure His word – just as you do. It is good to believe that there is a God who knows what we want better than we do ourselves, and Who helps us whenever we are in need of it. And it is also good to believe that now, just as in olden days, an angel is not far from those who are sad – strengthened unto God – not only to those who are nearly angels themselves, but particularly to those who want the help of a higher power to be preserved from the evil, from the badness which we know is in the world and not far away from us – not far from those who are broken-hearted and dejected in spirit. I have often read the story of Elijah with care; so often has it fortified me even to this day. [...]

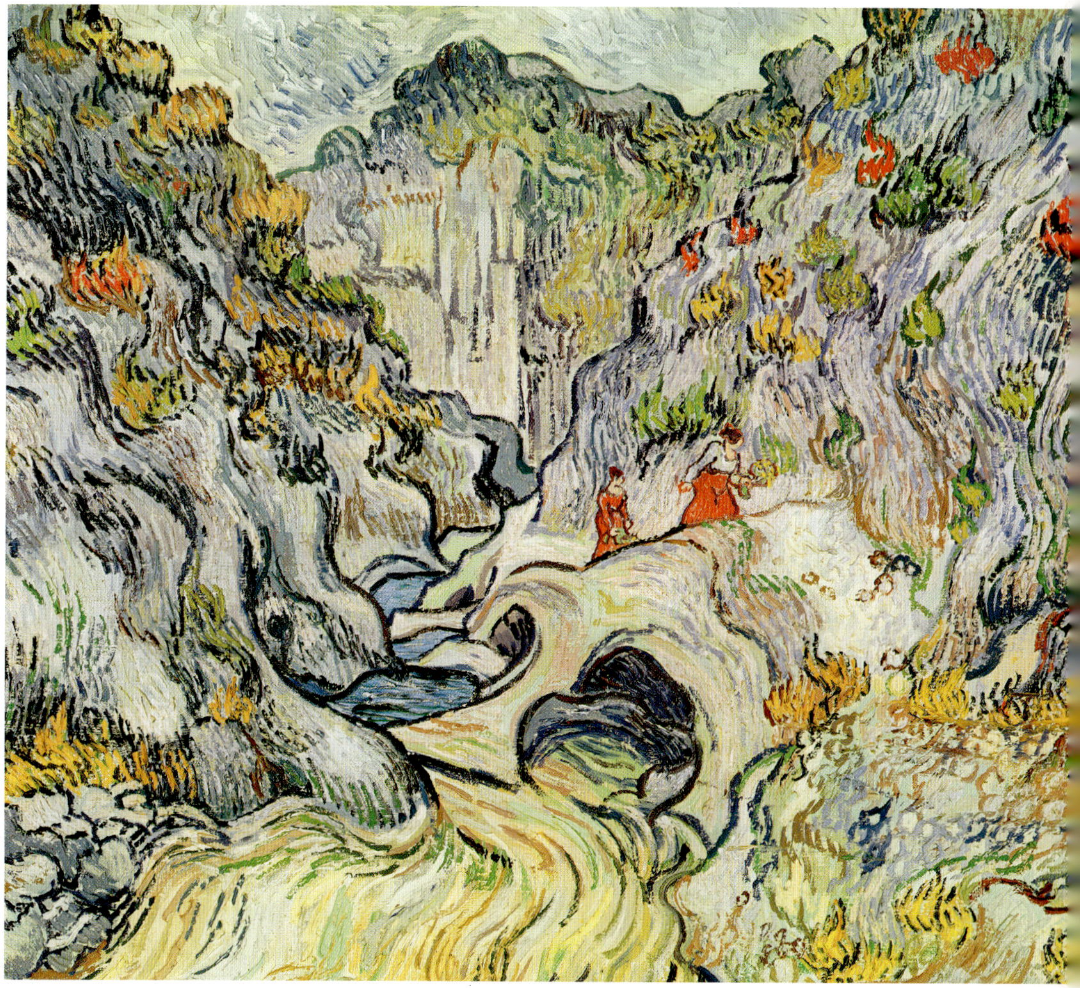

This afternoon there was a gale blowing here, and it rained, and I walked to the sea along the Jewish cemetery, and a few days ago I also took a walk to the spot of the Buitenkant near the East Railway where they are working on that sand embankment, etc. How beautiful and inspiring is that story of Jesus walking on the sea, Matthew 14:22–33. […]

Believe in God; through faith we may become 'sorrowful yet always rejoicing' and ever green, and we need not complain when our youth flies with the maturing of our strength. […]

Vincent states that it is his ambition to aspire to a religious vocation, to become a pastor, following his father's career. The long text he wrote to Theo is more a religious sermon than a letter.

Extract from Amsterdam, *3 March 1878*

[…] Heard the Reverend Mr Laurillard preaching this morning in the Oudezjide Chapel. Uncle Stricker was at church as well and I had coffee with him. […]

Uncle [Cor] told me that Daubigny had died. I freely confess that I was downcast when I heard the news, just as I was when I heard that Brion had died (his 'Bénédicité' hangs in my room), because the work of such men, if it is understood, touches us more deeply than one realizes. It must be good to die in the knowledge that one has done some truthful work and to know that, as a result, one will live on in the memory of at least a few

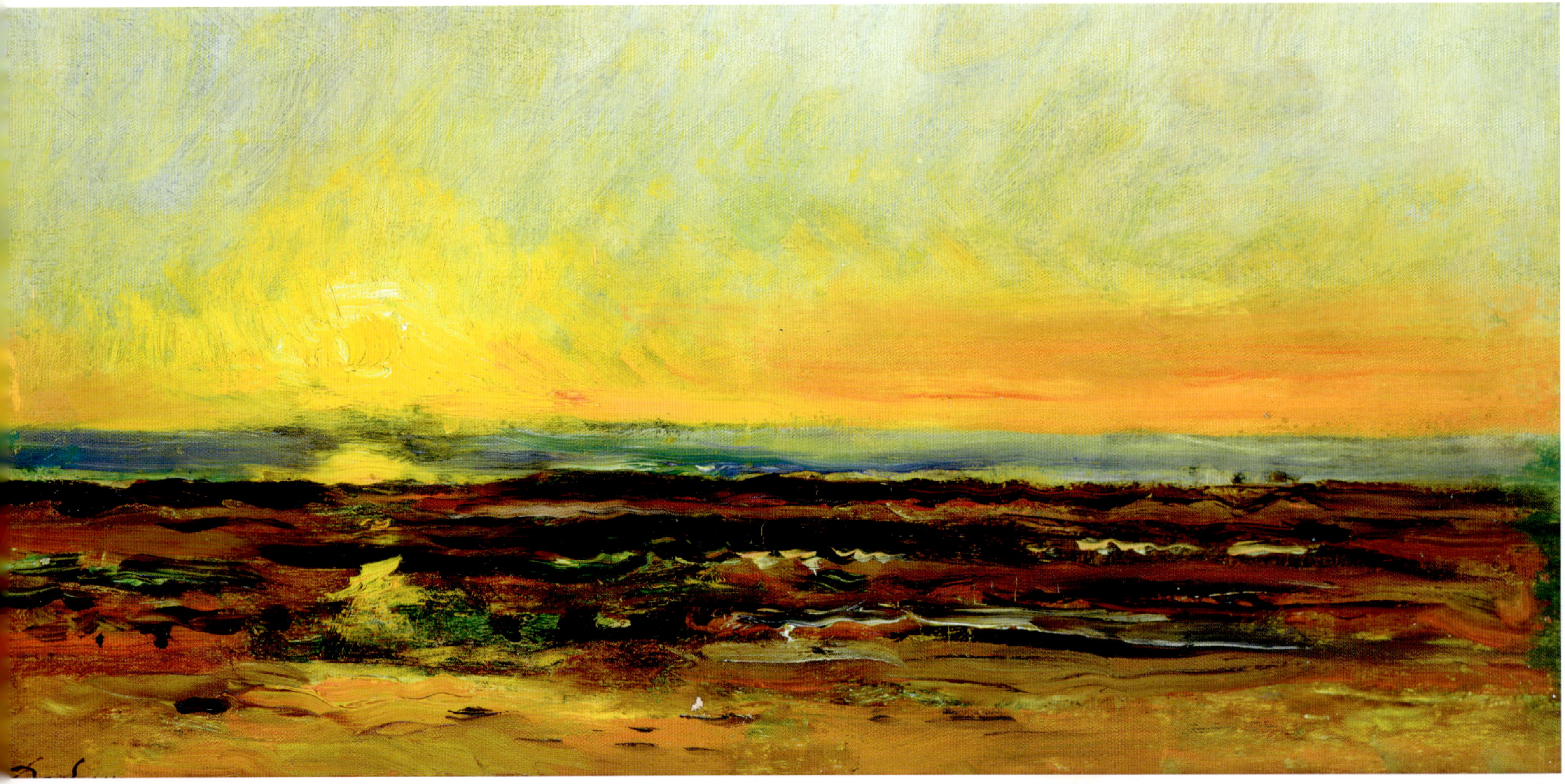

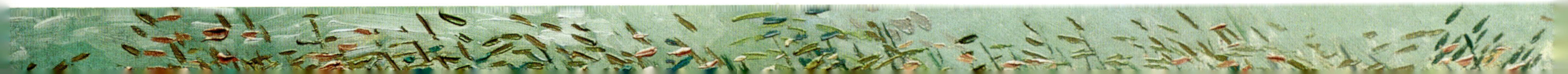

***Sunset on the Sea Coast,* date unknown, (detail) by Charles François Daubigny (1817–78)**
MEDIUM: Oil on panel
© Towneley Hall Art Gallery and Museum, Burnley, Lancashire/The Bridgeman Art Library

***Autumn Landscape,* 1890**
MEDIUM: Oil on canvas
Courtesy of Van Gogh Museum, Amsterdam, The Netherlands/ The Bridgeman Art Library

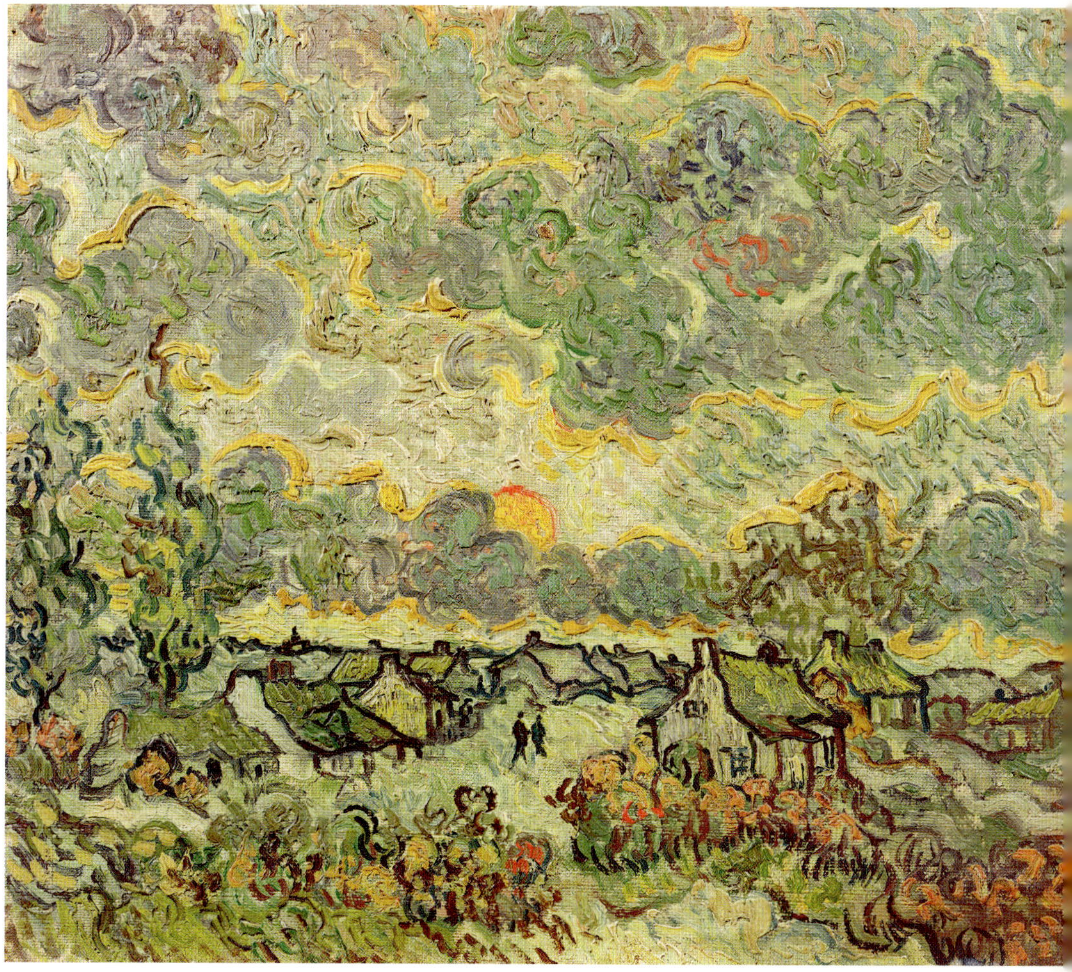

and leave a good example for those who come after. A work that is good may not last forever, but the thought expressed by it will, and the work itself will surely survive for a very long time, and those who come later can do no more than follow in the footsteps of such predecessors and copy their example. Speaking of good works, would you like to have a Flemish 'Imitation of Christ'? I hope to send it to you shortly, in a small book which, if need be, can easily be slipped into the pocket.

When Uncle told me about Daubigny, I thought of his etchings after Ruysdael ('Le buisson' and 'Le coup de soleil'), and Uncle has promised to get hold of them, as he did not know them at all. [...]

I have worked my way through the history of the Netherlands and have done an abstract of 30 closely written pages. (I was pleased to come across the battle of Waterloo and the 10-day campaign in it once again.) Do you know that Rochussen once painted the siege of Leyden? I mean the picture owned by Mr de Vos. Am now also working on general history.

[...] Have you read anything good lately? Be sure to get hold of the works of George Eliot somehow, you won't be sorry if you do, *Adam Bede*, *Silas Marner*, *Felix Holt*, *Romola* (the life of Savonarola), *Scenes from Clerical Life*. I shall reread them once more. Both the Reverend Mr McFarlane and Adler spoke to me about them, that is, they advised me to read them.

[...] Did you ever see an original etching by Millet of a man wheeling a barrow full of manure into a garden on a day like today, in early spring? And remember as well that he made an etching, 'Les becheurs'? If you ever do come across it you are unlikely to forget it in a hurry. I was thinking of the first this morning when Uncle Stricker was looking for texts in which the word manure, or dung, appears, e.g., 'Let it alone this year also, till I shall dig about it, and dung it.' Made a list recently of all the pictures by Brion I could remember. When you come here, you must tell me whether I have forgotten many of them. Lord, keep my memory green! That is something one should say over and over again. [...]

Vincent was saddened to hear news of the death of Charles-François Daubigny (1817–78), a French artist of the Barbizon School whom he admired. He contemplated that, 'It must be good to die in the knowledge that one has done some truthful work and to know that, as a result, one will live on in the memory of at least a few and leave a good example for those who come after.' It may have been a wish he held for himself too.

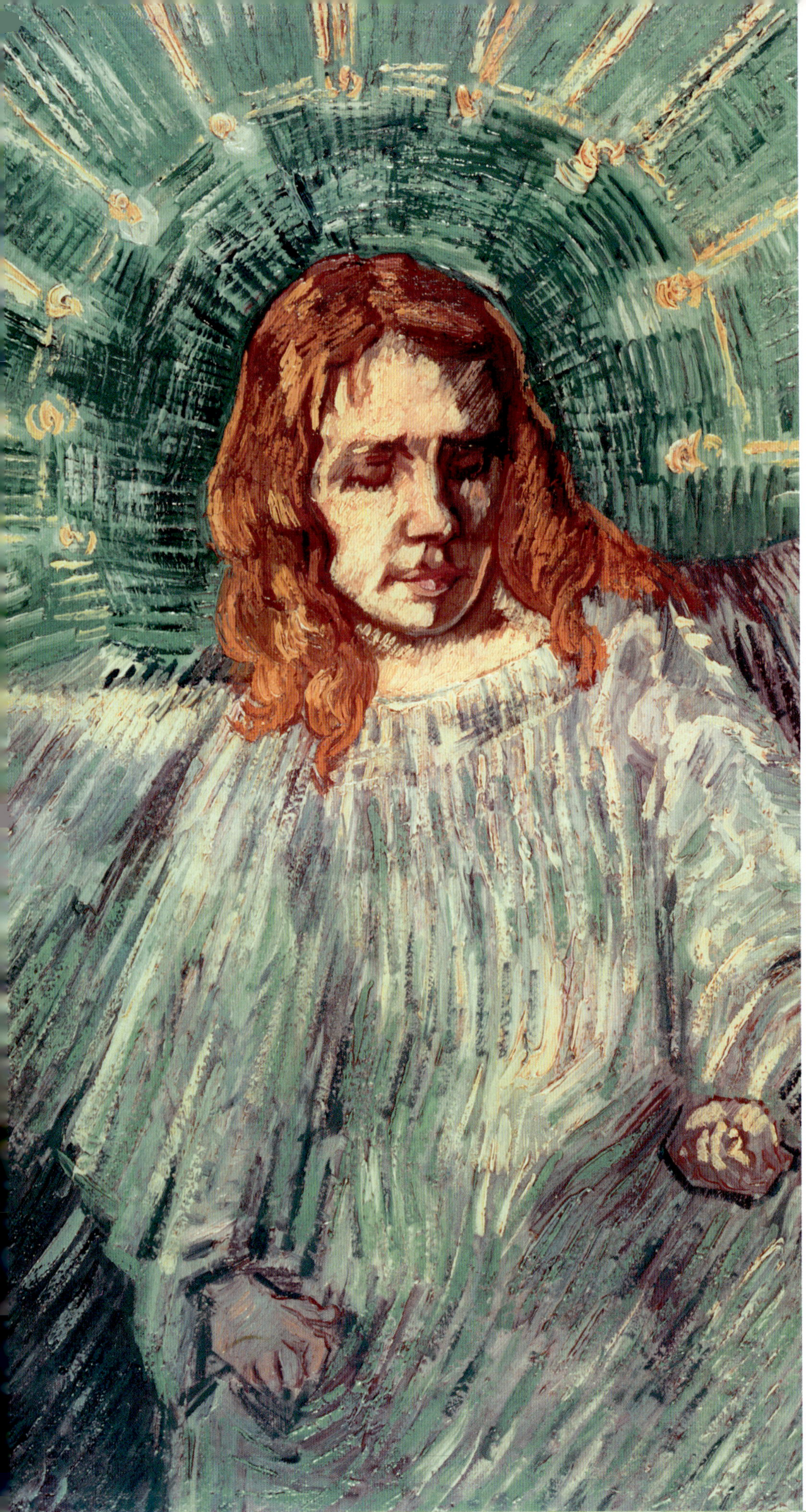

Extract from
Cuesmes, *July 1880*

I am writing to you rather reluctantly because, for a good many reasons, I have kept silent for such a long time. To some extent you have become a stranger to me, and I to you perhaps more than you think. It is probably better for us not to go on like that. It is probable that I would not have written to you even now, were it not that I feel obliged, compelled, to do so – because, be it noted, you yourself have compelled me to.

I heard in Etten that you had sent 50 francs for me. Well, I have accepted them. With reluctance, of course, with a feeling of some despondency, of course, but I have reached a sort of impasse, am in trouble, what else can I do? And so I am writing to thank you.

As you may know, I am back in the Borinage. Father said he would prefer me to stay somewhere near Etten, but I refused and I believe I was right to do so. To the family, I have, more or less, become a more or less objectionable and shady sort of character, at any rate a bad lot. [...]

Now, though it is a fairly hopeless task to regain the trust of an entire family, one which has perhaps never been wholly weaned from prejudice and other equally honourable and respectable qualities, I am not entirely without hope that, bit by bit, slowly but surely, the good relationship between one and all may be restored. In the first place I should be glad to see this good relationship – to put it no more strongly than that – restored at least between Father and me, and further, I set great store by

***The Angel (after Rembrandt)*, 1889, (detail)**
MEDIUM: Oil on canvas
Courtesy of Private Collection/ The Bridgeman Art Library

***Morning, Going out to Work*, 1888**
MEDIUM: Watercolour and ink on paper
Courtesy of Hermitage, St. Petersburg, Russia/The Bridgeman Art Library

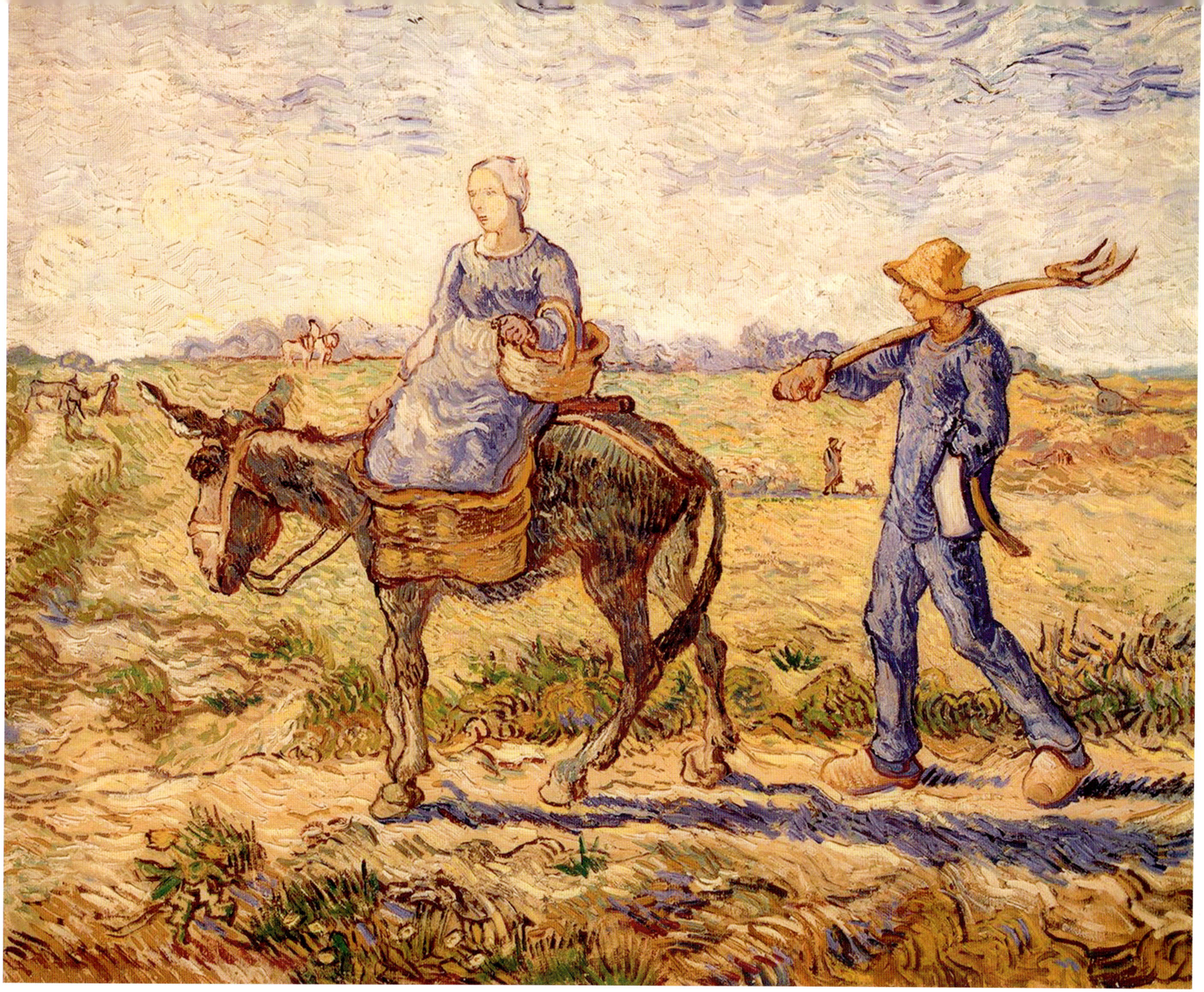

seeing it restored between the two of us. A good relationship is infinitely preferable to a misunderstanding.

Now I must trouble you with certain abstract matters, hoping that you will listen to them patiently. I am a man of passions, capable of and given to doing more or less outrageous things for which I sometimes feel a little sorry. Every so often I say or do something too hastily, when it would have been better to have shown a little more patience. Other people also act rashly at times, I think.

This being the case, what can be done about it? Should I consider myself a dangerous person, unfit for anything? I think not. Rather, every means should be tried to put these very passions to good effect.

To mention just one by way of an example, I have a more or less irresistible passion for books and the constant need to improve my mind, to study if you like, just as I have a need to eat bread. You will understand that. When I lived in other

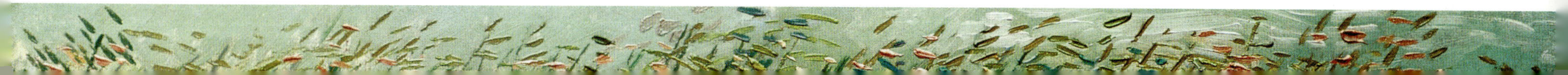

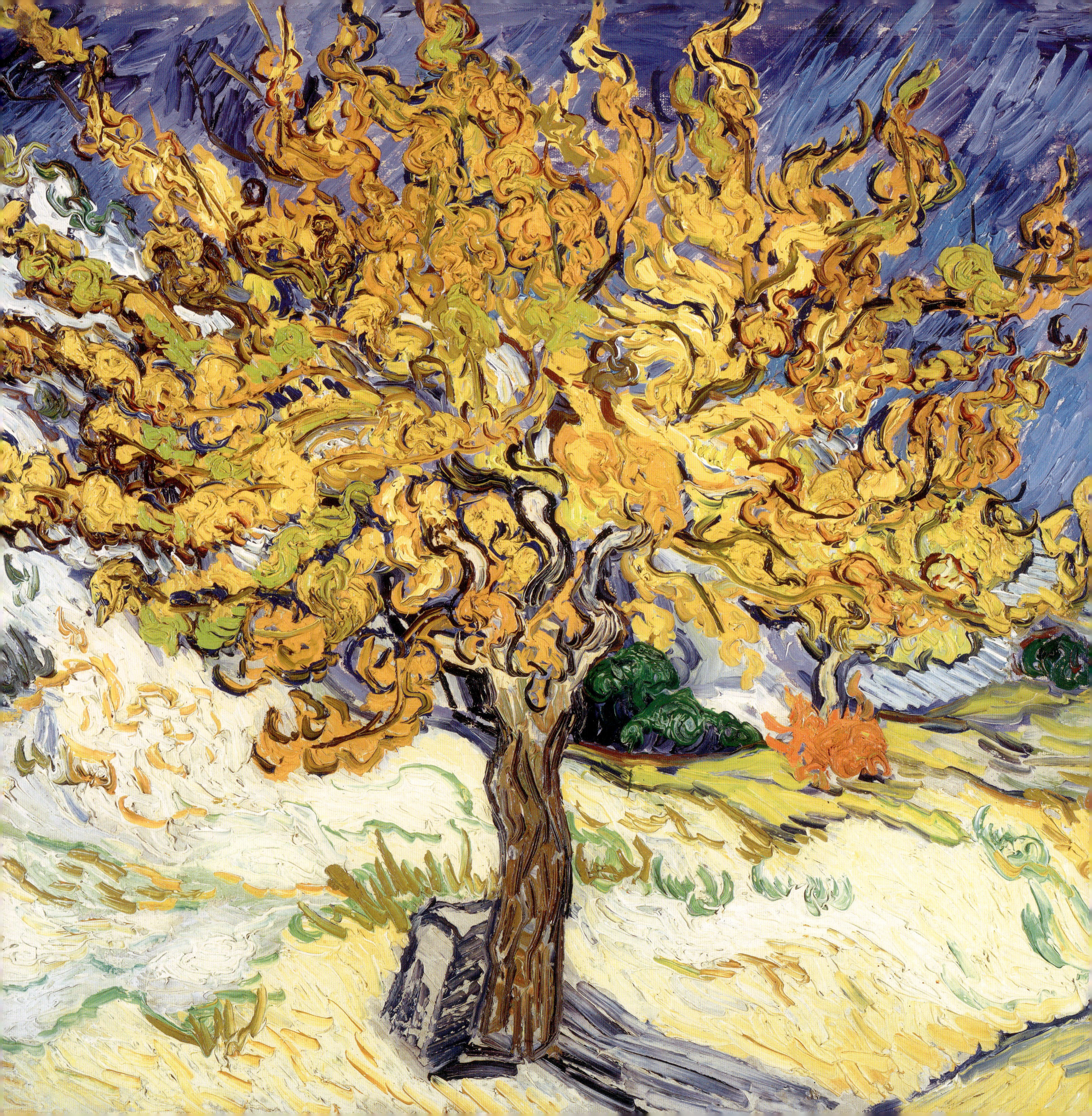

***Mulberry Tree*, 1889**
MEDIUM: Oil on canvas
Courtesy of Norton Simon Collection, Pasadena, CA, USA/The Bridgeman Art Library

***Landing Stage with Boats*, 1888**
MEDIUM: Oil on canvas
Courtesy of Museum Folkwang, Essen, Germany/Giraudon/The Bridgeman Art Library

surroundings, surroundings full of pictures and works of art, I conceived a violent, almost fanatical passion for those surroundings, as you know. And I do not regret that, and even now, *far from home, I often feel homesick for the land of pictures.* You may remember that I knew very well (and it may be that I know it still) what Rembrandt was or what Millet was or Jules Dupré or Delacroix or Millais or Matthijs Maris.

Well, today I am no longer in those surroundings, yet they say that what is known as the soul never dies but lives on for ever, continuing to seek for ever and again.

You know, for example, that I have often neglected my appearance. I admit it, and I also admit that it is 'shocking'. But look here, lack of money and poverty have something to do with it too, as well as a profound disillusionment, and besides, it is sometimes a good way of ensuring the solitude you need, of concentrating more or less on whatever study you are immersed in. [...] Now for the past five years or so, I don't know how long exactly, I have been more or less without permanent employment, wandering from pillar to post.
You will say, ever since such and such a time you have been going downhill, you have been feeble, you have done nothing. Is that entirely true?

What is true is that I have at times earned my own crust of bread, and at other times a friend has given it to me out of the goodness of his heart. I have lived whatever way I could, for better or for worse, taking things just as they came. It is true that I have forfeited the trust of various people, it is true that my financial affairs are in a sorry state, it is true that the future looks rather bleak. [...]"

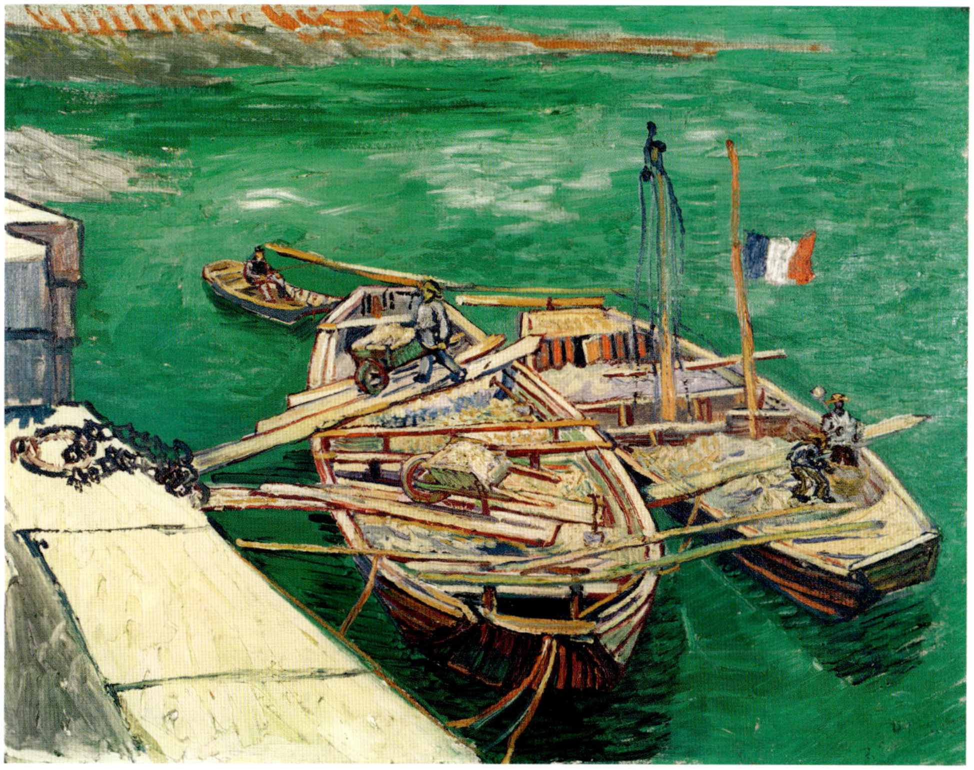

Vincent wrote a grudging thank-you note to Theo for 50 francs his brother had sent to him. He explains why he had been reluctant to write to him, aware that he had neglected many opportunities and neglected himself, and achieved what he considered little in his life to date.

Extract from Brussels, *15 October 1880*

"As you can see, I am writing you from Brussels. I thought it better to change my domicile for the present. And that for more than one reason. [...]

It had already been a long time since I have seen enough pictures or drawings etc., and the very sight of some good things here in Brussels has given me new inspiration and has strengthened my desire to make good things myself.

If Mr Schmidt would have the kindness to talk seriously about it to someone or other, I do not doubt that the thing could be satisfactorily arranged. He received me cordially, but still, if you yourself would put in a word or two on my behalf to recommend the thing to him, it would have more effect on him than I could make myself. It would be quite natural if he perhaps looked at me with some suspicion, because formerly I was with Goupil & Cie, left, and have now returned to the art field.

[...] Father wrote me that for the present I may count on receiving 60 fr. a month through his intermediary. There are several young men who are beginning to study drawing and are in the same position of not being rich either. The thing that gives one strength in such circumstances is not to be always alone, but to be in contact and relation with others in the same position. So you see, this is my great desire – that through Mr Schmidt I may have some chance to make the acquaintance of some of the young artists here. Will you do what I ask you to that effect, that is, write a little note to Mr Schmidt?

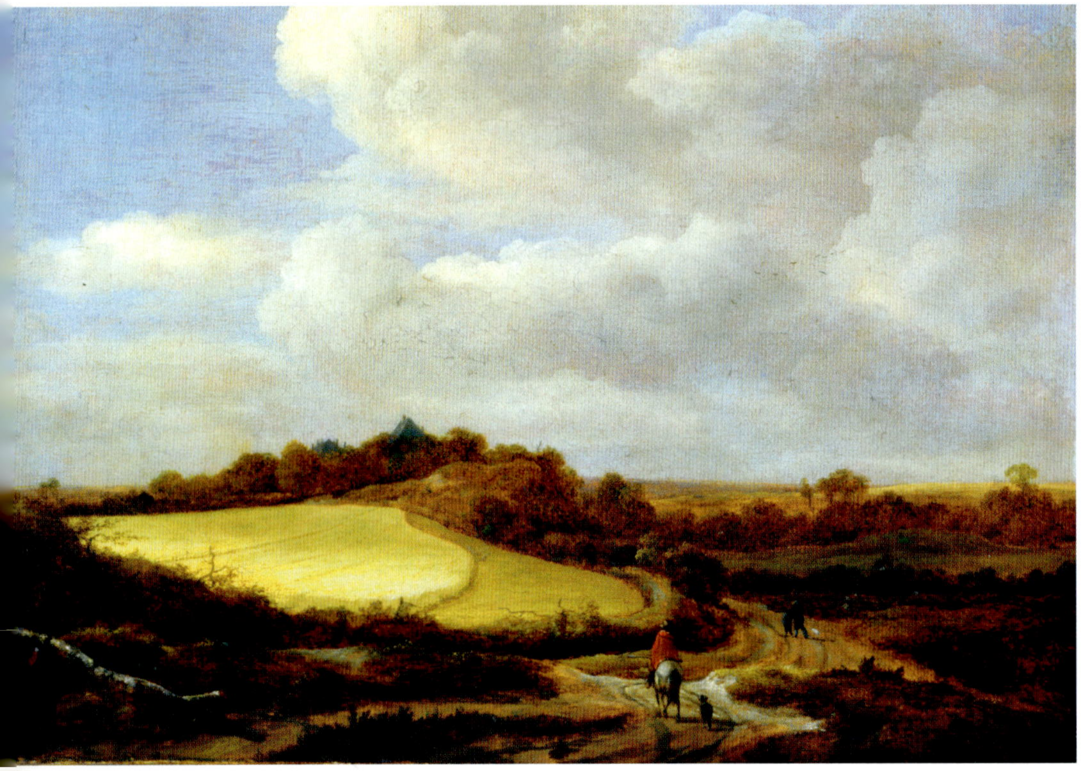

***The Wheatfield*, date unknown, (detail) by Jacob van Ruisdael (1628–82)**
MEDIUM: Oil on canvas
Courtesy of Musée des Beaux-Arts, Lille, France/Giraudon/The Bridgeman Art Library

***Ladies of Arles (Memories of the Garden at Etten)*, 1888**
MEDIUM: Oil on canvas
Courtesy of Hermitage, St. Petersburg, Russia/Giraudon/The Bridgeman Art Library

I have made another pen drawing after 'The Woodcutter' by Millet (the woodcut that you sent me). I think pen drawing is a good preparation, in case one should later want to learn etching. The pen is also very useful in accentuating pencil drawings, but one does not succeed in it at once. As to the drawing after 'Le Buisson' by Ruisdael, I will work with the pen on it especially, and prepare myself by using it on other drawings. [...]

In our interview Mr Schmidt spoke about my entering L'École des Beaux Arts here, but I told him frankly that I thought in my particular case it would be much better to work with some artist – especially since I have already finished two series of the Bargues and am on the third, which I could perhaps complete with the charcoal drawings by Allongé. However, I have not quite dismissed the idea of L'École des Beaux Arts; I might go there in the evening while I'm here if it is free or not too expensive.

But for the moment my aim must be to learn to make some drawings that are presentable and saleable as soon as possible, so that I can begin to earn something directly through my work. Because that is the necessity which is forced upon me. If you write me, please address your letters care of Mr Schmidt, for I do not know whether or not I shall stay at this hotel any longer. I think you will approve of what I say, for to progress, it is necessary to continue with vigour.

Once having mastered my pencil, or watercolouring, or etching, I can go back to the country of the mines or weavers and work from life better than I can now; but first I must learn more of the technique.

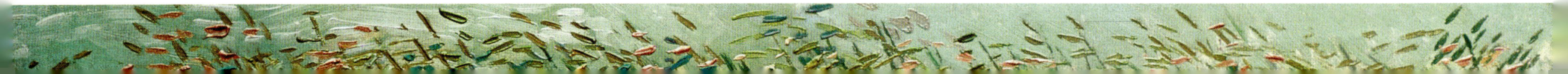

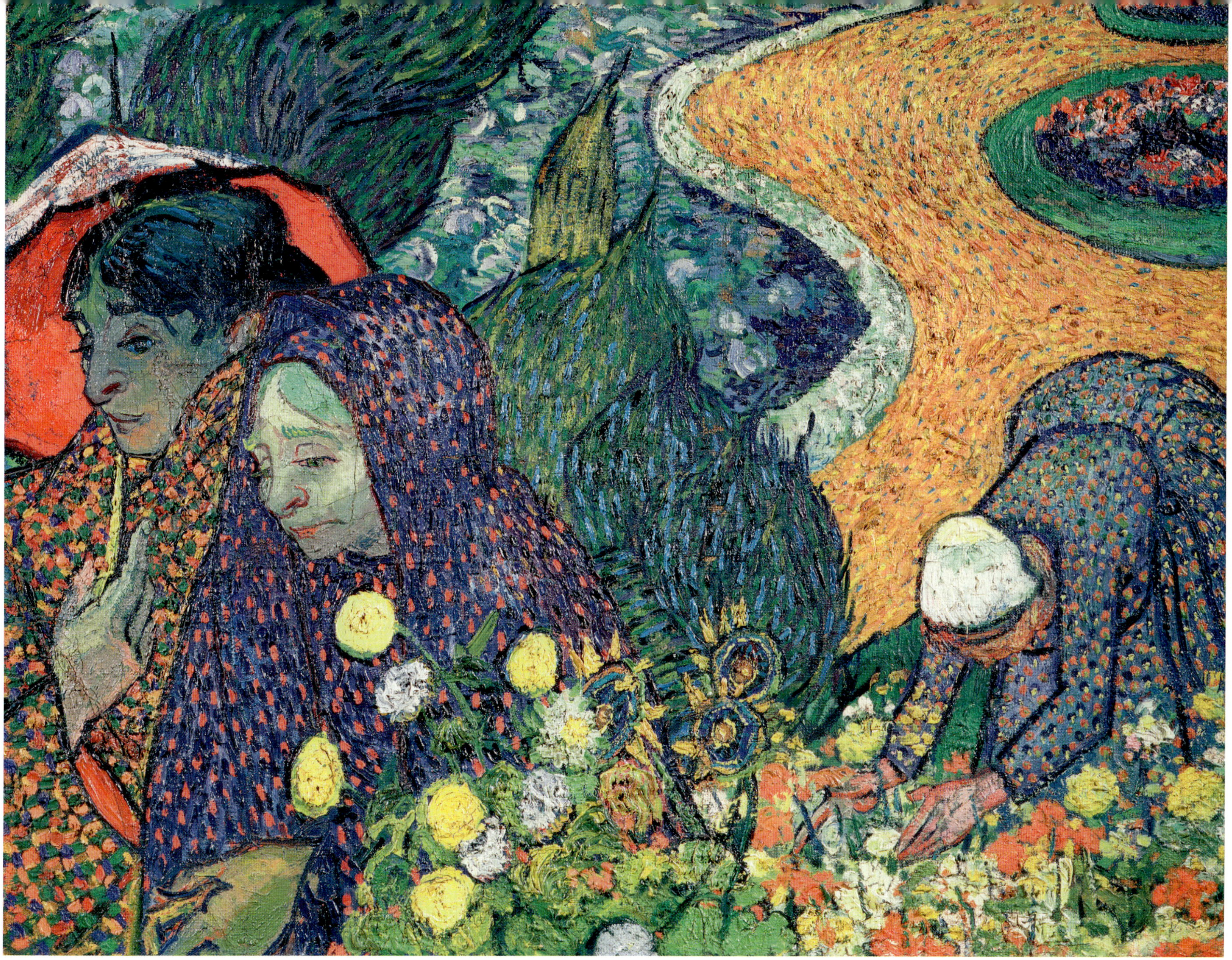

[…] I think that lodgings and perhaps food somewhat better than that of the Borinage will also help to set me right again. For I have undergone some misery in the Belgian 'Black Country', and my health has not been very good lately. But if I can only succeed someday in learning to draw well what I want to express. […] ”

Vincent, supported by his father with an allowance, is set on a career path as an artist. He is concentrating on drawing in the studio before venturing to work from life studies in the outdoors. Unsure about registering at L' École des Beaux Arts in Brussels, his current desire is to meet other artists. He asks Theo to write to a family friend Mr Schmidt for help: '…through Mr Schmidt I may have some chance to make the acquaintance of some of the young artists here. Will you do what I ask you to that effect, that is, write a little note to Mr Schmidt?' In his letter he discusses studying works by Millet and Jacob van Ruisdael (1620–82). His mind is set on making a living as a painter but he needs help from family to make it happen. From his letter to Theo, one senses the Vincent's determination to master drawing and watercolour and possibly etchings before tackling painting in oils.

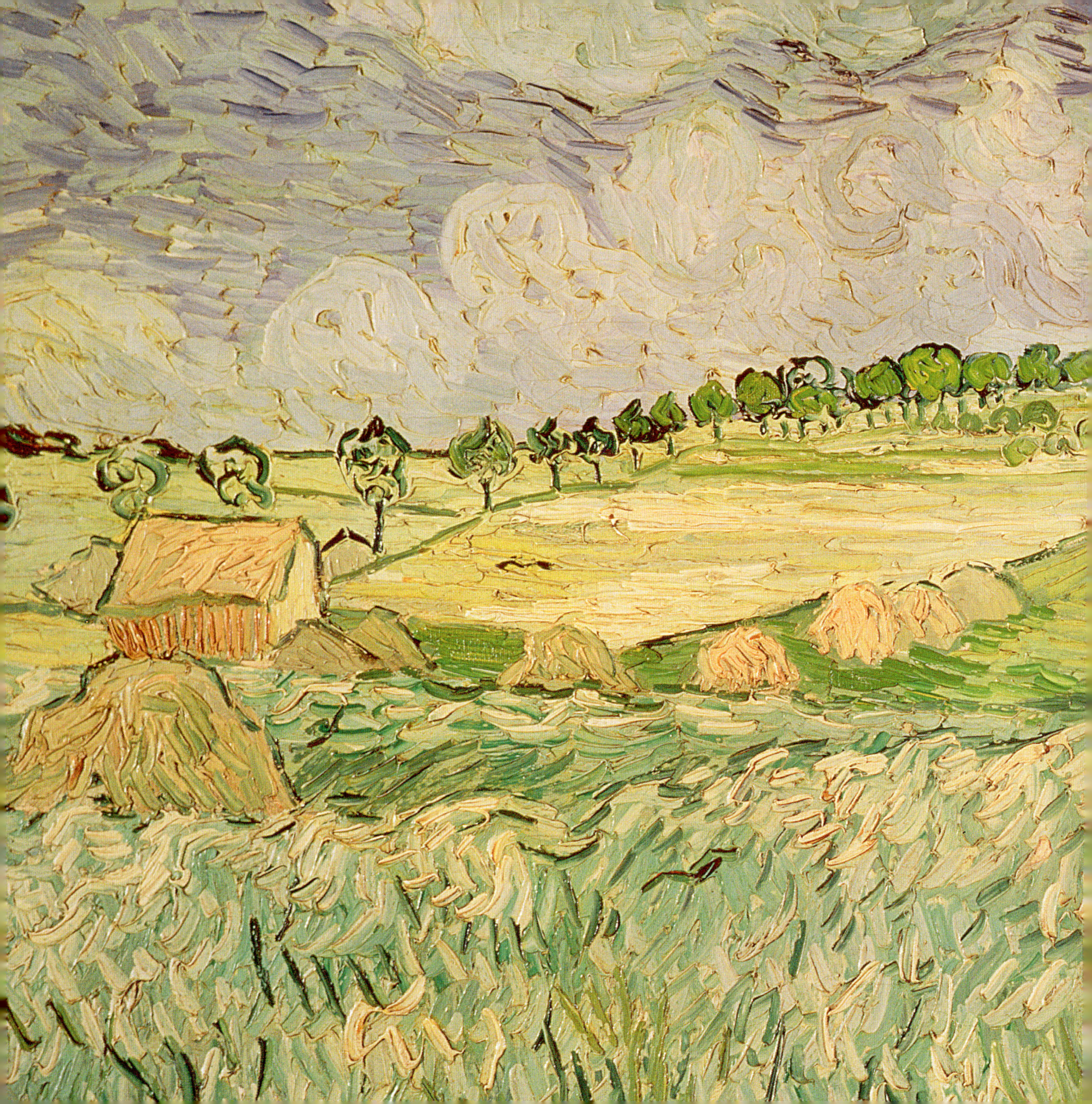

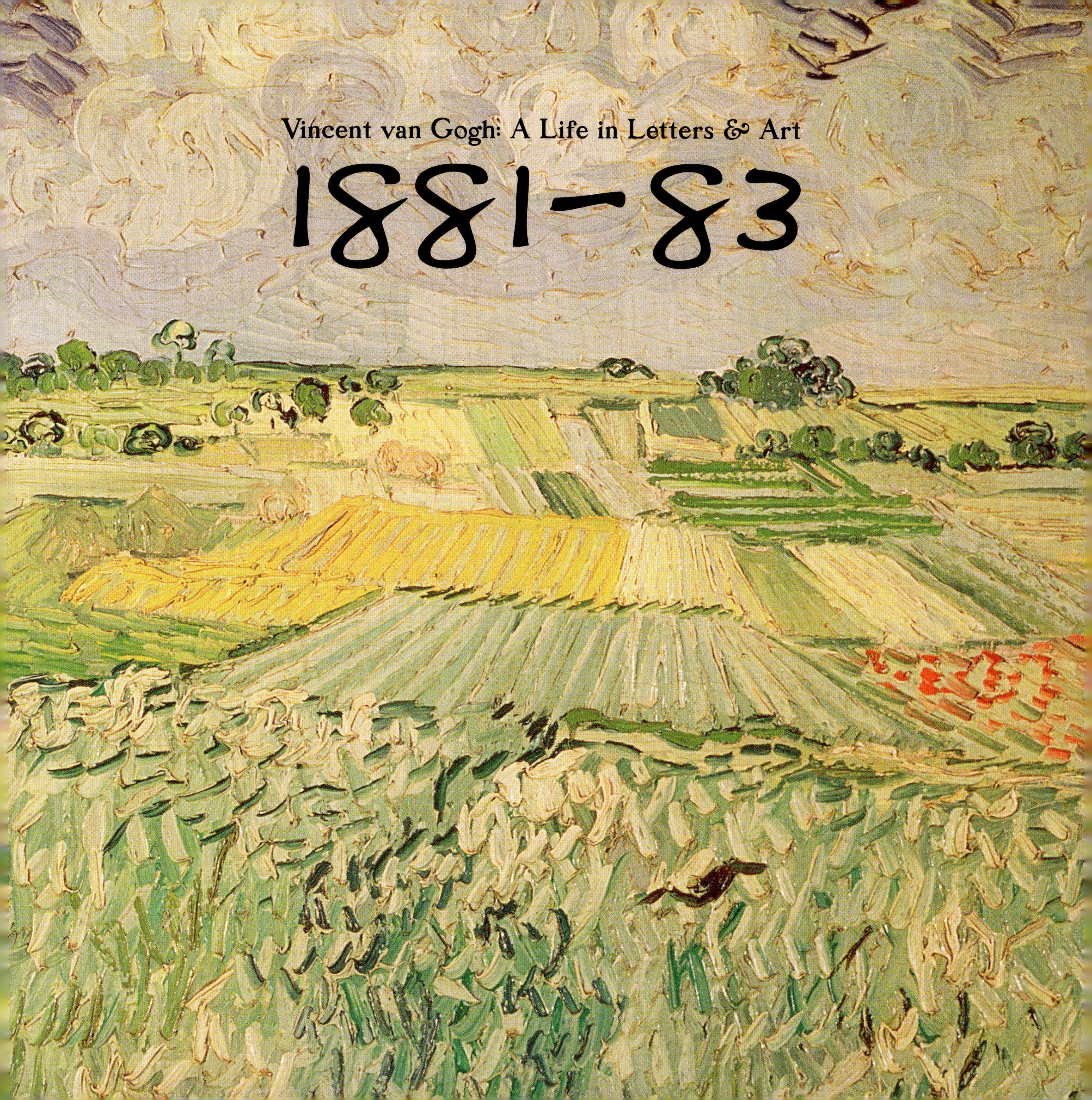
Vincent van Gogh: A Life in Letters & Art
1881–83

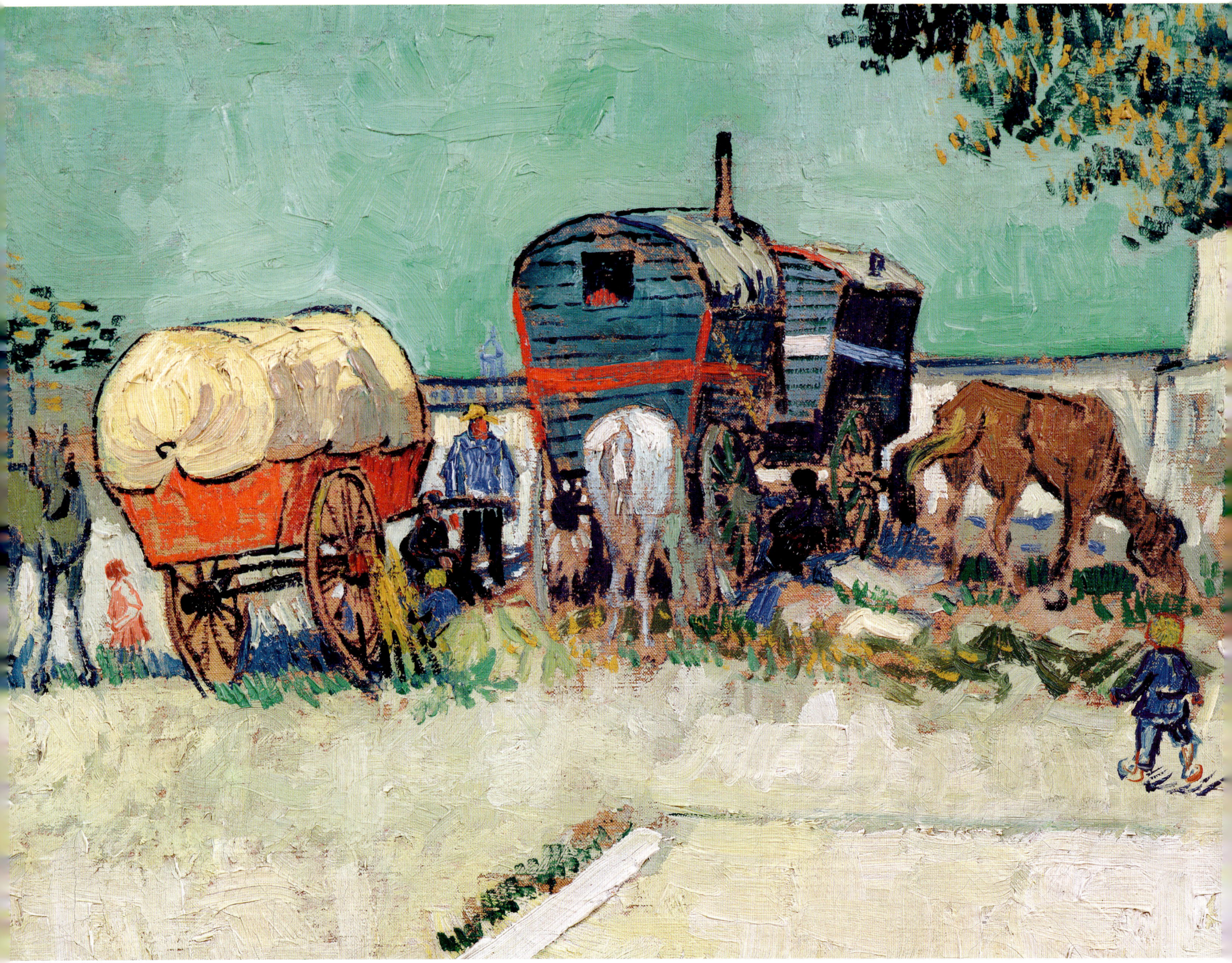

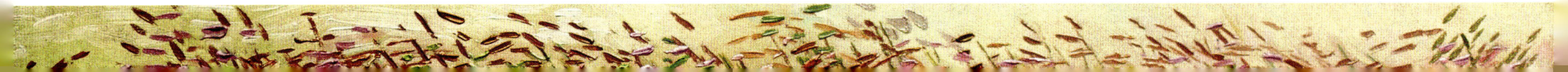

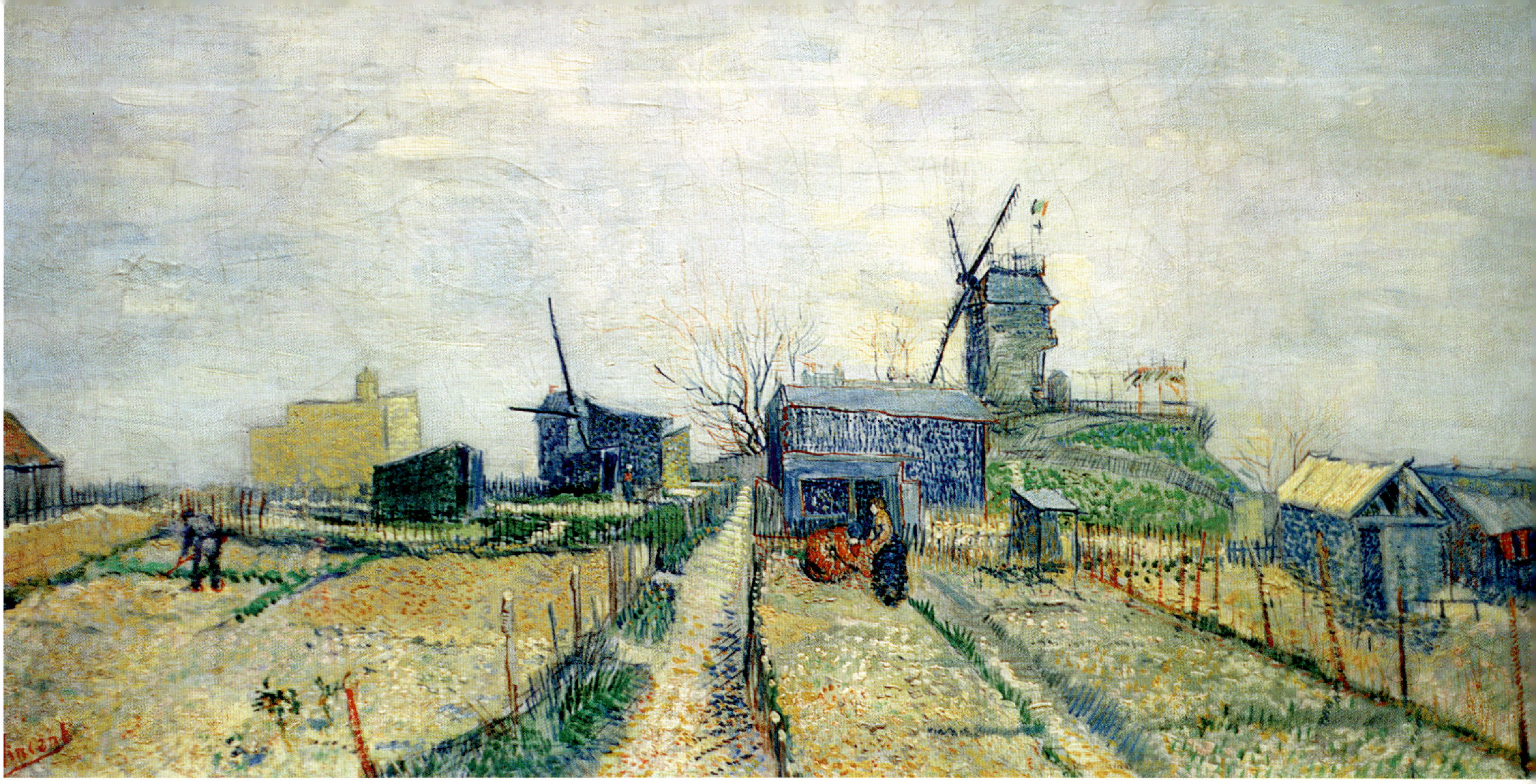

From Vincent van Gogh to

Theo van Gogh

Extract from

Brussels, *January* 1881

Mon très cher,

As I have not heard from you for so long – meaning, not for several months – nor even had the slightest answer to my last letter, perhaps it will not be out of place to ask you for some sign of life.

I must say it seems rather strange and rather unaccountable that you have not written me since the one letter I received on my arrival here. […] In thinking of you, I unconsciously said to myself, Why doesn't he write? If he is afraid of compromising himself in the eyes of Messrs Goupil & Cie by keeping in touch with me – is his position with those gentlemen so shaky and unstable that he is obliged to be so careful? Or is it that he is afraid I will ask him for money? But if this was the reason for your silence, you might at least have waited until I tried to squeeze something out of you, as the saying goes. […]

I have been drawing all winter until now, and I have also read a great deal, for indirectly that is very necessary to me. On the whole I can say I have made progress, but I ought to be able to get along more quickly. […] I have seen little of Van Rappard, because it seemed to me that he did not like to be disturbed. As long as I am not more advanced, I must avoid young artists, who do not always reflect on what they do or say. And yet I long very much to find one who, being more advanced than I, could help me progress. […]

I shake hands, awaiting a somewhat quicker reply. […]

***The Caravans, Gypsy Encampment near Arles,* 1888**
MEDIUM: Oil on canvas
Courtesy of Musée d'Orsay, Paris, France/Giraudon/The Bridgeman Art Library

***Vegetable Gardens and the Moulin de Blute-Fin on Montmartre,* 1887**
MEDIUM: Oil on canvas
Courtesy of Van Gogh Museum, Amsterdam, The Netherlands/ The Bridgeman Art Library

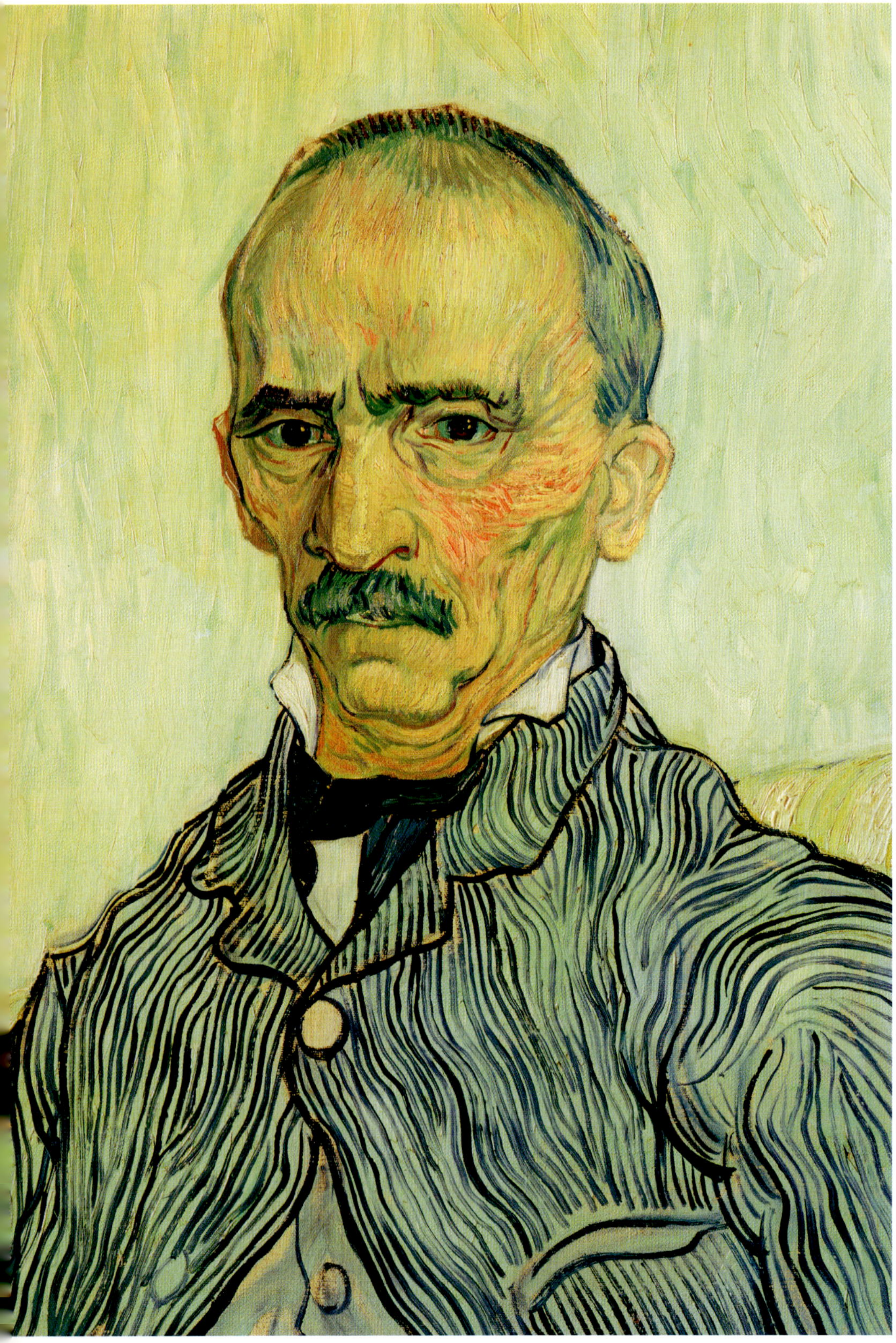

Extract from
Brussels, *January 1881*

"You will quite forgive me when you know that I wrote my last letter in a moment of spleen. My drawings went all wrong, and not knowing what to do, I began to write. I certainly ought to have waited for a better moment, and this will show you that I myself undoubtedly belong to that class of people of which I spoke in my last letter, namely, that class of people who do not always reflect on what they say or do. This being so, let us drop it.

I can tell you one thing; during these last days there has been a change for the better. I have finished at least a dozen drawings, or rather sketches in pencil and in pen and ink, which seem to me to be somewhat better. They vaguely resemble certain drawings by Lançon, or certain English wood engravings, but as yet they are more clumsy and awkward. They represent a porter, a miner, a snow shoveller, a walk in the snow, old women, a type of old man ('Ferragus' from Balzac's *L'histoire des treize*), etc. I am sending you two small ones, 'En Route' and 'Devant les Tisons' [In Front of the Wood Fire]. I see perfectly well that they are not good, but they are beginning to look like something.

I have a model almost every day, an old porter, or some working man, or some boy, who poses for me. Next Sunday perhaps one or two soldiers will sit for me. And because now I am no longer in a bad humour, I have quite a different and better opinion of you, and of the world in general. Also I have again drawn a landscape – a heath – a thing I had not done for a long time.

***Portrait of Superintendant Trabuc in St Paul's Hospital*, 1889**
MEDIUM: Oil on canvas
Courtesy of Kunstmuseum Solothurn, Switzerland/The Bridgeman Art Library

***Landscape at Saint-Rémy (The Ploughed Field)*, date unknown**
MEDIUM: Oil on canvas
Courtesy of Indianapolis Museum of Art, USA/Gift of Mrs James W. Fesler in memory of Daniel W. and Elizabeth C. Marmon/The Bridgeman Art Library

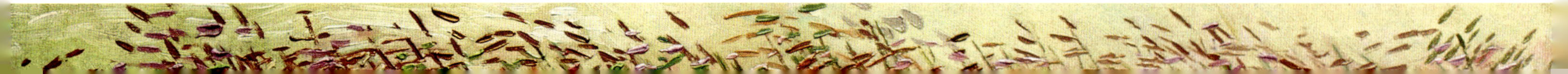

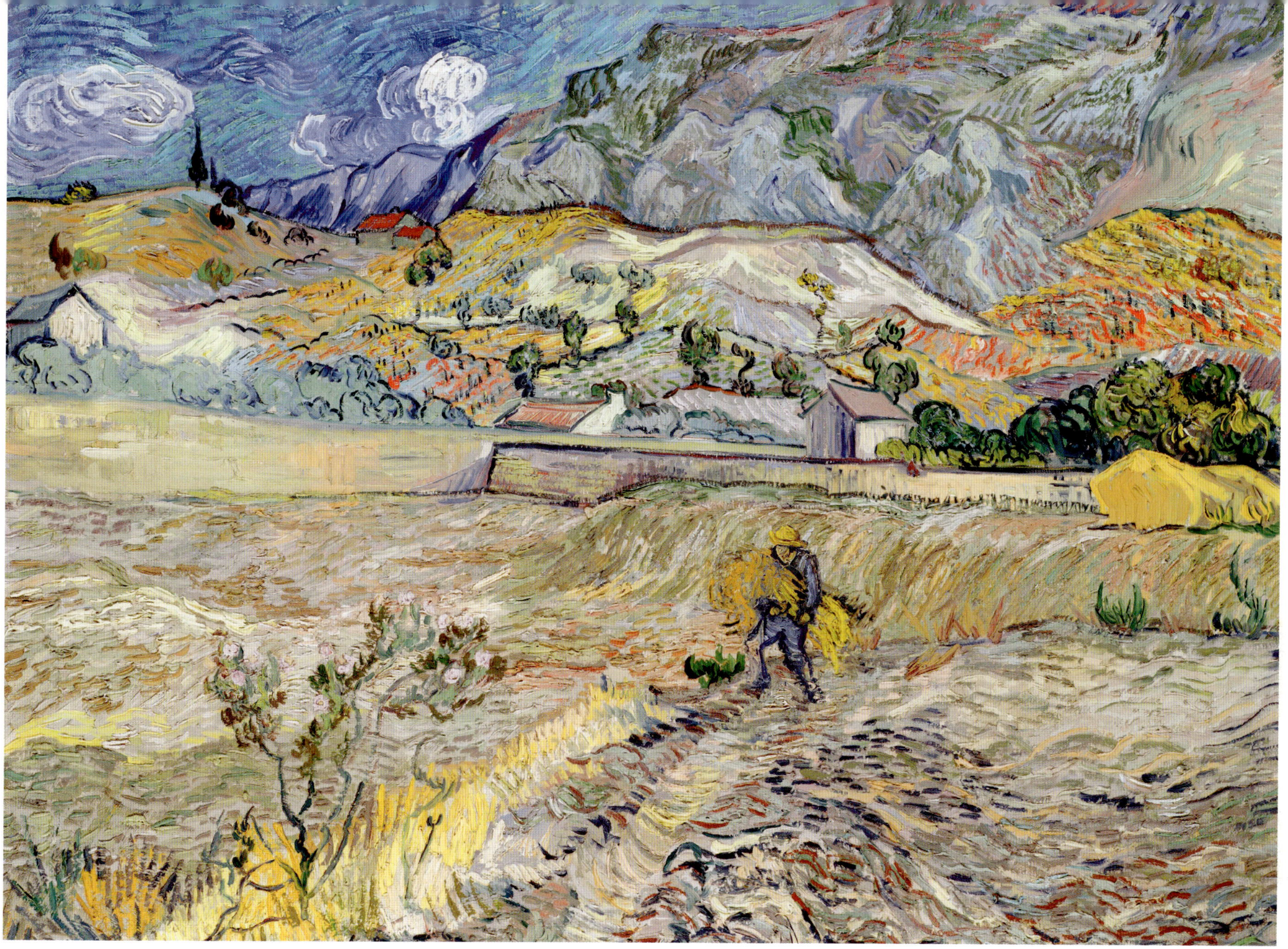

I love landscape very much, but I love ten times more those studies from life, sometimes of startling realism, which have been drawn so masterfully by Gavarni, Henri Monnier, Daumier, De Lemud, Henri Pille, Th. Schuler, Ed. Morin, G. Doré (e.g. in his 'London'), A. Lançon, De Groux, Félicien Rops, etc., etc. Now without in the least pretending to compare myself to those artists, still, by continuing to draw those types of working people, etc., I hope to arrive at the point of being able to illustrate papers and books. Especially when I am able to take more models, also female models, I shall make more progress – I feel it, and know it. And I shall also probably learn to make portraits. But the condition is to work hard, 'Not a day without a line,' as Gavarni said.

[…] As you vaguely spoke to me some time ago about coming to Paris, I must tell you that I wish no better than to go someday soon, provided I were sure of finding some work there which would give me a salary of at least 100 fr. a month. I must also tell you that as I have begun to draw, I do not intend to drop it, so I will try chiefly to get on in that line. […] ”

The letter is Vincent's apology for a dismissive letter sent earlier in January to Theo from whom he has not heard in several months. Theo had responded with news of his job at Goupil & Cie and changes to staff. Vincent updates him on his own progress, hoping to come to Paris but needing a secure income to do so.

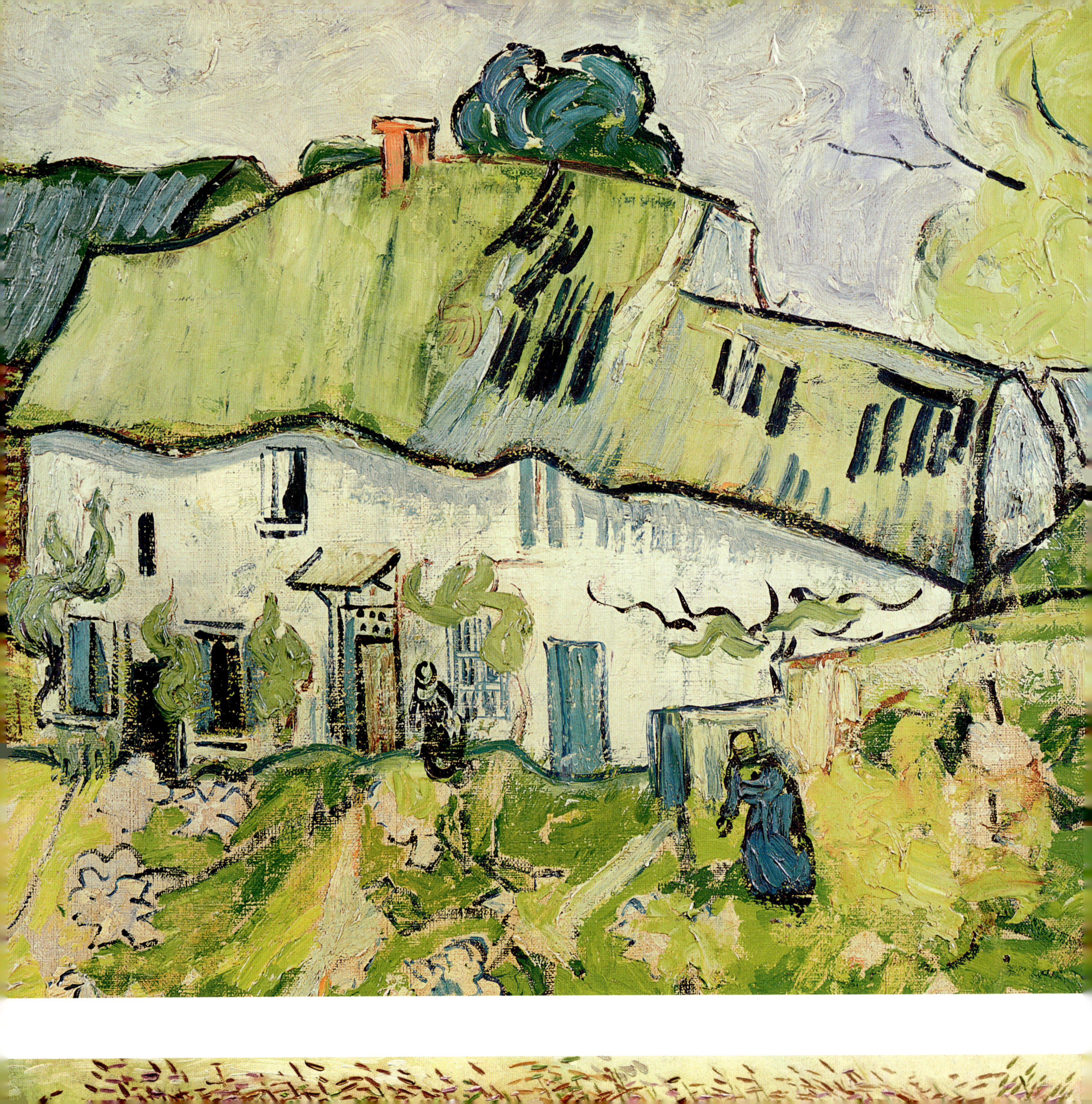

From Vincent van Gogh to his parents, Theodorus and Anna van Gogh

Extract from Brussels, *16 February 1881*

Dear Father and Mother,

I received your letter, which made me very happy, as I was already looking forward to it, especially because of Father's illness. I was glad to hear that there is some improvement. I am getting on pretty well with my work, though it is still far from perfect, and must become much better still. [...]

Now I must tell you another thing that I have done. As I told you, about a month ago I bought a pair of trousers and a coat, secondhand. It turned out so well that I bought another coat and pair of trousers from the same man. It's true that the first suit would have been quite sufficient, but it is much better to have two suits because they last longer when one can alternate them. Enclosed is a sample of the material. And I also had to replenish my underwear with three pairs of drawers, and paid 2.75 fr. apiece for them; besides, I bought a pair of shoes for 4 fr. The things I bought were really not superfluous. But altogether they have made a big hole in this month's money, and I shall have to stint myself in consequence, especially as I paid 5 fr. to that painter in advance for the lessons.

Do not worry about these expenses, however, and do not accuse me of extravagance, for really the contrary is rather my

***The Farm in Summer*, 1890**
MEDIUM: Oil on canvas
Courtesy of Van Gogh Museum, Amsterdam, The Netherlands/ Giraudon/The Bridgeman Art Library

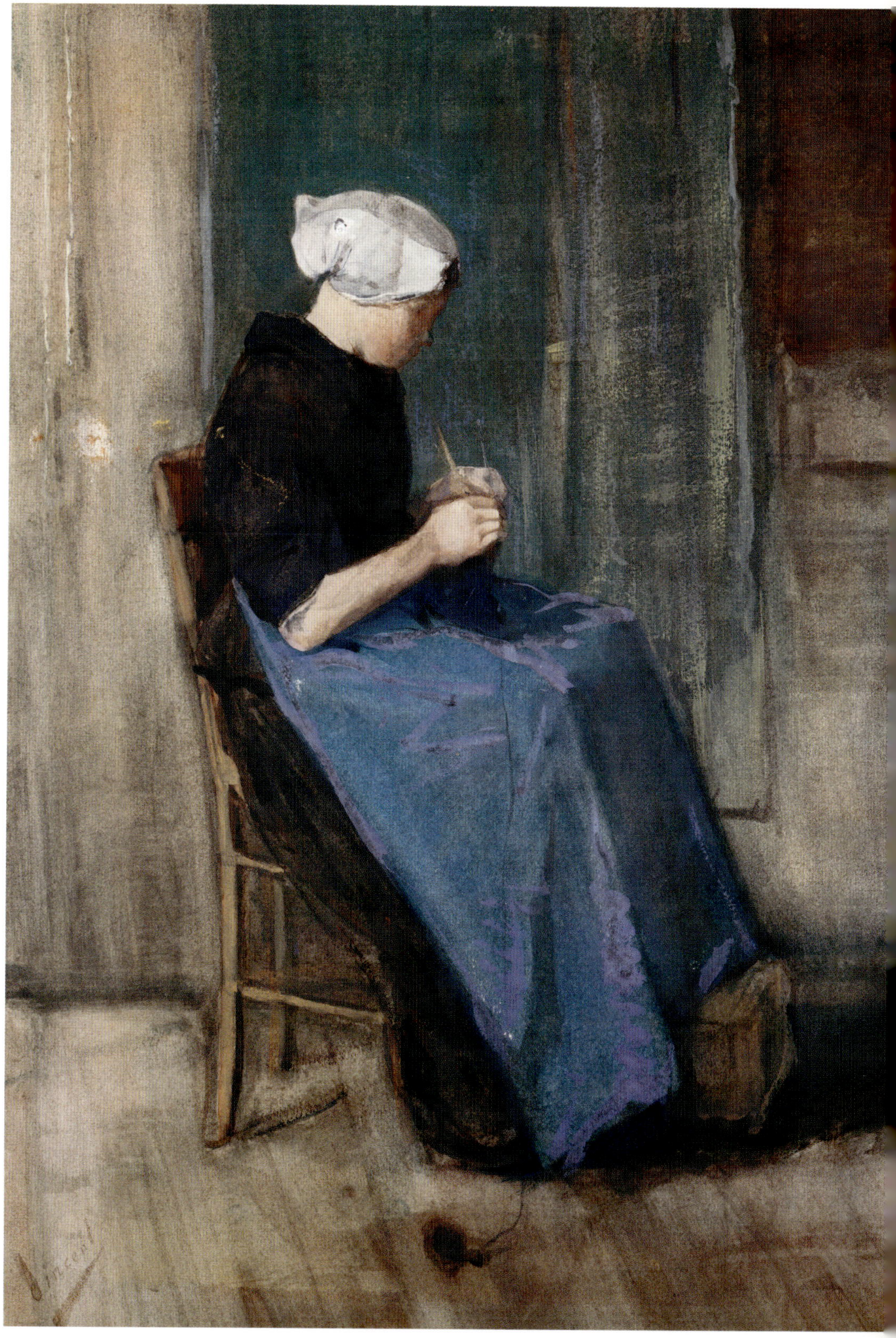

***Young Scheveningen Woman Knitting, Facing Right*, date unknown**
MEDIUM: Watercolour and gouache on paper
Courtesy of Private Collection/Photo © Christie's Images/The Bridgeman Art Library

fault of character, and if I could spend more, I should get on quicker and make more progress. If you can send me something extra this month without depriving yourselves, I hope you will. But if you cannot, there is no immediate hurry. I told my landlord that I should be rather hard up this month, and he agreed that I could pay at my convenience because he now knows me well enough not to demand my paying in advance, at least not for a full month.

I bought that suit for a reason other than wearing it myself as long as possible: when I can wear it no longer, it will serve me in another way. For you should know that eventually I must have a small collection of workmen's clothes in which to dress the models for my drawings. For instance, a Brabant blue smock, the grey linen suit that the miners wear and their leather hat, then a straw hat and wooden shoes, a fisherman's outfit of yellow oilskin and a sou'wester. And certainly also that suit of black or brown corduroy which is very picturesque and

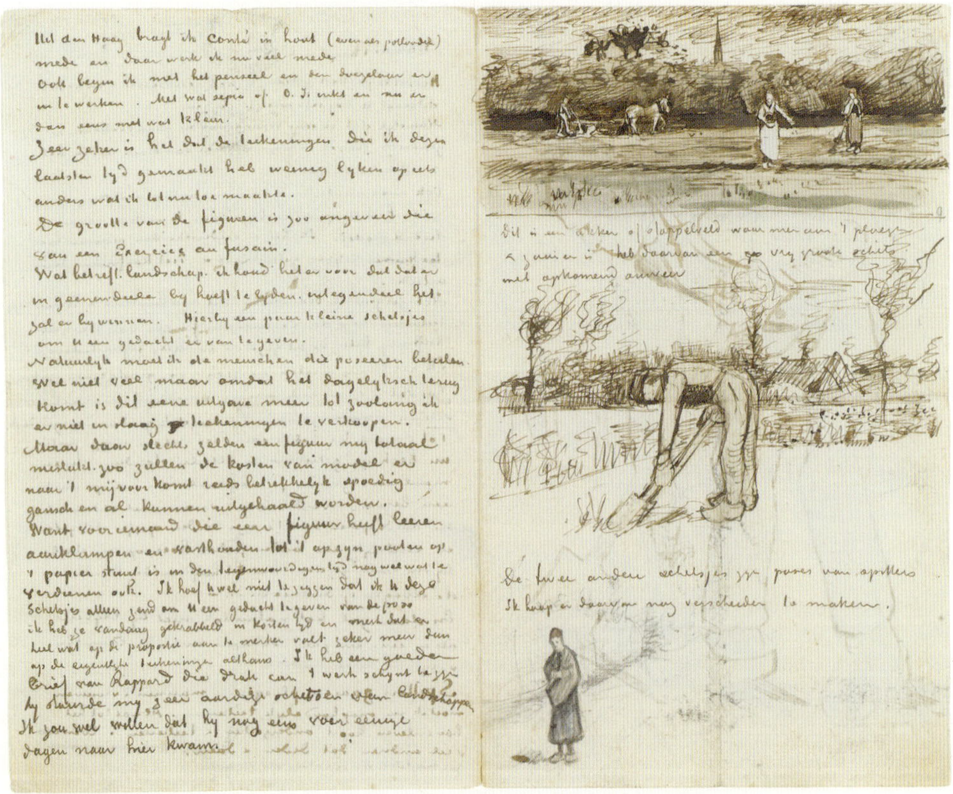

***The Haystacks*, date unknown**

MEDIUM: Oil on canvas

characteristic – and then a red flannel shirt or undervest. And also a few women's dresses, for instance, that of De Kempen [region in Brabant] and from the neighbourhood of Antwerp, along with the Brabant bonnet and, for instance, that of Blankenberg, or Scheveningen or Katwijk.

I certainly do not intend to buy all this at once, but to collect it gradually piece by piece. [...] Drawing the model with the necessary costumes is the only true way to succeed. Only if I study drawing thus seriously and thoroughly, always trying to portray truly what I see, shall I arrive; and then, notwithstanding the inevitable expenses, I shall make a living by it. For a good draughtsman can certainly find work nowadays: such persons are in great demand, and there are positions that are very well paid. [...]

And now I finish, with greetings to all, and my best wishes for A.'s birthday, and believe me,

Your loving

Vincent

The painter who gives me lessons now is making a very good picture of a Blankenberg fisherman.

Vincent updates his parents on his current lifestyle, noting to them how he has saved money by buying secondhand clothing but needing two sets of outer clothing, in order for the clothes to not wear out. He plans to use the spare clothes to dress his life models. Having explained how his money has been spent, he asks if they can send him some more.

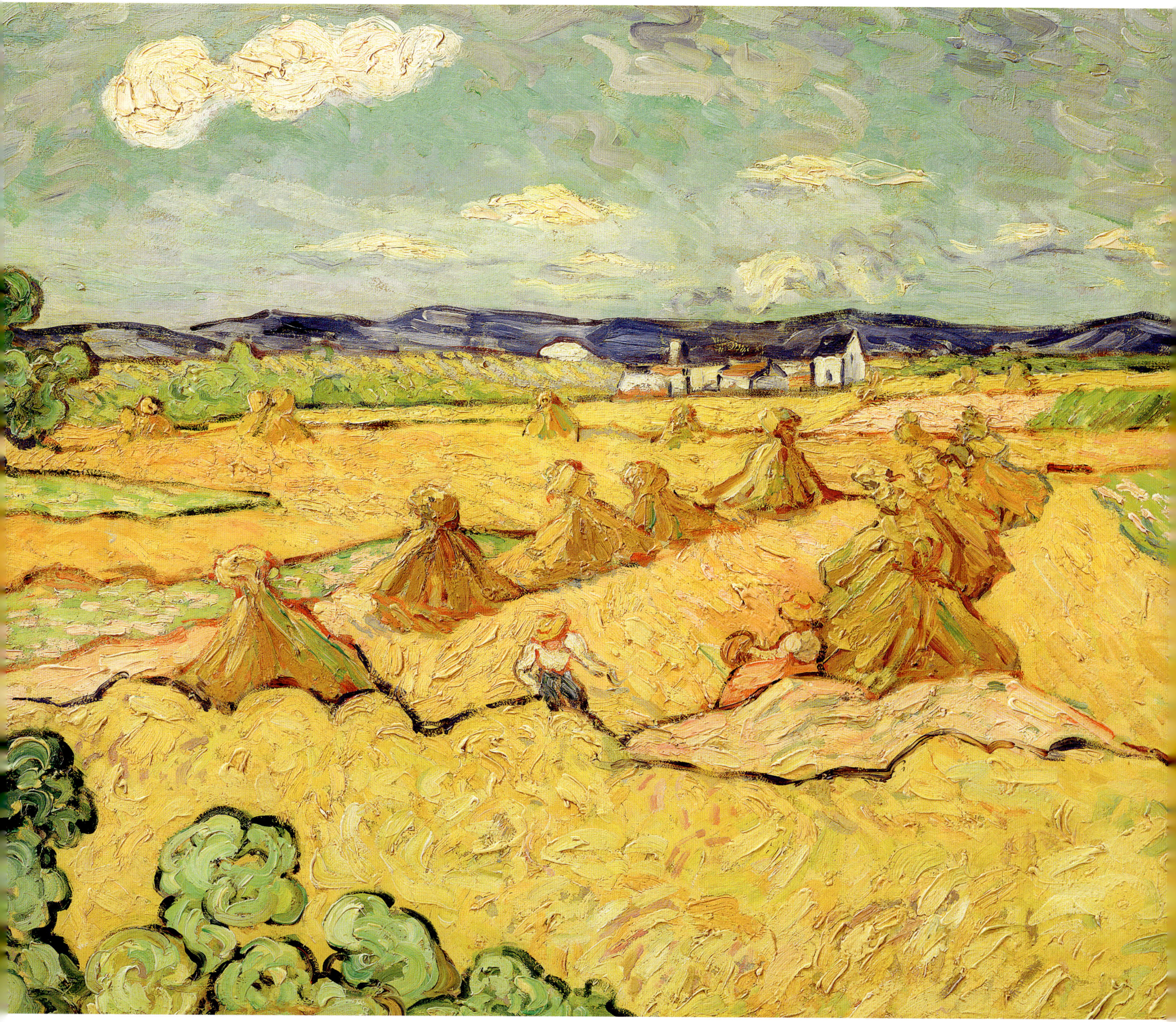
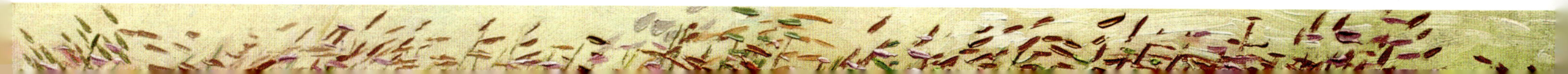

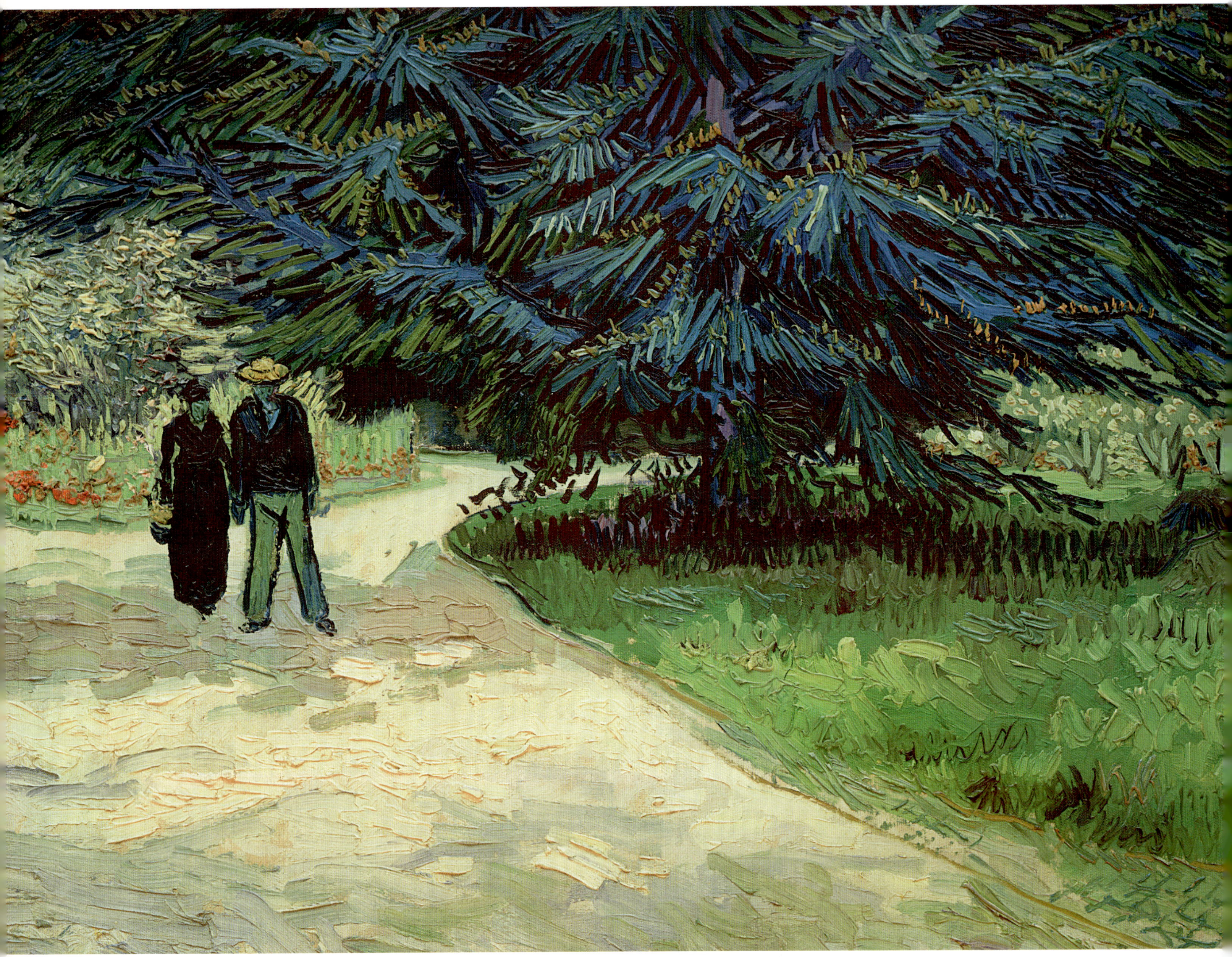

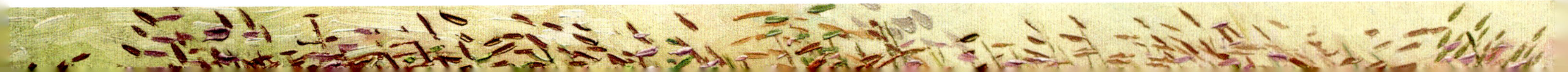

From Vincent van Gogh to

Theo van Gogh

Extract from

Etten, *3 November 1881*

Dear Theo,

There is something on my mind that I want to tell you about. You may perhaps know something of it already and it will not be news to you. I wanted to let you know that I fell so much in love with Kee Vos this summer that I can find no other words for it than, 'It is just as if Kee Vos were the closest person to me and I the closest person to Kee Vos' – and those words I spoke to her. But when I told her this, she replied that her past and her future remained as one to her so that she could never return my feelings.

Then I was in a tremendous dilemma about what to do. Should I resign myself to that 'never, no, never,' or consider the matter not yet settled and done with, keep in good heart and not give up?

I chose the latter. And to this day I do not regret this approach, although I am still up against that 'never, no, never'. [...]

One of the reasons why I have not written to you about all this before is that my position was so uncertain and unsettled that I was unable to explain it to you. Now, however, we have reached the point where I have spoken about it, not only to her but to Father and Mother, to Uncle and Aunt Stricker and to our Uncle and Aunt at Prinsenhage.

The only one to say to me, and that very informally and privately, that there really might be a chance for me if I worked hard and made progress, was someone from whom I least expected it: Uncle Cent. He was pleased with the way in which I reacted to Kee's 'never no, never', that is not making heavy weather of it but taking it in quite good humour, and said for instance, 'Don't give grist to the never, no, never mills which Kee has set up, I wish her all the best, but I rather hope those mills will go bankrupt.'

Couple in the Park, Arles, **1888**
MEDIUM: Oil on canvas
Courtesy of Private Collection/ The Bridgeman Art Library

Man Smoking, **1888**
MEDIUM: Oil on canvas
Courtesy of The Barnes Foundation, Merion, Pennsylvania, USA/ The Bridgeman Art Library

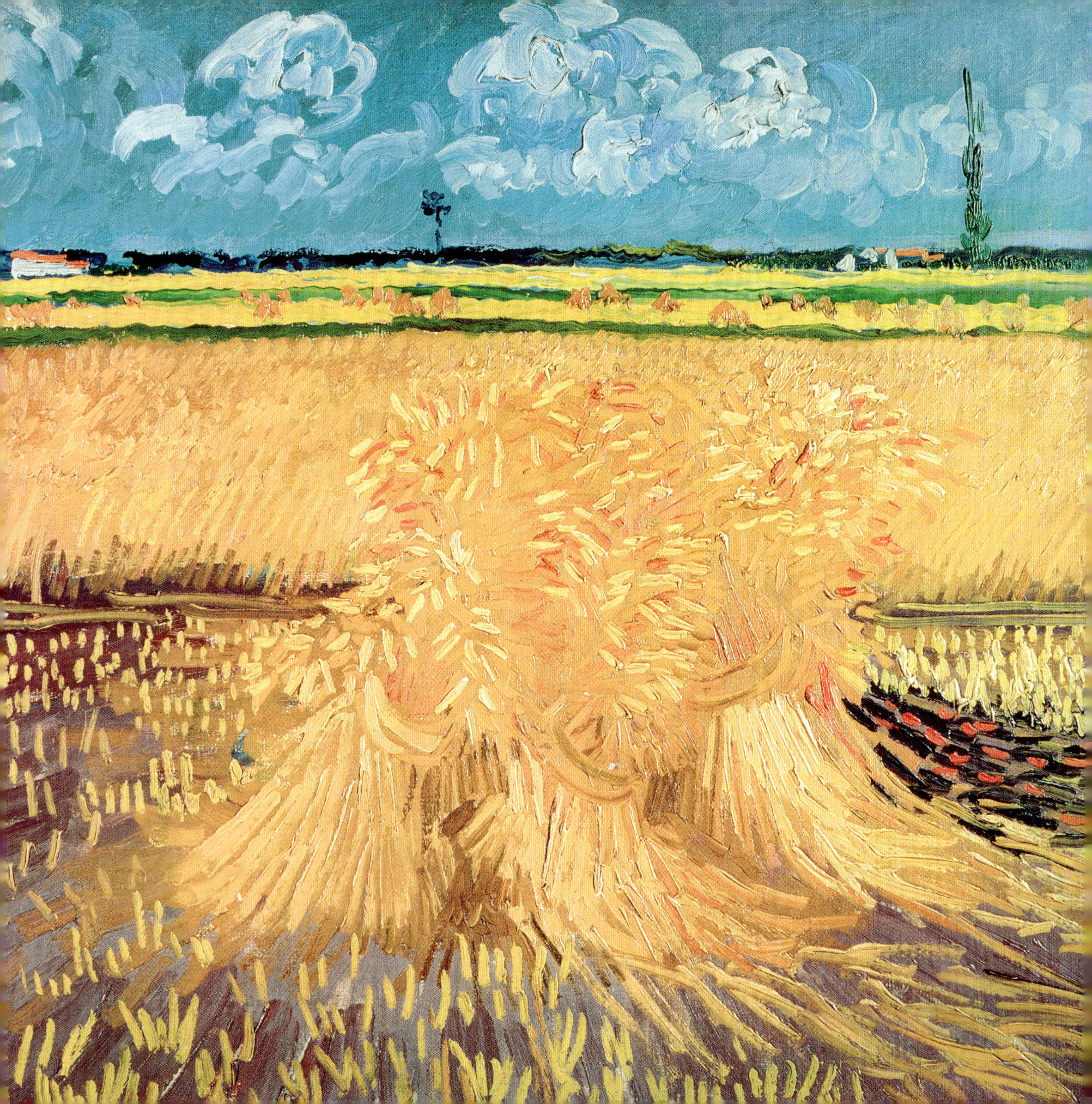

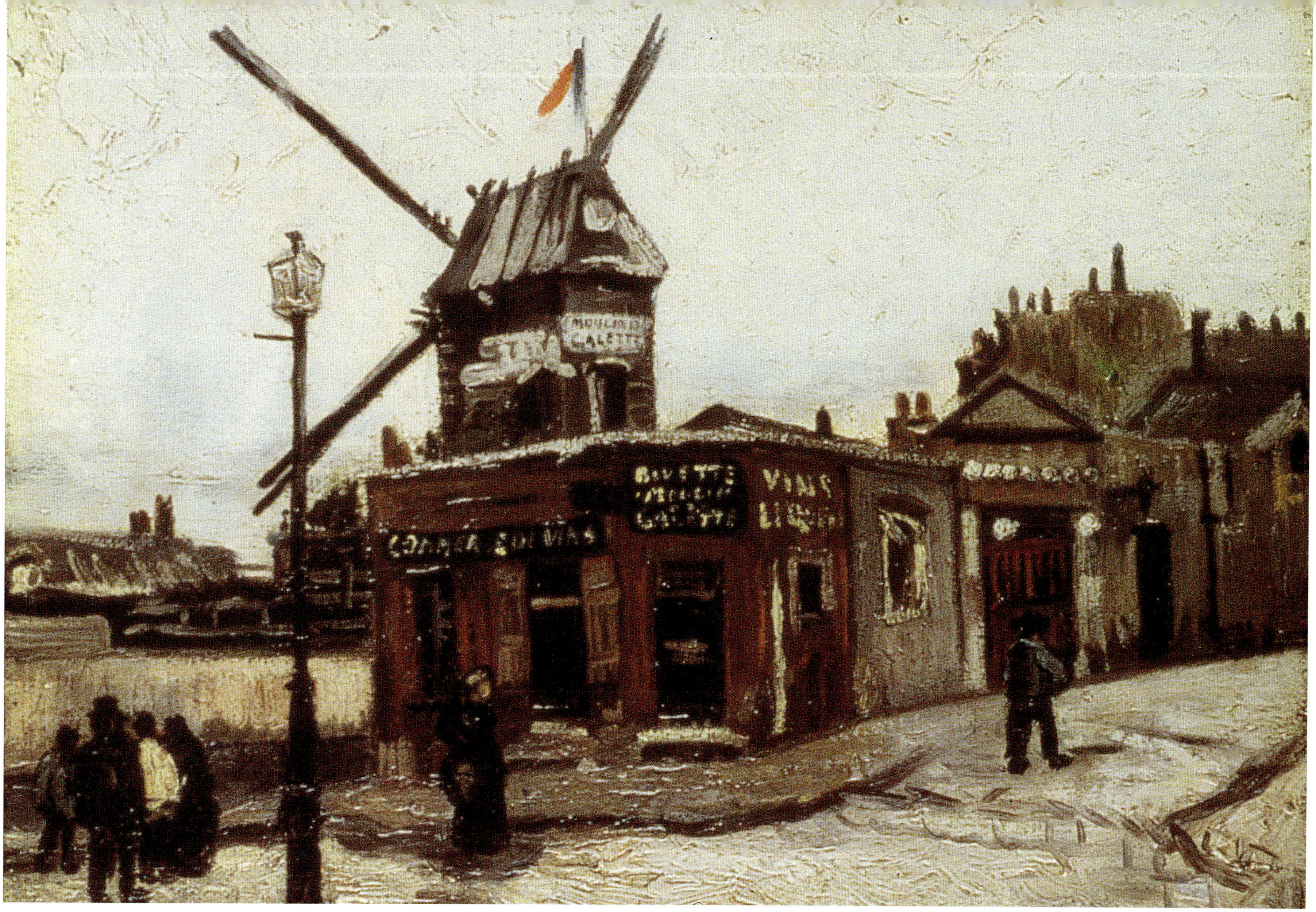

Similarly, I didn't take it amiss when Uncle Stricker said that there was the danger that I 'might be severing friendly relationships and old ties'. […]

For the time being, however, I think they'll go about it very gently, keeping me dangling and fobbing me off with fair words until Uncle and Aunt Stricker's big celebration (in December) is over [their silver wedding]. I fear they will be taking measures to get rid of me.

[…] I do believe that they are positively *against* it and I wanted to make that clear to you. They will try to make sure that Kee and I neither see or speak or write to each other, because they know very well that if we saw, spoke or wrote to each other, there would be a chance of Kee changing her mind. […]

The older people will change their minds about this affair, not when Kee changes her attitude but when I have become somebody who earns at least 1,000 guilders a year. Once again, forgive me the hard contours with which I am outlining matters. If I receive a little sympathy from the older ones, I believe that some of the younger ones will be able to understand my position.

***Wheatfield with Sheaves*, 1888**
MEDIUM: Oil on canvas
Courtesy of Honolulu Academy of Arts, Hawaii, USA/The Bridgeman Art Library

***The Moulin de la Galette*, 1886**
MEDIUM: Oil on canvas
Courtesy of Nationalgalerie, Berlin, Germany/The Bridgeman Art Library

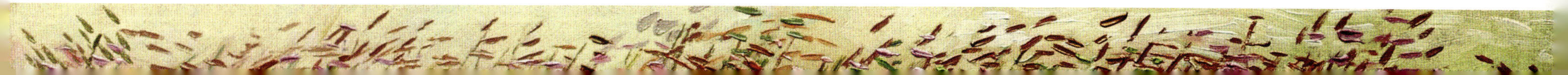

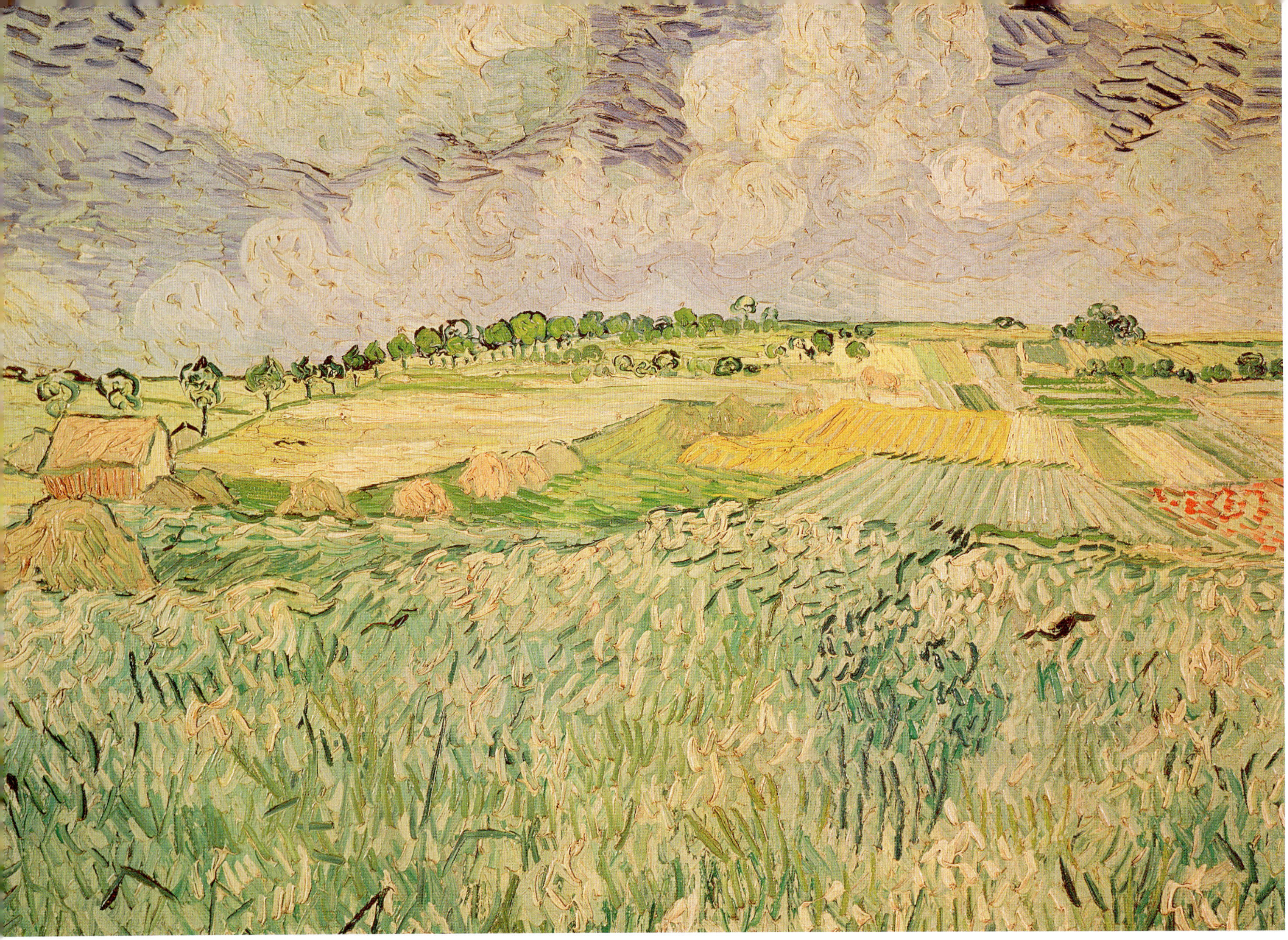

[…] But now you will realize that I hope to leave no stone unturned that might bring me closer to her, and that is my intention:

To go on loving her

Until in the end she loves me too. […]

Historians argue that the date of this letter might be 3 November 1881, which would coincide with Vincent's visit to the parental home of Cornelia 'Kee' Vos Stricker (1846–1918). In the spring of 1881, Vincent, now working as an artist, moved to his parents' house in Etten to save money. A widowed cousin, Kee Vos came to stay with her young son. As one would expect in a family home, she spent time with her cousin. Kee was the daughter of Vincent's mother's older sister and was seven years older than him. Unfortunately for both of them, Vincent misread her friendship as intimacy and fell in love with her. At his surprise proposal of marriage, Kee angrily refused him. In his letter he tells Theo that she chillingly replied 'Never, no, never.' Even after this explicit rejection he asks for advice on how to proceed. Following her refusal, she left the house in Etten the same evening. The episode was an embarrassment

to Vincent's and Kee's parents. This lengthy letter refers to Kee's family trying to keep him from seeing her. Nonetheless, Vincent decided to continue his pursuit.

Extract from
Etten, *7 November 1881*

In the first place I must ask you if it astonishes you at all that there is a love serious and passionate enough not to be chilled even by many 'never, no, nevers'?

[…] If you reply to this by saying, 'But there are people who put an end to their own life,' I simply answer, 'I really do not think I am a man with such inclinations.'

Life has become very dear to me, and I am very glad that I love. My life and my love are one. 'But you are faced with a "never, no, never",' is your reply.

My answer to that is, 'Old boy, for the present I look upon that "never, no, never" as a block of ice which I press to my heart to thaw.'

Following Vincent's rejection by Kee Vos, his letters to Theo – interspersed with references to his latest drawings – continue to discuss how the problem as he saw it could be solved: '…it would still be better for us [Vincent and Kee] to be together than not together. Vincent dismisses any thought or talk of suicide: 'I really do not think I am a man with such inclinations.'

***The Plain at Auvers*, 1890, (detail)**
MEDIUM: Oil on canvas
Courtesy of Neue Pinakothek, Munich, Germany/Giraudon/ The Bridgeman Art Library

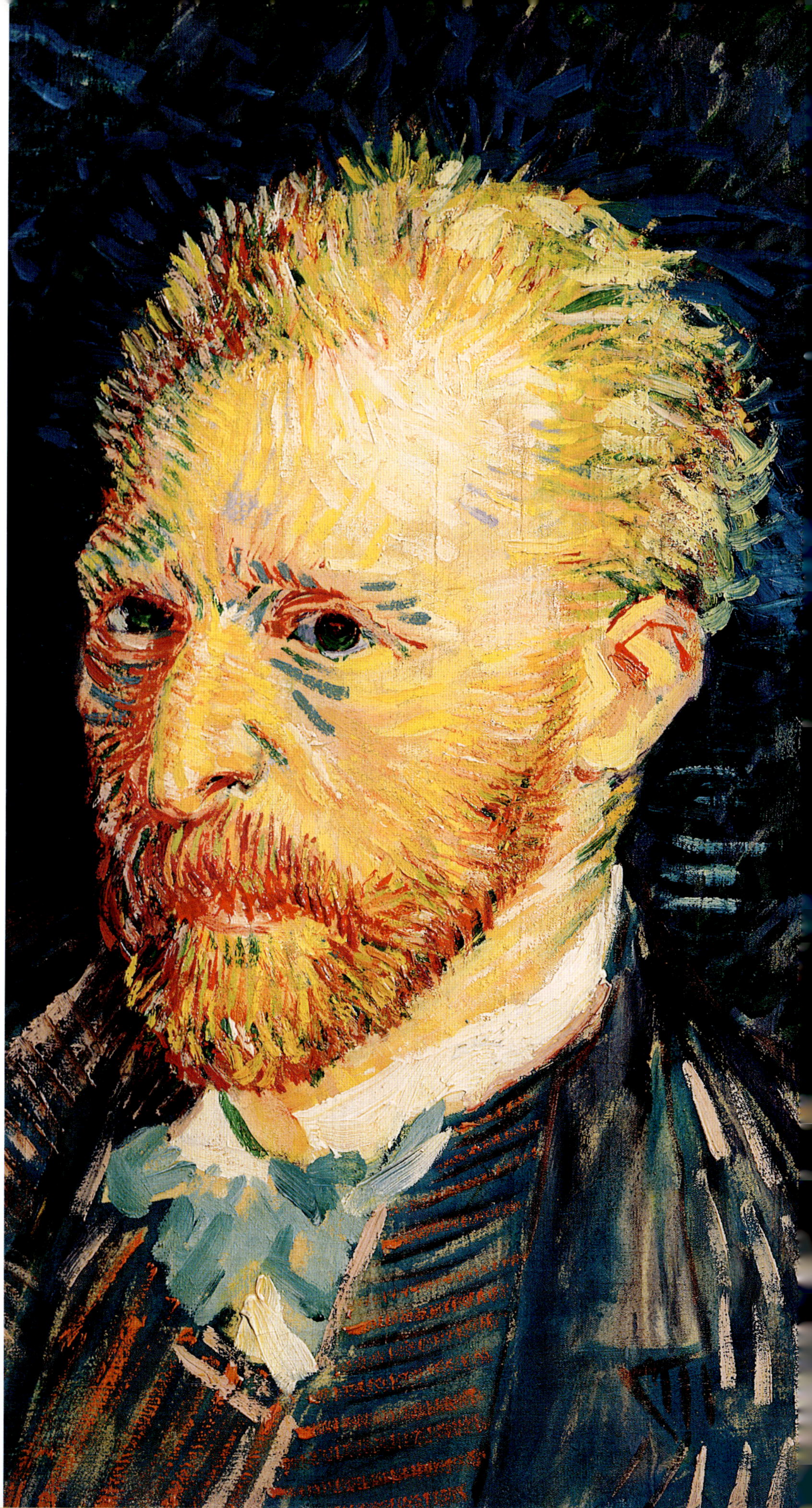

***Self Portrait*, 1887, (detail)**
MEDIUM: Oil on canvas
Courtesy of Musée d'Orsay, Paris, France/The Bridgeman Art Library

Extract from
Etten, *18 November 1881*

[…] As you know, Father and Mother on the one hand and I on the other do not see eye to eye about what should or should not be done with regard to a certain 'no, nay, never'. […]

Now while I am very distressed and sorry about it all, *I simply cannot agree* that a father who curses his son and (remember last year) proposes to send him to a lunatic asylum (which naturally I resisted with all my might) and who calls his son's love 'inappropriate and indelicate'!!!, is in the right. […]

There are things a man simply *cannot* let pass. If one hears people saying 'you are mad' or 'you are someone who severs family ties' or 'you are indelicate', then anyone with a heart in his body will protest with all his might. […]

Theo, I love her, her and no other, her forever. And, and, and, Theo, although the 'no, nay, never' still 'seems' to be in full sway, there is a feeling of something like redemption within me, and it is as if she and I had stopped being two and were united for all eternity.

Have my drawings arrived? […]

In his letter regarding the failed affair with Kee Vos, Vincent tries to convince Theo that the situation would be different if only the parents agreed to it. There had been many arguments. The disagreements over Vincent's unshakeable belief that Kee could love him pushed his parents to ask him

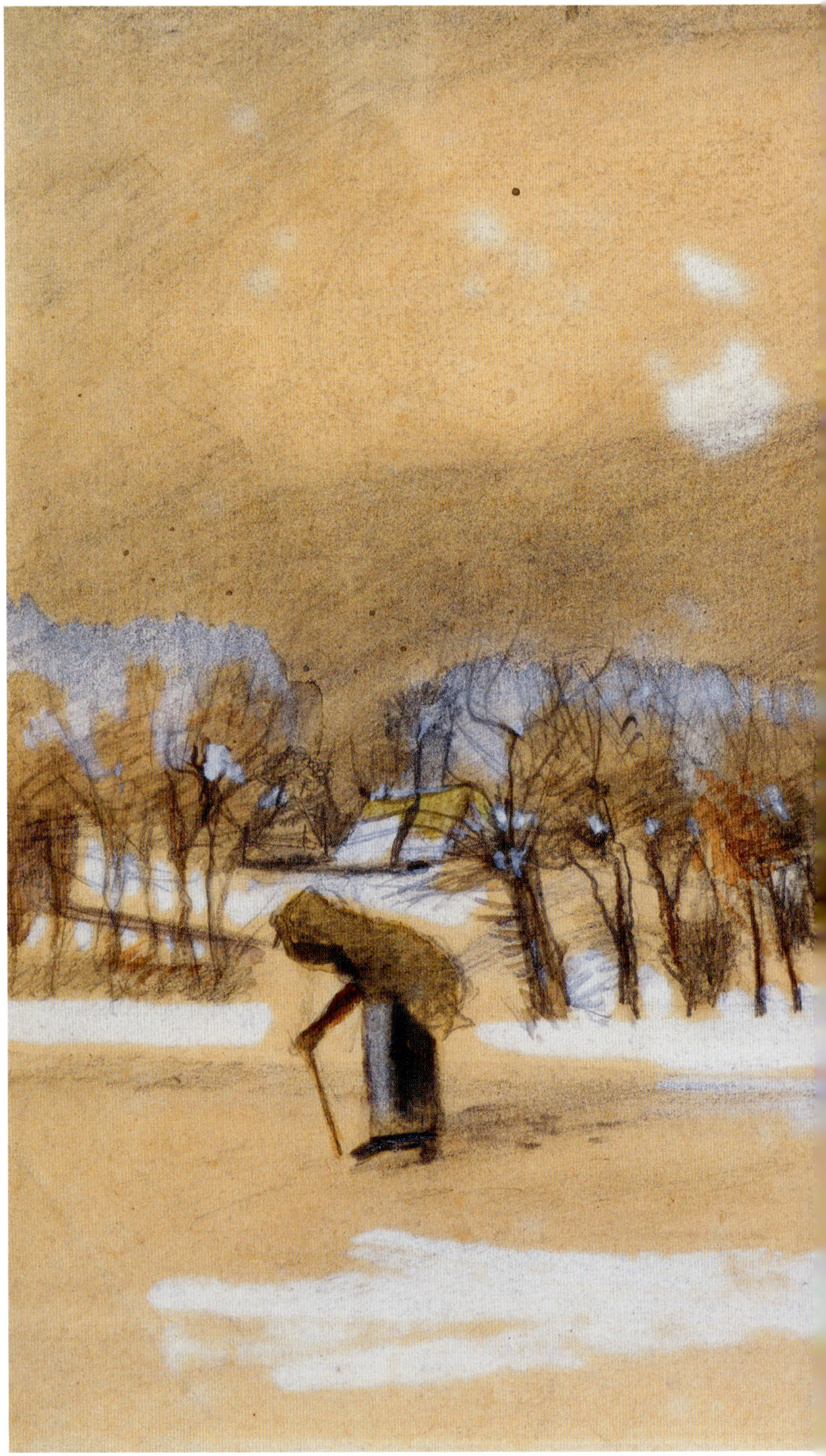

***Winter*, 1881**
MEDIUM: Pencil heightened watercolour on paper
Courtesy of Private Collection/Photo © Christie's Images/The Bridgeman Art Library

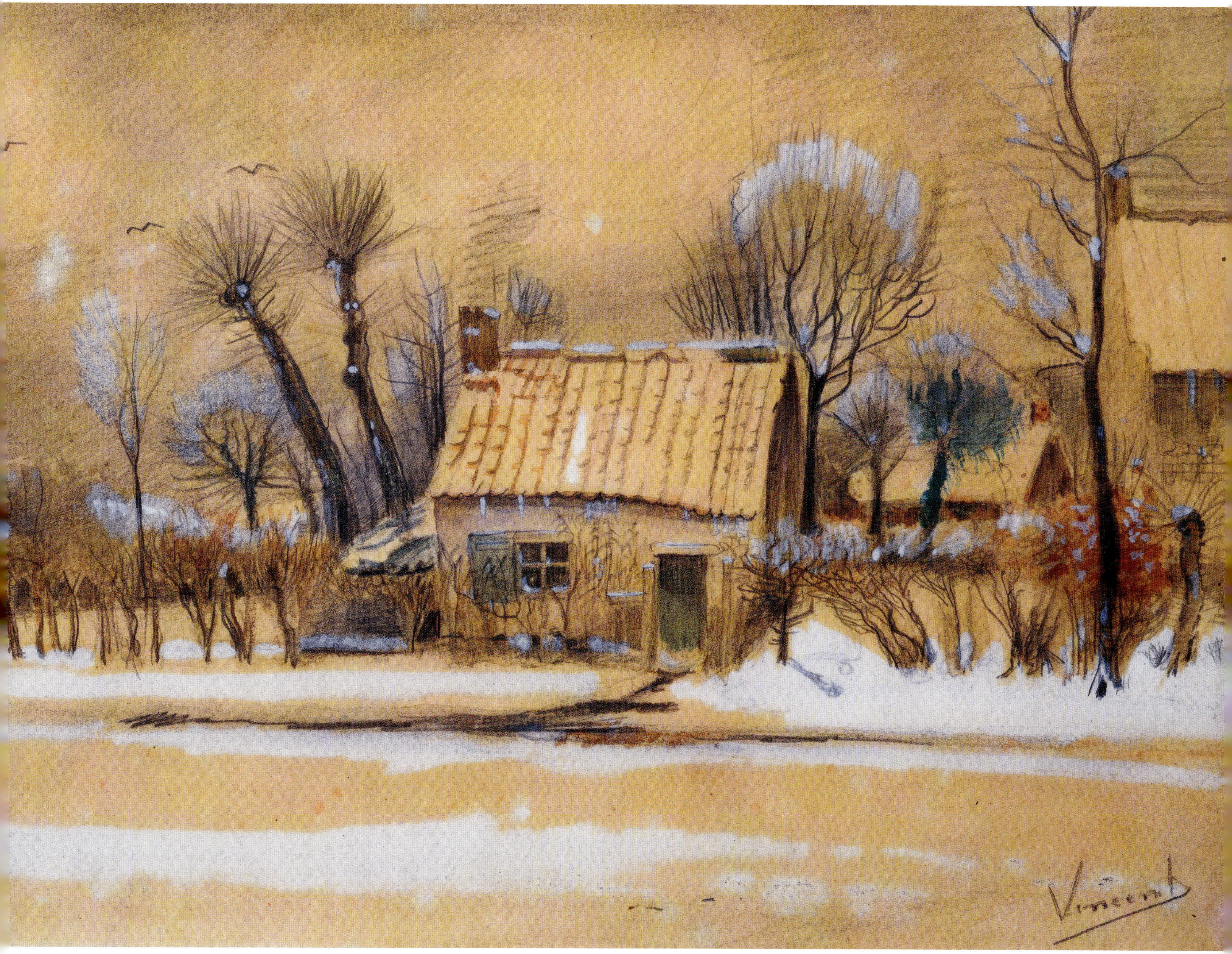
Vincent

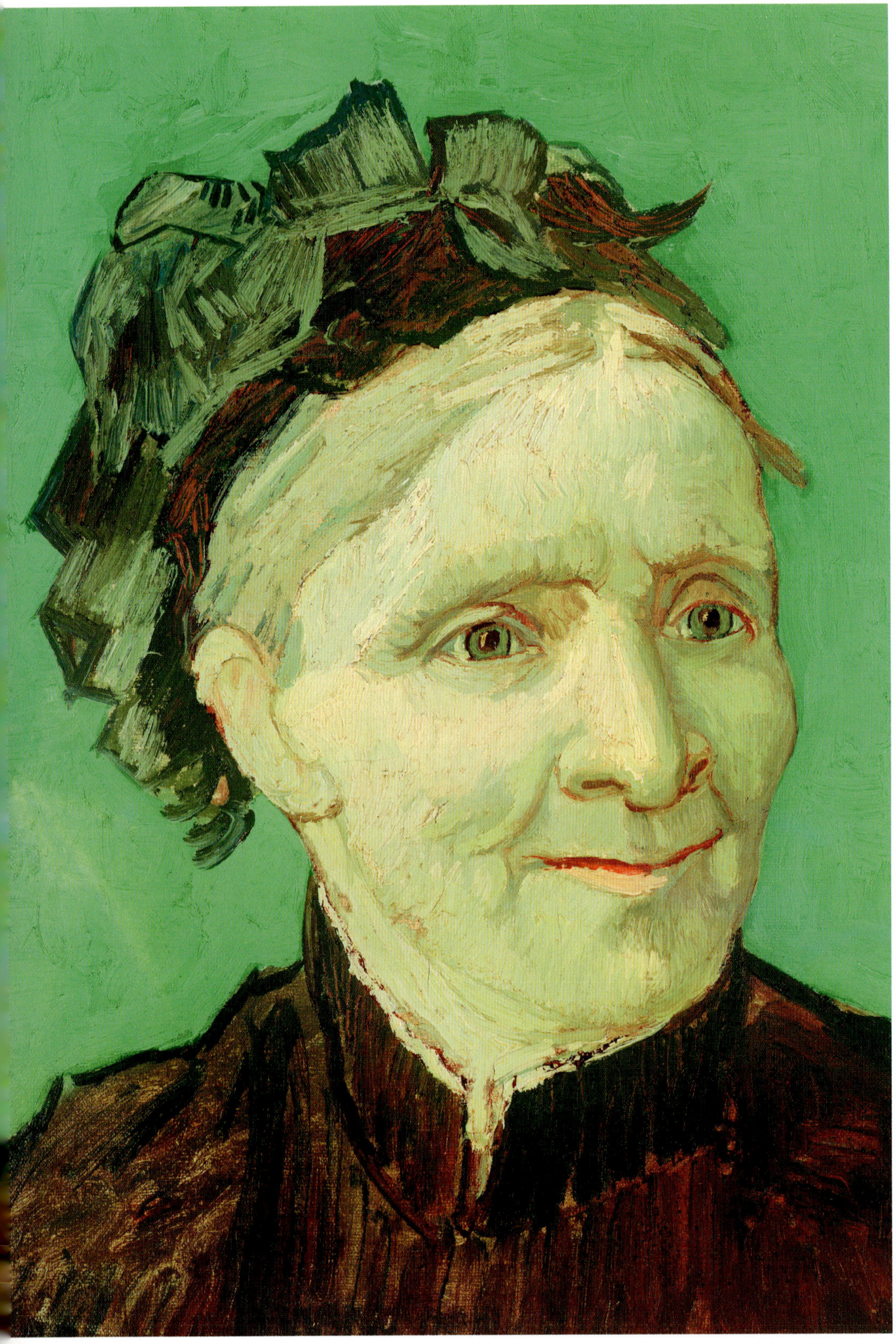

to leave the family home. He asks Theo for money to go to Amsterdam, although he did not want to leave with so many works in progress and argues that 'it would thwart me in my work'. He describes his latest drawings: 'I began to draw a man busy digging potatoes in a field [...] And I put in a little more of the surroundings [...] Some bushes in the background, and a streak of sky.' Vincent, self-taught as an artist, relied on Theo to give critical appraisal of his work.

Extract from
Etten, *23 November 1881*

I am very glad that you wrote to Father and Mother about a few things, as I asked you. I think it can only have a good influence – at least gradually. Of course you understand that I am not the man intentionally to grieve Father and Mother with anything. When I must do something contrary to their wishes and which often grieves them without cause, I feel very sorry about it myself. [...]

Now in regard to the 'case in question,' as Uncle Stricker calls what happened between Kee and me, I must tell you that I have risked an attack on the above-mentioned Mr. S.: by means of a registered letter. I was afraid unregistered letters would be ignored, but he will be obliged to read this one, and in it I have tried to draw his attention to some points which I fear he overlooked or which he would take no notice of. It is a very 'undiplomatic' letter, very bold, but I am sure it will at least make an impression on him. But perhaps at first it will cause him to use a certain expletive which he certainly would not use in a sermon.

***Portrait of the Artist's Mother*, 1888**
MEDIUM: Oil on canvas
Courtesy of Private Collection/Photo © Christie's Images/The Bridgeman Art Library

***The Diggers*, 1889**
MEDIUM: Oil on paper lined onto canvas
Courtesy of Detroit Institute of Arts, USA/Bequest of Robert H. Tannahill/The Bridgeman Art Library

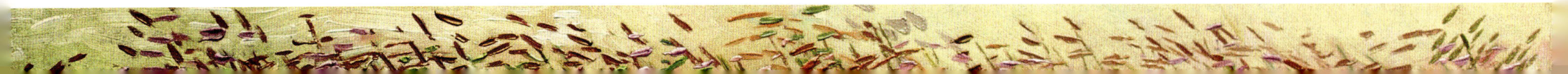

Extract from
The Hague, *29 December 1881*

Thanks for your letter and the enclosed. […] On Christmas Day I had a violent scene with Father, and it went so far that Father told me I had better leave the house. Well, he said it so decidedly that I actually left the same day.

The real reason was that I did not go to church, and also that if going to church was compulsory and if I was *forced* to go, I certainly should never go again out of courtesy, as I had done rather regularly all the time I was in Etten. But oh, in truth there was much more at the back of it all, including the whole story of what happened this summer between Kee and me.

I do not remember ever having been in such a rage in my life. […]

I went back to Mauve and said, 'Listen, Mauve, I cannot stay in Etten any longer, and I must go and live somewhere else, preferably here.'

'Well', Mauve said, 'Then stay.'

Extract from
The Hague, *c. 15–27 April 1882*

Since I wrote Mauve: 'Do you know that those two months you spoke of have long since passed? Let us shake hands, and then each go his own way, rather than have a quarrel between you and me,' I repeat, since I wrote this and received no sign in reply, my grief chokes me.

Because – and you know this – I love Mauve, and it is so hard that all the happiness he pictured to me will come to naught. For I am afraid that the better my drawings become, the more difficulty and opposition I shall meet. Because I shall have to

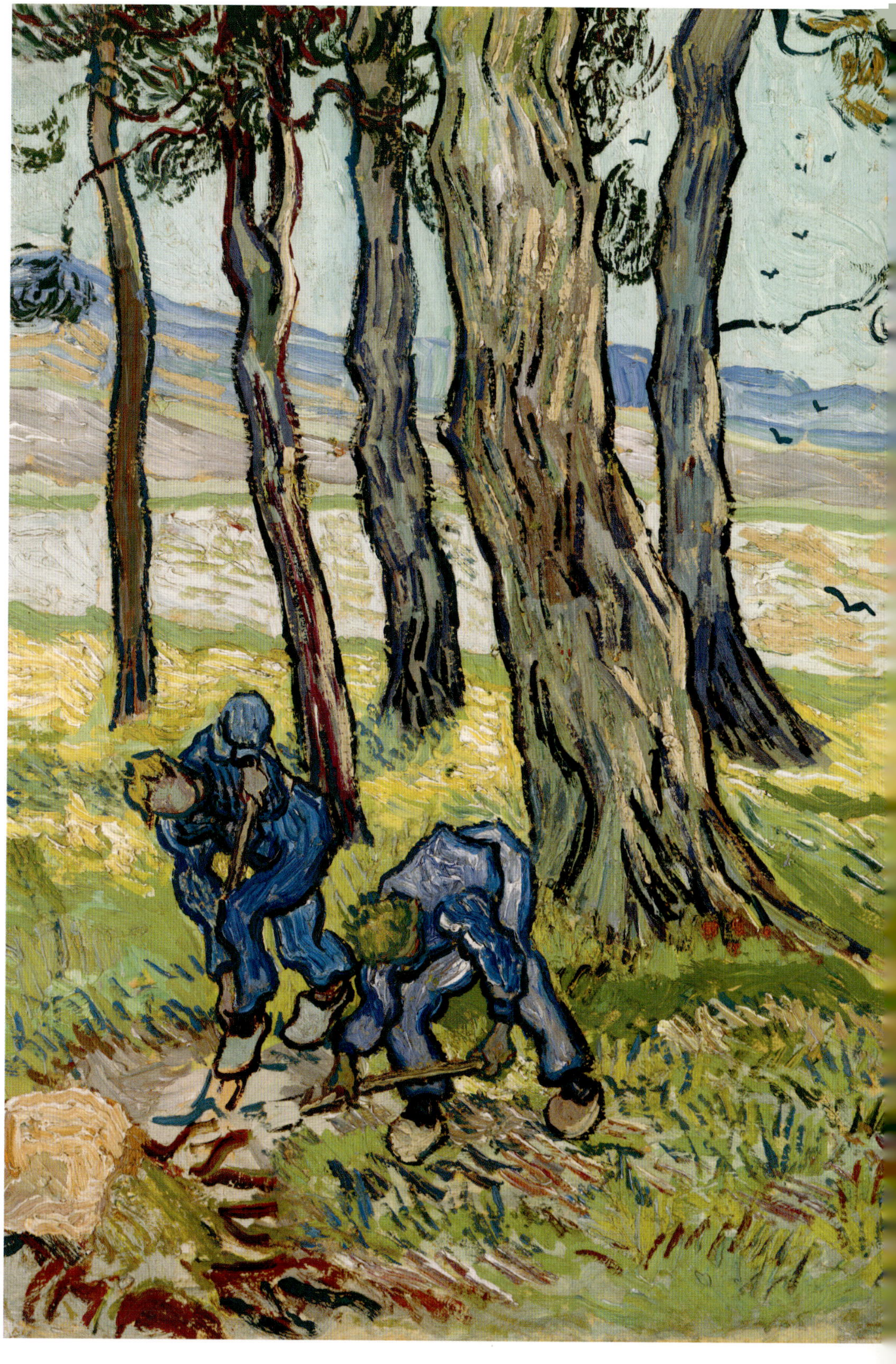

suffer much, especially from those peculiarities which I *cannot* change. First, my appearance and my way of speaking and my clothes; and then, even later on when I earn more, I shall always move in a different sphere from most painters because my conception of things, the subjects I want to make, inexorably demand it.

Enclosed is a little sketch of diggers, I will tell you why I'm sending it. Tersteeg said to me, 'You failed before and now you will fail again – it will be the same story all over again.' Stop – no, it is quite different now, and that reasoning is really nothing but a sophism. [...]

Vincent's financial dependence on Theo resulted in a falling out with his cousin-in-law, the painter Anton Mauve (1838–88), and Tersteeg (Hermanus Gijsbertus Tersteeg, 1845–1927, Vincent's mentor at Goupil & Cie), with Tersteeg telling Vincent that 'Mauve and I will see to it that there is an end to this'. Vincent blamed Tersteeg for Mauve's sudden change of feeling toward him. He had written in annoyance to Theo, explaining that Tersteeg wanted 'saleable' works and that '... it causes me a great deal of worry ... when those whom I thought I could depend on for sympathy, like Mauve and Tersteeg, become indifferent or hostile and spiteful'. He had written to Mauve to explain his thoughts but received no reply, something that 'choked' him with grief. In the letter he encloses a sketch of diggers for Theo, quoting Tersteeg's words, 'You failed before and now you will fail again.'

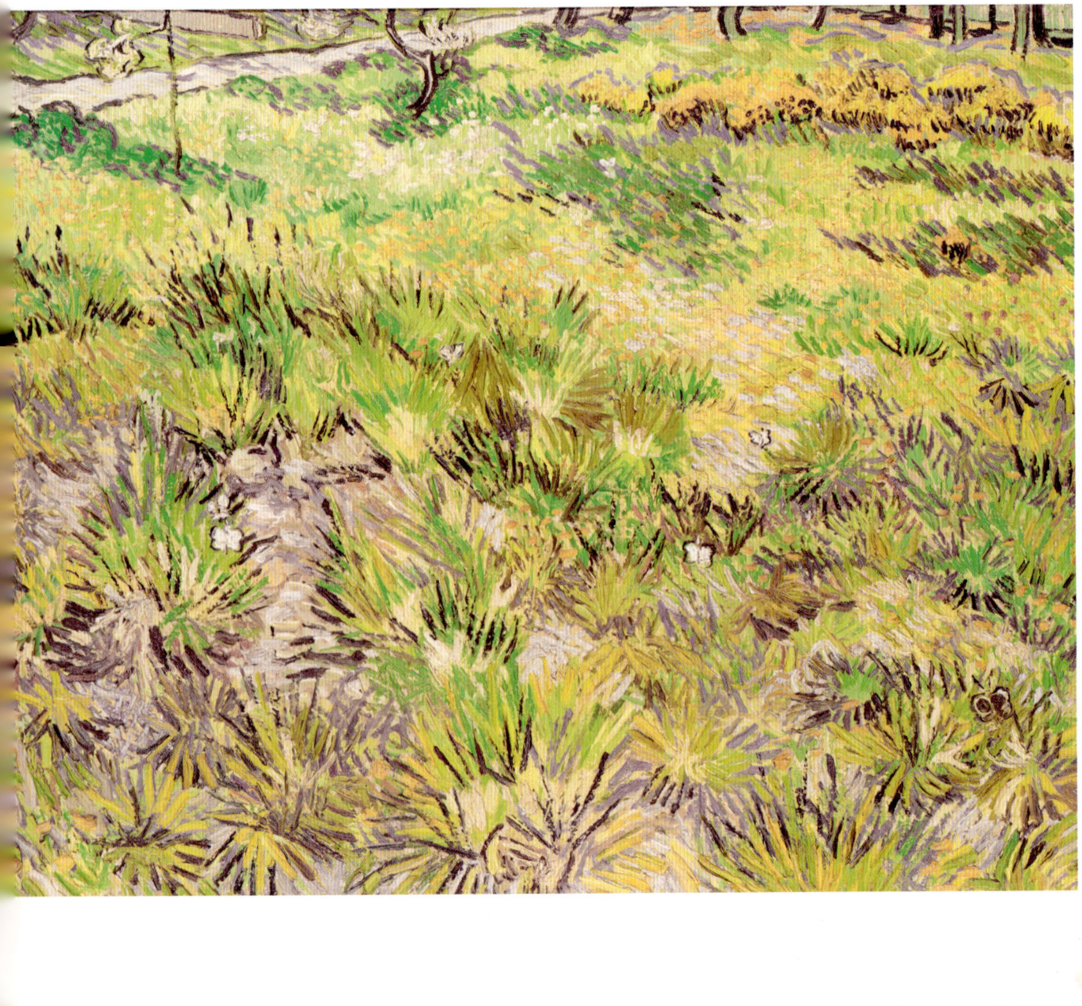

Extract from The Hague, *3–12 May 1882*

Last winter I met a pregnant woman, deserted by the man whose child she was carrying. A pregnant woman who walked the streets in the winter – she had her bread to earn, you'll know how. I took that woman on as a model and have worked with her all winter. I couldn't pay her a model's full daily wages, but I paid her rent all the same, and thus far, thank God, I have been able to save her and her child from hunger and cold by sharing my own bread with her.

When I first came across this woman, she caught my eye because she looked so ill. I made her take baths and as many restoratives as I could manage, and she has become much healthier. I have been with her to Leyden, where there is a maternity hospital in which she will be confined.

***Meadow with Butterflies*, 1890**
MEDIUM: Oil on canvas
Courtesy of National Gallery, London, UK/The Bridgeman Art Library

***Moonlit Landscape*, date unknown**
MEDIUM: Oil on canvas
Courtesy of Museu de Arte, Sao Paulo, Brazil/The Bridgeman Art Library

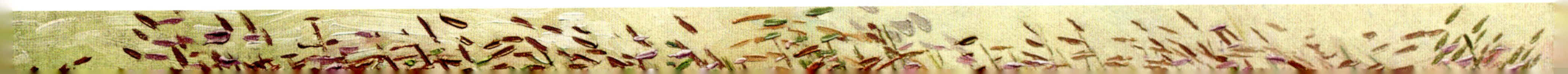

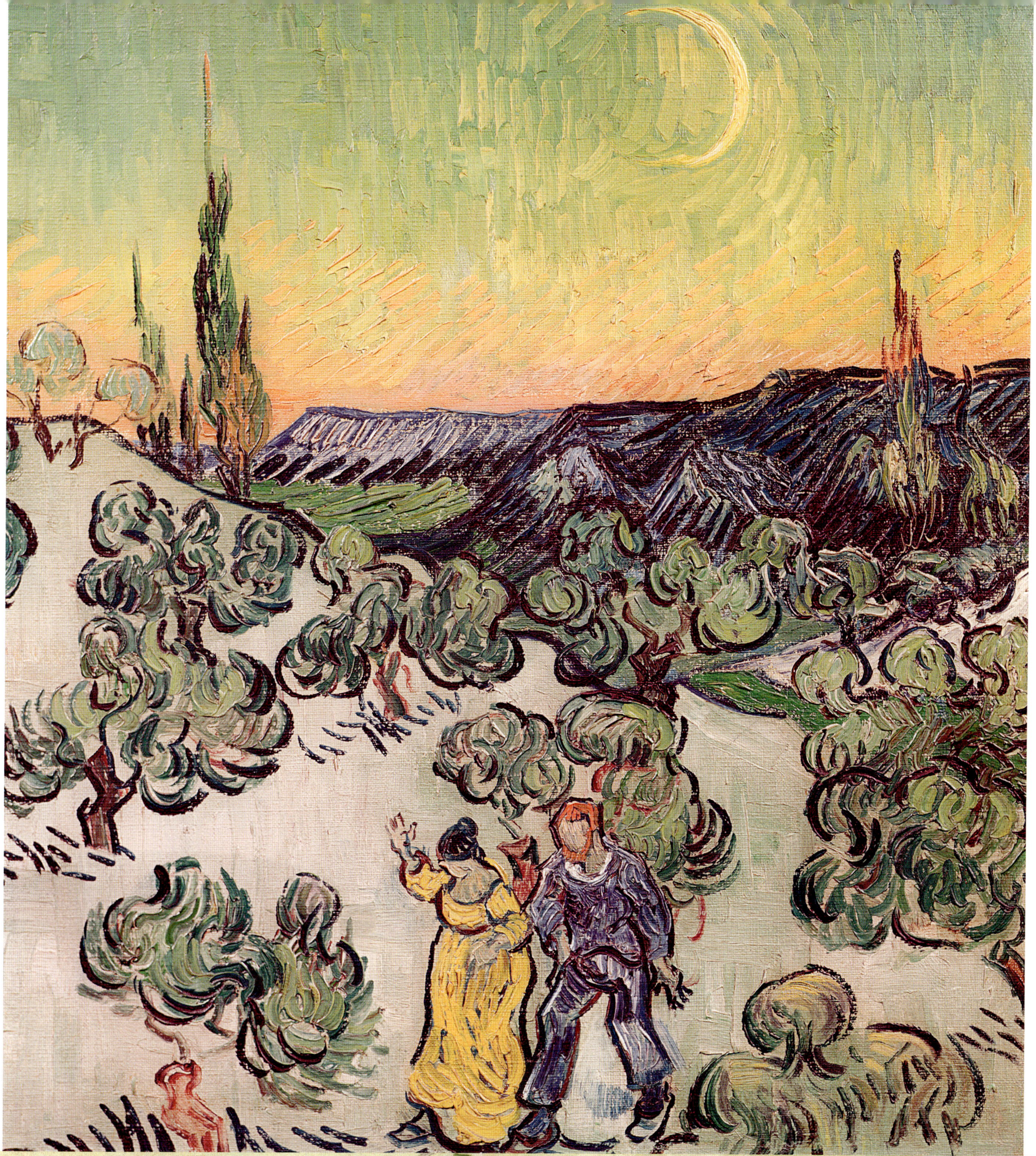

It strikes me that any man worth his salt would have done the same in a case like this. I consider what I did so simple and natural that I thought I could keep it to myself. She found posing difficult, yet she has learned, and I have made progress with my drawing because I have had a good model. The woman is now attached to me like a tame dove. For my part, I can only get married once, and when better than now, and to her, because it is the only way to go on helping her and she would otherwise be sent back by want on to the same old path which leads to the abyss. She has no money, but she is helping me to earn money with my work. "

The pregnant woman is thought to be Clasina Maria Hoornik, also known as Sien, and her young daughter Maria Wilhemina Hoornik. When Vincent met her at the end of January 1881, he had found someone more in need of love and companionship than himself. He took them in, supporting Sien when she gave birth to a baby boy. His letter speaks of marrying Sien but nothing more is said and there are no records of the marriage, although Sien later stated that they had been married.

Extract from
The Hague, *1–2 June 1882*

" I want to tell you something about what you seem to be afraid of, namely the possibility that the family may want to take steps to place me under legal guardianship. If you really think '*a few witnesses (and even then false ones) are all that would be needed to*

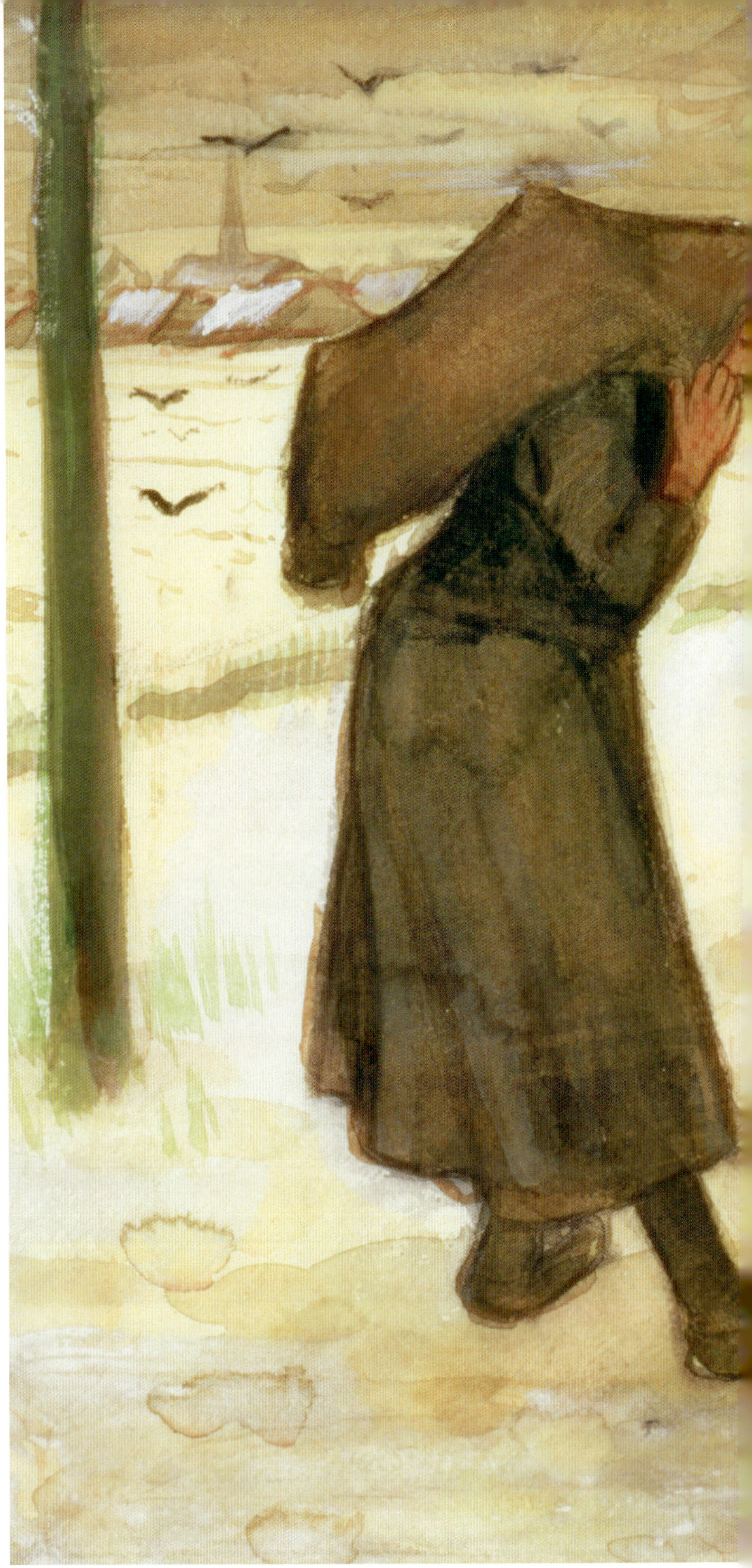

***Miners' Wives Carrying Sacks of Coal*, 1882**
MEDIUM: Watercolour on paper
Courtesy of Rijksmuseum Kroller-Muller, Otterlo, Netherlands/The Bridgeman Art Library

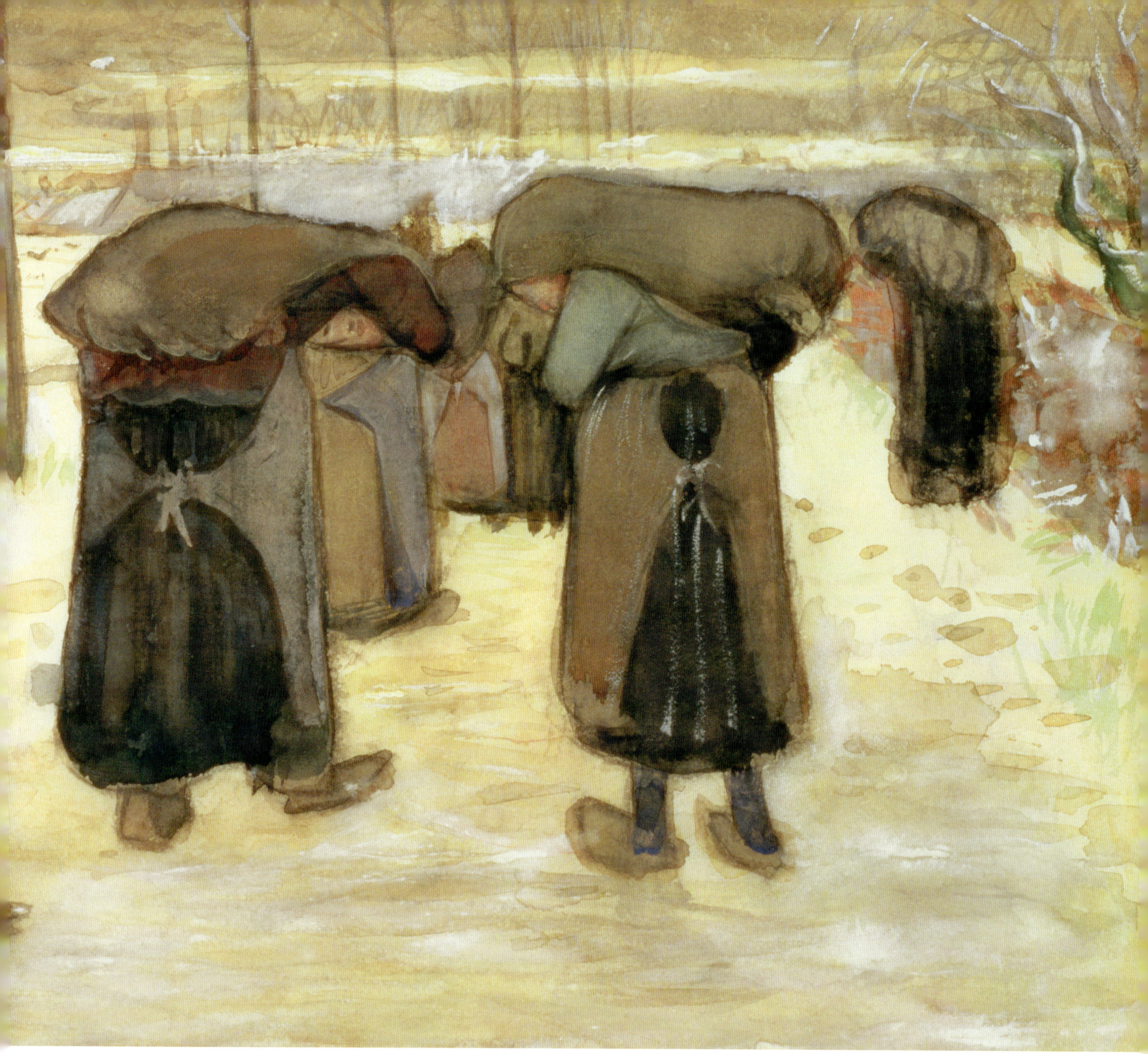

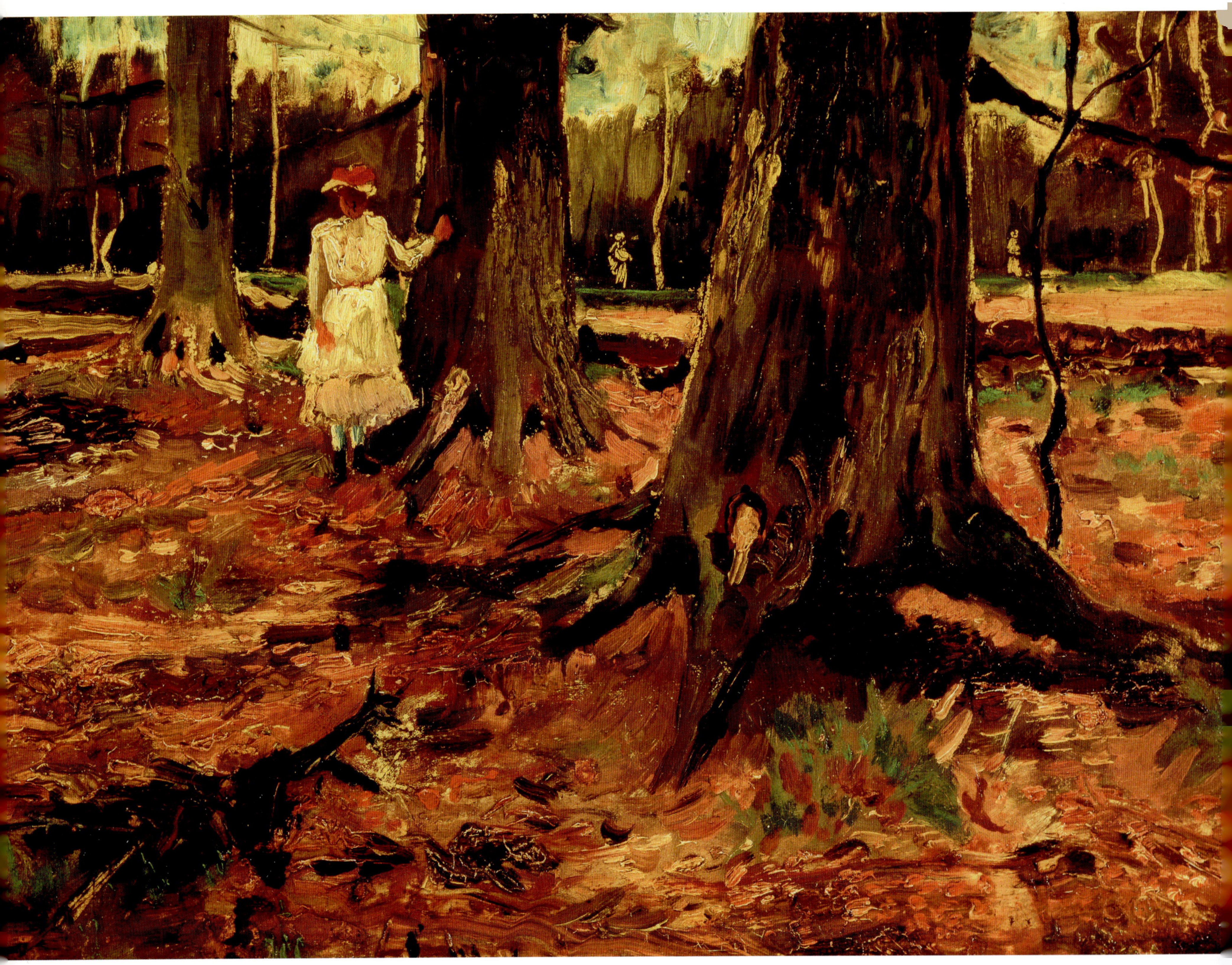

testify that you cannot manage your financial affairs and that would be enough to entitle Father to deprive you of your civil rights and place you under guardianship,' if, I say, you really think that this sort of thing is so easy to do these days, then I take the liberty of questioning it.

The legal procedure of guardianship, which has been disgracefully abused so often in order to get rid of individuals considered 'troublesome' or 'unpleasant' (*mauvais coucheur* [awkward customer]), can no longer be applied quite so easily these days. And the law gives the accused the right to appeal and many another remedy.

Theo had written to Vincent worried that their father was going to take steps to place Vincent under a guardianship restriction. Vincent argued in his letter as to why he rejected it and said he would fight it. Nothing more was done by his parents.

Extract from The Hague, *2 July 1882*

As I told you in yesterday's letter, I have been to Leyden. Sien was confined last night; has had a very difficult delivery, but thank God has come out of it alive and with a particularly nice little boy as well.

Her mother and little girl and I went there together – you can imagine how very anxious we were, not knowing what we should hear when we asked the orderlies in the hospital about her. And how tremendously glad we were when we heard: 'Confined last night … but you mustn't talk to her for long….' I shall not easily forget that 'you mustn't talk to her for long'; for it meant 'you can still talk to her,' when it could easily have been, 'you will never talk to her again.' […]

With her earlier misfortune behind her, a completely new period of her life will start, and though she cannot regain her spring, which is past and was but barren, her *midsummer growth* will be all the greener for it. You will know how in the middle of the summer, when the greatest heat is over, the trees put out fresh young shoots, a new young layer of green over the old, weathered one.

[…] Well, brother, you are to blame for my being so happy today that it made me cry. Thanks for everything, my dear fellow, and believe me, with a handshake in my thoughts, […]

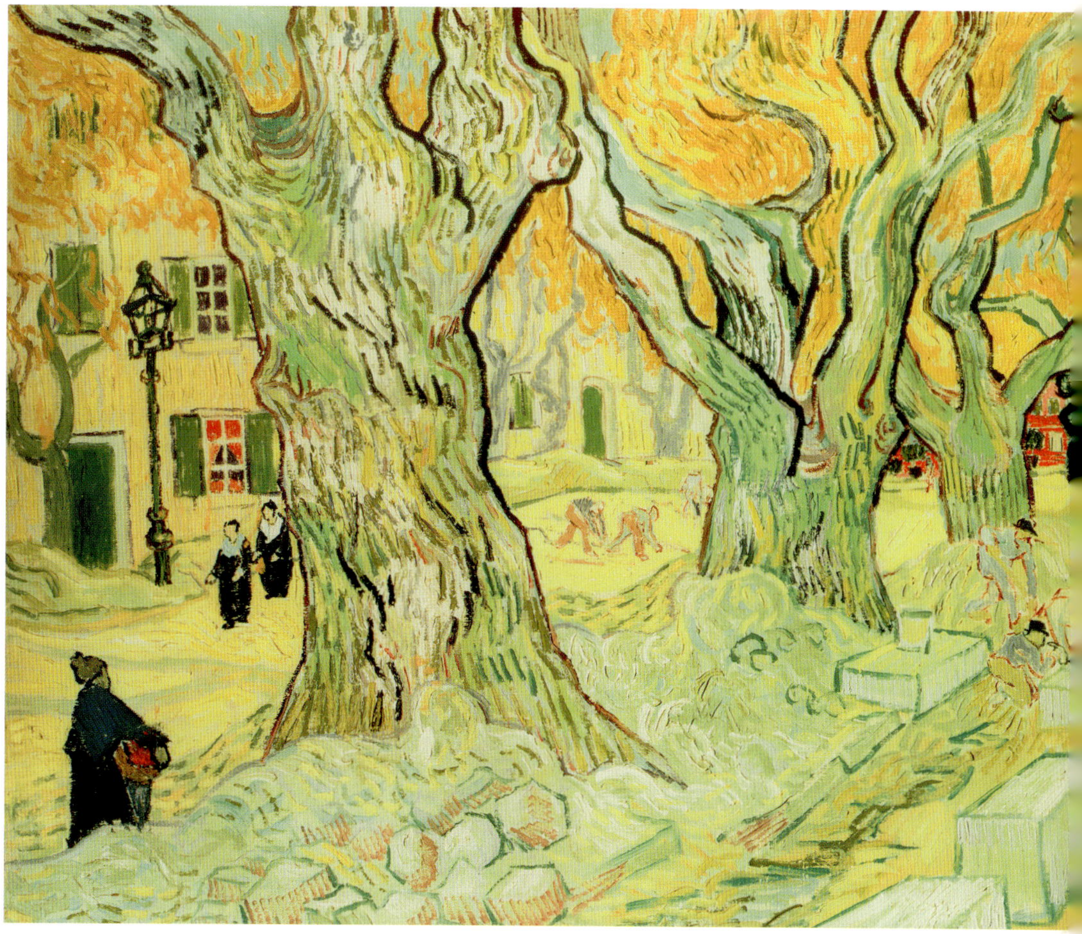

***Girl in White in the Woods*, 1882, (detail)**
MEDIUM: Oil on canvas
© akg-images/Electa

***The Road Menders*, 1889**
MEDIUM: Oil on canvas
Courtesy of Phillips Collection, Washington DC, USA/The Bridgeman Art Library

Sien had given birth to a son in hospital, a brother to the daughter she already had. Theo had, as usual, helped with funds. Vincent had visited her with Sien's mother and daughter. He looked forward to her making a good recovery and planned for them to all live together.

Farmhouses at Saintes-Mairies, **1888**
MEDIUM: Oil on canvas
Courtesy of Private Collection/Photo © Christie's Images/The Bridgeman Art Library

Extract from
The Hague, *5 or 6 August 1882*

In my last letter you will have found a little sketch of that perspective frame I mentioned. I just came back from the blacksmith, who made iron points to go on the sticks and iron corners for the frame.

It consists of two long stakes; the frame may be attached to them either upright or horizontally with strong wooden pegs.

So on the shore or in the meadow or in the fields one can look through it as *through a window*, the vertical lines and the perpendicular line of the frame and the diagonal lines and the point of intersection, or else the division in squares, certainly give a few basic markers, with the help of which one can make a firm drawing, from the indication of the main lines and proportions – at least for those who have some instinct for perspective and some understanding of the reason why and the manner in which perspective gives an apparent change of direction to the lines and a change of size to the lines and to the whole mass. [...]

[...] With long and continuous practice it enables one to draw quick as lightning, - and once the drawing is established to paint quick as lightning also. [...]

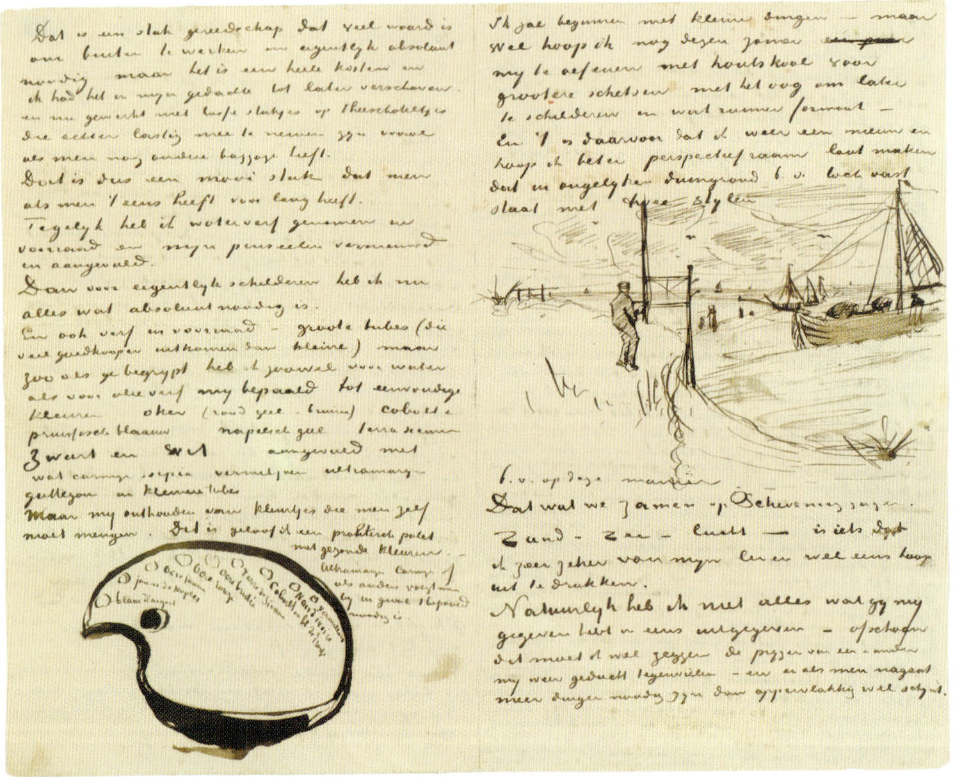
Dat is een stuk gereedschap dat veel noodig is om buiten te werken en eigentlijk absoluut noodig maar het is een heele kosten en ik had het in mijn gedachte tot later verschoven en nu gewerkt met losse stukjes op theeschoteltjes die echter lastig mee te nemen zijn vooral als men nog andere bagage heeft.
Dat is dus een mooi stuk dat men als men 't eens heeft voor lang heeft.
Tegelijk heb ik waterverf genomen en voorraad en mijn penseelen vernieuwd en aangevuld.
Dan voor eigentlijk schilderen heb ik nu alles wat absoluut noodig is.
En ook verf in voorraad – groote tubes (die veel goedkooper uitkomen dan kleine) maar zoo als ge begrypt heb ik zoowel voor water als voor olieverf my bepaald tot eenvoudige kleuren oker (rood geel bruin) cobalt & pruissisch blaauw napelsch geel terra sienna zwart en wit aangevuld met wat carmin, sepia vermiljoen ultramarijn gutegom in kleinere tubes
Maar my onthouden van kleurtjes die men zelf moet mengen. Dit is geloof ik een praktisch palet met gezonde kleuren. – Ultramarijn carmin enz. als anders voegt men by in geval 't absoluut noodig is.

Ik zal beginnen met kleine dingen – maar wel hoop ik nog dezen zomer my te oefenen met houtskool voor grootere schetsen met het oog om later te schilderen in wat ruimer formaat –
En 't is daarvoor dat ik weer een nieuw en hoop ik beter perspectiefraam laat maken dat in ongelyken duingrond b.v. best vast staat met twee stylen
b.v. op deze manier
Dat wat we samen op Scheveningen zagen.
Zand – zee – lucht – is iets dat ik zeer zeker van myn leven wel eens hoop uit te drukken.
Natuurlyk heb ik niet alles wat gy my gegeven hebt in eens uitgegeven – ofschoon dit moet ik wel zeggen de prijzen van een en ander my weer geducht tegenvielen – en er als men nagaat meer dingen noodig zyn dan oppervlakkig wel schynt.

Vincent was excited about his new perspective frame, which had iron spikes and two long legs. He explains to Theo that it is 'fixed' by means of strong wooden pegs either horizontally or vertically. He includes a sketch to explain the mechanics of it.

Extract from
The Hague, *20 August 1882*

I have just received a nice letter from home which gave me very real pleasure, and from which it is clear that your visit and the things you told them about me and my work have had a reassuring effect on them. [...]

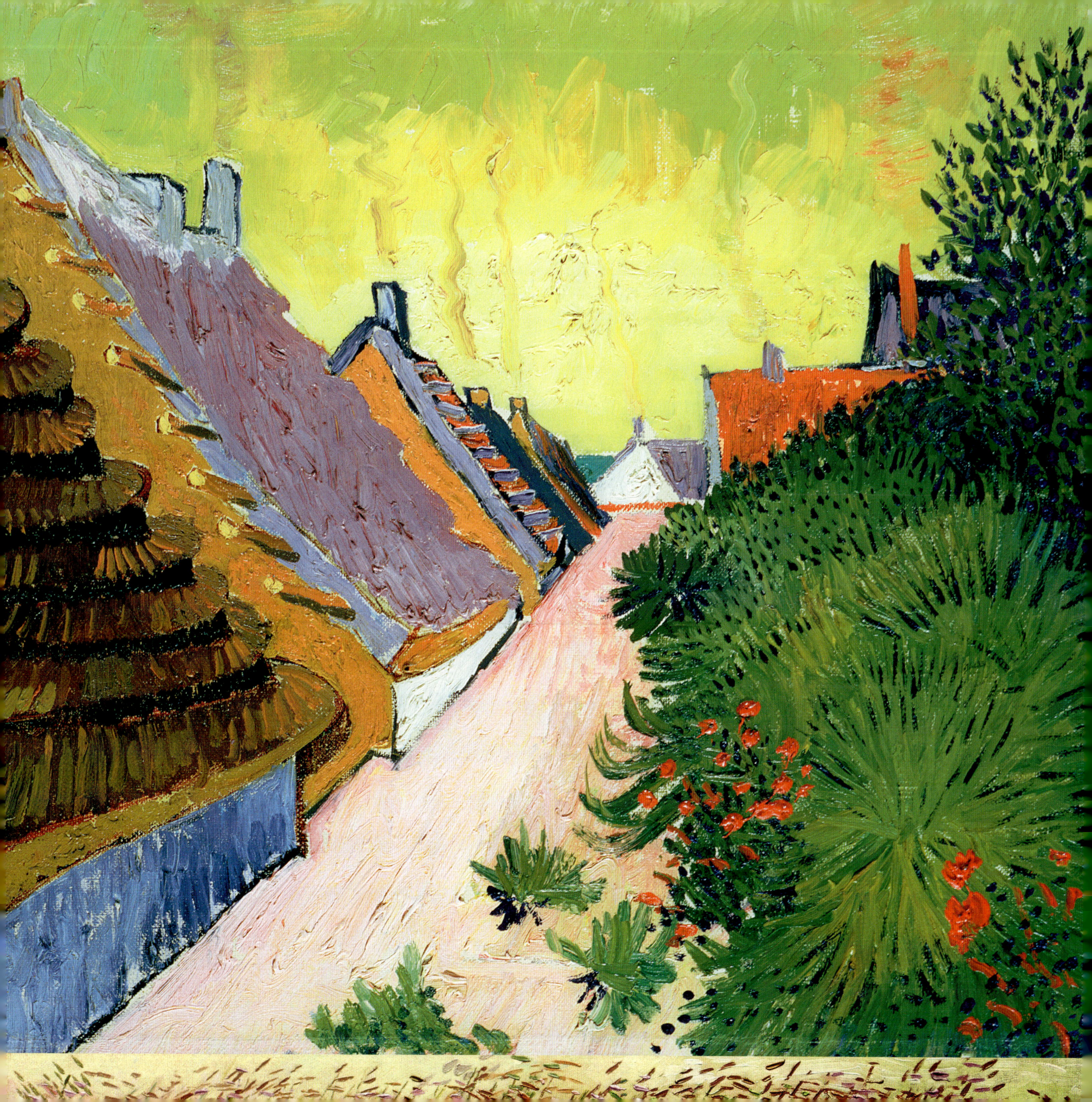

***The Bakery in de Geest*, 1882**
MEDIUM: Pencil and charcoal on vellum
Courtesy of Haags Gemeentemuseum, The Hague, Netherlands/The Bridgeman Art Library

***The Bridge at Trinquetaille*, date unknown**
MEDIUM: Oil on canvas
Courtesy of Private Collection/Photo © Christie's Images/The Bridgeman Art Library

[…] This week I have painted some rather large studies in the wood, which I tried to carry out more thoroughly and vigorously than the first ones.

The one which I believe succeeded best is of nothing but a piece of dug-up earth – white, black and brown sand after a pouring rain. […]

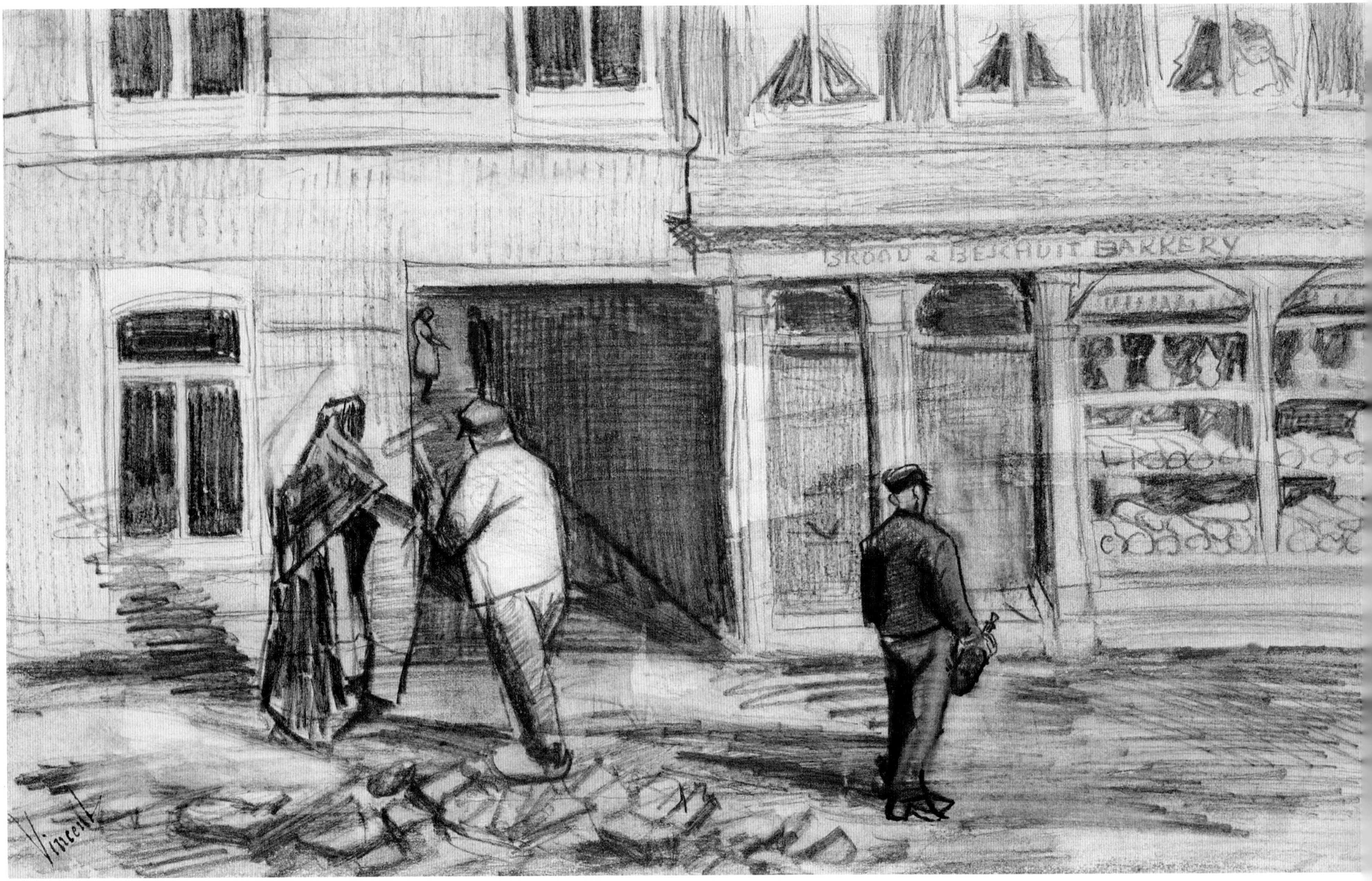

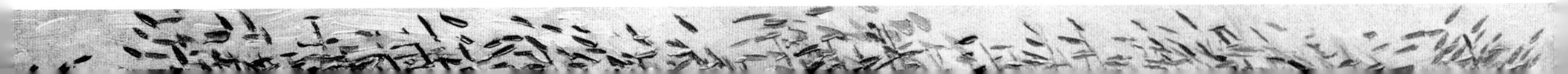

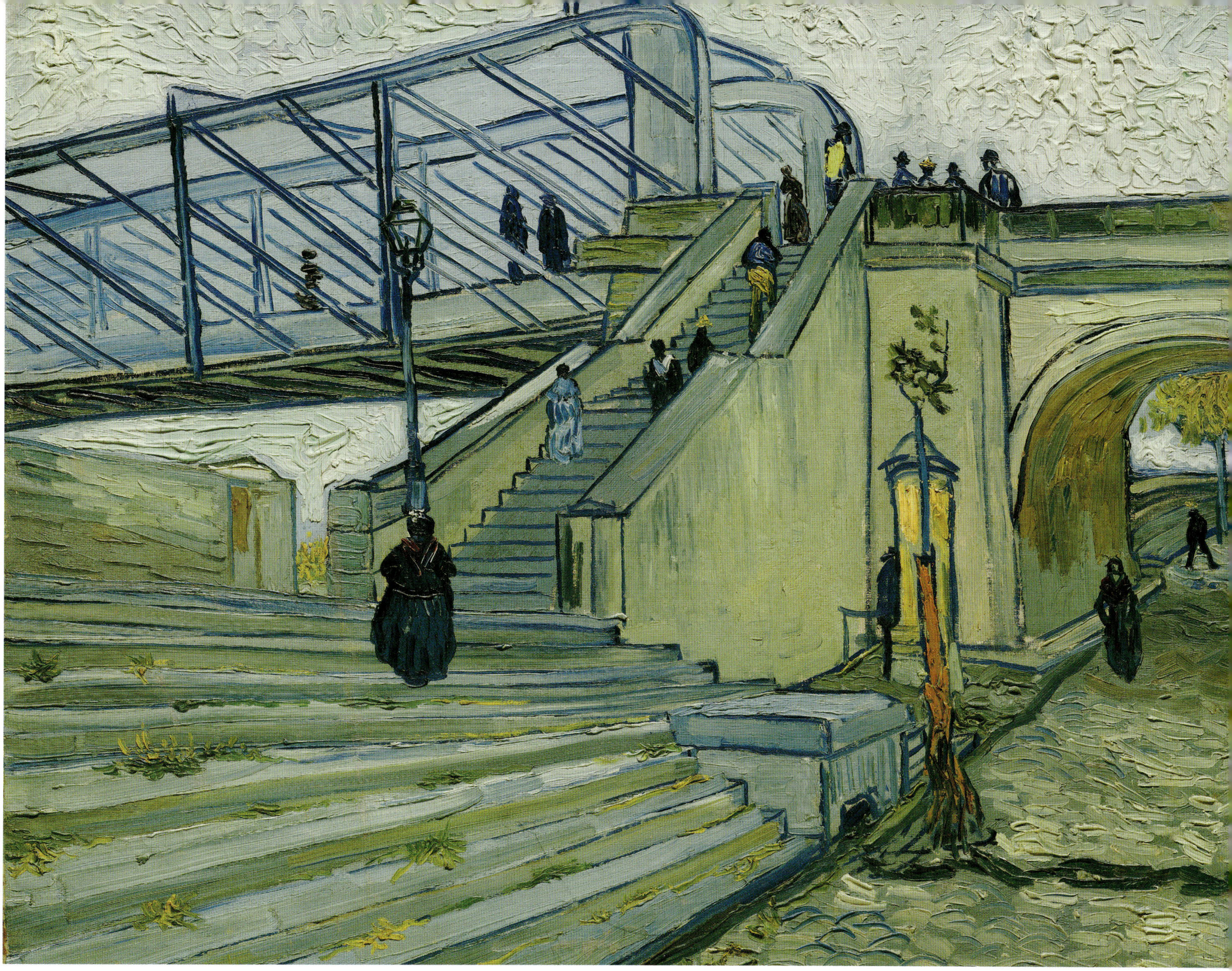

The other study in the wood is of some large green beech trunks on a stretch of ground covered with dry sticks, and the little figure of a girl in white. […] It was with extreme pleasure that I made these two studies. […]

At all events, drawing in charcoal is something I am sure I must study now more than ever – at all events, I have enough to do and can go on. Even when I restrain myself a little in painting, I can work just as hard. […]

Landscape, as I have taken it up now, decidedly requires the figure too. They are studies for backgrounds which one must do so thoroughly because the tone of the figure and the effect of the whole depend on it.

What I like so much about painting is that with the same amount of trouble which one takes over a drawing, one brings home something that conveys the impression much better and is much more pleasant to look at – and at the same time, more

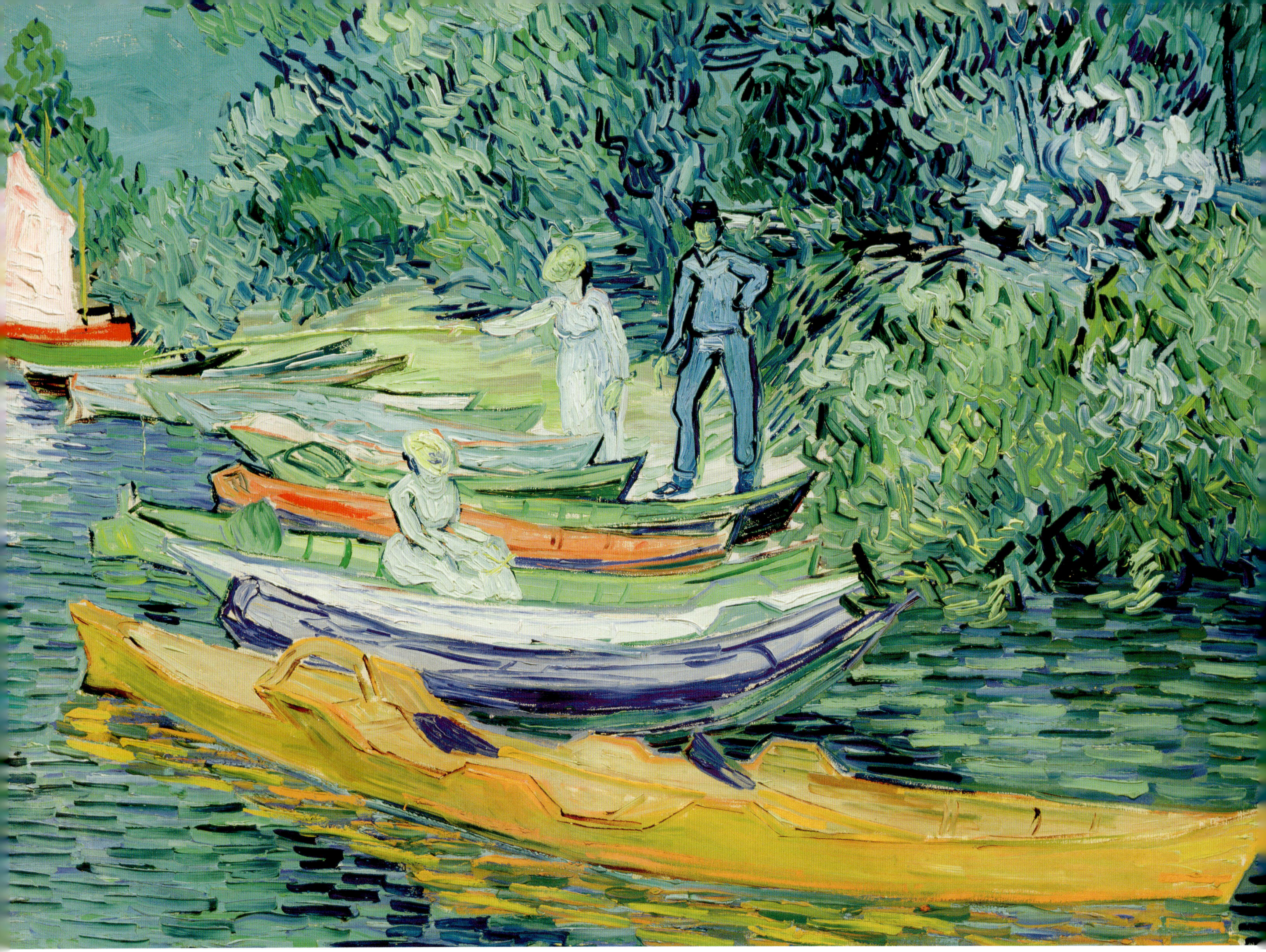

correct too. In a word it is more gratifying than drawing. But it is absolutely necessary to be able to draw the right proportion and the position of the object pretty correctly before one begins. If one makes mistakes in this, the whole thing comes to nothing.

I am longing for autumn. I must be sure to have a stock of colours and other things against that time. I love so much, so very much, the effect of the yellow leaves; the green beech trunks stand out so well against them, and figures, too.

I regret that it will be a year perhaps before you will see all my paintings (even though I might send you something now and then) and before we can talk things over. I assure you that the things I have painted now will prove useful to me. Perhaps I

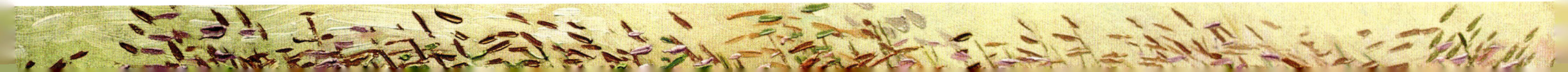

shall succeed now where I did not succeed in January. [...] Please do not suspect me of being indifferent to earning money; I am trying to find the shortest way to that end. [...]

If you saw that my painting would have the best chance, of course I should not refuse to paint more. But if it would be a long time before it became saleable, I would be the first to say. Meanwhile we must practise the greatest economy, and, by drawing, many expenses are avoided and one makes solid though slow progress. I see a change in these painted things, and I am writing you about it because you can tell better than I how it may affect the eventual saleability. [...] At all events it seems to me that the painted studies have a *more pleasant aspect* than my drawings.

Personally, I attach less value to the more pleasant, less meager effect; my goal is the expression of more severe and virile things, for which I still have to drudge a great deal.
But if you said, work on those landscapes or woods scenes or marines, I would have nothing against it, as it would not prevent my attempting larger or more serious things. I should only want the assurance that they are worth the brushes, the paint and the canvas, and that it is not throwing money away to do them, but that they are worth what they cost. [...]

If the painted ones are unsaleable, then certainly it will be more advantageous to draw with charcoal or something. But if it were possible to make good the expense of painted studies, then I want to tell you that in principle I have nothing against it, now that I see that they turn out rather well and may perhaps turn out to be a source of good fortune. In principle I am only against wasting paint on things which one can learn just as well another way, when there is no chance of selling them at present. [...]

Vincent regularly discussed his work with Theo. In this letter he explains what he has been drawing and painting and how hard he is working. The subject of the 'saleability' of his work was in the forefront of his mind, yet he determines that 'studying nature is more important to me than studying the prices of pictures'.

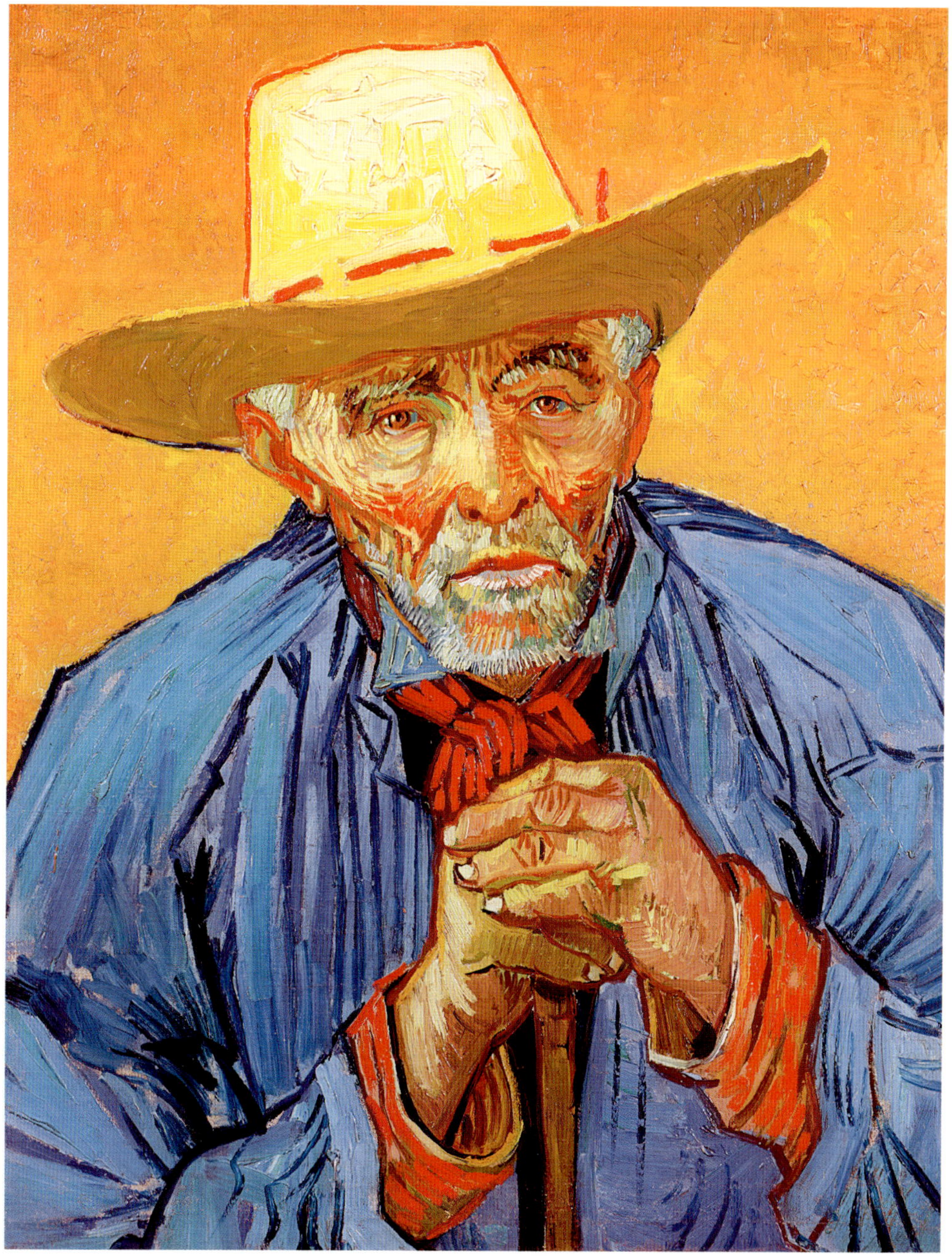

Bank of the Oise at Auvers, 1890
MEDIUM: Oil on canvas
Courtesy of Detroit Institute of Arts, USA/Bequest of Robert H. Tannahill/ The Bridgeman Art Library

Portrait of Patience Escalier, 1888
MEDIUM: Oil on canvas
Courtesy of Private Collection/Photo © Lefevre Fine Art Ltd, London/ The Bridgeman Art Library

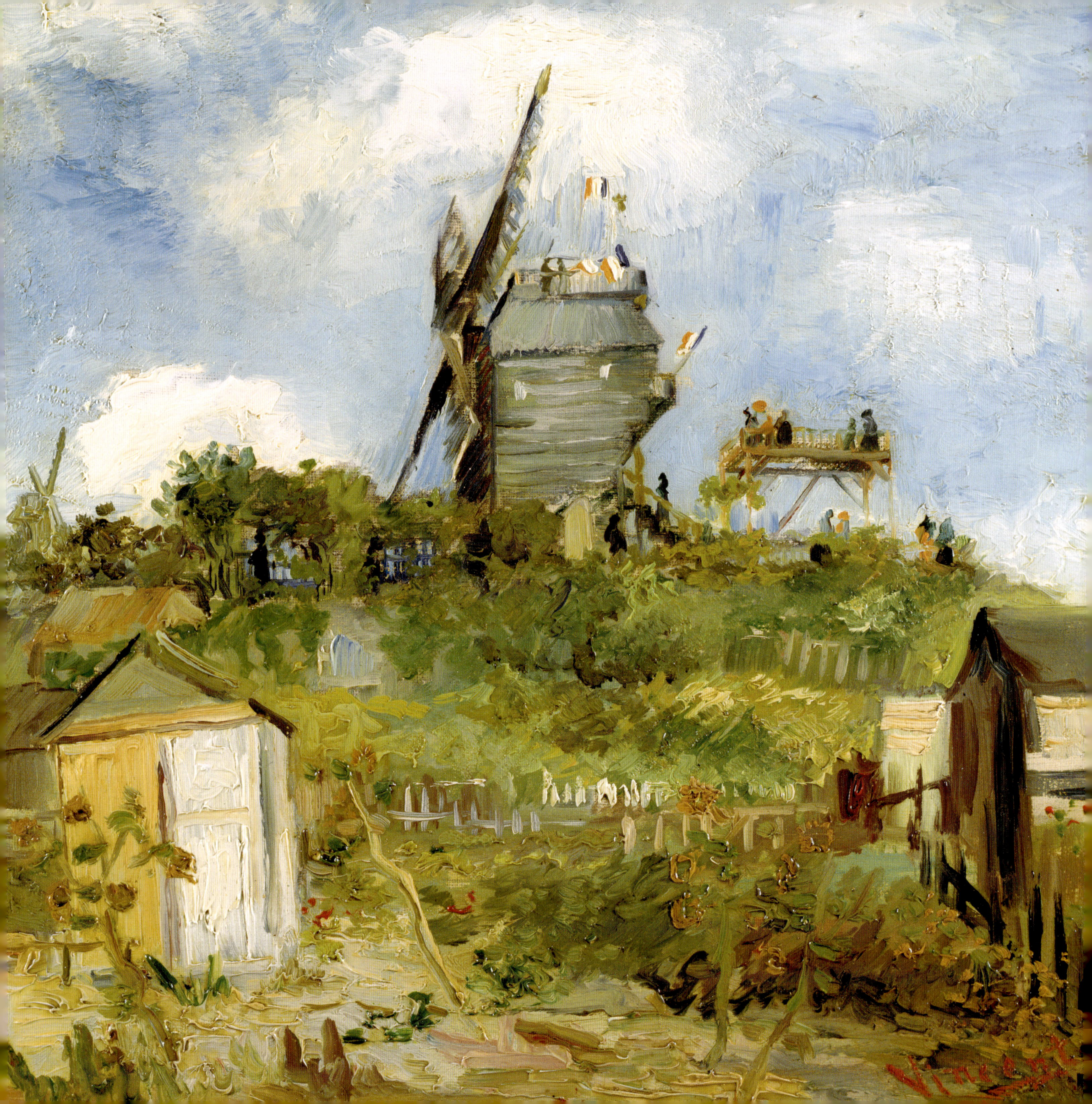
Vincent

Extract from

The Hague, *3 September 1882*

I have just received your very welcome letter and, as am taking some rest today, I am answering it at once. Thank you very much for it and for the enclosure, and for the various things you say in it.

And many thanks for your description of that scene with the workmen at Montmartre, which I found very interesting because you convey the colours so well that I can see them. I am glad you are reading the book on Gavarni. I found it very interesting, and it made me love G. twice as much.

Paris and its environs may be beautiful, but we have no complaints here either.

This week I did a painting that I think would remind you a little of Scheveningen as we saw it when we walked there together: A large study of sand, sea and sky – a big sky of delicate grey and warm white, with a single small patch of soft blue shimmering through – the sand and the sea light, so that the whole becomes golden, but animated by the boldly and distinctively coloured figures and fishing smacks, which tend to set the tonal values. The subject of the sketch I made of it is a fishing smack weighing anchor. The horses stand ready for hitching up before pulling the smack into the sea. I am enclosing a little sketch of it.

It was really hard to do. I just wish I'd painted it on a panel or on canvas. I tried to get more colour into it, that is, depth, strength of colour.

How strange it is that you and I so often seem to have the same thoughts. Yesterday evening, for instance, I came home from the woods with a study, having been deeply preoccupied with the question of depth of colour the whole week, and particularly at that moment. And I should very much have liked to have talked to you about it, especially with reference to the study I had done

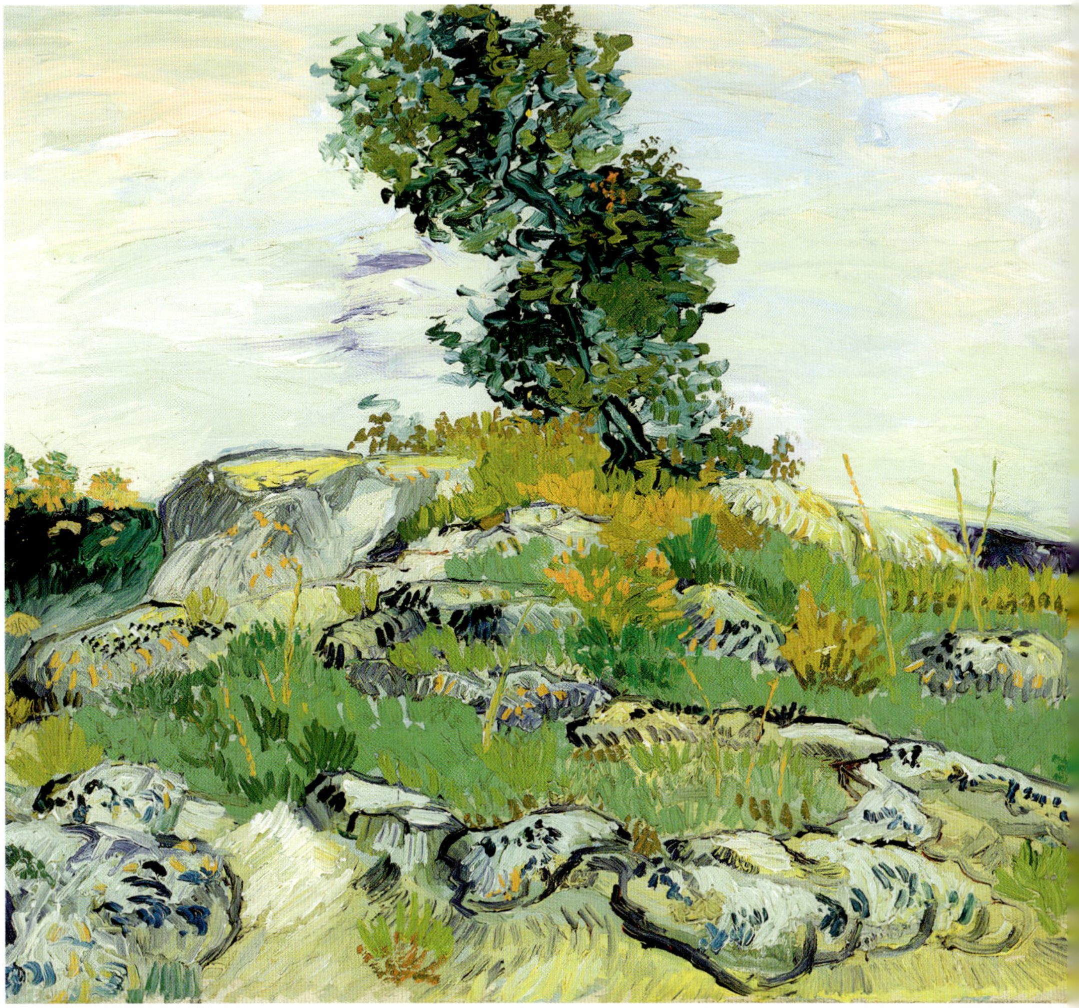

– and lo and behold, in this morning's letter you chance to mention that you were struck by the very vivid, yet harmonious, colours of Montmartre. I don't know if it was precisely the same thing that struck the two of us, but I do know that you would most certainly have been affected by what struck me so particularly and would probably have seen it in the same light.

***Le Moulin de Blute-Fin, Montmartre*, 1886**
MEDIUM: Oil on canvas
Courtesy of Art Gallery and Museum, Kelvingrove, Glasgow, Scotland/ © Culture and Sport Glasgow (Museums)/ The Bridgeman Art Library

***The Rocks*, 1888**
MEDIUM: Oil on canvas
Courtesy of Museum of Fine Arts, Houston, Texas, USA/Gift of Audrey Jones Beck/ The Bridgeman Art Library

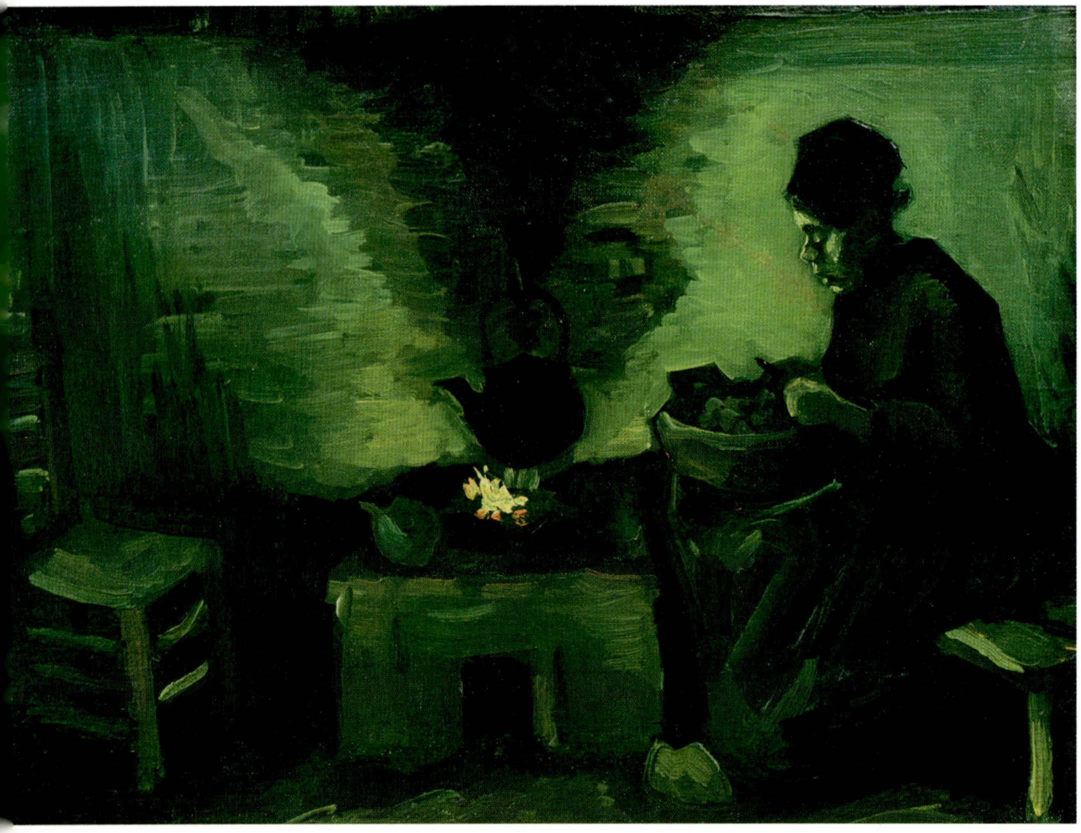

As a start, I am sending you a little sketch of the subject and I shall tell you what the problem was.

The woods are becoming thoroughly autumnal, and there are colourful effects I don't often see in Dutch paintings.

Yesterday evening I was working on a slightly rising woodland slope covered with dry and mouldering beech leaves. The ground was light and dark reddish brown, emphasized by the weaker and stronger shadows of trees casting half-obliterated stripes across it. The problem, and I found it a very difficult one, was to get the depth of colour. [...] A few figures of wood gatherers are foraging about, dark masses of mysterious shadows. The white cap of a woman bending down to pick up a dry branch stands out suddenly against the deep reddish-brown of the ground. A skirt catches the light, a shadow is cast, the dark silhouette of a man appears above the wooded slope. A white bonnet, a cap, a shoulder, the bust of a woman show up against the sky. [...]

In a way I am glad that I never *learned* painting. In all probability I would then have learned to ignore such effects as this. Now I can say to myself, this is just what I want. If it is impossible, it is impossible, but I'm going to try it even though I don't know how it ought to be done. *I don't know myself* how I paint it, I just sit down with a white board in front of the spot that appeals to me, I look at what is in front of my eyes, and I say to myself: that white board has got to turn into something. [...]

One thing I should like to bring to your attention as a matter of importance – wouldn't it be possible to obtain paint, panels, brushes, etc., at *discount* prices? I am having to pay the *retail* price at the moment. Have you any connection with Paillard or someone like that? If so, I think it would be much more economical to get paints, say, wholesale, for instance white, ochre, sienna, and we could then come to some arrangement about the money. Everything would be cheaper, it goes without saying. Do think it over.

One doesn't paint well by using a lot of paint, but in order to do a ground effectively or to get a sky bright, one must sometimes not spare the tube. [...]

Well, if there could be a little extra this month, that would be wonderful. If not, then not. I shall work as hard as I can.

Vincent was delighted to discover that he and Theo had both focused on the depth of colour they had observed in two different scenes: Vincent in the local woodlands, the colours of which he had found hard to capture, and Theo in Paris, commenting on the 'very vivid, yet harmonious colours of Montmartre'.

***Peasant Woman by the Hearth*, c. 1885**
MEDIUM: Oil on canvas laid on board
Courtesy of Musée d'Orsay, Paris, France/Giraudon/The Bridgeman Art Library

***Fishing in the Spring, Pont de Clichy*, 1887, (detail)**
MEDIUM: Oil on canvas
Courtesy of The Art Institute of Chicago, IL, USA/Giraudon/The Bridgeman Art Library

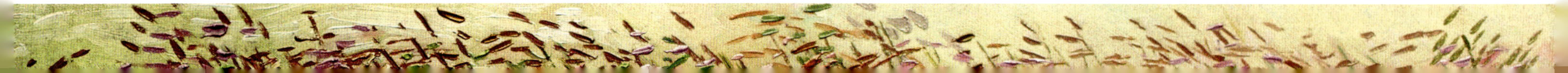

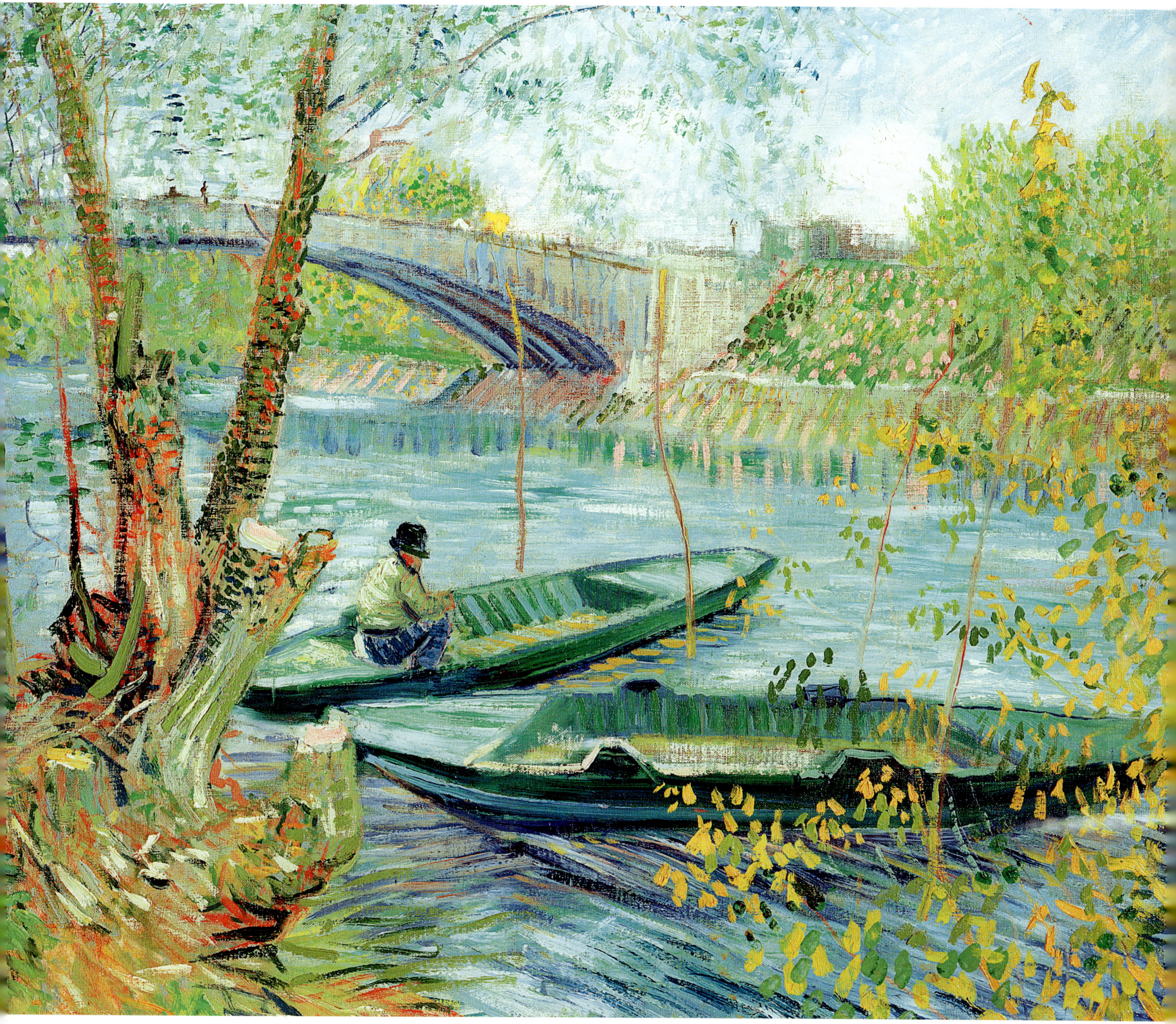

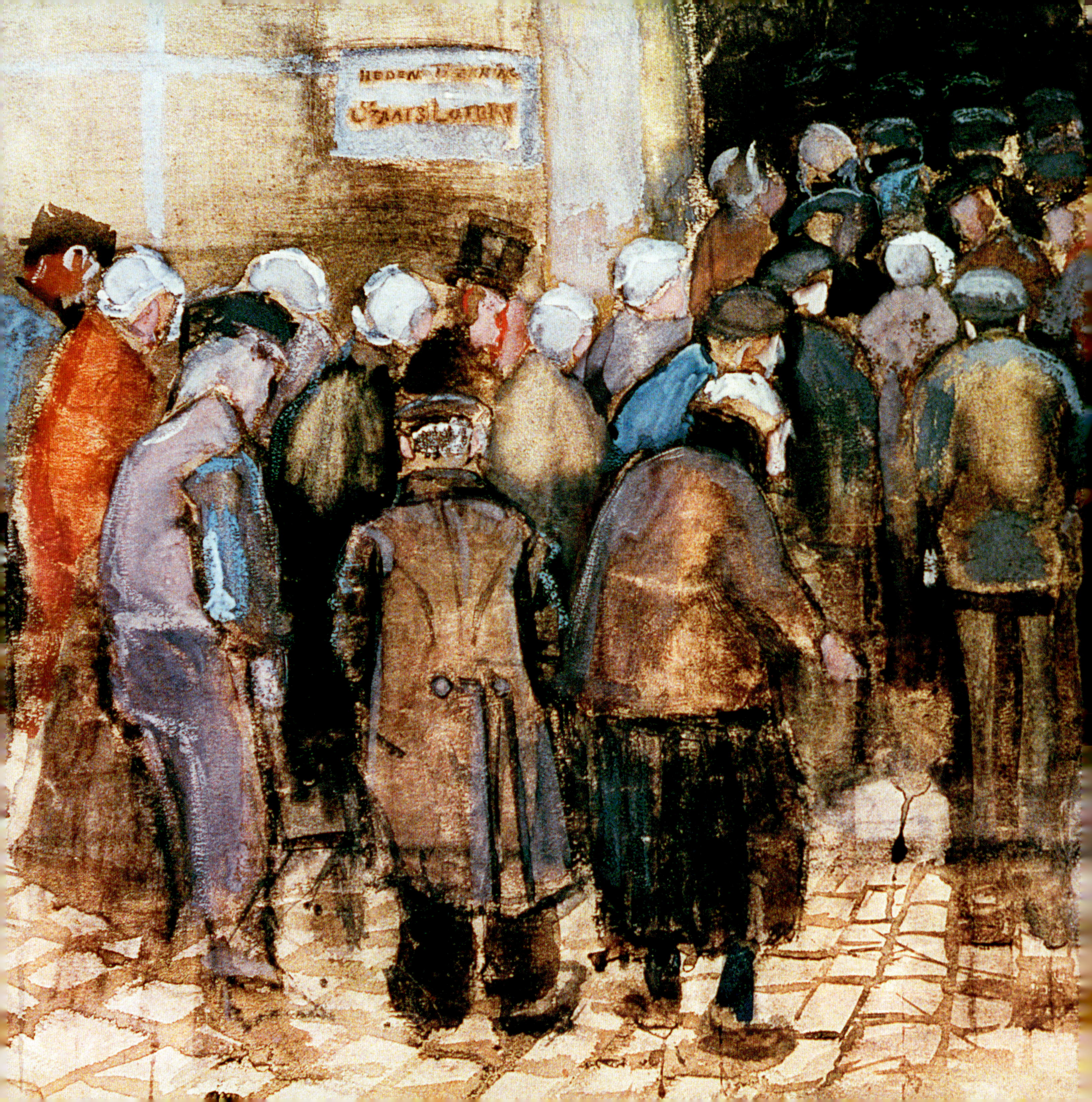
HEDEN

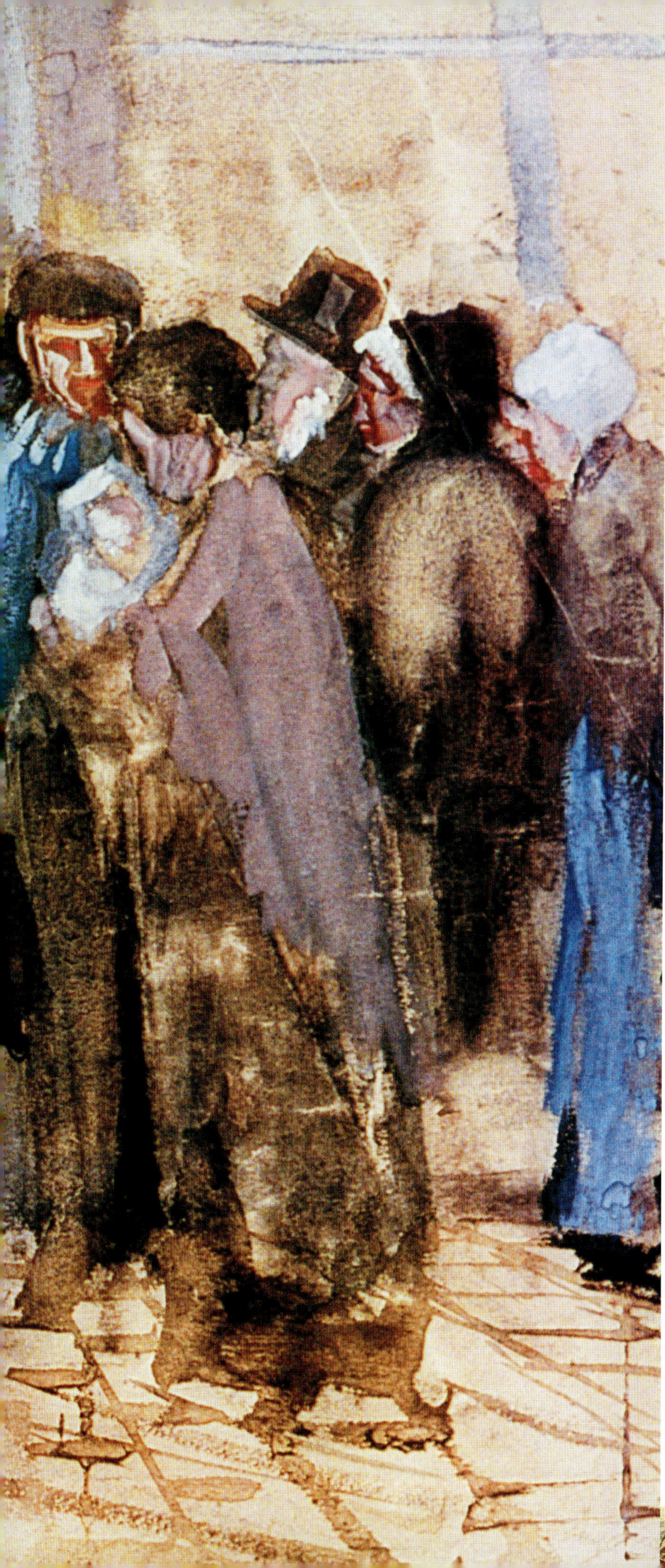

Extract from
The Hague, *1 October 1882*

[…] You may remember Mooijman's State Lottery office at the top of Spuistraat. I passed it one rainy morning when a crowd of people were standing outside waiting to get their lottery tickets. Most of them were little old women and the sort of people of whom one cannot tell what they do or how they live, but whom evidently scrape and struggle to make their way through life. Of course, superficially a small crowd of people like that so patently interested in 'Today's Draw' is something to make you and me smile, neither of us giving two pins for the lottery.

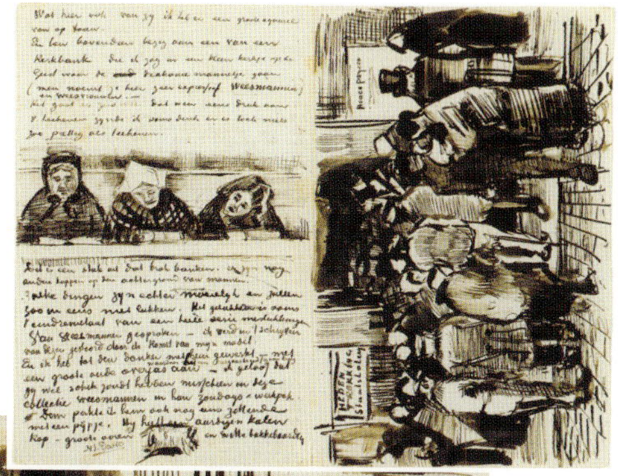

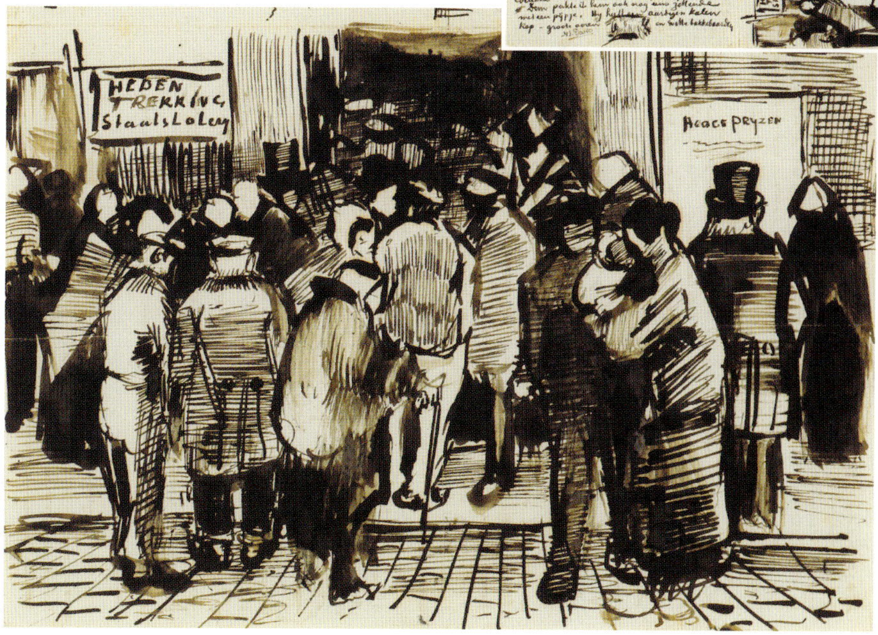

The State Lottery, 1882
MEDIUM: Watercolour on paper
Courtesy of Van Gogh Museum, Amsterdam, The Netherlands/The Bridgeman Art Library

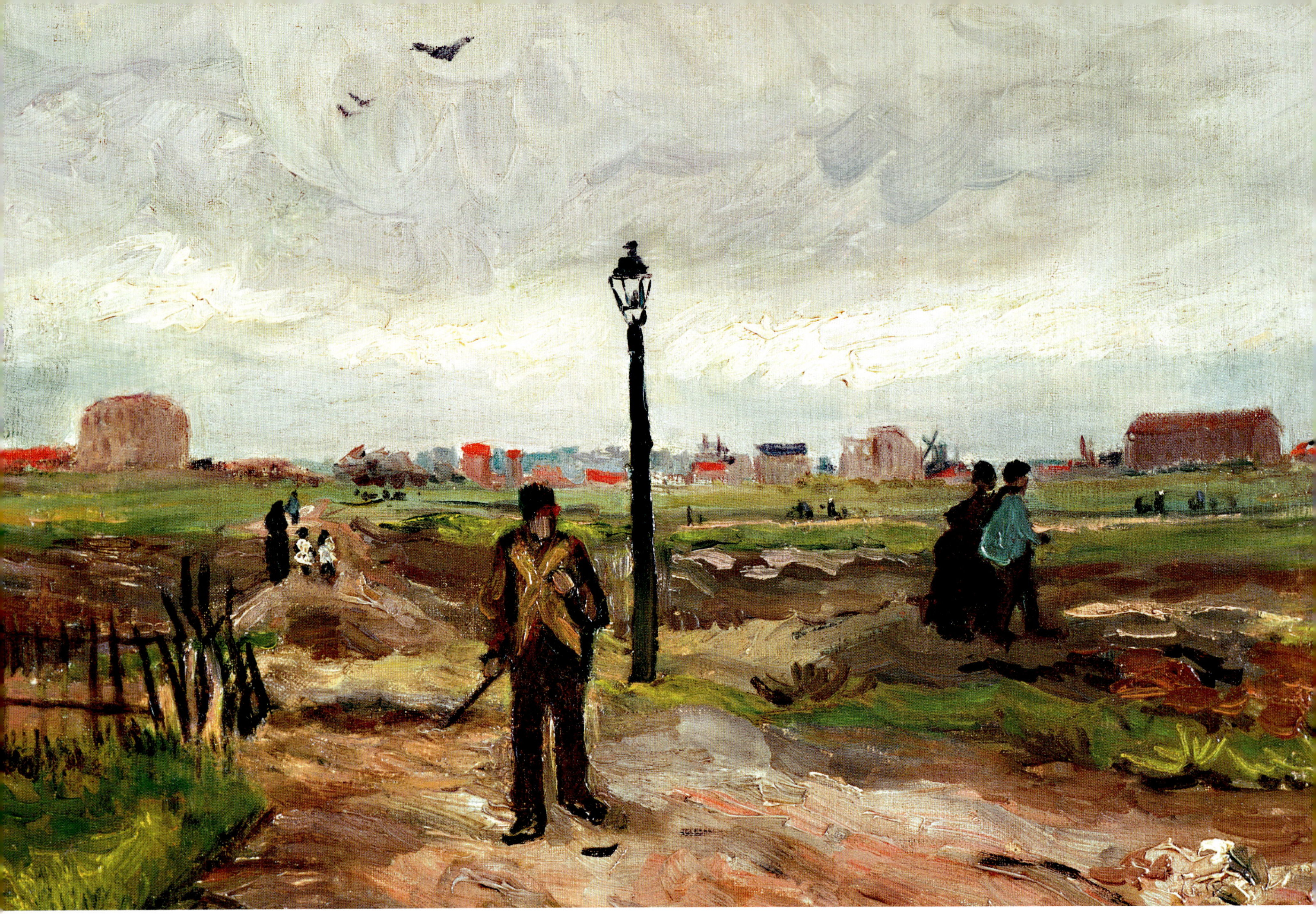

But I was struck by that small group and their expectant expressions, and while I did the sketch it assumed a greater and deeper significance for me than it had at first sight. It seems to me that it takes on more significance when one views it as: *the poor and money*. However, that is true of nearly all groups of figures – one must think about them before one can tell what one is looking at. The keen interest in, and the illusions about, the lottery may seem rather childish to us, but are serious indeed when we think of their counterpart, the misery and the sort of *efforts de perdus* [forlorn efforts] of those poor wretches to find salvation, as they think, through a lottery ticket possibly paid for with their last pennies, money that should have gone on food.

Be that as it may, I am trying my hand at a large watercolour of it. ”

In watercolour on paper Vincent painted a vibrant depiction of a small crowd of people swarming around the entrance of Mooijman's State Lottery office in Spuistraat. *The State Lottery*, 1882 shows a scene filled with older people and poorer people, huddling together toward the entrance.

Extract from
The Hague, *c. 11 January 1883*

"When I read your letter this morning, I was greatly touched by what you wrote. This is one of those things of which the world sometimes says, 'Why should he meddle with it?'. And yet it is not so much our own will as circumstances which drive us to do it. And once we understand the situation, such a deep, fathomless pity is roused in us that we can no longer hesitate. And this is the case with you, I think. [...] what else can I say, but that it seems to me that in such cases we must follow our impulses.

If one has such an encounter, one must expect it to cause a struggle, especially a struggle with oneself, because sometimes one literally does not know what to do or what not to do. But isn't this struggle – and even the mistakes one may make – better, and doesn't it develop us more than if we systematically avoid emotions? The latter thing is, in my opinion, what makes many so-called strong spirits into nothing but weaklings in reality.

You have my full sympathy in this matter, and as I myself am standing in the midst of realities and can tell you my experience since we spoke about it last, if you wish to hear something about it, or wish to speak about the future, or consult about whatever it may be, I am always entirely at your disposal.

And your writing that you will come to Holland before long is very welcome news indeed.

Perseverance is the great thing in love, once it has taken hold of us. That is, if the love is returned, for if it is decidedly not returned, one is literally absolutely helpless.

Well, I thank you for your confidence, and when I think it over, I am relatively confident of the result. Such a feeling is not 'passion,' for a deep, fathomless pity is at the root of it. [...]

The Outskirts of Paris, 1886
MEDIUM: Oil on cardboard
Courtesy of Private Collection/Photo © Christie's Images/The Bridgeman Art Library

The Fish Drying Barn at Scheveningen, c. 1882
MEDIUM: Pencil on paper
Courtesy of Private Collection/Giraudon/The Bridgeman Art Library

At all events, write me soon, and be assured of my full sympathy in regard to what you wrote me. Adieu, boy. A handshake in thought [...]"

Theo had confided in Vincent about a torrid relationship he was in with a woman called Marie. Not much is known about her but from Theo's letters we know she was a Roman Catholic, born in Brittany and was a sickly woman. Parallels were drawn by Vincent, regarding his own relationship with the once sick and homeless Sien and her children.

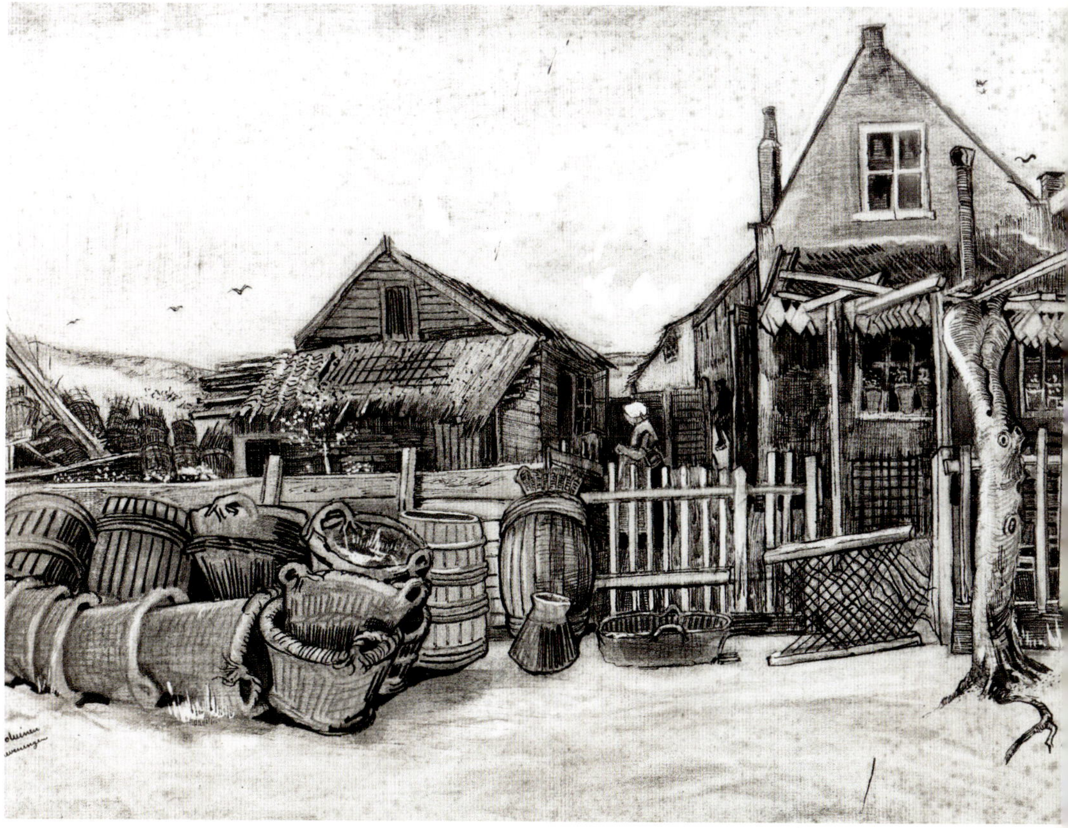

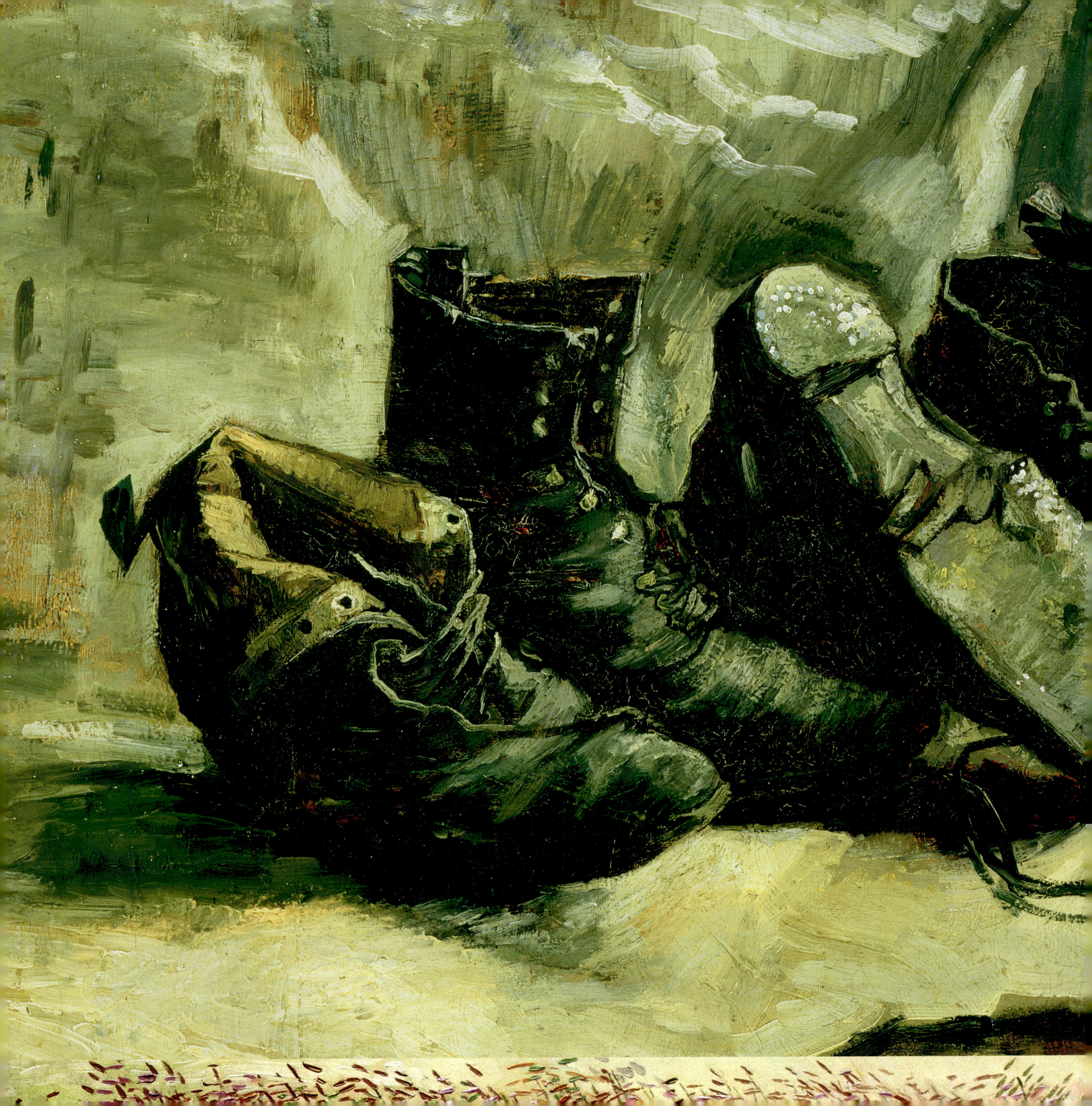

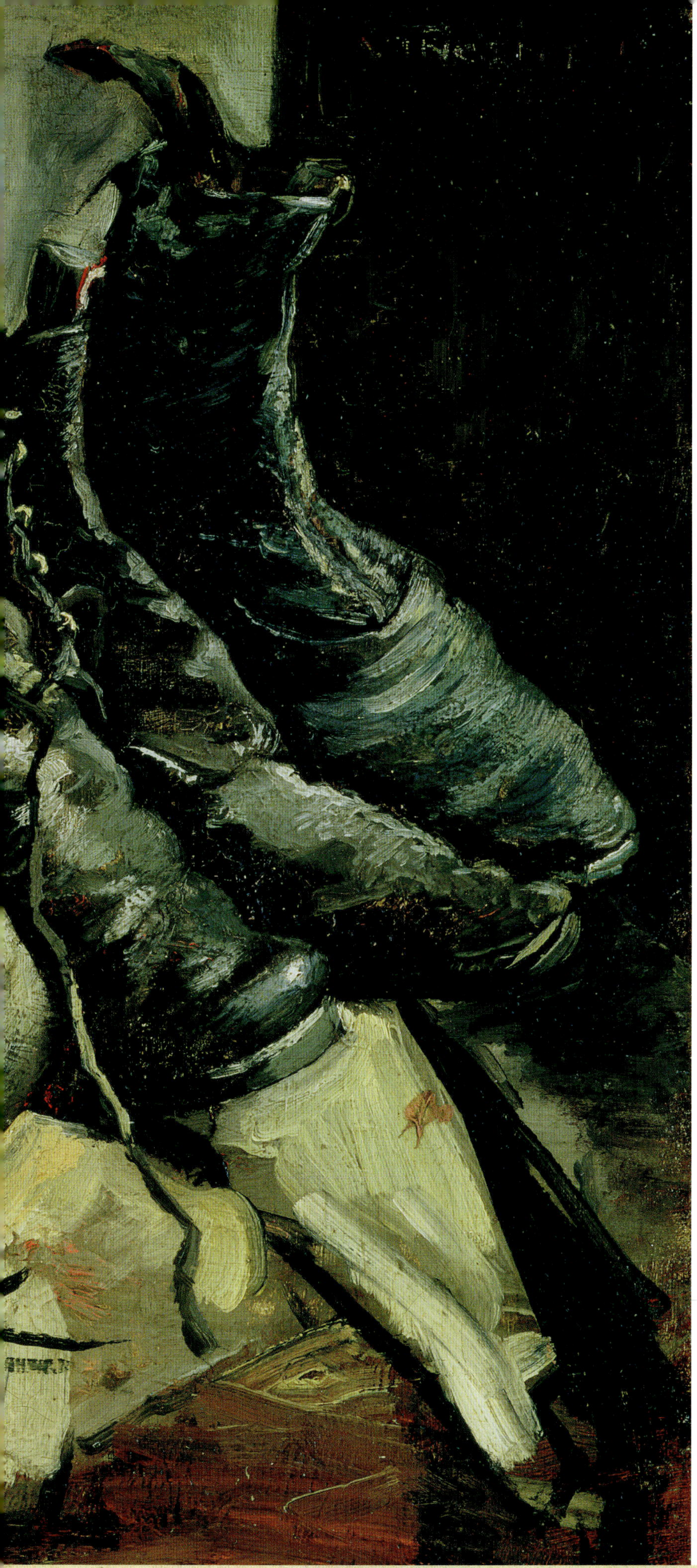

Extract from
The Hague, *3 March 1883*

I enclose a little sketch which I made in the soup kitchen. They sell the soup in a large passage where the light falls from above, through a door to the right.

Now I tried to find that same effect in the studio. In the background I put a white screen, and on that I drew the hatch, according to its real position and measurements; I closed the farthest window entirely, and the middle window at the bottom, so that the light falls from *P*, exactly as in the place itself.

You see, when I have the models posing there, I get exactly the same effect as in the real soup kitchen.

In the sketch above, you see the grouping in the studio. I have put a line around the part I wanted to draw.

Of course I can study the poses of the figures as long and as much and as correctly as I like, yet generally remaining true to what I have seen. […]

In the above sketch, the wall is white, with wainscot painted grey, the floor, darker. By paying attention to those things, one gets the local colour so much more correctly. I have a few of these things already, and also many *real* clothes. Yesterday, for instance, I bought a very picturesque patched smock of coarse linen. I am always on the lookout for such things; by paying some attention to them, the models give more satisfaction than if one leaves it all to chance.

***Three Pairs of Shoes*, 1886–87**
MEDIUM: Oil on canvas
Courtesy of Fogg Art Museum, Harvard University Art Museums, USA/Bequest from the Collection of Maurice Wertheim, Class 1906/The Bridgeman Art Library

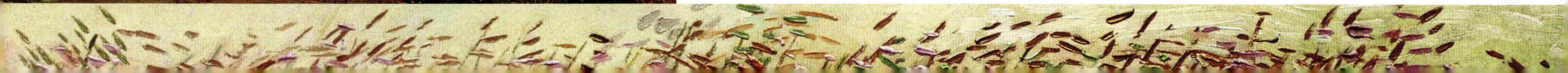

I love my studio the way a sailor loves his ship. I know that in time it will become just what I want, but my purse doesn't always allow me to do what I should like. But the things which one buys in this way are things that last, and *now* I have a chance which perhaps I shouldn't get again later.

The change in the studio brings even more expenses – indirectly rather than directly – for I won't consider it finished before I have many more things which are necessary to make it practical.

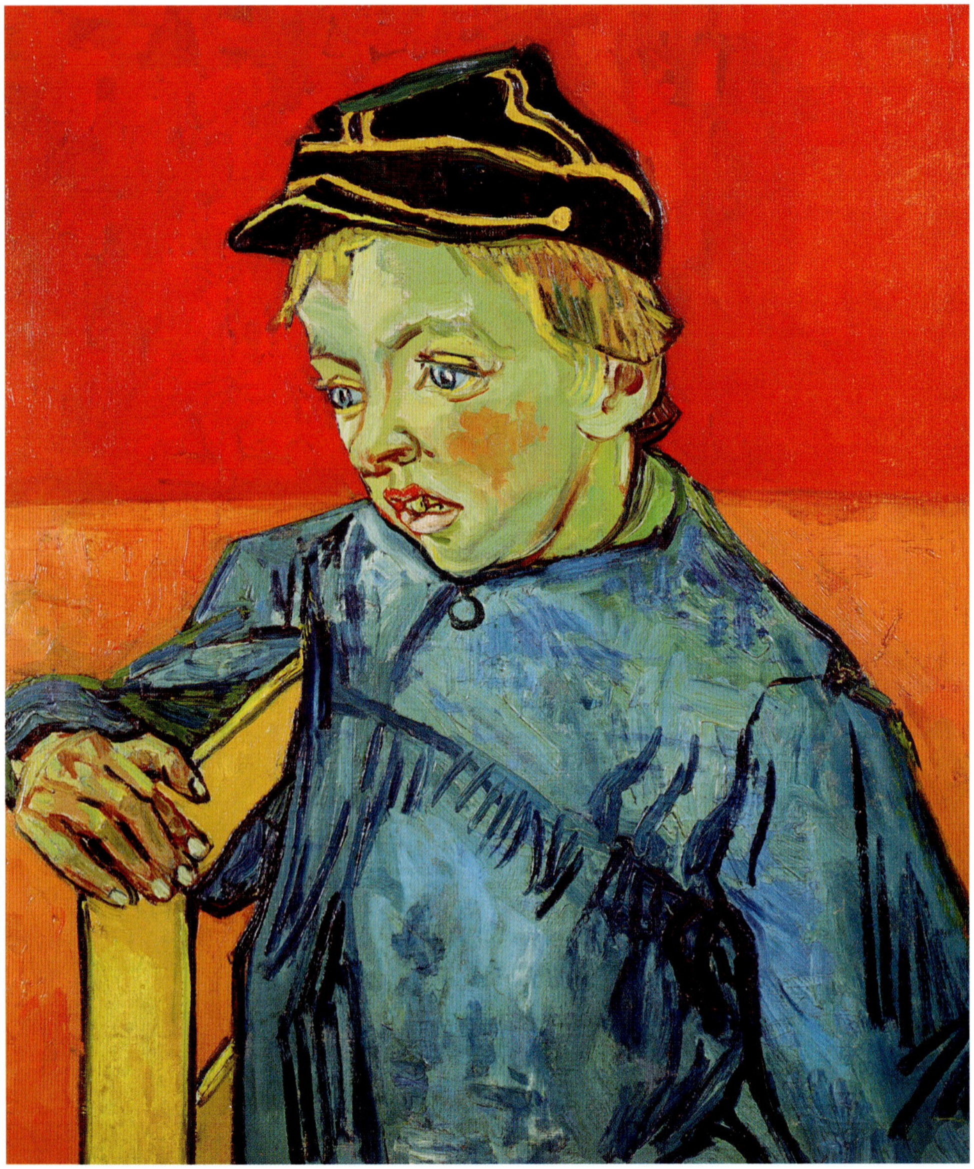

***The Schoolboy*, 1889–90**
MEDIUM: Oil on canvas
Courtesy of Museu de Arte, Sao Paulo, Brazil/The Bridgeman Art Library

***Farmhouse After the Rain*, 1883**
MEDIUM: Oil on canvas on panel
© akg-images

[…] This and many other things give me a strong desire to push on vigorously.

At all events, whether you can send me something or not, I can promise you better drawings before long. […]

Among the studies of heads – old men, etc. – which I still have, there are some which I will not be able to improve at once, because there is unquestionably some touch of nature in them, and at the same time something with which I am, of course, not quite satisfied; so I dare not say 'I shall do it better in a few days'.

[…] At all events, one thing I can promise you now, tomorrow I'll have the house full of people, that is, the woman's mother, and her younger sister, and a boy from the neighbourhood, and all these persons, together with my own people, will pose for the drawing of which this is the first rough sketch.

Adieu. My best wishes for your patient [Marie] or rather, your convalescent.

Extract from
The Hague, *22 July 1883*

It may be feverishness, or nerves, or something else, I don't know, but I don't feel well. Perhaps I am thinking more than is necessary about that expression in your letter concerning various things; I hope so. And I have an uneasy feeling I can't shake off, though I have tried to overcome it.

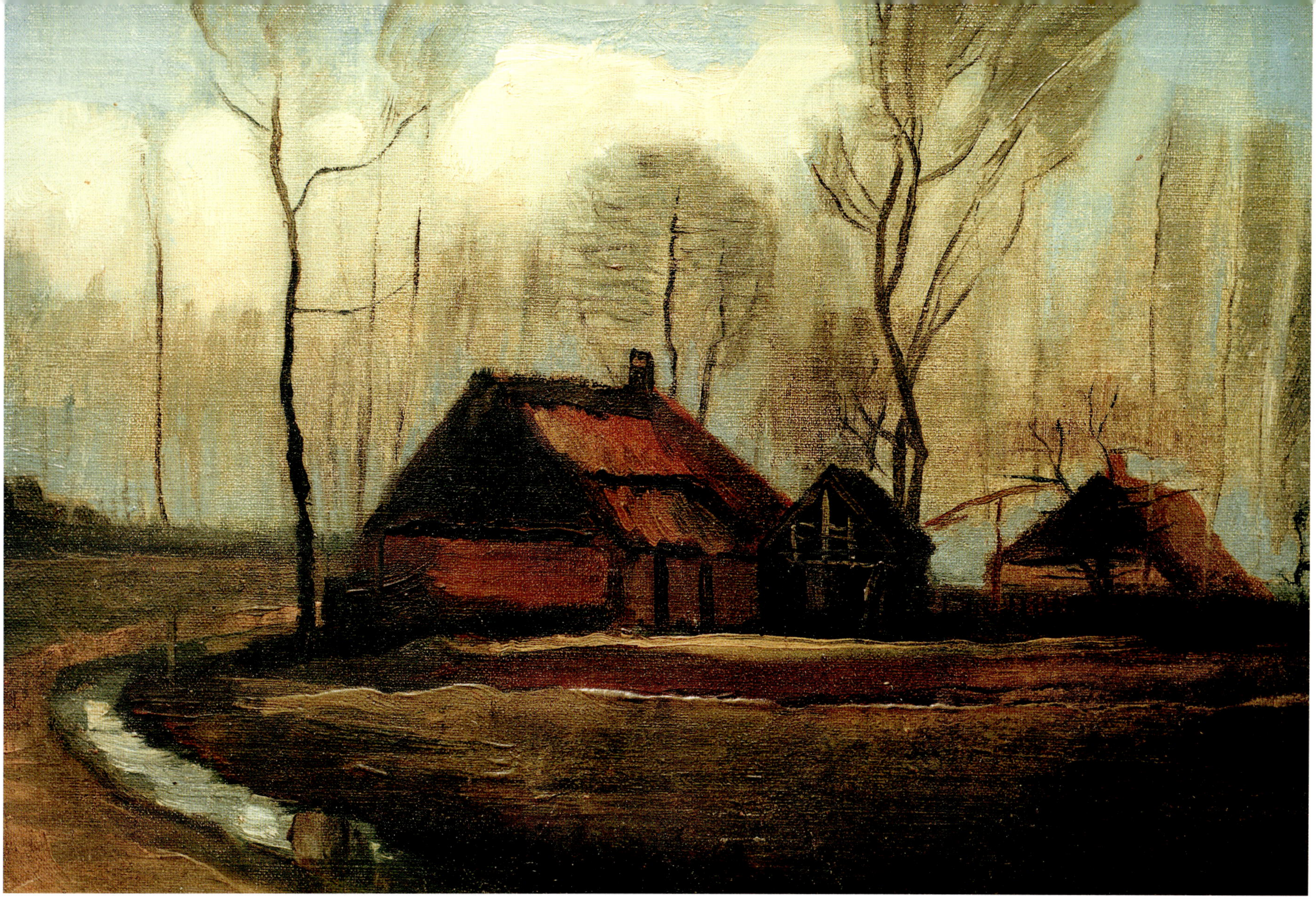

There isn't any reason for it, is there? If there is anything, then tell me straight out what kind of obstacles there are.

At all events, write too, by return of mail if possible, whether there is anything or not. I can't help it if there is no reason for it, but all at once I'm in the dumps. It may be a reaction from my overexerting myself. [...]

Yours sincerely

Vincent

In fact, I have no real friend but you, and when I am in low spirits, I always think of you. I only wish you were here, that we might again talk together about moving to the country.

Except for what I told you about, there is nothing the matter with me, and things are going well – but perhaps I am a little feverish or something – I feel miserable. I had to pay money right and left – landlord, paint, baker, grocer, shoemaker, heaven knows what – and only a little is left. But the worst is that after many such weeks, one feels one's resistance ebbing, and is overcome by a pervading feeling of weariness.

If you can't send anything at once, brother, at all events try to write me by return of mail if possible. And as to the future, if there is some danger, tell it straight out, '*homme avisé en vaut deux*' [a man in the know is better than one that is not], it is better to know exactly what one has to fight against.

Things are looking dark right now. If it were only for me, but there is the thought of the woman and the children, poor

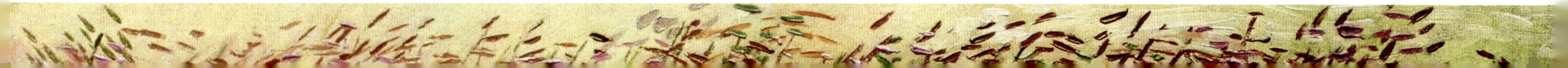

creatures whom one would keep safe, and feels responsible for. [...] I cannot talk about it with them, but for myself it became too much today. Work is the only remedy; if that does not help, one breaks down.

And you see the trouble is that the possibility of working depends on selling the work, for there are expenses – the more one works, the greater the expenses are (though the latter is not true in every respect). When one does not sell and has no other income, it is impossible to make the progress which would otherwise follow of its own accord. "

Extract from
The Hague,
4–8 August 1883 – postscript

" For no particular reason, I cannot help adding a thought that often occurs to me. Not only did I start drawing relatively late in life, but it may well be that I shall not be able to count on many more years of life either. [...]

So, as to the time I still have ahead of me for work, I think I may safely presume that my body will hold up for a certain number of years *quand bien même* [in spite of everything] – a certain number between 6 and 10, say. (I can assume this the more safely as there is for the time being no immediate *quand bien même*.) [...]

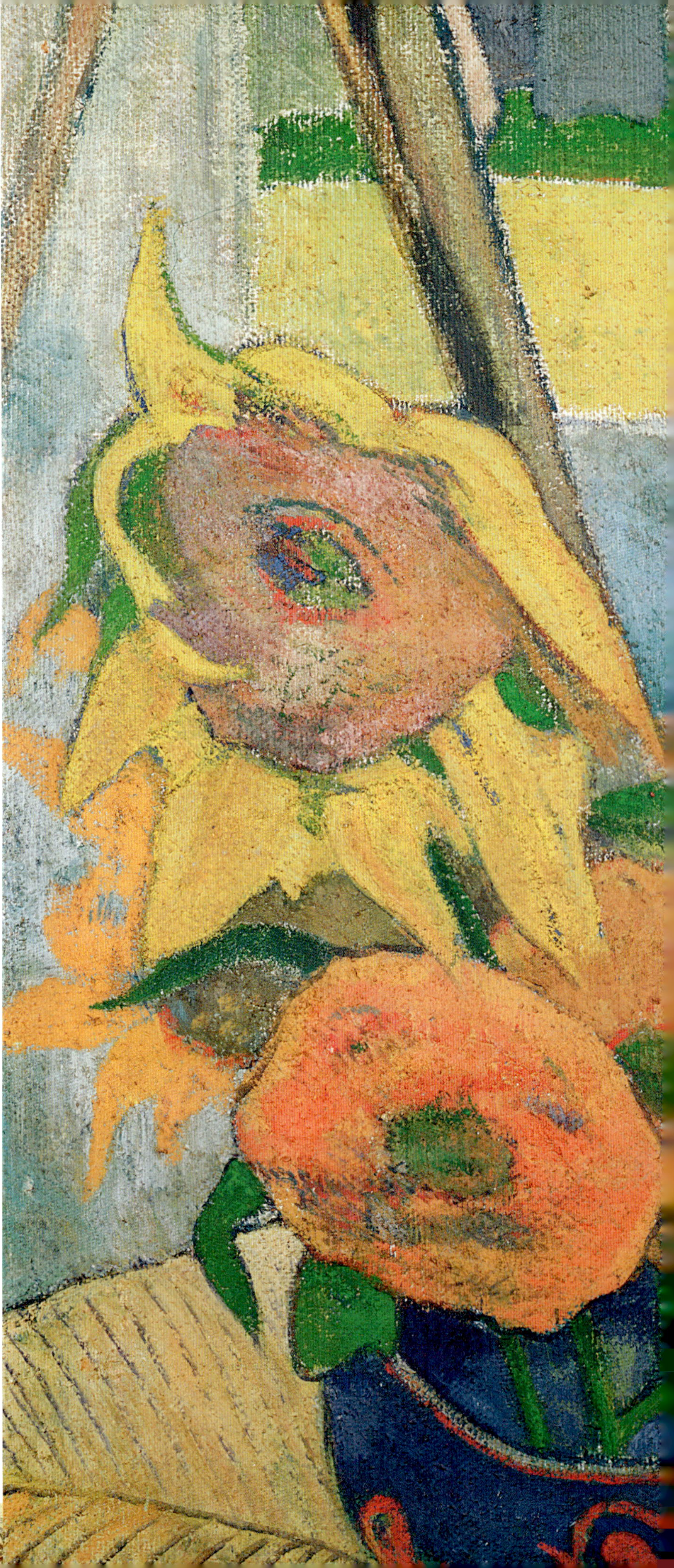

***Van Gogh Painting Sunflowers*, 1888**
by Paul Gauguin (1828–1909)
MEDIUM: Oil on canvas

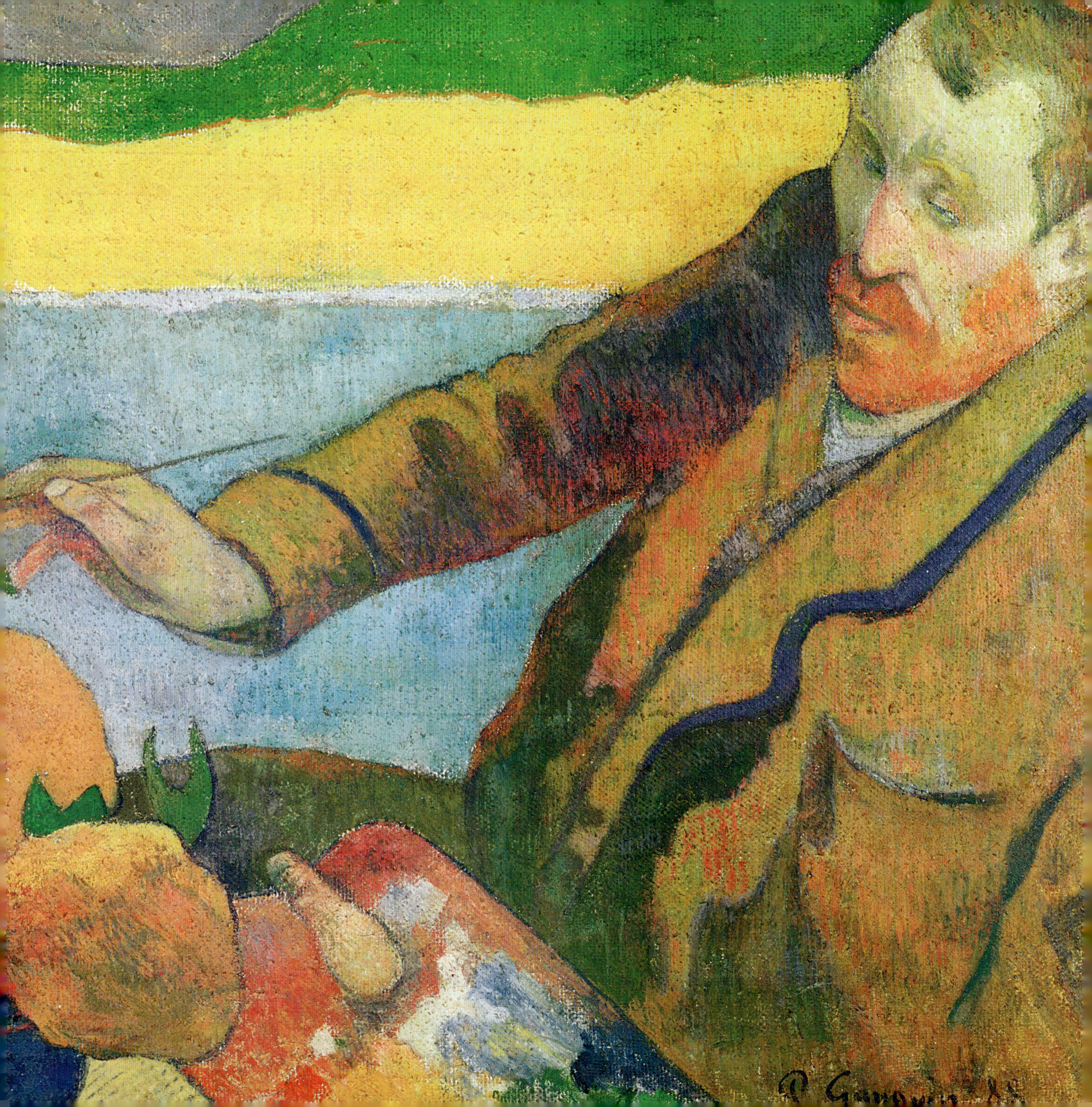

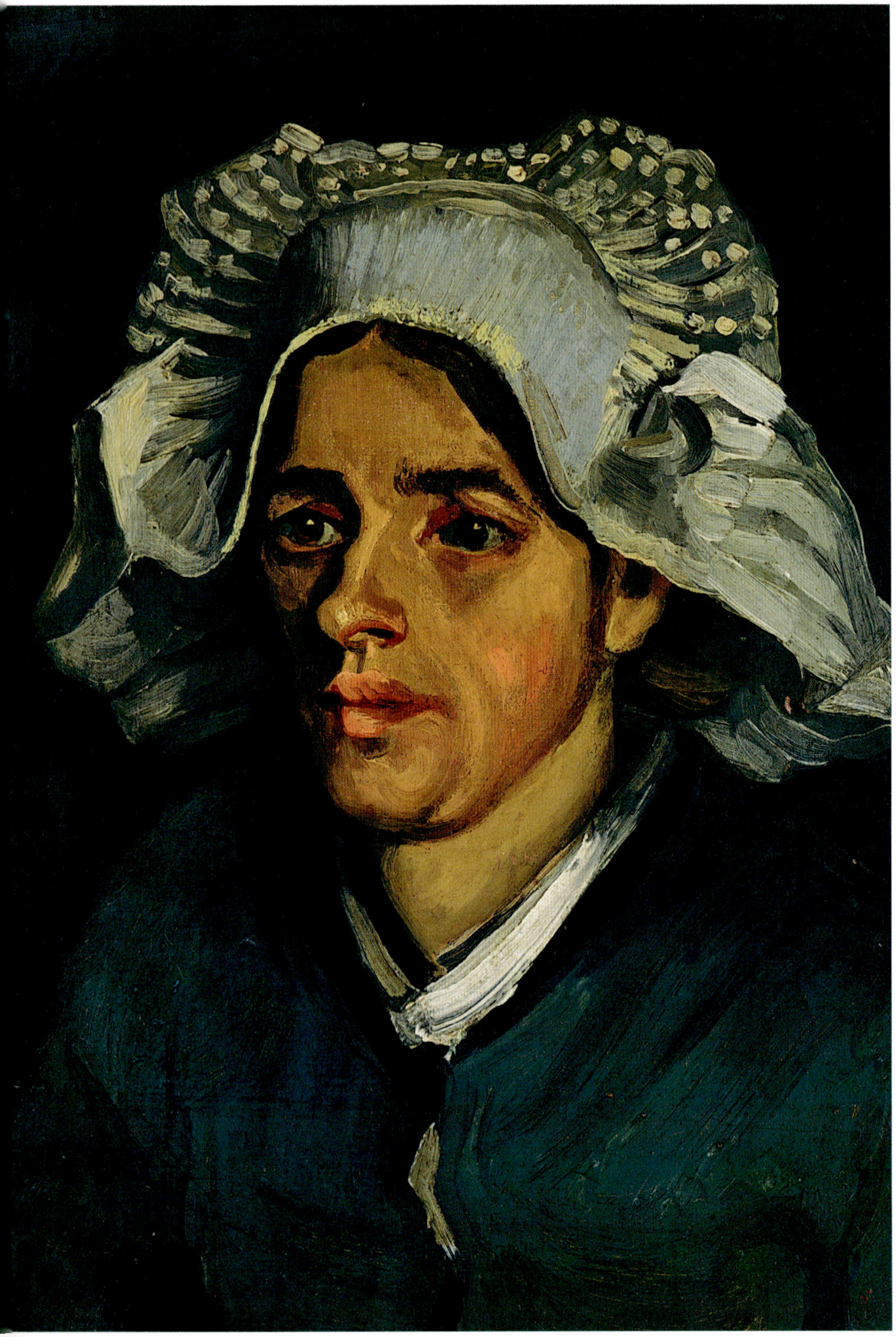

That is how I regard myself, as having to accomplish in a few years something full of heart and love, and to do it with a will. Should I live longer, *tant mieux*, [so much the better] but I put that out of my mind. *Something must be accomplished* in those few years, this thought guides all my plans. […]"

Vincent worries that money is going to dry up from Theo and the worry prevents him from working. In his postscript he adds that he feels he has another six to 10 years to live (a sadly accurate prediction), adding that 'Something must be accomplished in those few years….'

Extract from The Hague, *18 August 1883*

"[…] My firm resolve is to be dead to anything except my work. But it is very hard for me to speak about those things, simple in themselves, but which unfortunately link up with much deeper things.

There is no anguish greater than the soul's struggle between duty and love, both in their highest meaning. When I tell you I choose my duty, you will understand everything.

A simple word said about it during our walk, made me feel that absolutely nothing is changed in me in that respect, that it is and remains a wound which I carry with me, while it lies deep and cannot be healed. After years it will be the same as it was the first day.

[…] I have never suspected *her*, nor do I suspect her now, nor shall I ever suspect her, of having had any but right and proper financial motives. She went as far as was reasonable, other people exaggerated. But for the rest, you understand that I do not hold any delusive convictions about love for me, and what we talked of on the road remains between us. Since then, things have happened that would not have taken place, if at a certain

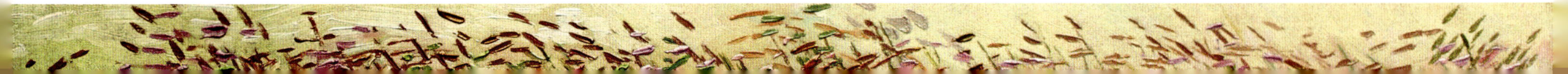

moment I had not had to face in the first place a decided 'no,' and secondly a promise that I would not stand in her way. I respected in her a sense of duty – I never have suspected, shall never suspect her of anything mean. [...]

Yours

Vincent

You will understand, however, that I must avoid everything which might tempt me to hesitate, so that I *must* avoid everything and everybody that would remind me of *her*. [...]"

After the failure of his relationship with Sien, Vincent moved to Drenthe, in the northern Netherlands, in order to forget her, to begin his life over and to concentrate on his art: 'My firm resolve is to be dead to anything except my work.' However, he missed her and the children very much.

Extract from Drenthe, *c. 15 September 1883*

"Now that I have been here for a few days and have done a good deal of walking about in various directions, I can tell you more about the area in which I have ended up. I am enclosing a quick little scratch of the first study I painted here, a cottage on the heath. A cottage made entirely of turfs and sticks. I have seen the inside of some 6 or so like this, too, and more studies of them will follow. [...]

To mention one of the many fresh impressions and feelings I have gained on my exploratory outings, let me tell you for instance about the barges drawn by men, women, children, white or black horses, laden with peat, *in the middle of the heath*, just like the ones you see in Holland, say on the Rijs-wijk towpath. [...] There are 4 or 5 canals in the village, to Meppel, to Dedemsvaart, to Coevorden, to Hollands Veld. Following them, one now and then sees a curious old mill, farmhouse, boatyard, or lock. And always the bustle of peat barges. [...]

I often think with melancholy of the woman and the children, if only they were provided for; oh, it's the woman's fault, one might say, and it would be true, but I am afraid her misfortunes will prove greater than her guilt. I knew from the beginning that her character was spoiled, but I hoped she would improve; and now that I do not see her any more and ponder some things I saw in her, it seems to me more that she was too far gone for improvement. And this only increases my feeling of pity, and it becomes a melancholy feeling because it is not in my power to redress it.

Theo, when I meet on the heath such a poor woman with a child on her arm, or at her breast, my eyes get moist. It reminds me of her, her weakness; her untidiness, too, contributes to making the likeness stronger. *I know that she is not good*, that I have an absolute right to act as I do, that I *could not* stay with her back there, that I really *could not* take her with me, that what I did was even sensible and wise, whatever you like; but, for all that, it cuts right through me when I see such a poor little figure feverish and miserable, and it makes my heart melt inside. [...]"

When Vincent had moved to Drenthe he had looked for a place to set up an artists' colony. Pleased with the rural setting, he described it to Theo. However, his mind was still on Sien and her young family, and every time he came across a poor young woman on the heath, he was painfully reminded of them. After six weeks in Drenthe, he returned to his parents' home in Nuenen.

***Head of a Peasant Woman*, 1885**
MEDIUM: Oil on canvas laid on millboard

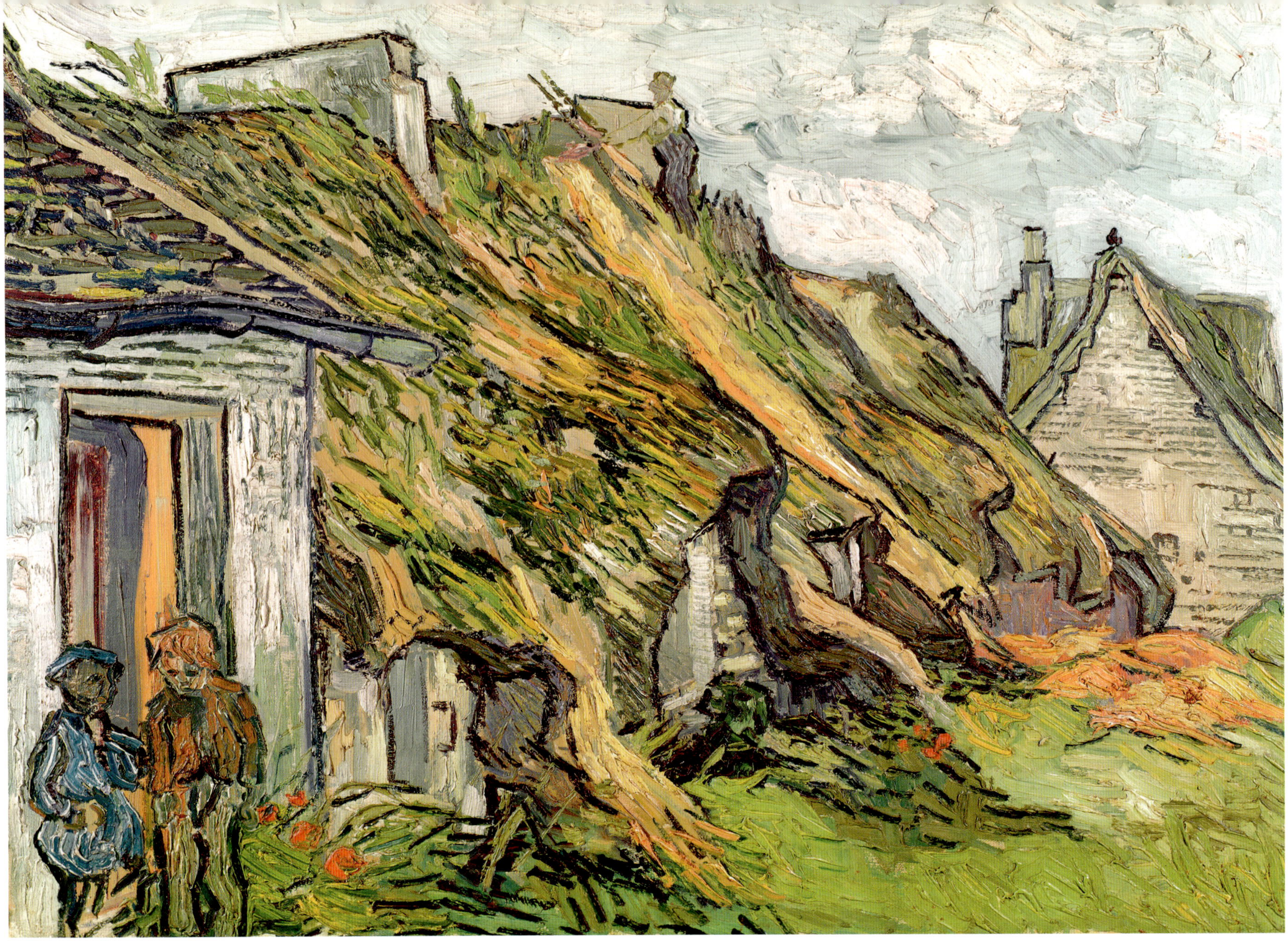

Extract from
Nuenen, *17 December 1883*

"I sense what Father and Mother *instinctively* (I do not say *intelligently)* think about me. They shrink from taking me into the house as they might from taking a big shaggy dog who is sure to come into the room with wet paws – and is so very shaggy. He will get in everyone's way. *And his bark is so loud*. In short, he is a filthy beast. [...]

This house is also too good for me, and Father and Mother and the family are so exceedingly refined (though not sensitive underneath), and – and – there are clergymen, lots of clergymen. The dog appreciates that if they do keep him, they are only putting up with him, only just tolerating his presence 'in this house,' so he will try to track down a kennel elsewhere. [...] In fact this dog used to be Father's son once upon a time, and it was Father who left him out in the streets a little too long, so he was bound to become rougher, but seeing that Father forgot this many years ago and has never thought *deeply* about what the bond between father and son means, we had best say nothing about it. [...]

The only thing the dog regrets is that he came back, because it wasn't as lonely on the heath as it is in this house – despite all that kindness. The poor beast's visit was a weakness, which I hope will be forgotten, and which he will avoid repeating in the future. Because I have had no expenses since I have been here, and because I have twice received money from you, I paid for the journey myself and also for the clothes Father bought me because mine weren't good enough, and at the same time I have repaid the 25 guilders to friend Rappard. I'm sure you'll be pleased about this, everything was such a mess.

Dear Theo, enclosed is the letter I was writing when I received yours. Which I shall now answer, having carefully read what you say.

I shall start by saying I think it noble of you that, believing that *I am making things difficult* for Father, you take his part and give me a brisk dressing-down. I value this in you. [...]

You do realize, don't you, that I'm sure *you have saved my life* and I shall *never* forget that. *Even after we have put an end* to relations which, I fear, would place us into a false position, I shall still not only be your brother, your friend, but I shall also owe you an infinite debt of loyalty because you held out your hand to me and because you have gone on helping me. [...] Money *can* be repaid, not kindness such as yours.

[...] Please send me the usual by return of mail, if you can, then I shan't have to ask Father for anything when I leave, which I *ought to do as soon as possible*.

I gave all the 23.80 guilders you sent on December 1 to Father, for 14 guilders borrowed and 9 guilders for shoes and trousers. I gave all the 25 guilders you sent on December 10 to Rappard. I still have a quarter and a few cents in my pocket. So that is the financial position. [...] From here I shall go to Rappard's. And from Rappard's, perhaps to Mauve's. My intention is thus to try to do everything in a calm and orderly fashion.

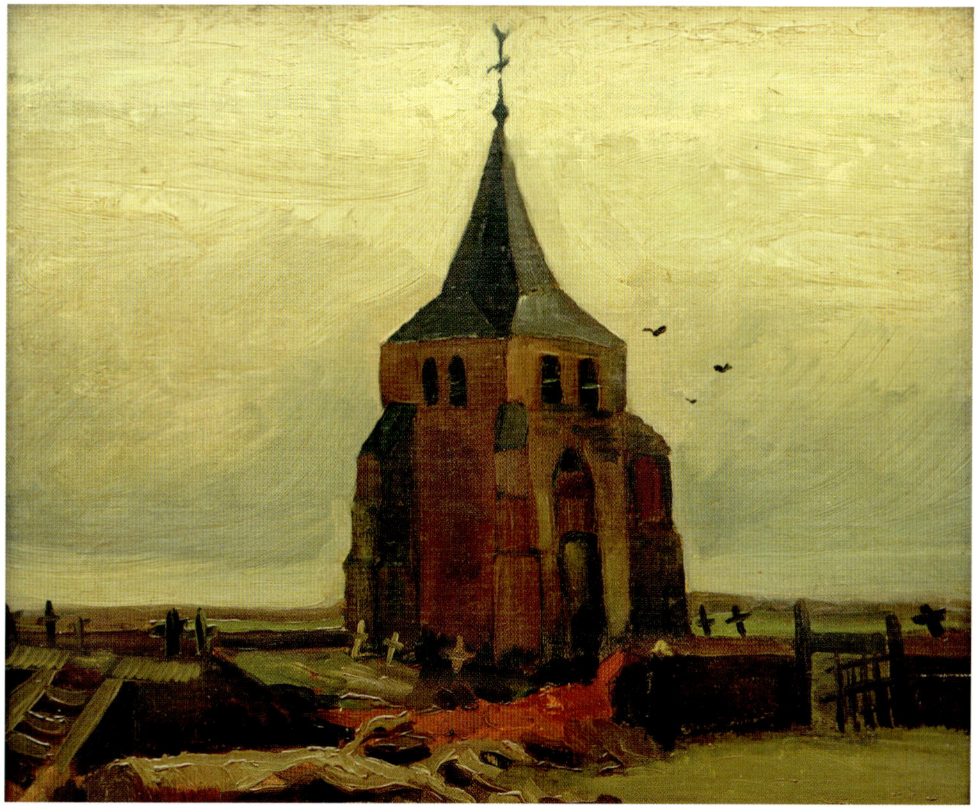

There is too much in my candidly expressed opinion of Father which I cannot take back in the circumstances. [...] Allow me to tell you that I never knew that someone of 30 was 'a boy', particularly when he has probably had more experience than most during those 30 years. But do think of my words as the words of a boy if you want. I am not responsible for how you view what I say, am I? That is *your* business. [...]

In any event I am neither Father's enemy nor yours, nor shall I *ever* be."

Vincent had returned home after reaching a low ebb in Drenthe, a move he describes as a mistake. He likens himself to a shaggy dog that is not welcome in his parents' house. Theo had written to Vincent lightly admonishing him for arguing with their Father. Vincent was not happy that his brother and confidant had criticized his behaviour and, while admitting that he owed his life to Theo for his generosity, he could not agree with him on this point.

***Thatched Cottages in Chaponval, Auvers-sur-Oise*, 1890**
MEDIUM: Oil on canvas
Courtesy of Kunsthaus Zurich, Switzerland/ The Bridgeman Art Library

***The Old Tower at Nuenen*, 1884**
MEDIUM: Oil on canvas
© akg-images

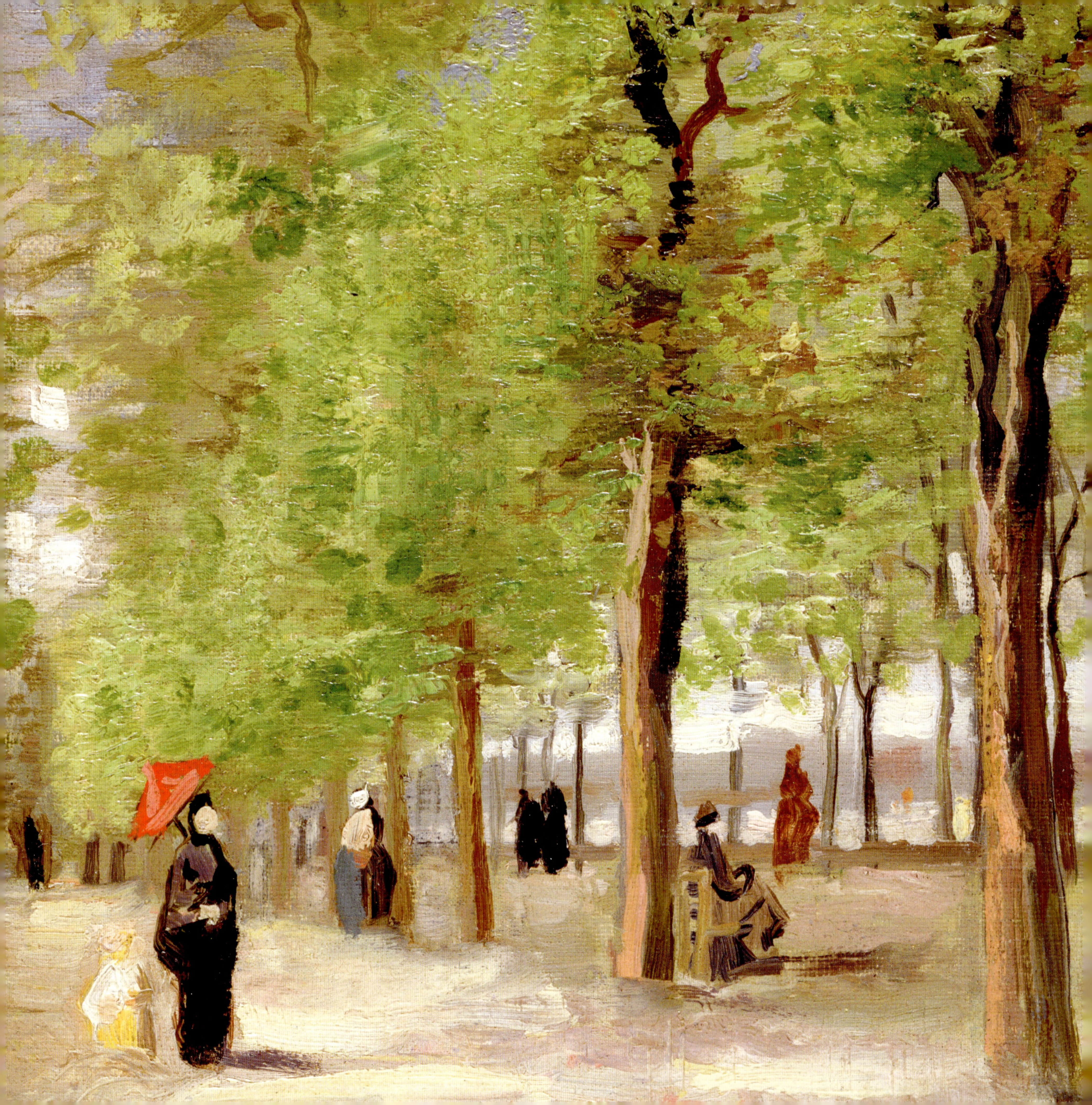

Vincent van Gogh: A Life in Letters & Art

1884–86

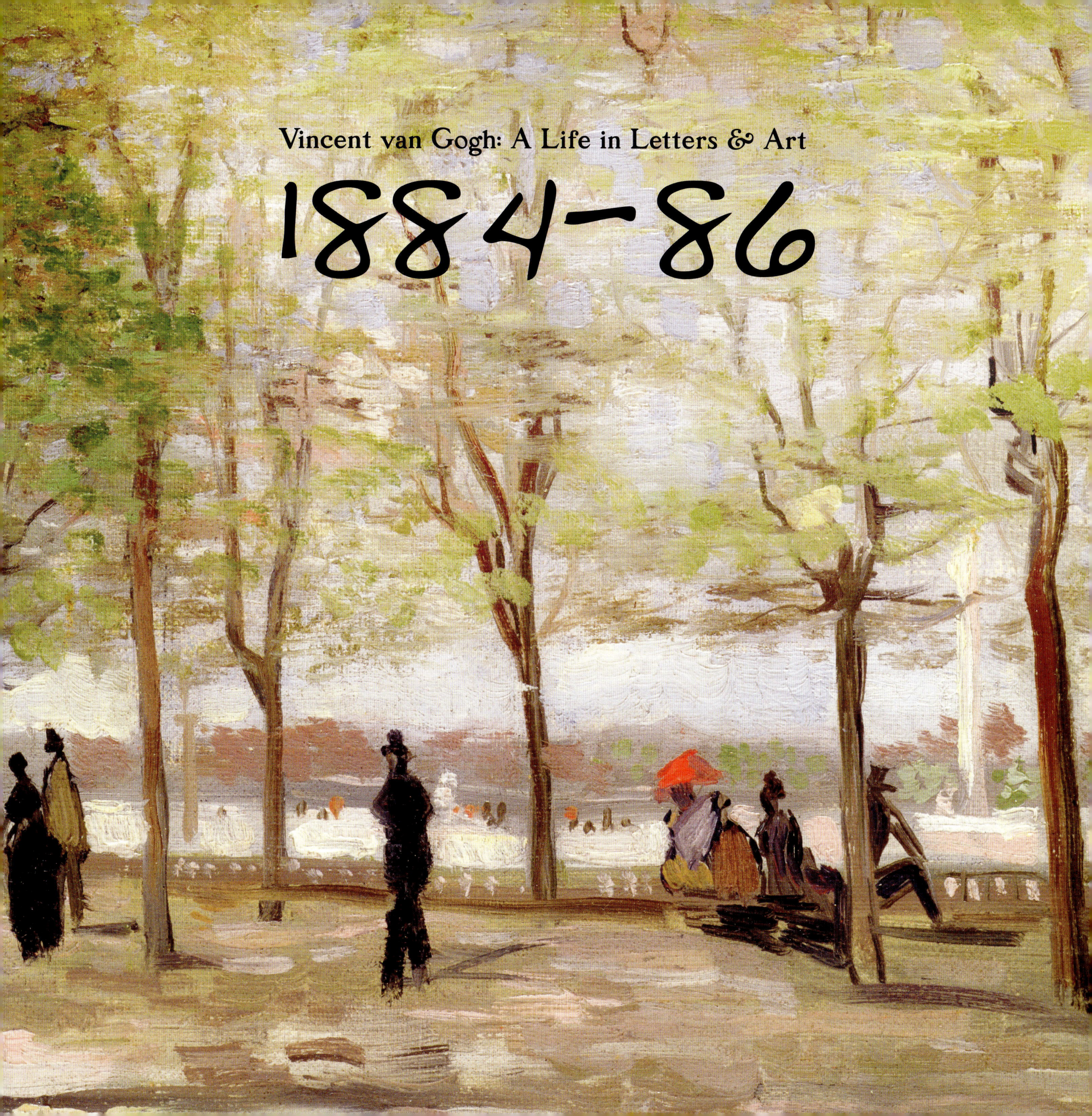

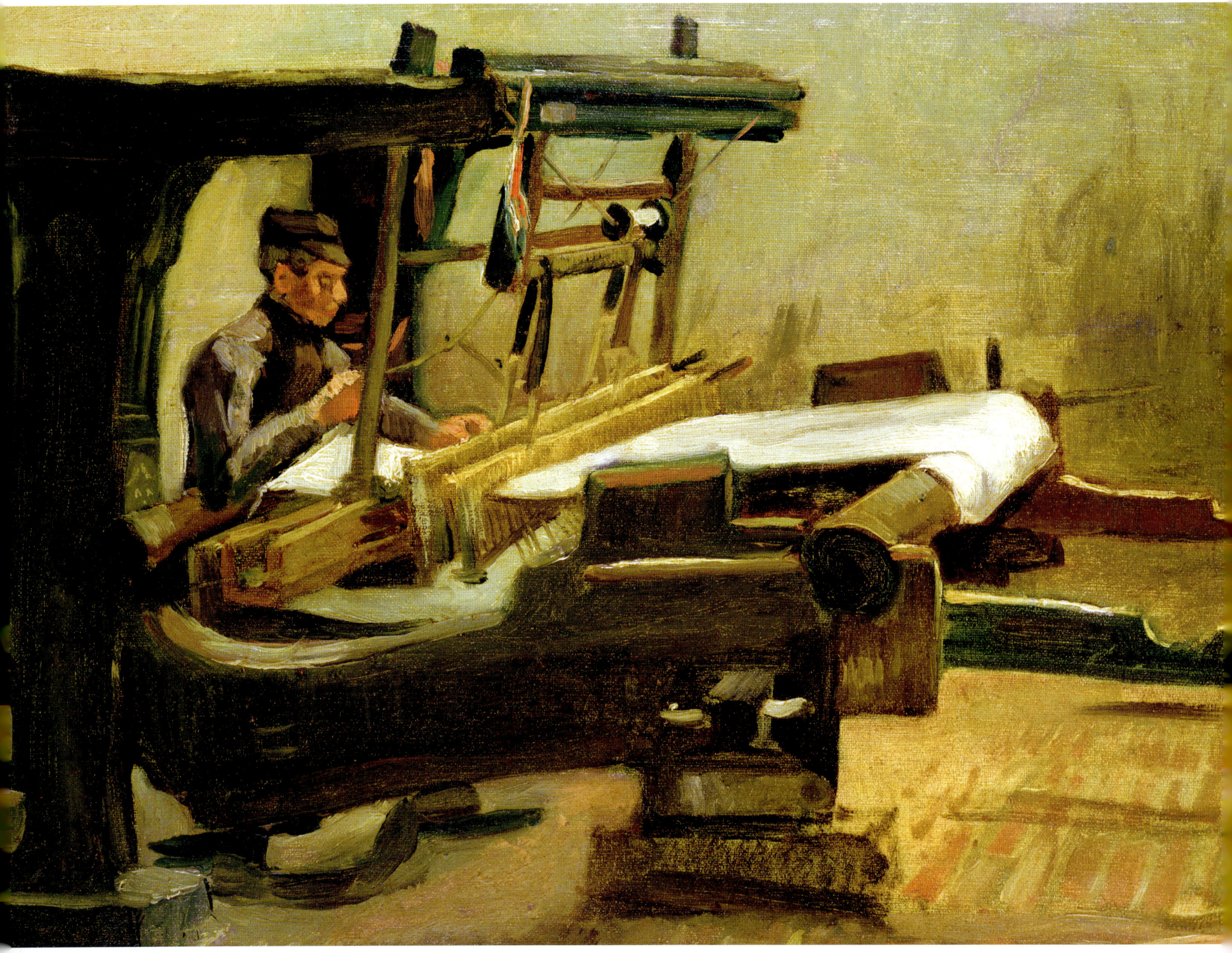

From Vincent van Gogh to
Theo van Gogh
Extract from
Nuenen, *1 March 1884*

Dear Theo,

"[…] I'm sure you're right to say that my work must improve a great deal, but at the same time I also think that your efforts to do something with it could become a bit more determined. You have *never yet* sold a *single thing* I have done – whether for a lot or a little – *in fact, you haven't even tried.* […]

As far as saleability or unsaleability is concerned, that's a dead horse I don't intend to go on flogging. […] It's become very clear to me by this time that you couldn't care less about my doings…. I also foresee that I shall grow cooler and cooler towards you. […]

What you write about Marie is quite understandable – if a woman isn't all milk-and-water, I can well imagine her not showing much enthusiasm for moping about in the company of cantankerous fathers as well as spiritual sisters. In any event, a woman no less than a man would feel sorely tempted to end the stagnation *quand même* [at all costs] – stagnation which may start out as splendid resignation, but which, alas, one will generally be made to regret as soon as one feels one is going to freeze solid in the end. […]

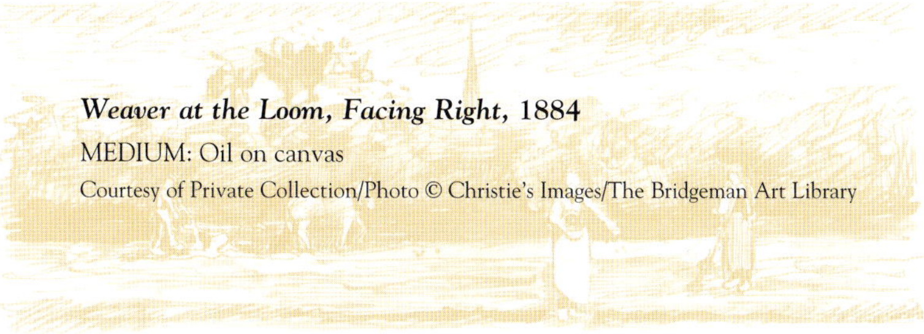

***Weaver at the Loom, Facing Right,* 1884**
MEDIUM: Oil on canvas
Courtesy of Private Collection/Photo © Christie's Images/The Bridgeman Art Library

[…] you say you leave me completely free, it seems to me that ultimately, for example, if I keep company with a woman of whom you and others do not approve, perhaps rightly, though sometimes I don't give a damn about that, there is a small tug at the purse strings to make me feel that it is 'in my own interests' to defer to your opinion.

When it came to that business with the woman, you also had your way, and it came to an end, but […] I'm damned if I'll practise morality in order to get a little bit of money. […]

Just think it over, my dear fellow – I do not hide my innermost thoughts from you […]"

Vincent and Theo were at loggerheads over money, Vincent was not happy that Theo had not sold his drawings or paintings and suggested that he was not trying hard enough. Theo's argument was that the works may not be saleable. Anger at being unjustly treated by his family comes through in Vincent's words; he does not appreciate that, should he choose a woman not approved by the family, the threat of an end to financial support is used to make him to break off the relationship.

From Vincent van Gogh to
Anthon van Rappard
Extract from
Nuenen, *late March 1884*

Dear friend Rappard,

"[…] I have noticed that you sometimes disapprove of things in your own work which in my opinion are rather good. […]

Anyway, I've been painting quite a bit lately, a seated girl winding shuttles for the weavers and a weaver on his own. I'm

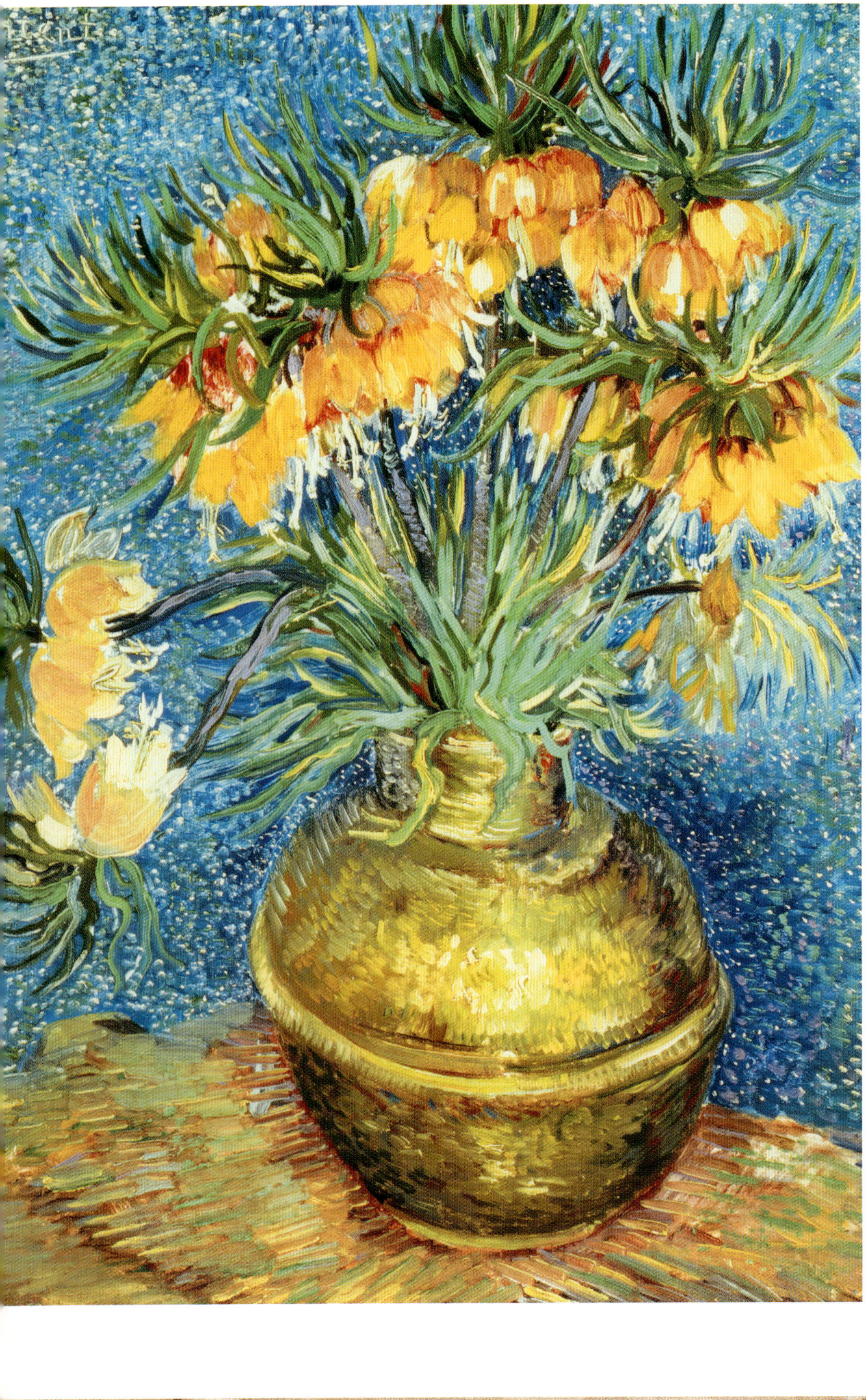

rather anxious that you should see my painted studies one of these days. [...]

I detest writing or talking about *technique* in general, Rappard – though I may occasionally get the urge none the less to discuss how to execute some idea or other of mine, be it with you or with someone else, and I never make light if the practical value of such discussions. But that doesn't gainsay my first thought – which I may not have expressed properly. [...]

But to change the subject, it is fiendishly difficult not to feel anything, not to be affected when those bloody idiots say 'does he paint for money?'. One hears that drivel day in, day out, and one gets angry with oneself later for having taken it to heart. [...] when I write to you about certain expressions of yours I do so only in order to ask you: are you certain that those who are so loud in their praises of technique are *de bonne foi* [of good faith]? I'm only asking because *I know that your aim is to avoid studio chic.*

Having fallen out with his brother Theo, Vincent turned to his friend Anthon van Rappard (1858–1892) for conversation on art and theoretical and practical advice on painting. At times he rants through his personal dislikes of the arts world in long letters. What comes across is his great respect for van Rappard and his appreciation of the man's art.

From Vincent van Gogh to
Theo van Gogh
Extract from
Nuenen, *c. 1 April 1884*

Dear Theo,

I just received your letter and enclosed 250 francs. [...] I want to consider the money I receive from you as money I have earned.

Of course I will send you *my work every month*. As you say, that work will be your property then, and I perfectly agree with you that you have every right to do anything with it; even I couldn't make any objection if you should want to tear it to pieces.

Theo suggested that all the artworks that Vincent sent him should become his property in return for funding. Vincent had accused Theo of not trying hard enough to sell the works. The need for a return on his money led Theo to this decision. From Vincent's tone one can see that he is quite hurt and angered by the arrangement, teasing Theo that he could tear up any of his works as soon as he had paid for them if he wanted.

Extract from
Nuenen, *early August 1884*

I just wanted to drop you a line while you are in London.

[…] Last week I was in the fields every day during the harvest, of which I made a composition.

I made this for somebody in Eindhoven who wants to decorate a dining room. He intended to do this with compositions of various *saints*. I begged him to consider whether the appetite of the worthy people who would have to sit down at that table would not be more stimulated by six illustrations from peasant life in the Meierij [Manor District]. He is a man with whom I want to remain on good terms – a former goldsmith. […] He is

***Crown Imperial Fritillaries in a Copper Vase*, 1886**
MEDIUM: Oil on canvas
Courtesy of Musée d'Orsay, Paris, France/Giraudon/The Bridgeman Art Library

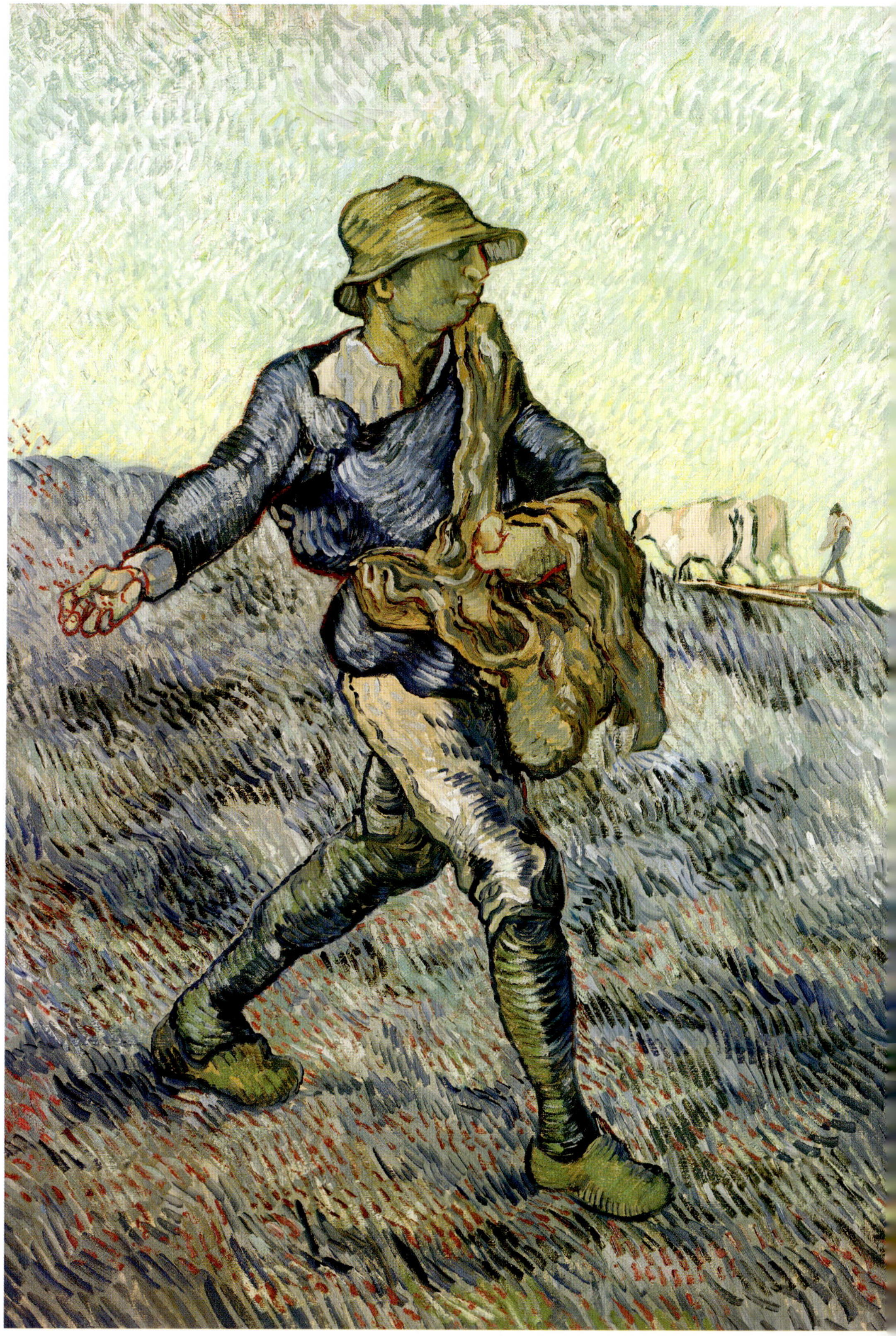

***The Sower (after Millet)*, 1890**
MEDIUM: Oil on canvas
Courtesy of Private Collection/ The Bridgeman Art Library

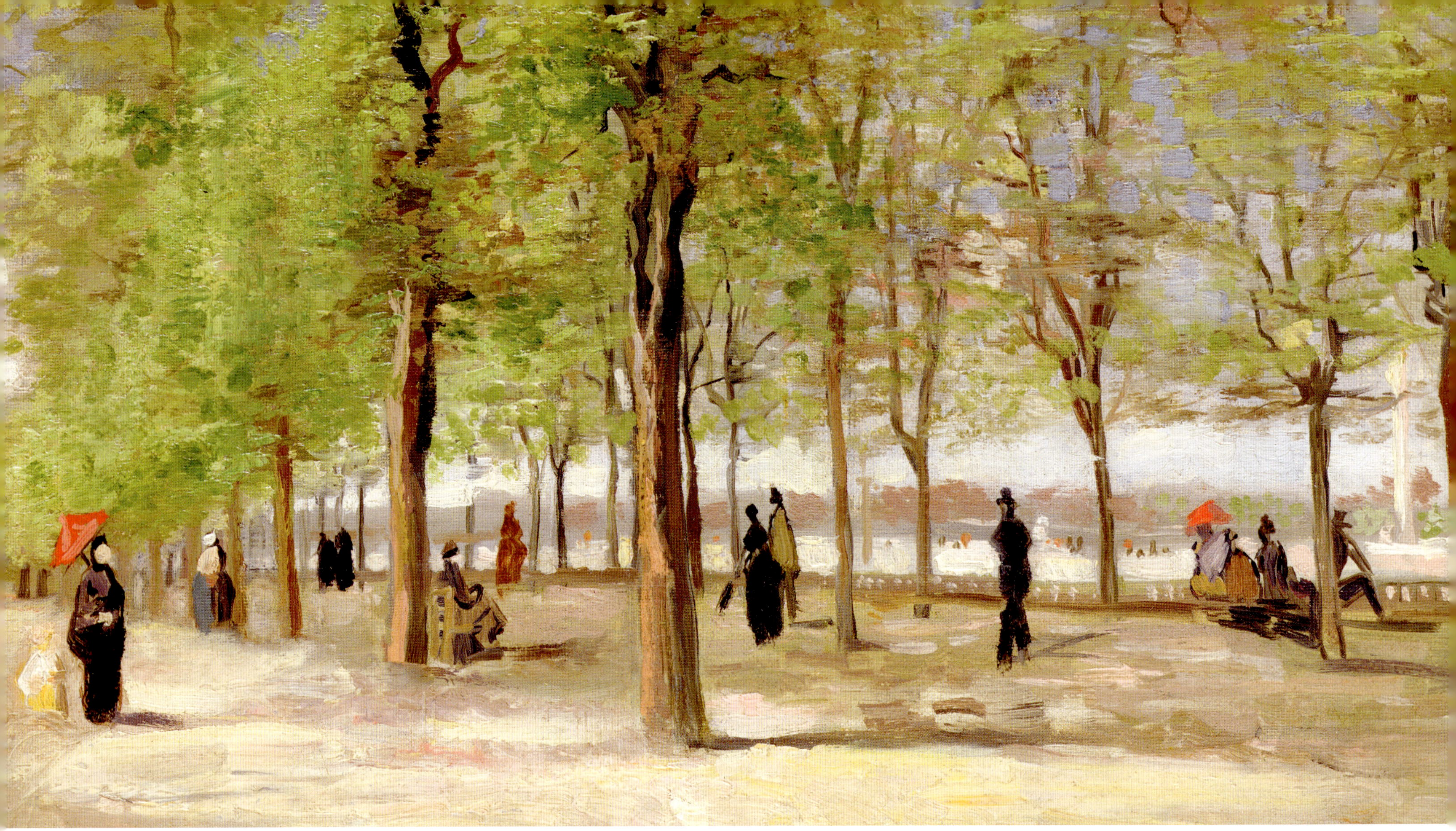

decorating the ceilings and walls himself. […] But he positively wants 'painting' in the dining room, and has begun to paint twelve panels of flowers.

There are six panels left on the longest wall, and for these I gave him preliminary sketches of a sower, ploughman, shepherd, harvest, potato digging, ox wagon in the snow.

But he is pleased with this first panel, as well as with my sketches for the other subjects."

Vincent had been given a commission to design six panels for a dining room of a wealthy patron, Antoon Hermans, in Eindhoven. Hermans wanted images of individual saints in the panels, but Vincent persuaded him to adopt his favourite pastoral themes including images of a sower, reaper, ploughman and shepherd. The patron painted the panels himself.

Extract from Nuenen, *2 October 1884*

"Thanks for your letter, thanks for the enclosure.

[…] Now, there are people who say to me 'Why did you have anything to do with *her* [Margot]?' – that's *one* fact. And there are people who say to her, 'Why did you have anything to do with *him*?' – that's another fact.

Apart from that, both she and I have grief enough and trouble enough, but as for regrets – neither of us have any. Look here – I believe without question, or have the certain knowledge, that she loves me. I believe without question, or have the certain knowledge, that I love her. […] Theo, I feel so much confounded pity for this woman, just because her age and

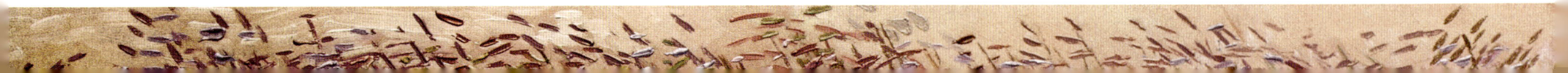

Terrace in the Luxembourg Garden, 1886
MEDIUM: Oil on canvas
Courtesy of Sterling and Francine Clark Art Institute, Williamstown, USA/The Bridgeman Art Library

Avenue of Poplars, 1884, (detail)
MEDIUM: Oil on canvas
© akg-images

just *possibly* a liver and gallbladder complaint hang so threateningly over her head. And this is aggravated by emotions. For all that, we shall find out what can or what, fatally, cannot be done. However I shall not do anything without a *very good* doctor, so *I* shall do her no *harm*.”

Vincent discusses the problems he faces with his latest girlfriend Margot Begemann. It is clear from the tone of the letter that Vincent has no interest in Theo's opinion of her or the opinions of other family members. However, Margot's sisters had opposed the relationship and she had attempted suicide. Instead he discusses the works of Jean-François Millet (1814–75), Émile Zola (1840–1902) and Jules Breton (1827–1906), in relation to women.

Extract from
Nuenen, *late October 1884*

“[…] The last thing I made is a rather large study of an avenue of poplars, with yellow autumn leaves, the sun casting, here and there, sparkling spots on the fallen leaves on the ground, alternating with the long shadows of the stems. At the end of the road is a small cottage, and over it all the blue sky through the autumn leaves.

[…] As a result of things I talked over with him [Rappard], it may be that I shall stay here and work on here rather than go elsewhere. His visit has given me new ideas for my own work again, and there are so many things in my mind which I should like to make that, after all, I can hardly put off starting work on them.”

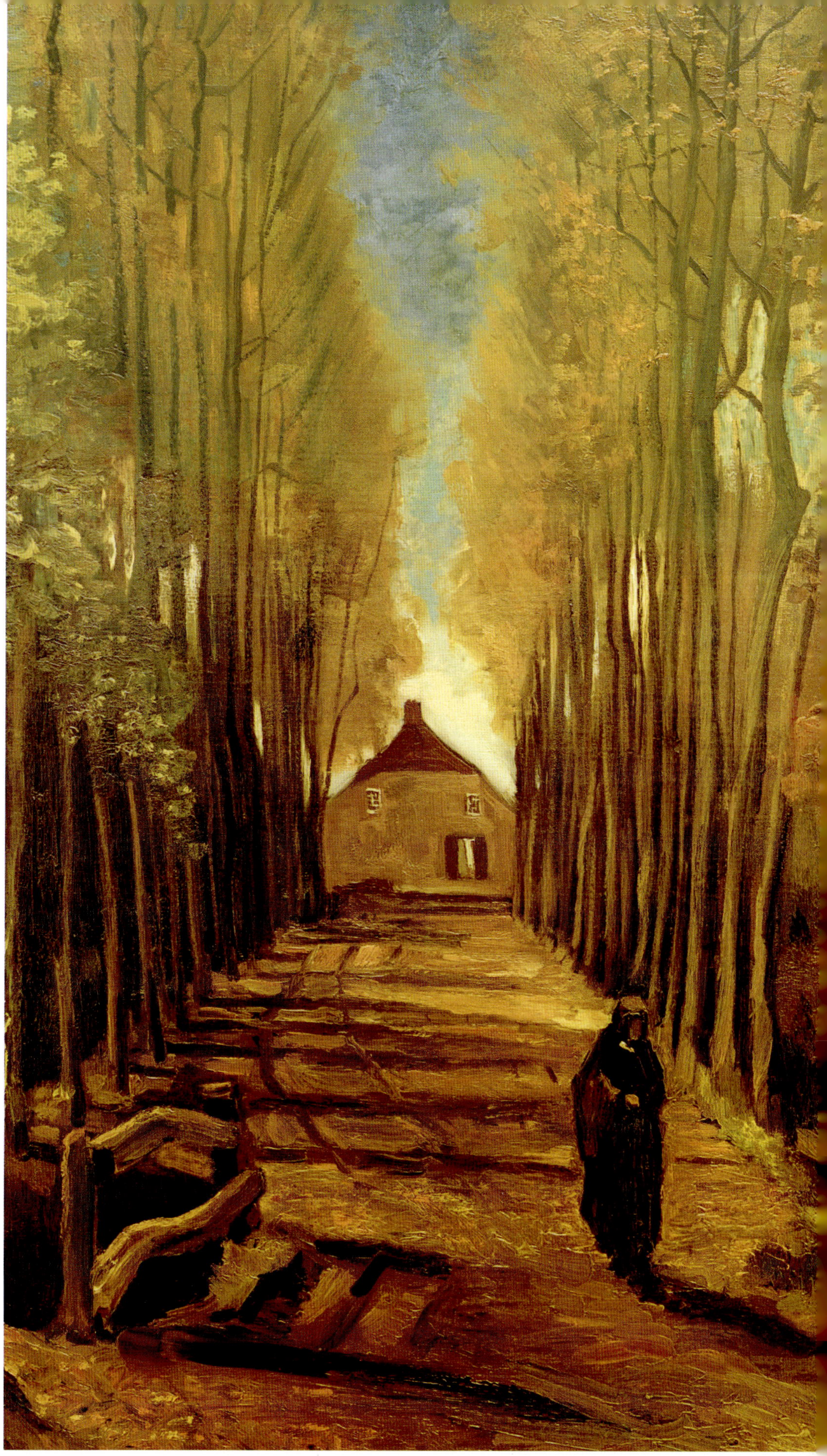

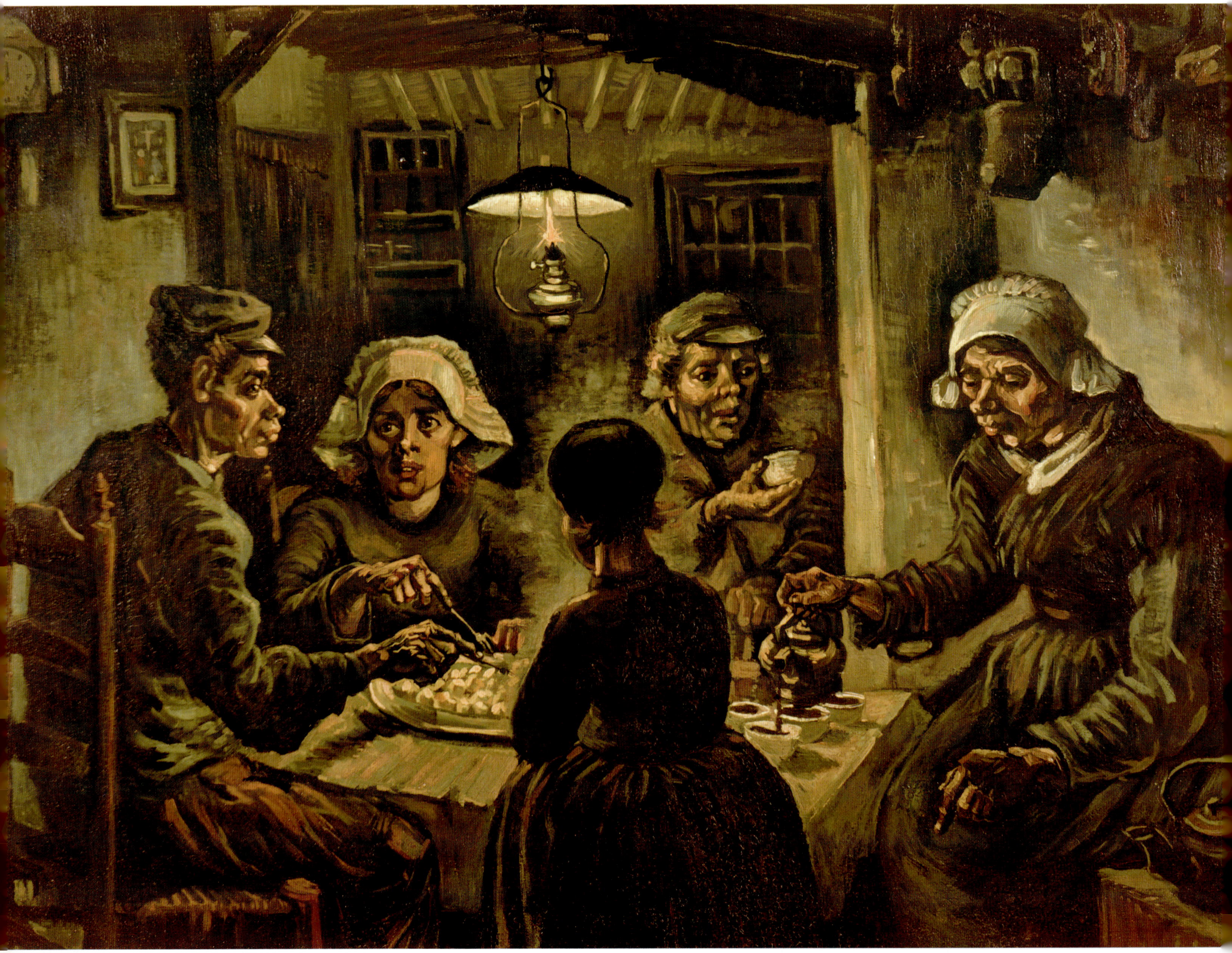

Vincent and van Rappard continued their discussions on art and their appreciation of Impressionism. Vincent decides that he may stay on in Nuenen rather than move.

Extract from Nuenen, *mid-November 1884*

Yesterday I brought home that study of the water mill at Gennep, which I painted with pleasure, and which has procured me a new friend in Eindhoven [Anton Kerssemakers], who passionately wants to learn to paint, and to whom I paid a visit, after which we set to work at once. [...] I intend to make these people gradually pay, not in money, but by telling them, You must give me *tubes of paint*. [...]

On 26 March 1885, Vincent's father, Theodorus van Gogh (1822–85), died suddenly after suffering a stroke at the age of 63. Vincent's relationship with his father had been at times a difficult one. Though he had held great hopes for his eldest son, his unease over Vincent's unsteady relationships with women, failure as a pastor, failure as an art dealer and unemployed status as an artist caused dissonance. To Vincent his father, a theologian and pastor, was a kindly, somewhat dull man set in his ways. Correspondence between father and son has not survived, but a week after Theodorus's death Vincent wrote to Theo:' Life for anybody is not long, and the problem is only to make something of it'.

Extract from Nuenen, *13 April 1885*

[...] I went to Eindhoven today to order a small lithographic stone, as this is to become the first of a series of lithographs, on which I intend to start again. When you were here I asked you about the costs of reproduction by the G. & Co. process. I think you said it would be 100 francs. Well, the old-fashioned, almost neglected, ordinary lithographic process is quite a lot cheaper – especially in Eindhoven, perhaps. I get the use of the stone, graining, paper and the printing of 50 copies for *3 guilders*.

Anyway, I intend to do a series of subjects from peasant life – *les paysans chez eux* [peasants at home]. [...]

You write that the public attitude – that is, indifference to Millet's work, as you have just had occasion to observe at the exhibition – is not encouraging, either for artists or for those who have to sell paintings. I quite agree – but Millet himself felt and knew what I hope never to forget is that '*il s'agit d'y aller en sabots*' [because I go about in clogs I shall manage], that

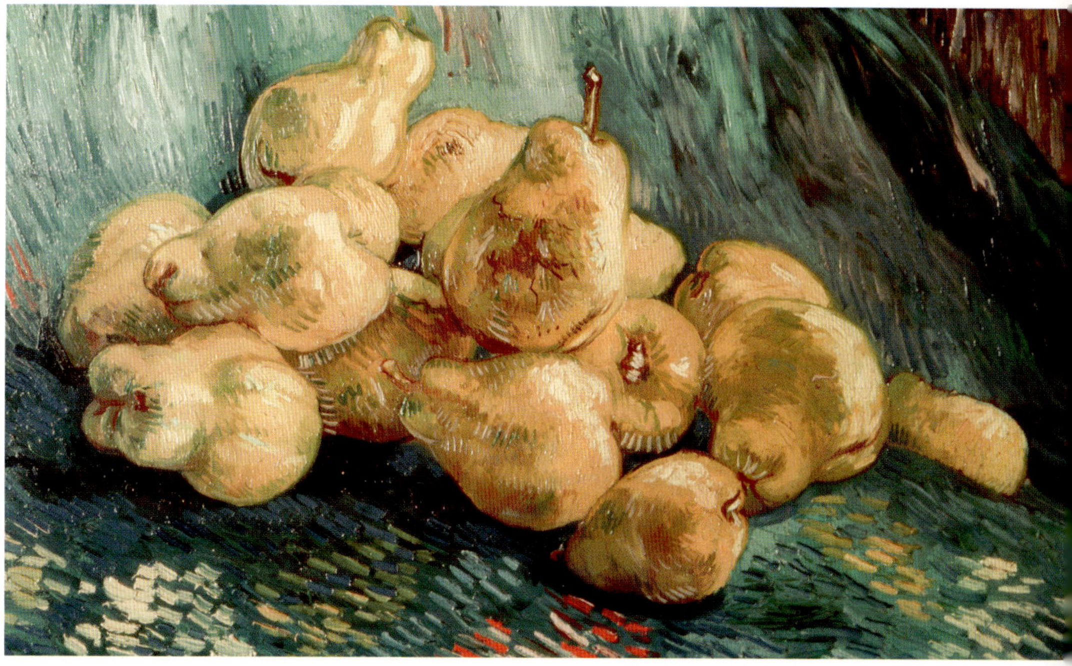

***The Potato Eaters*, 1885**
MEDIUM: Oil on canvas
© akg-images

***Still Life with Quinces*, 1888, (detail)**
MEDIUM: Oil on canvas
Courtesy of Galerie Neue Meister, Dresden, Germany/© Staatliche Kunstsammlungen Dresden/The Bridgeman Art Library

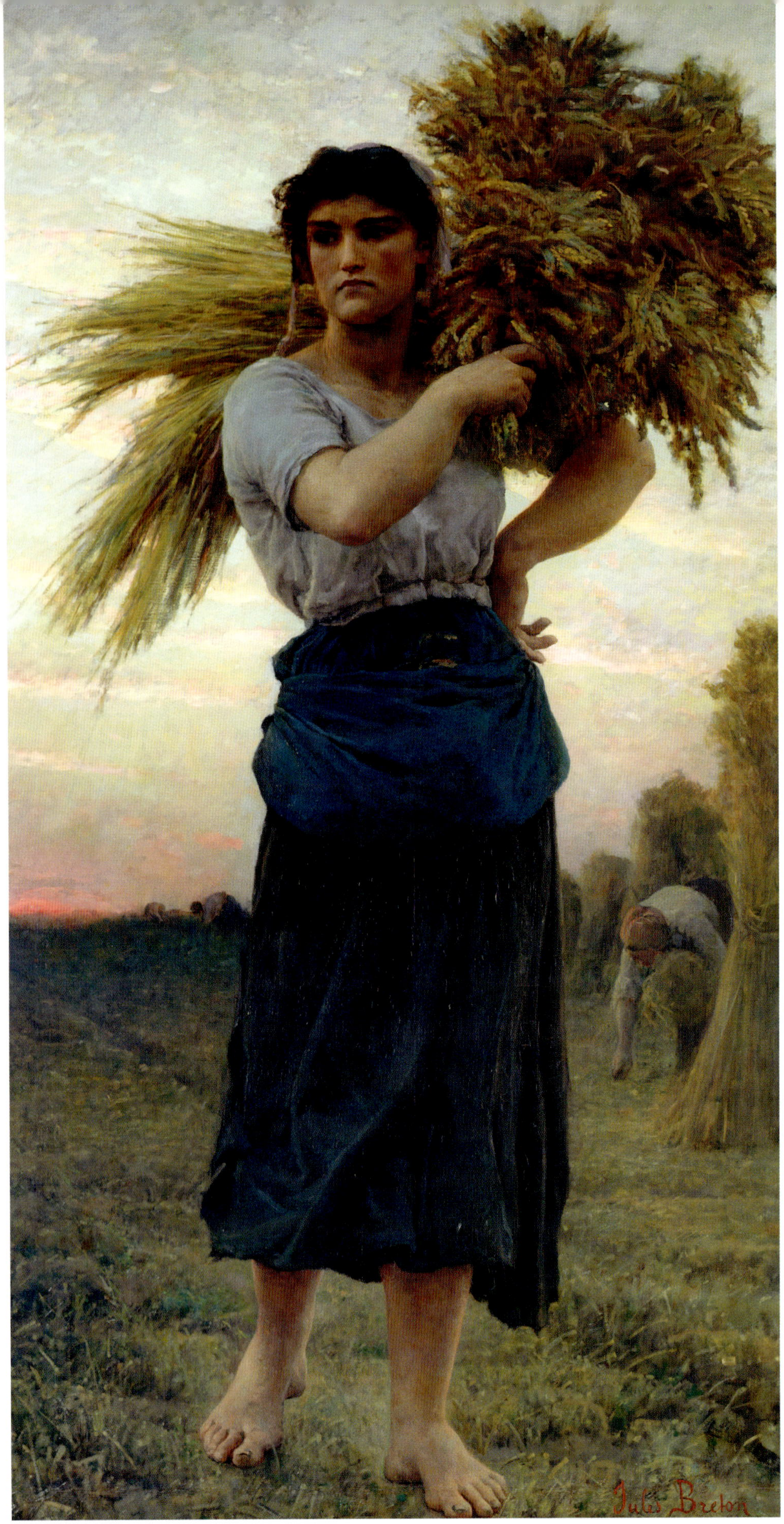

is, being content with the kind of food, drink, clothes and sleeping arrangements with which the peasants are content. [...]

If you come across the '*Chat noir*' people, you might show them this small sketch *to be going on with, but I can do a better one if they like, for this one was done in a great rush* and is simply meant to give you a clearer idea of the effect and the composition than the first one. Regards and thanks, with a handshake. "

Vincent mentions is this letter that Theo could show some of his work to the people at 'Chat noir'. *Le chat noir* was a leading magazine at the time and it is clear that Vincent considered submitting illustrations to them.

From Vincent van Gogh to
Anthon van Rappard
Extract from
Nuenen, *June 1885*

Amice Rappard,

" [...] To come to the point – the reason I am writing you – though it was *you* who insulted me in the first place, and not *I* who insulted you – is simply that I have known you so long that I do not consider this a reason to break off all intercourse with you.

What I have to say to you I say as one painter to another – and this will be true as long as you and I are painting – whether we keep up our acquaintance or not.

***The Gleaner*, 1877**
by Jules Breton (1827–1906)
MEDIUM: Oil on canvas
Courtesy of Musée des Beaux-Arts, Arras, France/Giraudon/The Bridgeman Art Library

***Plain at Auvers*, 1890**
MEDIUM: Oil on canvas
Courtesy of Private Collection/ Giraudon/The Bridgeman Art Library

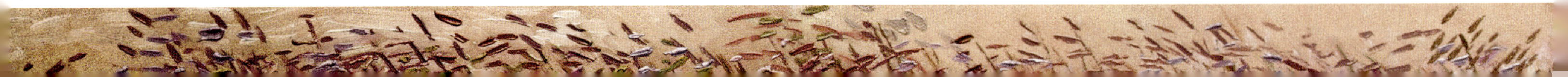

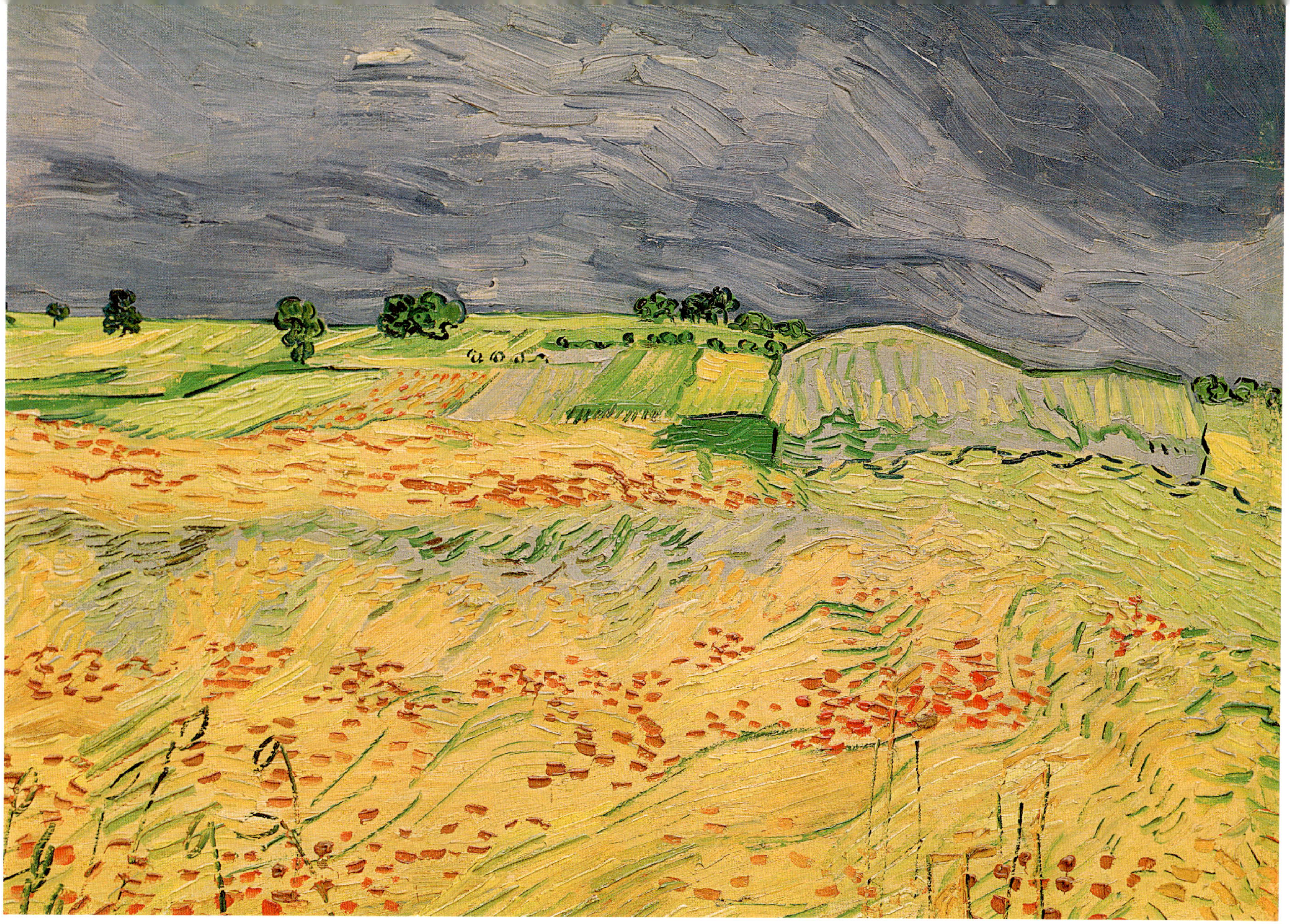

[...] The reason I am writing you again is just my love for Millet, for Breton and for *all those* who paint *peasants* and the *common people*, and I count you among them.

Believe me, don't quarrel with me about Millet. Millet is a man I will not quarrel about, although I don't refuse to talk about him."

Van Rappard had been critical of Vincent's lithograph *The Potato Eaters*, and derided Vincent for alluding to Millet in reference to his own work. Vincent, incensed by the slur from his friend, demands to know the real reason behind the insult, questions academic figure drawing in relation to contemporary art, and defends his admiration for Millet and all painters of peasant scenes.

From Vincent van Gogh to
Theo van Gogh
Extract from
Nuenen, *July 1885*

Dear Theo,

"[...] Nowadays, when connoisseurs stand in front of a painting like the one by Benj, Constant, or like some reception given by some cardinal by I don't know which Spaniard – it's the custom to say, with a meaningful air, something about 'clever technique'. But as soon as those same connoisseurs are confronted by a subject from peasant life or a drawing by, say, Raffaelli, they criticize the technique with the same knowing air. […]

You may think I'm wrong to comment on this, but I'm so struck by the fact that all these exotic pictures were painted *in the studio*. Just try going outside and painting things on the spot! All sorts of things happen then. I had to pick off a good hundred or more flies from the 4 canvases you're about to receive, not to mention dust and sand, etc., not to mention the fact that if one carries them through heath and hedgerows for a couple of hours, a branch or two is likely to scratch them, etc. Not to mention the fact that when one arrives on the heath, one feels tired and hot after a couple of hours' walk in this weather. Not to mention the fact that the figures don't stand still like professional models, and that the effects one wants to capture change as the day wears on. […]

Vincent voiced his opinion that many works of art, scenes of markets and harems or bullfights were usually painted in the studio, whereas his peasant paintings and landscapes were painted outdoors, with all the problems that attended painting in the open air.

Extract from
Nuenen, *early September 1885*

[…] These last two weeks I have had a lot of trouble with the reverend gentlemen of the clergy […] believing like so many others that they were obliged to intervene – that I ought not to be too familiar with people below me in station. But while they put the matter to me in these terms, they used quite a different tone with the 'people of lower station', namely, threatening them if they allowed themselves to be painted. This time I went straight to the Burgomaster and told him all about it, pointing out that it was no business of the priests. […]

A girl I had frequently painted was about to have a baby and they suspected me, though I had nothing to do with it. But I heard what had really happened from the girl herself, namely that a member of the priest's own congregation in Nuenen had played a particularly ugly part in the affair, and so they could not get at me. […]

After a local girl whom Vincent had used as a model became pregnant, suspicion fell on Vincent. The clergy were not happy that local girls were used as models and tried to get the practice stopped. The local people supported Vincent, preferring to get money to work for him than go begging to the church.

Extract from
Nuenen, *10 or 11 October 1885*

I have been to Amsterdam this week. I hardly had time to see anything but the museum. I was there three days, I went on Tuesday and came back on Thursday. The result is that I am *very* glad I went in spite of the cost, and I made up my mind not to go so long without seeing pictures again. […]

As to connections for my work, I spoke with somebody about it, and whenever I go again, I shall take some work with me. There is a general slackness which makes it easy enough to find an occasion for exhibition. […]

After Vincent's visit to Amsterdam and the magnificent paintings he had viewed in the Rijksmuseum, his letters between October and November 1885 are full of discussion about his own painting techniques, explaining to Theo the advantages and disadvantages of painting outdoors, his method of colour mixing, use of black, and of complementary colours. The major news was that he was moving. After paying his rent he had given notice that he would quit his studio. The continuing problems over his use of local models,

and the interference of the local priest in his relations with local people, had made his decision to leave final. 'I am greatly handicapped by the neighbours, and I notice that people are still afraid of the priest [...] the best thing is a radical change'.

Extract from Antwerp, *28 November 1885*

I just wanted to send you a few more impressions of Antwerp. This morning I took a long walk in the pouring rain, the object of the outing being to fetch my things from the custom house. The various warehouses and storage sheds on the quays look splendid.

One of de Goncourt's sayings was, 'Japonaiserie for ever'. Well, those docks are one huge Japonaiserie, fantastic, peculiar, unheard of – or at any rate, that's one way of looking at them. I would love some day to take a walk there in your company, just to find out if we see things in the same way. [...]

My studio isn't at all bad, especially now that I've pinned up a lot of small Japanese prints which I enjoy very much. You know, those small female figures in gardens or on the beach, horsemen, flowers, gnarled thorn branches.

[...] My little room has turned out better than I expected and certainly doesn't look dreary.

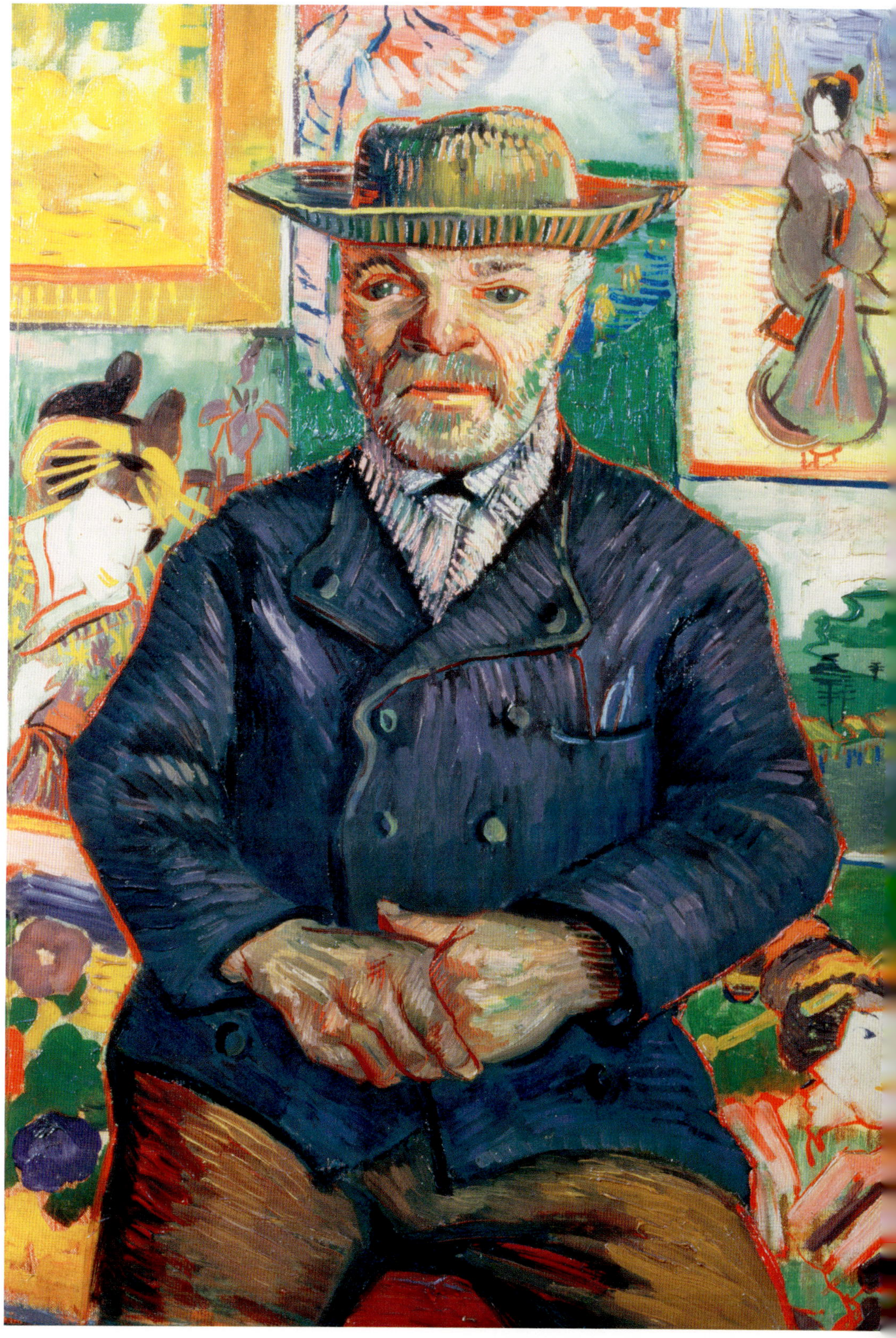

***Père Tanguy*, 1887–88**
MEDIUM: Oil on canvas
Courtesy of Private Collection/The Bridgeman Art Library

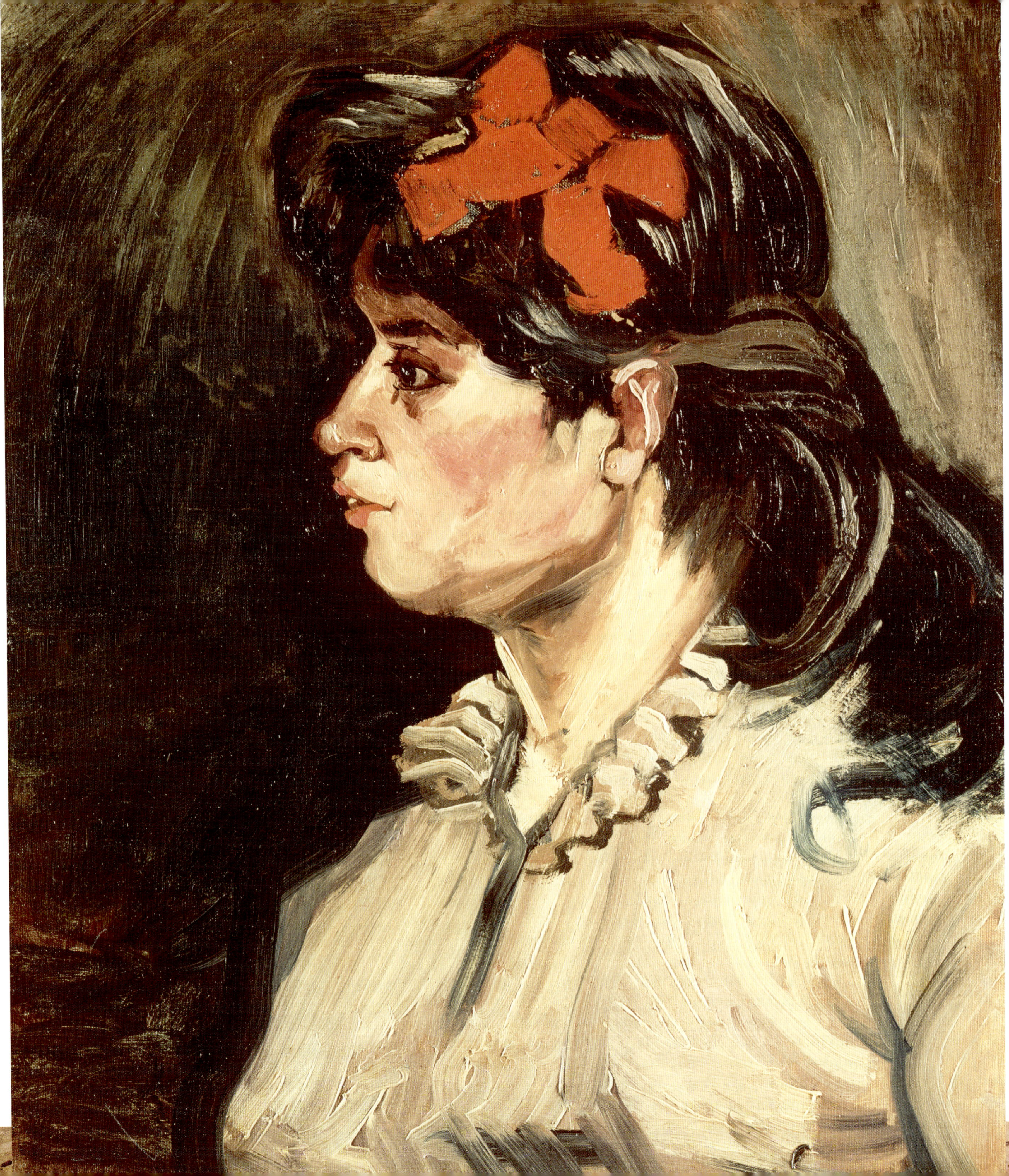

***Portrait of a Woman with a Red Ribbon*, 1885**
MEDIUM: Oil on canvas
Courtesy of Private Collection/The Bridgeman Art Library

***The Restaurant de la Sirène at Asnières*, 1887**
MEDIUM: Oil on canvas
Courtesy of Musée d'Orsay, Paris, France/Giraudon/The Bridgeman Art Library

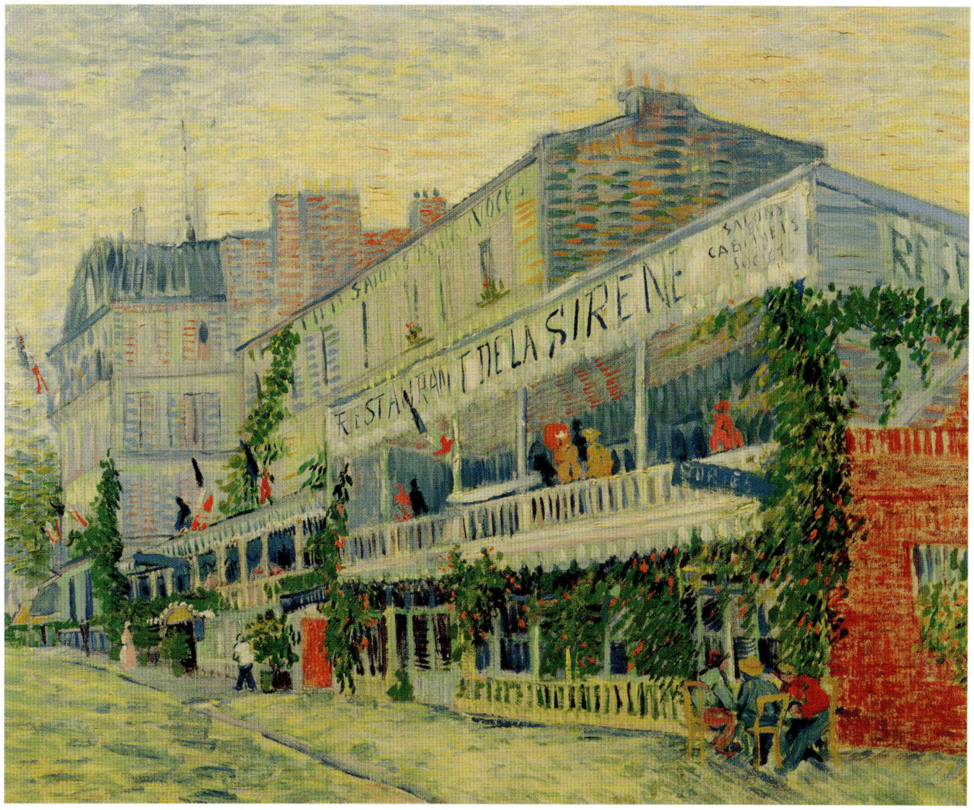

Extract from
Antwerp, *28 December 1885*

It's more than time I thanked you for the 50 fr. you sent, which enabled me to get through the month, although from today onwards things will be more or less back to normal.
But – a few more studies have been done and the more I paint the more progress I think I make. The moment I received the money I took on a beautiful model and did a life-sized painting of her head. [...]

Anyway, here is the colour range: a flesh colour full of tonal values, with more bronze in the neck, jet-black hair – black which I had to do with carmine and Prussian blue – off-white for the little jacket, light yellow, much lighter than the white, for the background. A touch of flame in the jet-black hair and again a flame-coloured bow in the off-white.

She's a girl from a *café-chantant* [singing café] and yet the expression I was looking for was somewhat Ecce Homo-like. But that was because I was aiming for the truth, especially in the expression, though I also wanted to put my own thoughts into it. [...]

What rather pleased me was that the girl who posed for me wanted to have one of the portraits for herself, preferably just like the one I'd done. And that she's promised to let me paint a study of her in a dancer's costume at her room, as soon as possible. It can't be done right away because the man who runs the café where she stays objects to her posing, but she's about to take lodgings with another girl, and both she and the other girl would like to have their portraits done. And I really very much hope that I'll get her back, for she has a remarkable head, and she's witty. [...]

This is something new for me, and I want to achieve it at all costs. Manet has done it and Courbet – well, *sacrebleu*, I've the same ambition too, the more so as I've felt the infinite beauty of the study of women by the giants of literature – Zola, Daudet, de Goncourt, Balzac – in the very marrow of my bones. [...]

From a business point of view I can only say that we are in what people have already begun to call '*la fin d'un siècle*'– that the women have the same charm as at the time of revolution – and just as much to say – and that one would be '*retiré du monde*' [dead to the world] if one worked without them. It is the same everywhere, in the country as much as in the city – one has to take women into account if one wants to be up to date.

Goodbye, have a happy New Year, with a handshake. [...]

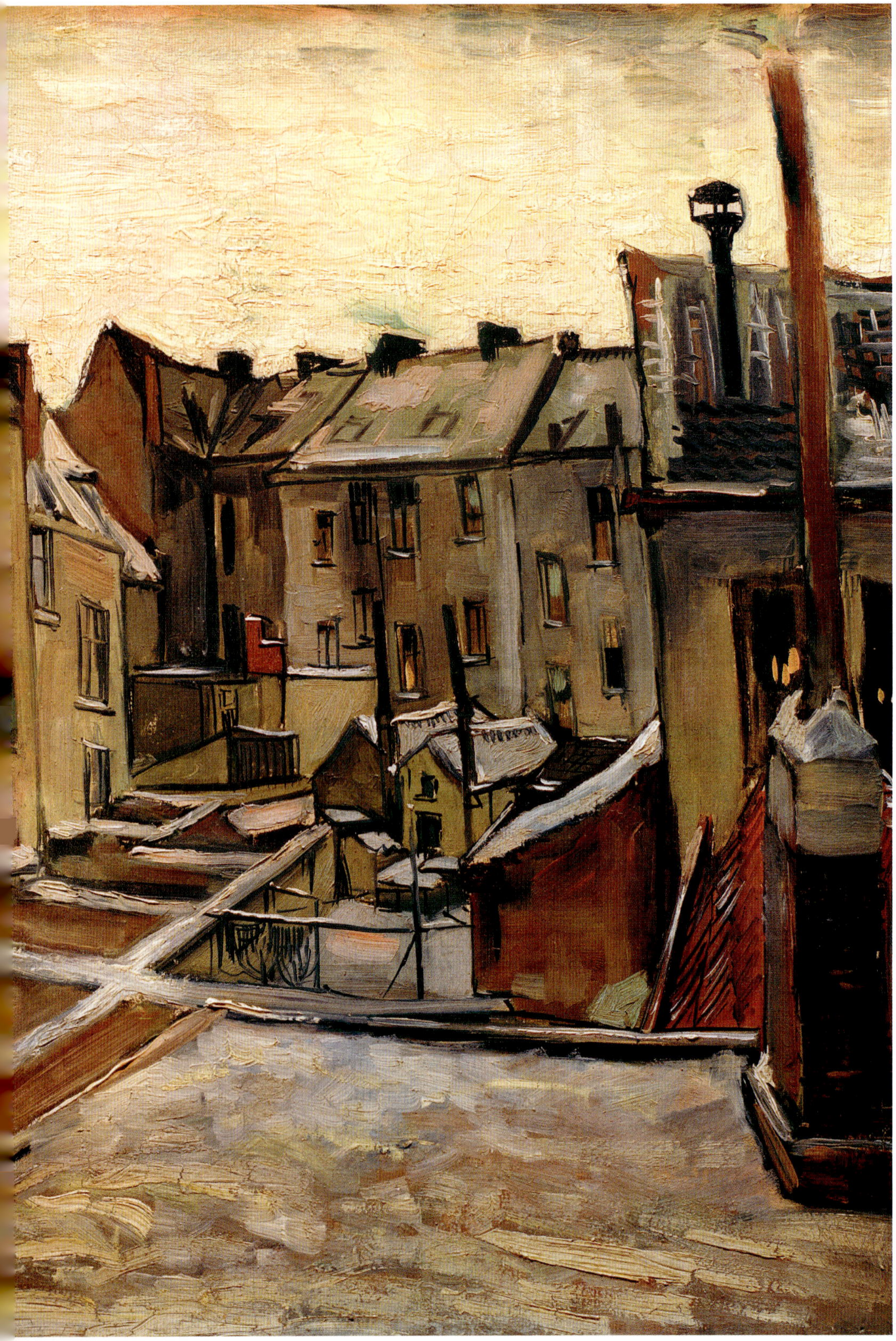

Extract from
Antwerp, *c. 22 January 1886*

"I have now been painting at the academy for a few days, and I must say that I like it pretty well. Especially because there are all kinds of painters there, and I see them work in the most varied ways, something I have never experienced before – I mean seeing others work.

It would be by far the best thing for me to stay here a long time, for their models are good, and it will save a great deal of expenses of painting and models, and it is much more difficult than you seem to know, especially if one works alone. But let's hope that in this way things will improve.

Next Monday we shall get new models; in fact, then I shall begin in earnest, and for Monday I ought to have had a large canvas; they also told me that I must definitely have other brushes, etc.

But I haven't any money left, so it is really pressing, and I wish you would do what you can, for I am also doing what I can, and almost all the time it is such that hardly anything is left for food.

In the evening I also go there to draw, but I think the fellows in the drawing class all work badly and in an absolutely wrong way.

The painting class is better and, as I think I wrote you already, there are all kinds of people and of all ages, about five of them even older than I am. [...]"

***Backyards in Antwerp*, 1885**
MEDIUM: Oil on canvas
© akg-images

***View from Window, Paris*, 1887, (detail)**
MEDIUM: Oil and pencil on board
Courtesy of Private Collection/Photo © Christie's Images/The Bridgeman Art Library

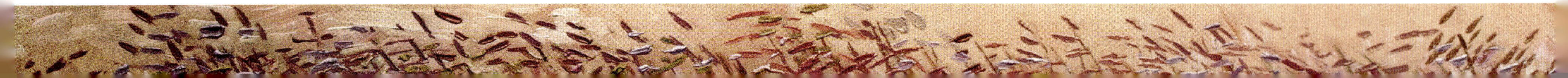

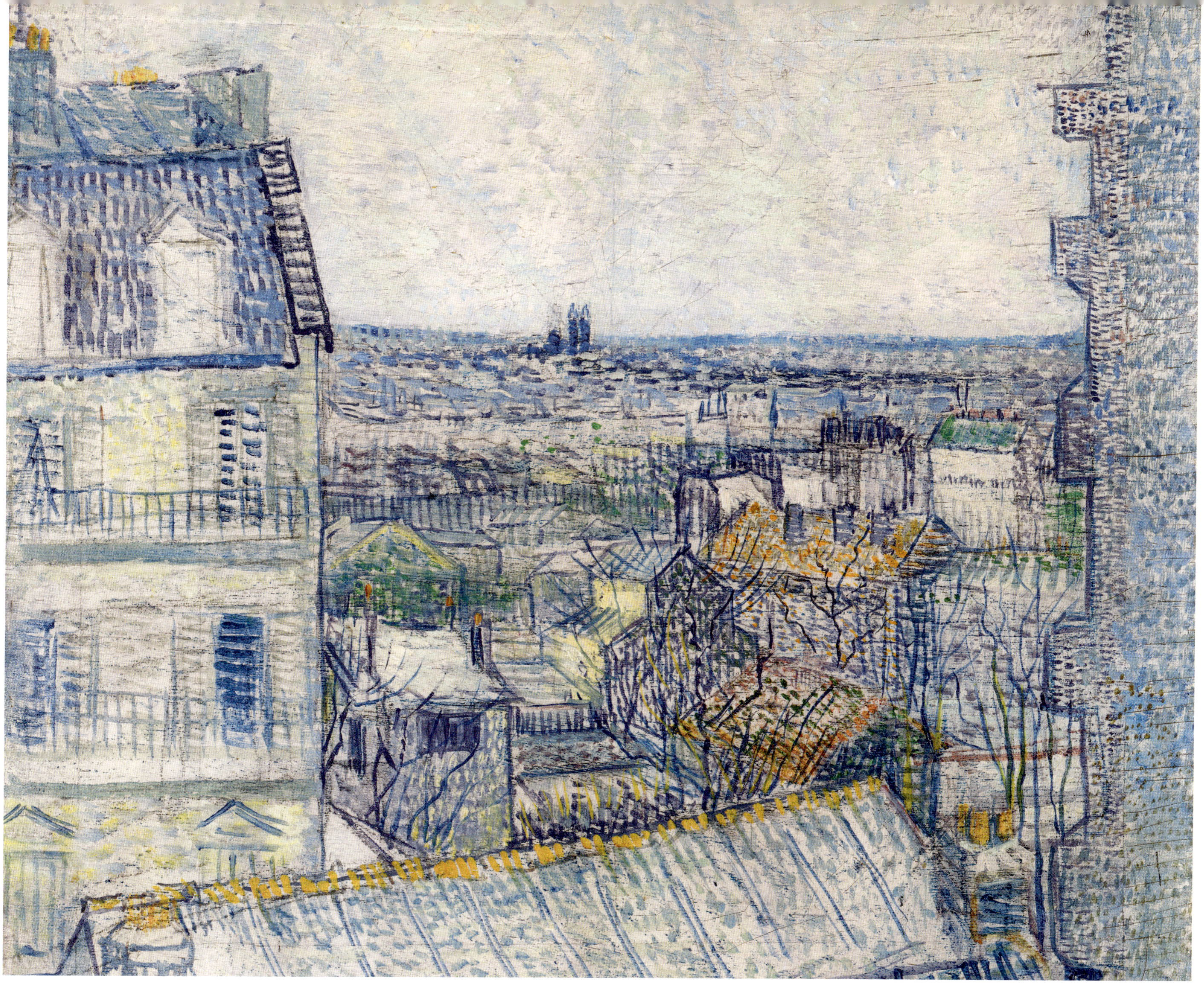

Extract from

Paris, *c. 1 March 1886*

"Don't be angry with me for arriving out of the blue. I've given it so much thought and I'm sure we'll gain time this way. Shall be at the Louvre from midday onwards, or earlier if you like.

Please let me know what time you can get to the Salle Carrée. As far as expenses are concerned, I repeat that it won't make much difference. I still have some money left, of course, and I want to talk to you before spending any of it. We'll sort everything out, you'll see.

So come as soon as you can. I shake your hand,"

Ever yours

Vincent

Vincent was upset that Theo did not write more to him about the project of working together: 'Founding a studio together would perhaps be a *good* thing but we must feel sure we can carry it through ...' Theo wanted to wait a few months until he could rent a larger apartment for them to live in but Vincent wanted to advance the plan: '... would you approve of me coming to Paris earlier than June or July ... If I rent a garret in Paris, and bring my paintbox and drawing materials with me...'. Vincent wrote to Theo that the time had come to make a decision. He was going to come as soon as his dental treatment was finished, which required money. Theo obliged with the money. Vincent made a sudden move from Antwerp to Paris in March 1886, three months earlier than Theo had requested. Vincent wrote to Theo, seeking understanding for the sudden move: 'Do not be cross with me for having come all at once like this ... I believe in this way we shall save time. I shall be at the Louvre from midday or sooner if you like. ... We'll fix things up you'll see'. The note, hurriedly scribbled in crayon, was written to Theo as soon as Vincent had disembarked from the Antwerp train. He sent a porter to Theo's apartment, to announce his arrival.

From Vincent van Gogh to
Horace Mann Livens
Extract from
Paris, *August–September 1886*

My dear Mr Livens,

Since I am here in Paris I have very often thought of yourself and work. You will remember that I liked your colour, your ideas on art and literature and I add, most of all your personality. I have already before now thought that I ought to let you know what I was doing, where I was. [...] In Antwerp I did not even know what the Impressionists were, now I have seen them and though *not* being one of the club yet I have much admired certain Impressionists' pictures – *Degas* nude figure – *Claude Monet* landscape.

[...] I have made a series of colour studies in painting, simply flowers, red poppies, blue corn flowers and myosotys, white and rose roses, yellow chrysanthemums – seeking oppositions of blue with orange, red and green, yellow and violet. [...]

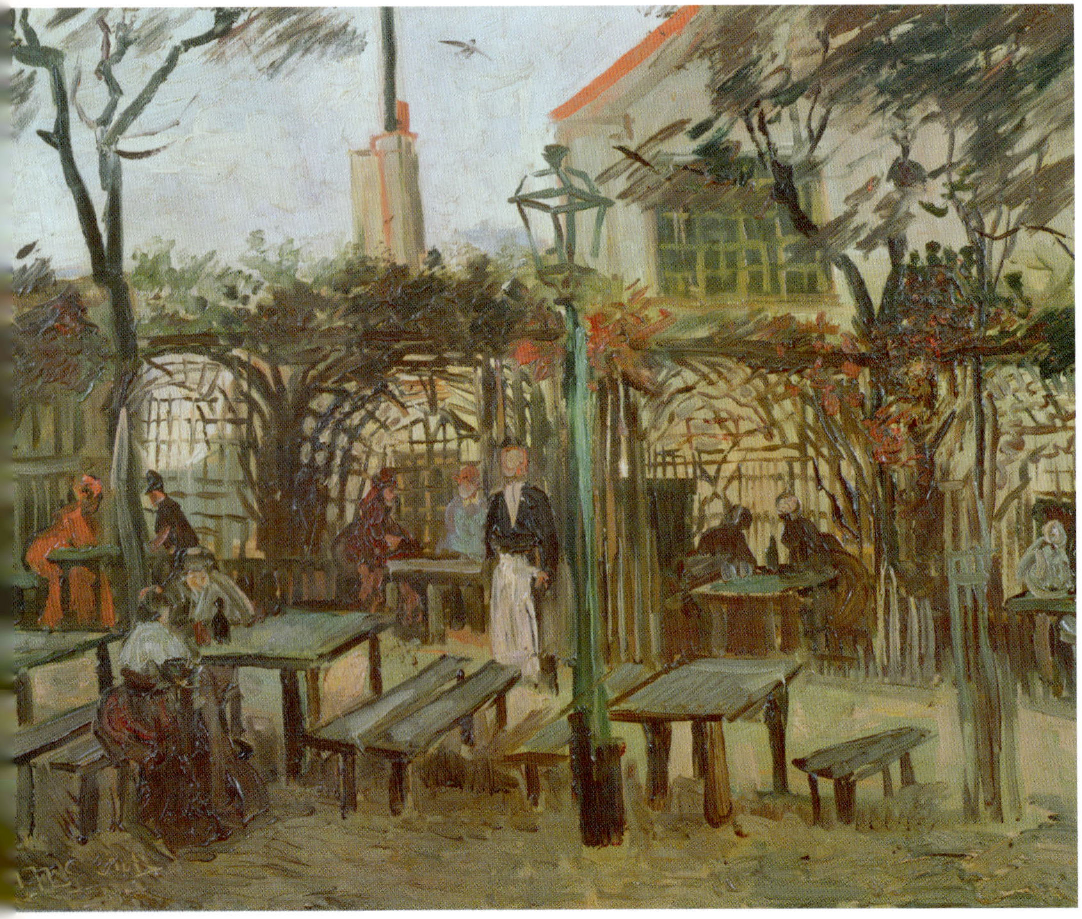

***Pleasure Gardens at Montmartre*, 1886**
MEDIUM: Oil on canvas
Courtesy of Musée d'Orsay, Paris, France/The Bridgeman Art Library

***Tulip Fields with the Rijnsberg Windmill*, 1886, (detail) by Claude Monet (1840–1926)**
MEDIUM: Oil on canvas
Courtesy of Musée d'Orsay, Paris, France/The Bridgeman Art Library

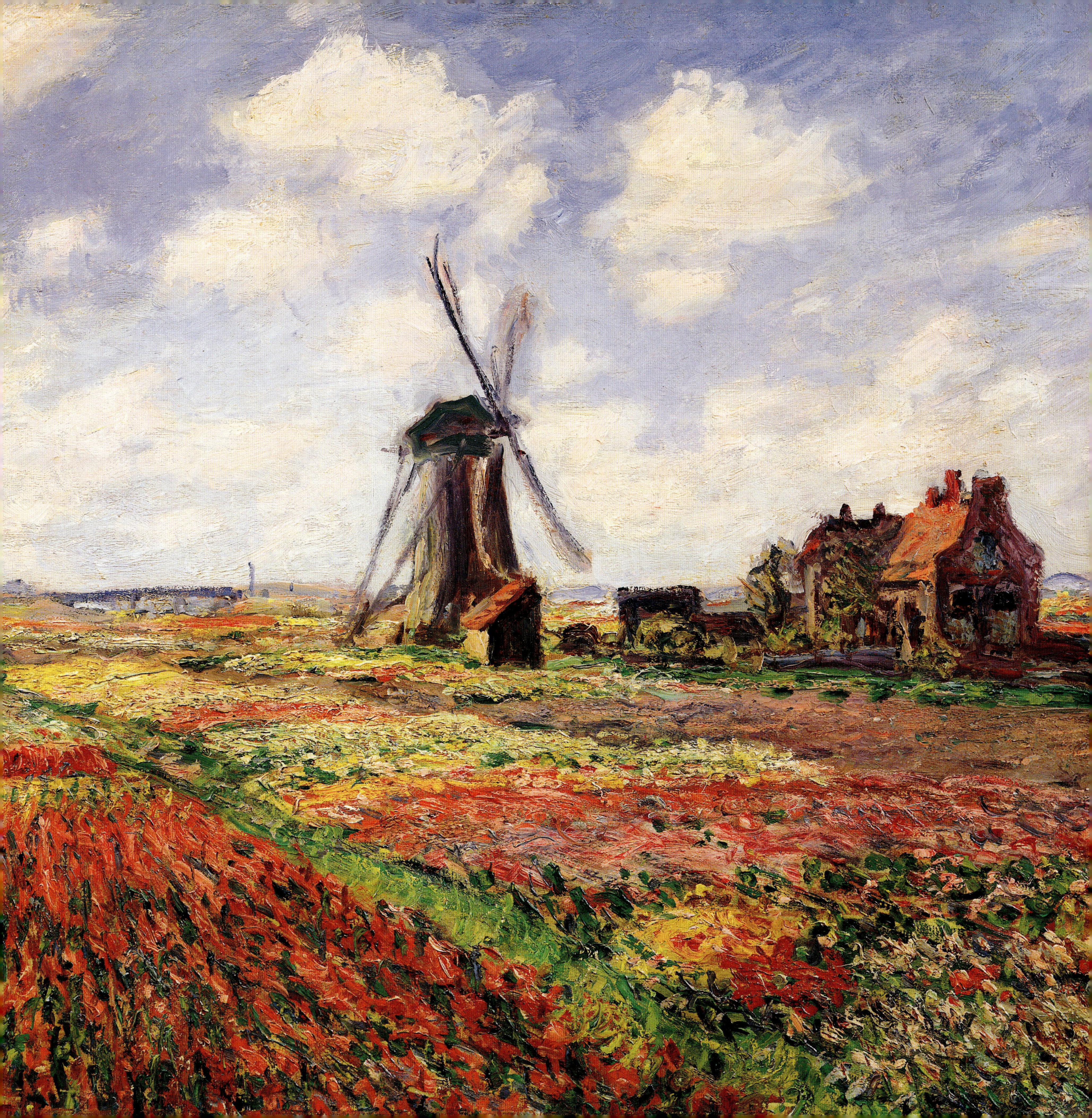

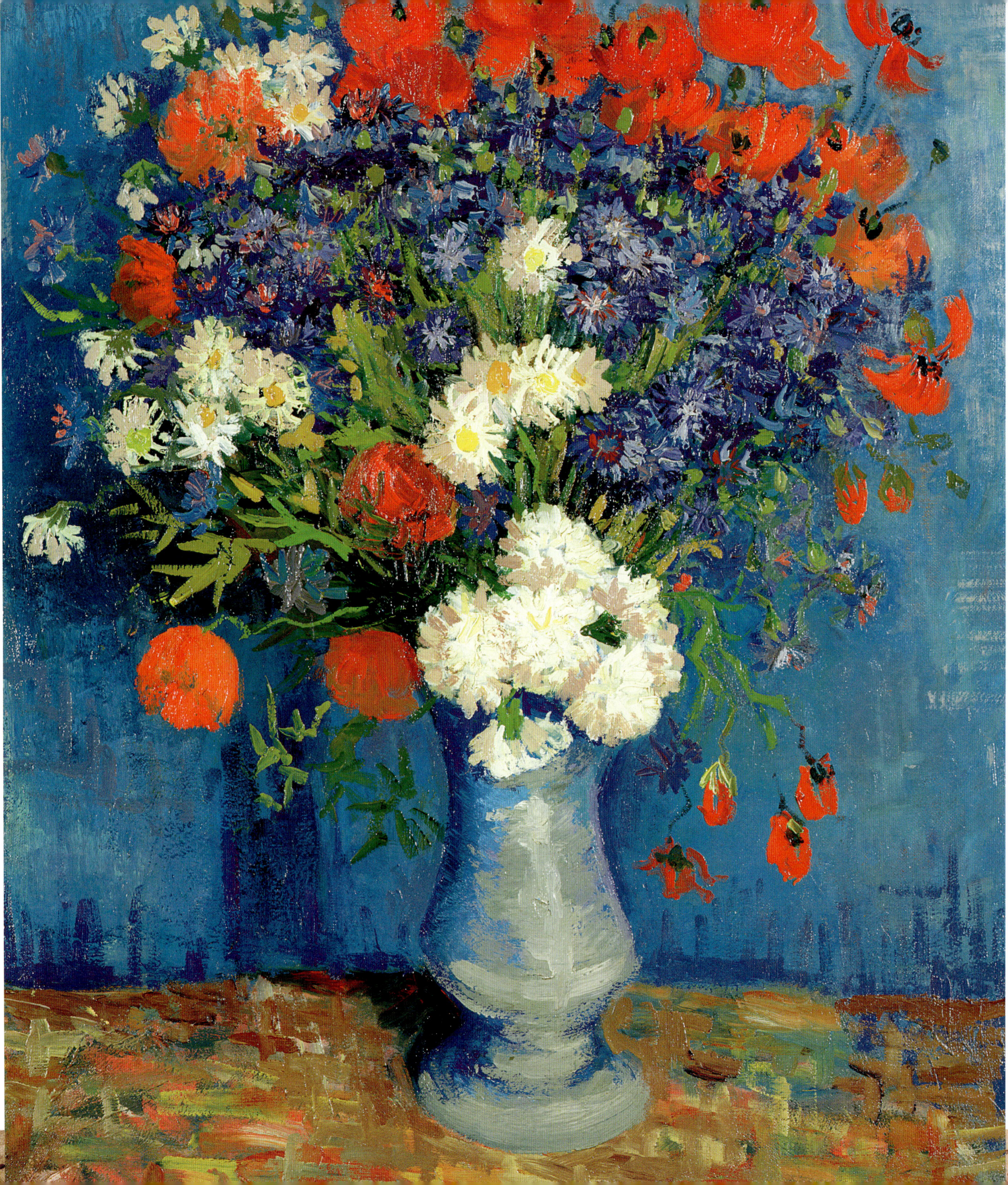

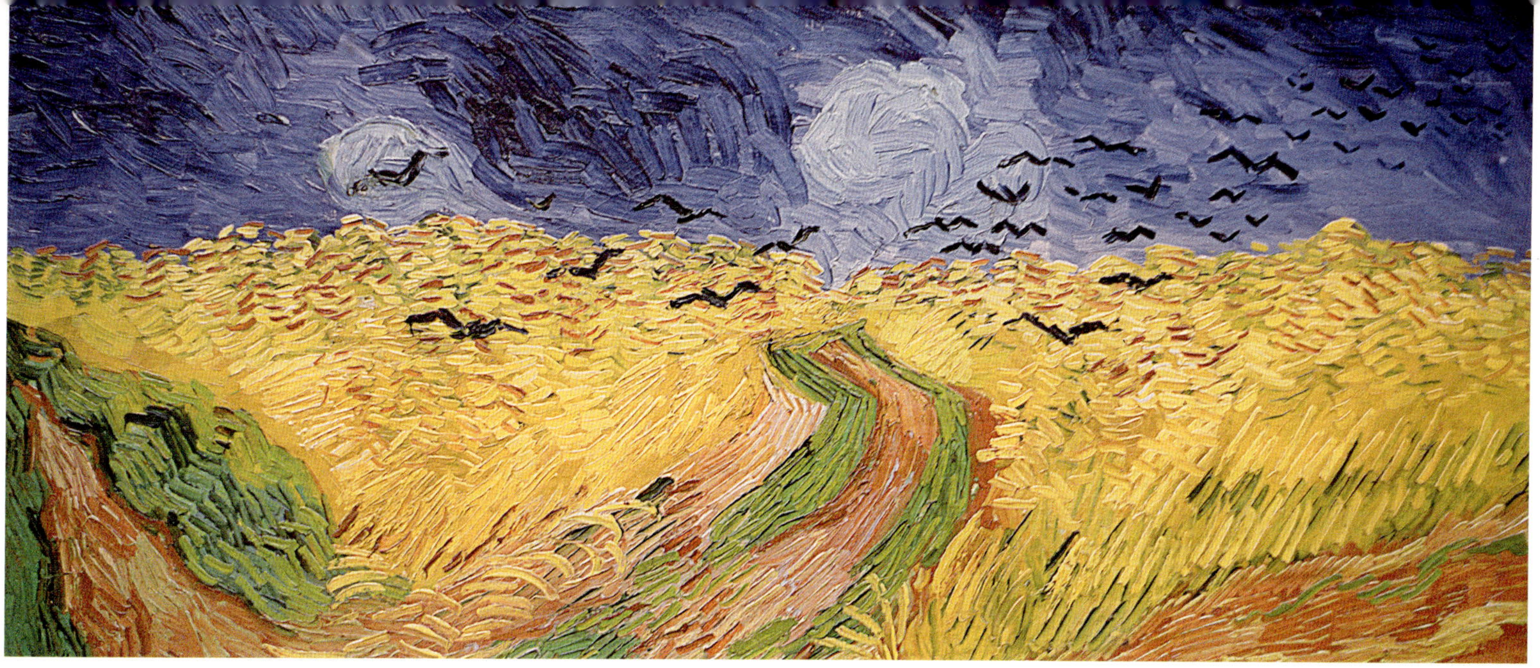

So as we said at the time: in *colour* seeking *life* the true drawing is modelling with colour. I did a dozen landscapes too, frankly *green* frankly *blue*.

[…] If ever you did come here, write to me before and I will, if you like, share my lodgings and studio with you so long as I have any. In spring – say February or even sooner I may be going to the South of France, the land of the *blue* tones and gay colours.

Write to me in any case. Remember me to Allen, Briet, Rink, Durant but I have not often thought of them as I did think of you – almost daily.

Shaking hands cordially.

Yours truly

Vincent

Between August and September 1886, Vincent wrote to the young English painter, Horace Mann Livens (1862–1936) whom he had met in Antwerp. Livens had discussed the art of the Impressionists. Vincent now wrote to him: 'I did not know what the Impressionists were, now I have seen them and though *not* being one of the club yet I have admired certain Impressionists' pictures – *Degas* nude figure – *Claude Monet* landscape.' Vincent's letter to Livens discusses many matters but the main topic was the use of colour in painting. His vibrant use of colour is visible in his paintings from this period in Paris, such as *Pleasure Gardens at Montmartre*, 1886, and *View from Window, Paris*, 1887. The network of artists in Paris expanded Vincent's circle of friends. He spent time with Émile Bernard (1868–1941) and Paul Signac (1863–1935), and Henri de Toulouse-Lautrec (1864–1901), who painted the pastel *Portrait of Vincent van Gogh*, 1887. Toulouse-Lautrec and Van Gogh, both seeking solace in alcohol, were steady drinking partners, regularly meeting in the cafés of Montmartre.

***Vase with Cornflowers*, 1887**
MEDIUM: Oil on canvas
Courtesy of Private Collection/ Photo © Lefevre Fine Art Ltd, London/The Bridgeman Art Library

***Wheatfield with Crows*, 1890**
MEDIUM: Oil on canvas
Courtesy of Van Gogh Museum, Amsterdam, The Netherlands/ The Bridgeman Art Library

From Vincent van Gogh to
Theo van Gogh
Extract from
Paris, *August 1886*

Dear Theo,

[…] That you are not suited to S. and S. is not suited to you is, I think, incontrovertible, as well as that you must part company – but how? It would be a good thing if you accepted the idea

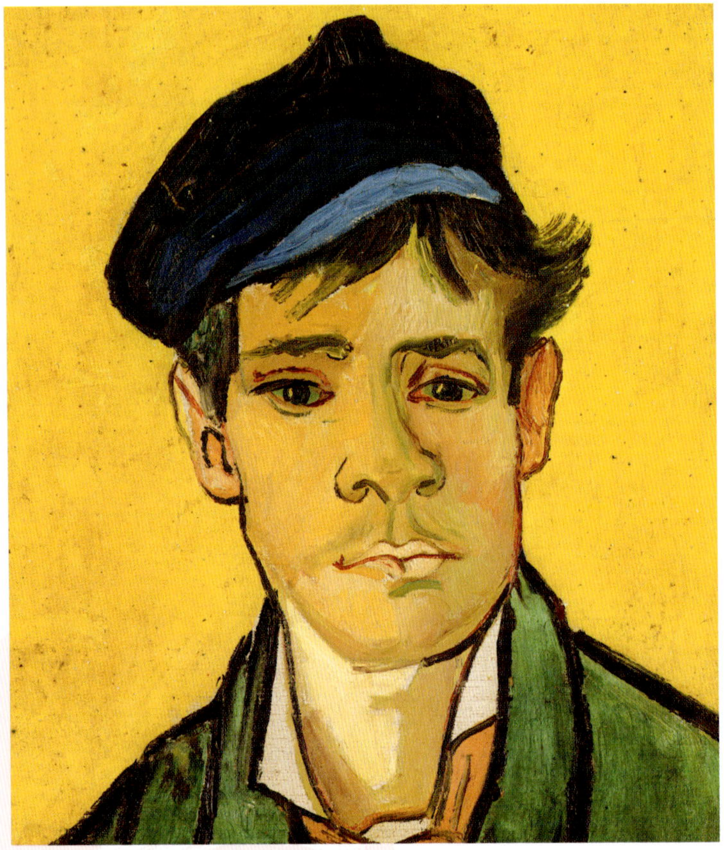

that the affair cannot be settled in the way you propose, by treating her harshly you would immediately drive her to suicide or insanity, and the repercussions on you would be sad indeed and leave you a broken man.

So no catastrophes, please! Well, I told Bonger [Andries Bonger] what I told you, namely that you should try and pass her on to somebody else, and I told him more explicitly what my feelings on the subject are that an amicable arrangement, which would seem obvious, could be reached by your passing her on to me. So it is certain that, if you could reconcile yourself to it, and S. too, I am ready to take S. off your bands, preferably *without* having to marry her, but if the worst comes to the worst *even* agreeing to a marriage de raison. [...]"

Vincent writes to Theo whilst he is in Holland. He advises on the subject of a woman known as 'S.' in the text, whom Theo has been seeing but now wants to stop the affair.

From Willemina van Gogh to her friend Line Kruysse

Extract from Nuenen, *26 August 1886*

"[...] My second brother, Theo, from Paris, left yesterday; he really is a dear boy. He told us so many good things about Vincent, the eldest, who is living with him. His paintings are getting so much better and he is beginning to exchange them for those of other painters, so everything's sure to come right in time. According to Theo, he is definitely making a name for himself. But we are under no illusions, and are only too grateful that he is having some slight success. You don't know what a hard life he has had, and who can say what is still in store for him. His disappointments have often made him feel bitter and have turned him into an unusual person. That was difficult for my parents, who could not always follow him and often misunderstood him. My father was strict, and attached to all sorts of conventions of which my brother never took any particular notice; needless to say, that often led to clashes and to words spoken in anger, which neither party was quick to forget. So during the past eight years Vincent has been a bone of contention with many, and all too often one tended to forget all the good there was in him, the appearances to the contrary. During the past few years he has been working at home with us; after my father's death, Anna [her sister] thought it would be more peaceful for Mother if he stopped living at home, and saw to it that he left us. He took that so badly that from then on he has not been in touch with us, and it is only through Theo that we have news of him. [...]"

***Young Man with a Hat*, 1888**
MEDIUM: Oil on canvas
Courtesy of Private Collection/Giraudon/ The Bridgeman Art Library

***Sunflowers*, 1887**
MEDIUM: Oil on canvas
Courtesy of Metropolitan Museum of Art, New York, USA/The Bridgeman Art Library

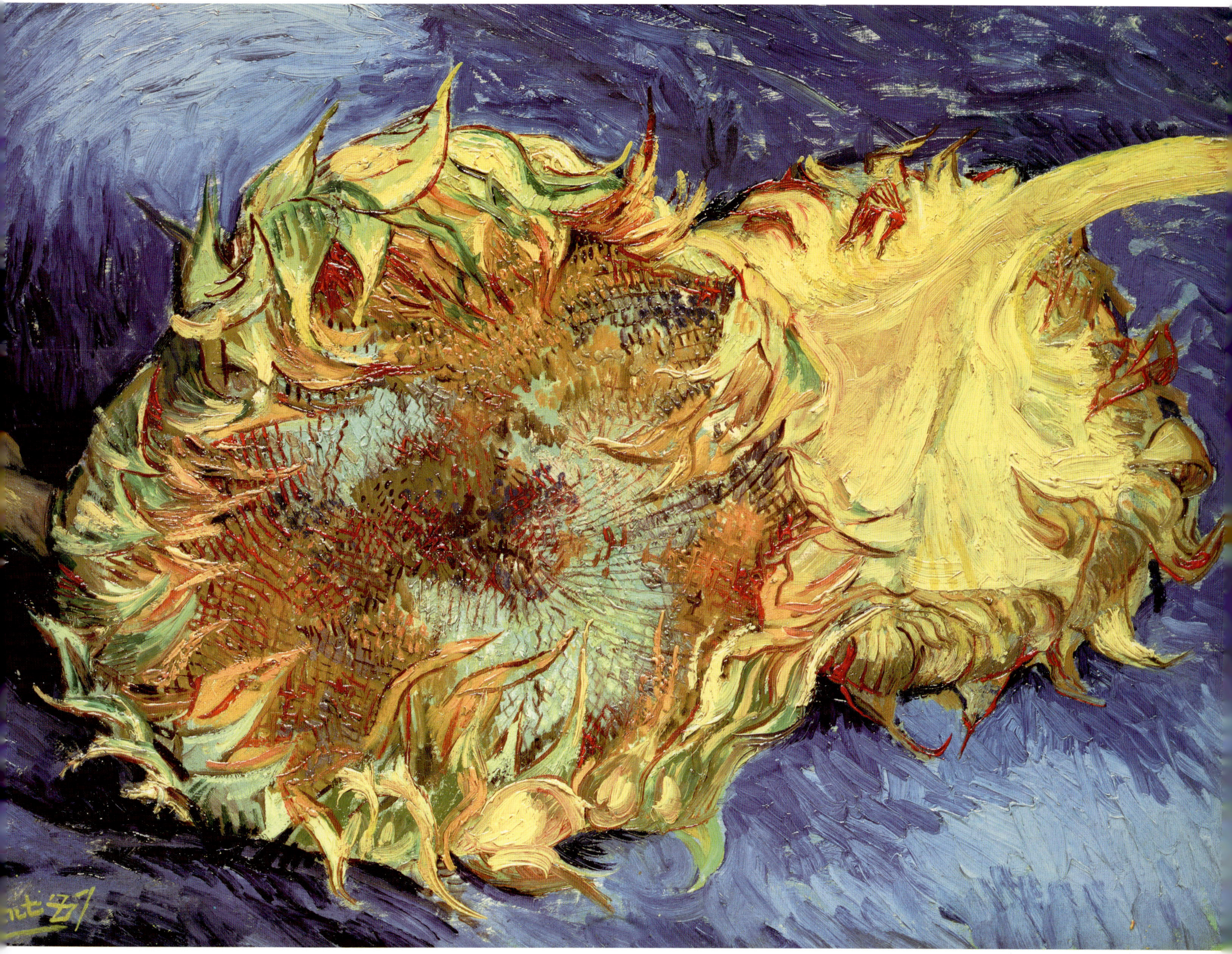

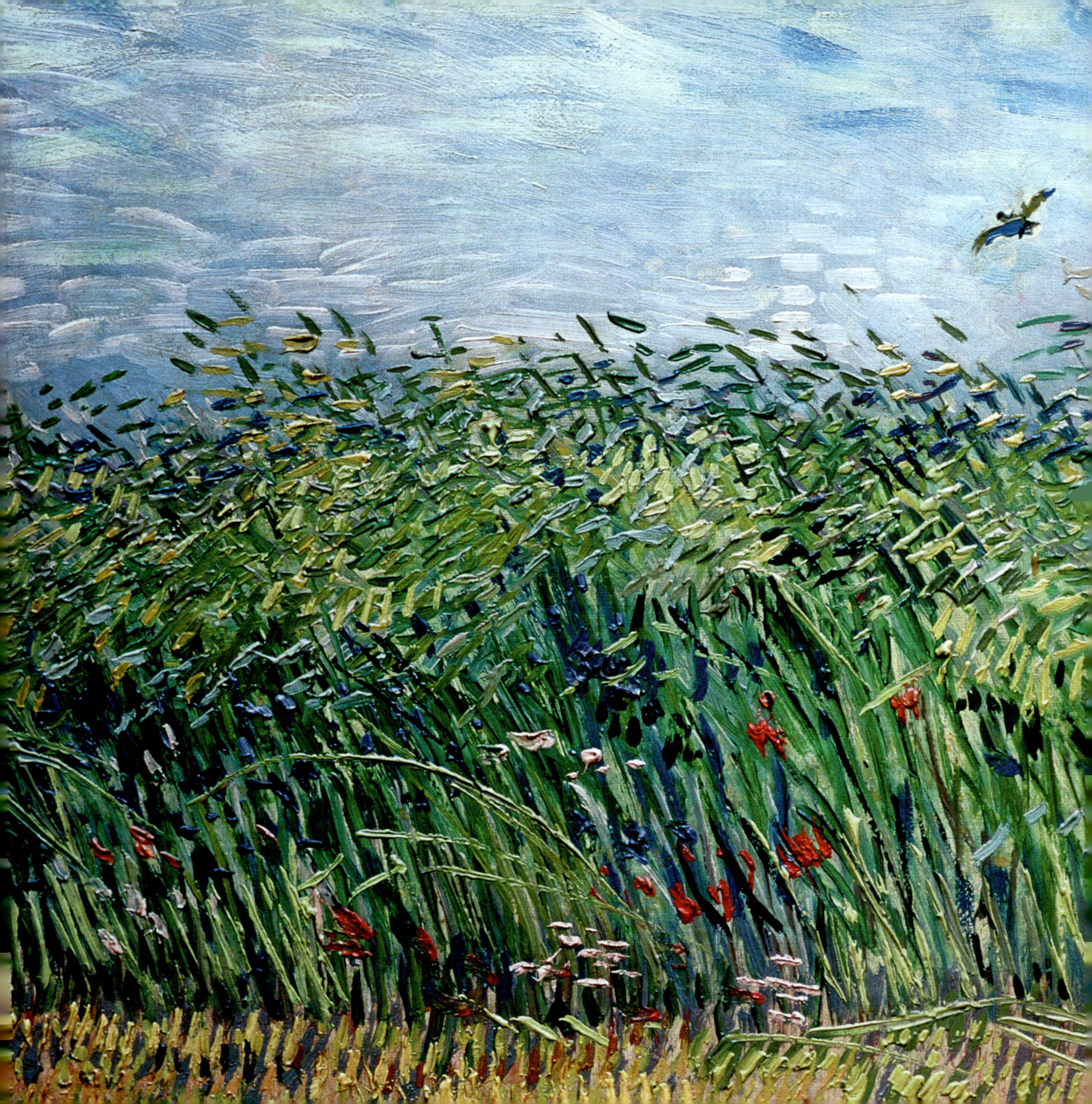

Vincent van Gogh: A Life in Letters & Art

1887–88

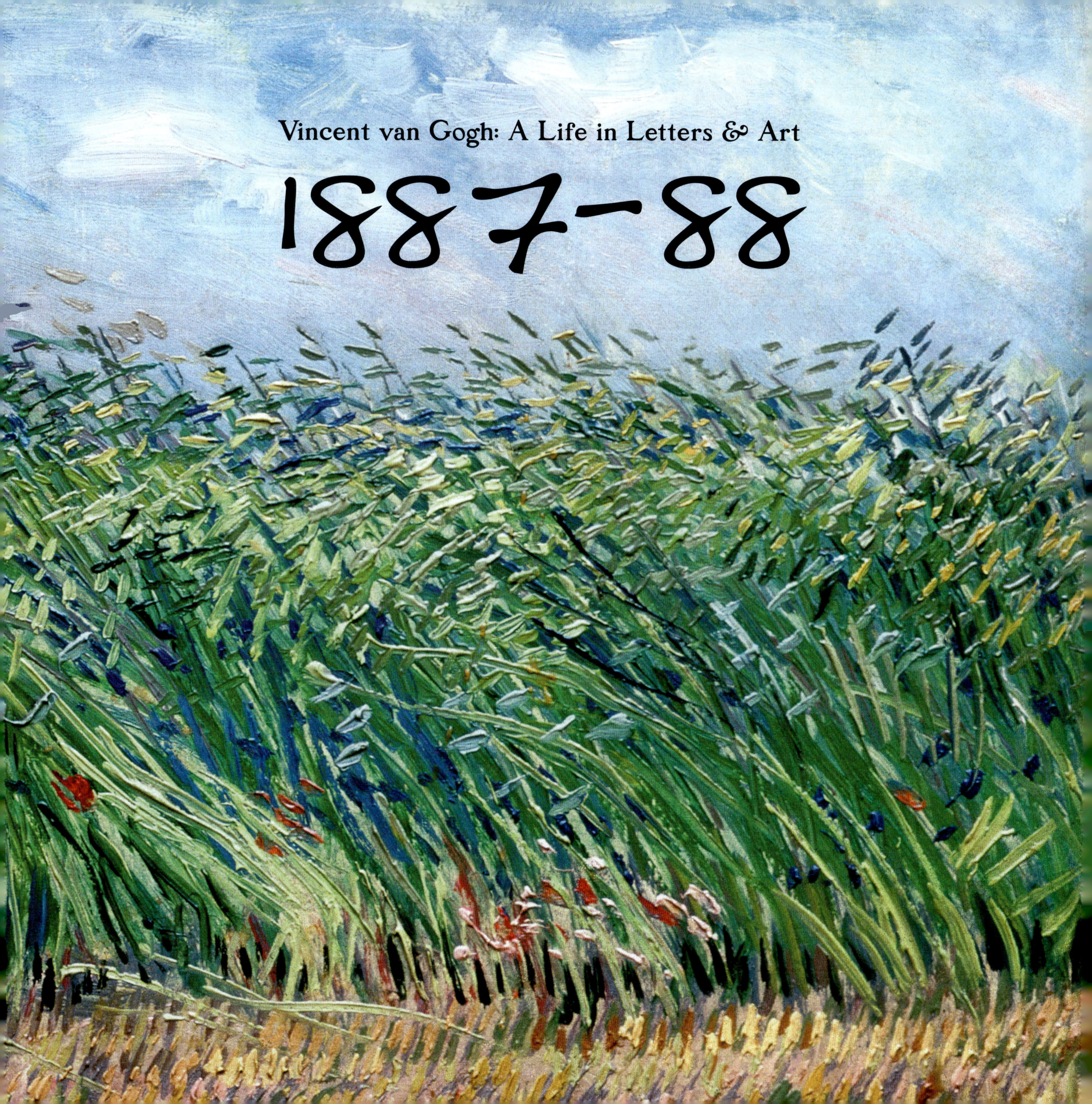

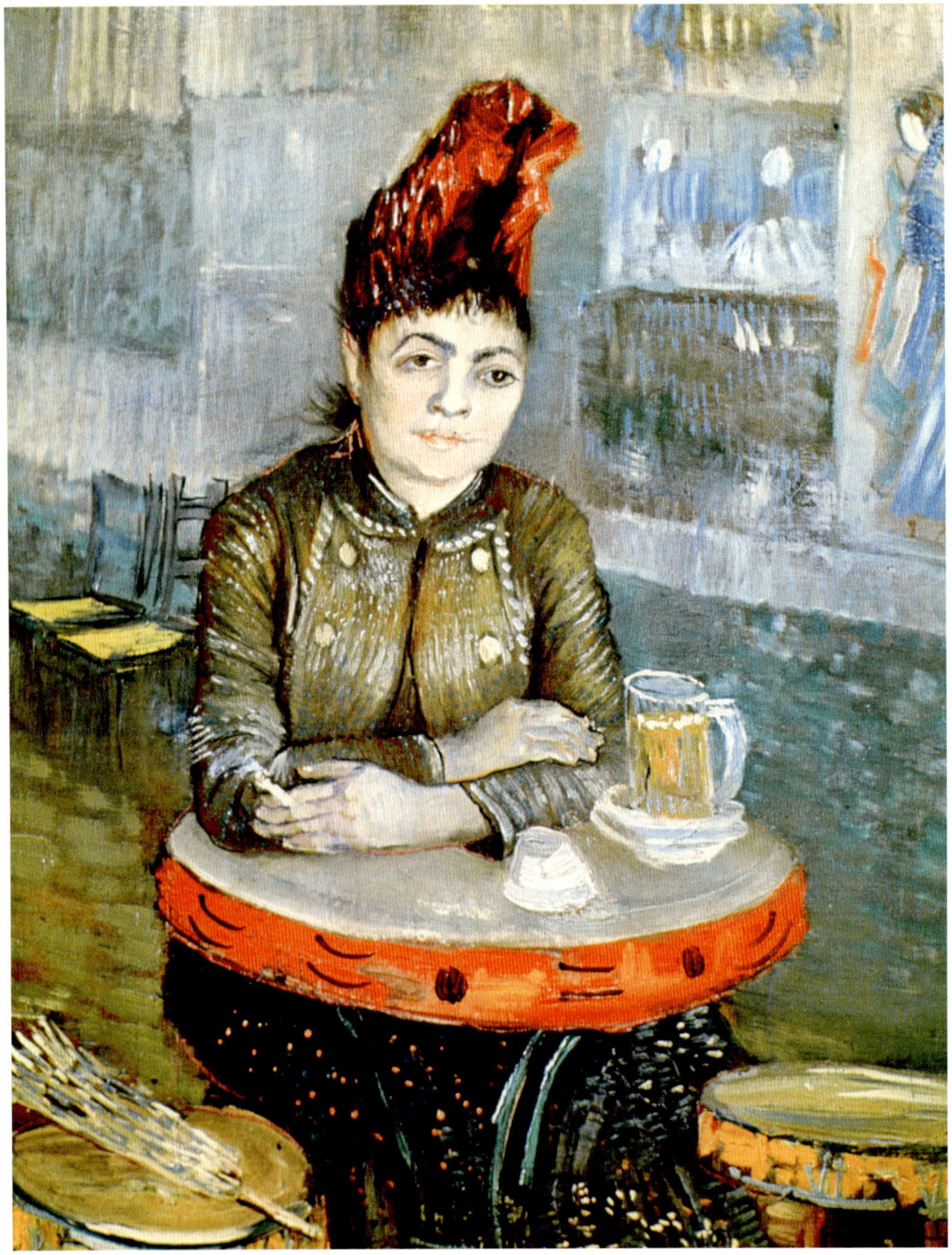

Vincent van Gogh to
Theo van Gogh
Extract from
Paris, *August 1887*

My dear friend,

"Enclosed is a letter which arrived yesterday, but which the concierge didn't give me straight away. I've been to the Tambourin, since if I hadn't gone, they would have thought I was afraid. And I told la Segatori [Agostina Segatori (1841–1910), proprietress of Café La Tambourin] that I wouldn't pass judgement on her in this matter, but that it was for her to judge herself. That I had torn up the receipt for the pictures – but that she had to return *everything*. That if she had not had a hand in what had happened to me, she would have seen me the next day. That as she didn't come to see me, my feeling was that she knew they were trying to pick a quarrel with me, but that she had tried to warn me by saying, 'Go away,' which I hadn't understood, and furthermore, perhaps didn't want to understand.

To which she replied that the pictures, & all the rest, were at my disposal. She maintained that it was I who had tried to pick a quarrel – which doesn't surprise me – knowing that if she sided with me they would take it out on her. I also saw the waiter when I went in, but he made himself scarce. I didn't want to take the pictures immediately, but I said that when you returned we would discuss the matter because these pictures belong to you as much as to me, and in the meantime I advised her to think about what had happened again. She didn't look well and was white as a sheet, which isn't a good sign. She didn't know that the waiter had gone up to your place. If that's true, I would be more inclined to believe she had tried to warn me they were trying to pick a quarrel with me than that she had plotted the whole thing herself. She cannot do as she likes. I'm awaiting your return now before taking any action.

I've done two pictures since you left."

***Woman in the Café Tambourin*, 1887**
MEDIUM: Oil on canvas
Courtesy of Van Gogh Museum, Amsterdam, The Netherlands/ The Bridgeman Art Library

***The Italian: Agostina Segatori*, 1887**
MEDIUM: Oil on canvas
Courtesy of Musée d'Orsay, Paris, France/Giraudon/The Bridgeman Art Library

Extract from
Paris, *August 1887*

Thank you for your letter, and for that which it contained. I feel sad that even successful paintings do not cover their costs.

I was touched by what you wrote about home, 'They are fairly well but yet it is sad to see them'. A dozen years ago one would have sworn that, come what may, the family would always prosper and do well. It would give Mother much pleasure if your marriage came off; and you also ought not to stay single for the sake of your health and business.

As for me, I feel the desire for marriage and children leaving me, and now and then I'm rather depressed that I should be like this at 35, when I ought to be feeling quite the opposite. And sometimes I blame it all on this rotten painting. It was Richepin who said somewhere: the love of art is the undoing of true love. I think that's absolutely right, but on the other hand true love makes one weary of art.

And although I already feel old and broken, I can still be amorous enough at times to feel less passionate about painting. One must have ambition to succeed, and ambition seems to me absurd. I wish above all I were less of a burden to you – and that needn't be impossible from now on, for I hope to make such progress that you'll be able to show what I do in full confidence without compromising yourself. And then I'll retire somewhere in the Midi so as not to see so many painters who fill me with disgust as men.

You can be sure of one thing – I shan't be trying to do any more work for the Tambourin – I think it's about to change hands anyway, and I most certainly don't object to that. As for la Segatori, that is quite a different matter. I still feel affection for her and I hope that she, too, still feels some for me. But at the moment she is in a difficult situation, she is neither a free agent nor mistress in her own house, on top of which she's suffering and sick. Although I wouldn't say so in public – I'm convinced she's had an abortion (unless, that is, she did have a miscarriage) – whatever, in her case I don't hold it against her.

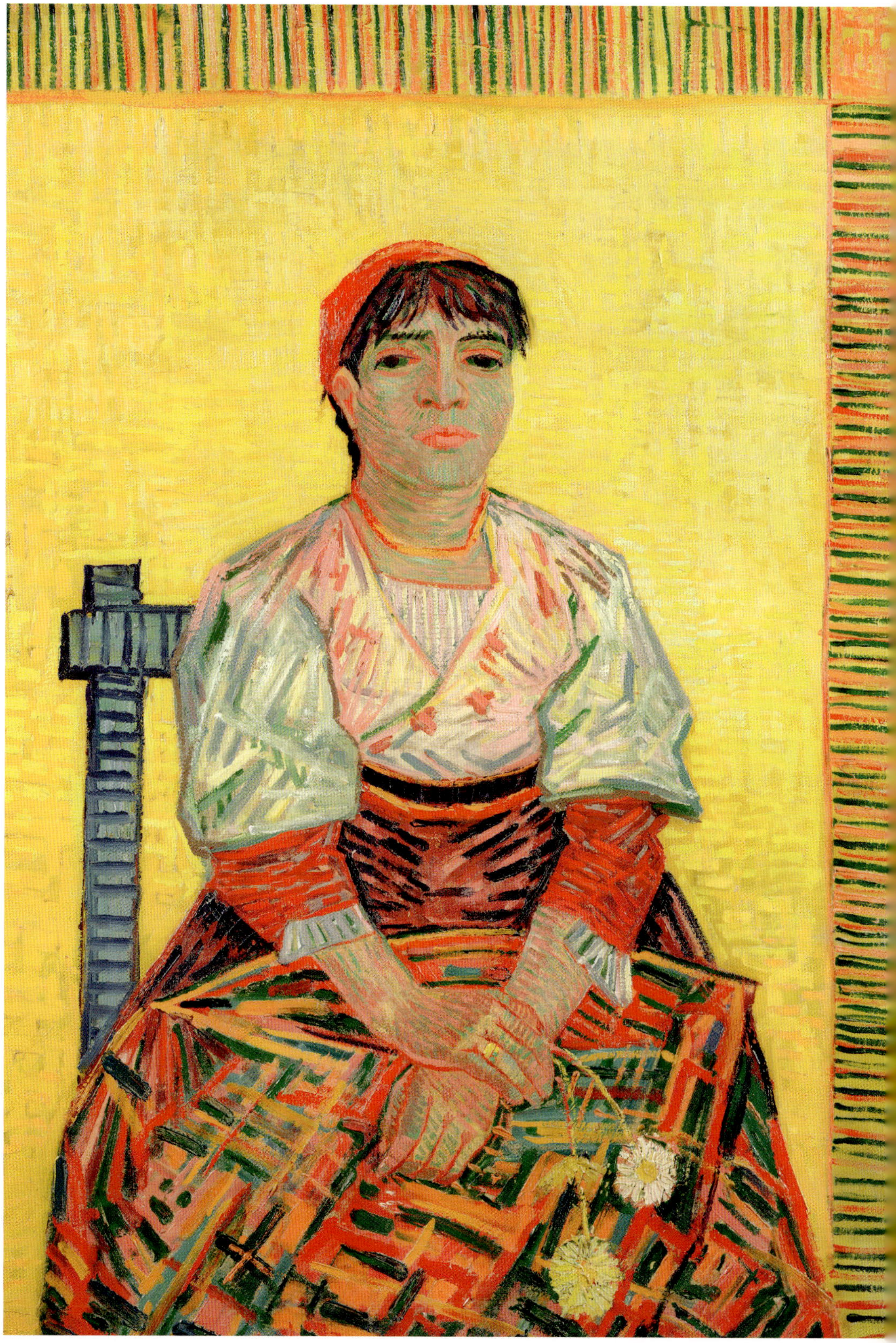

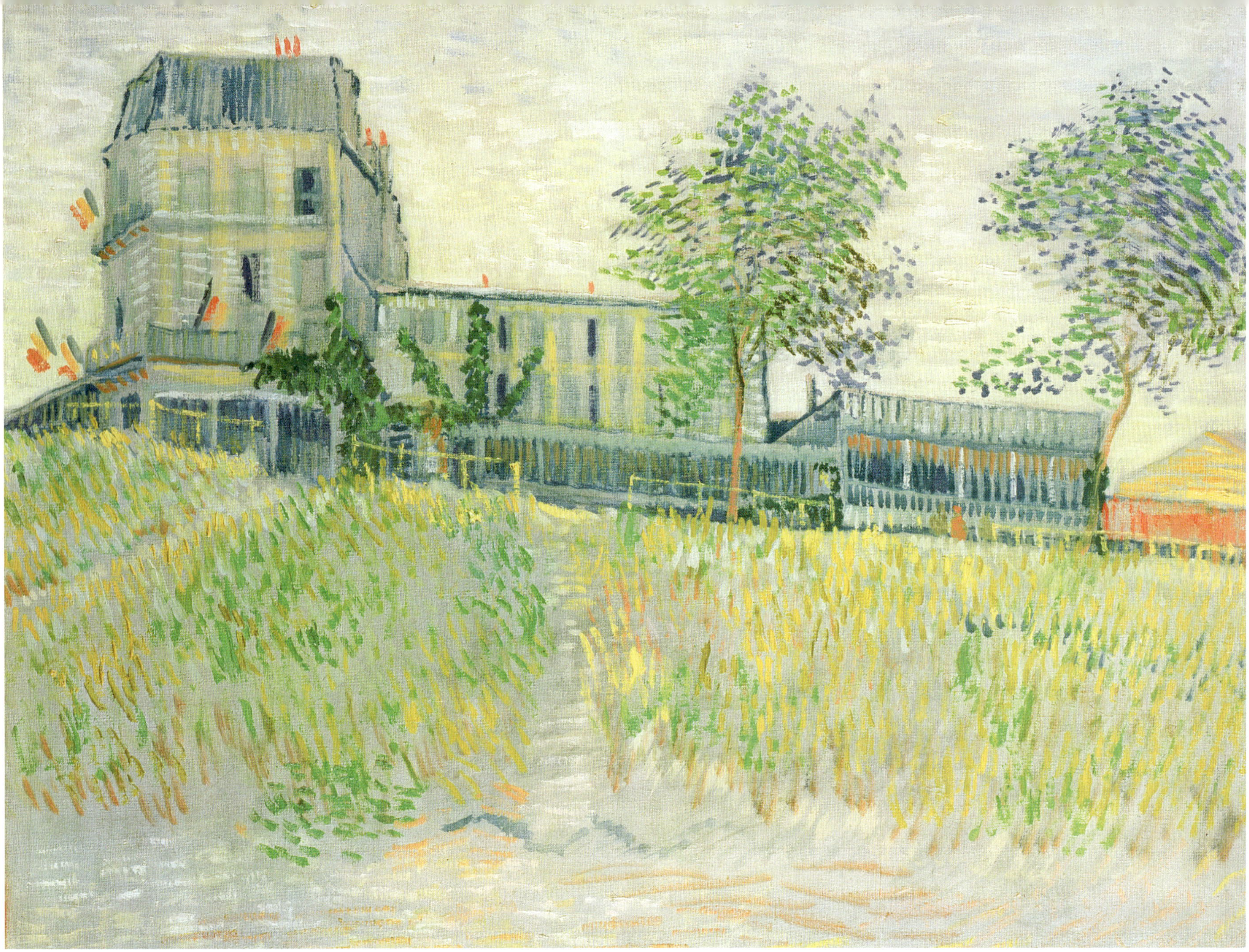

Vincent van Gogh to

Willemina van Gogh

Extract from

Paris, *Summer/Autumn 1887*

My dear little sister,

"I thank you very much for your letter, but for my part I hate writing these days. Still, there are some questions in your letter which I should like to answer.

To begin with, I must disagree with you when you say you thought Theo looked 'so wretched' this summer. Personally, I think that on the contrary Theo's appearance has become a great deal more distinguished during the past year. One has to be strong to stand life in Paris for as many years as he has done.

Is the Bible enough for us? These days I think Jesus himself would say again to those who sit down in melancholy, 'It is not here, it is risen. Why seek ye the living among the dead?' [...] I, for my part, am always glad that I have read the Bible more carefully than many people do nowadays, just because it gives me some peace of mind to know that there used to be such lofty ideals. [...]

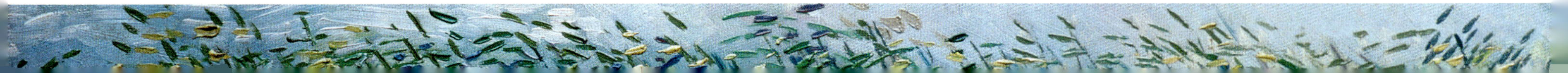

My own adventures are confined chiefly to making swift progress toward growing into a little old man – you know, with wrinkles, a tough beard and a number of false teeth, and so on. But what does all that matter? I have a dirty and difficult trade – painting. [...] If I didn't have Theo, I should not be able to do justice to my work, but having him for a friend, I'm sure I shall make progress and things will fall into place. As soon as possible I plan to spend some time in the south, where there is even more colour and even more sun.

I should be most obliged if you could let me know how Margot Begemann is and how things are with the de Groots, how did that business turn out? Did Sien de Groot marry her cousin? And did her child live?

Of my own work I think that the picture of peasants eating potatoes I did in Nuenen is *après tout* [above all] the best I've done. But since then I've had no chance of getting models, though on the other hand I did have the chance to study the colour question. And if I should find models again for my figures later, then I would hope to be able to show that I am after something other than little green landscapes or flowers.

Last year I painted almost nothing but flowers so as to get used to colours other than grey, vis. pink, soft or bright green, light blue, violet, yellow, orange, glorious red.

And when I was painting landscapes at Asnières this summer, I saw more colour in them than I did before. Now I'm going to try it with a portrait. And I must say that I'm not painting any the worse for it, perhaps because I could tell you of a very great deal that's wrong with both painters and paintings if I wanted to, quite as easily as I could tell you something that's good about them.

[...] Give Mother much love from me,

Vincent

Vincent had written in response to his sister Willemina's (1862–1941) letter. The range of topics they cover is vast, from her bible studies and the possibility of her becoming an artist, to Vincent's current painting projects in and around Paris.

***The Restaurant de la Sirène at Asnières*, 1887**
MEDIUM: Oil on canvas
Courtesy of Ashmolean Museum, University of Oxford, UK/The Bridgeman Art Library

***The Zouave*, 1888**
MEDIUM: Oil on canvas
Courtesy of Private Collection/Photo © Lefevre Fine Art Ltd., London/ The Bridgeman Art Library

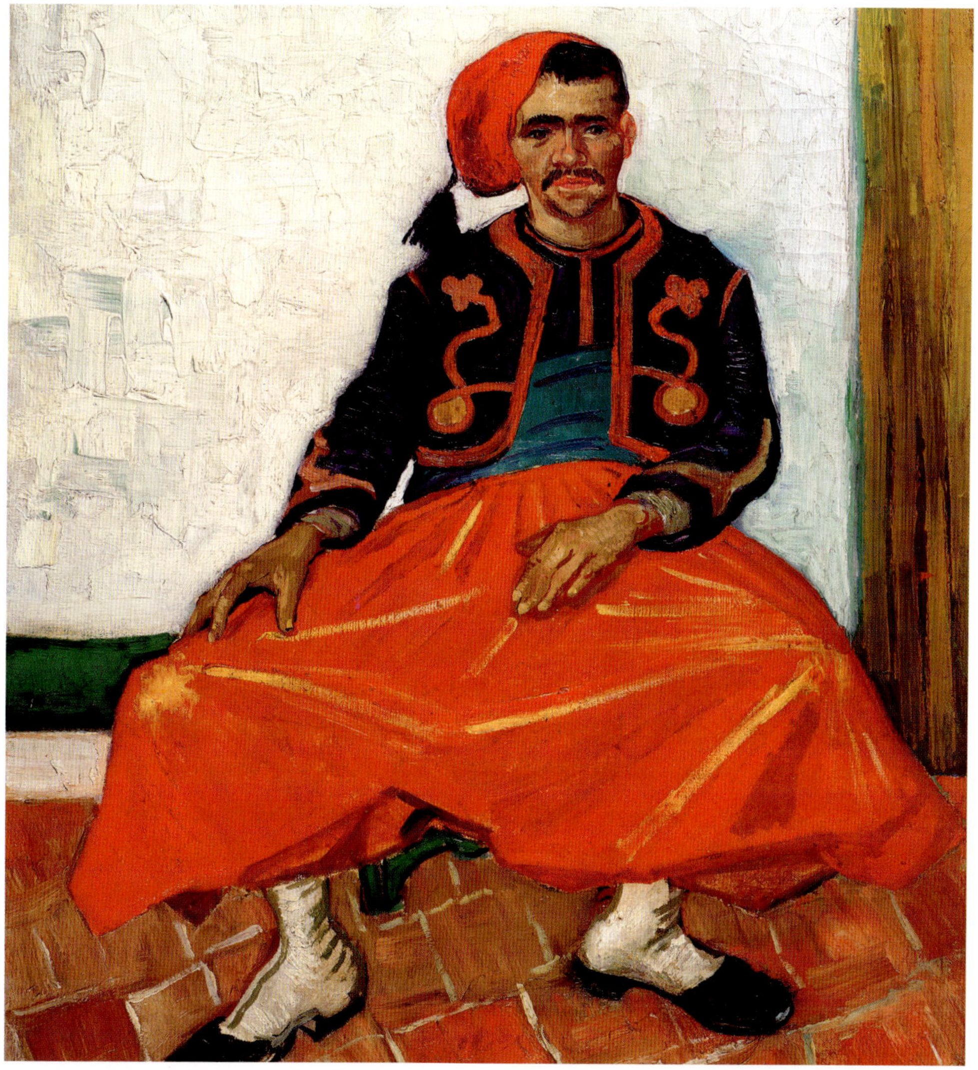

Vincent van Gogh to

Theo van Gogh

Extract from

Arles, *21 February 1888*

My dear Theo,

"During the journey I thought of you at least as much as I did of the new country that I was seeing.

Only I told myself that maybe later on you will often come here yourself. It seems to me almost impossible to be able to work in Paris unless one has a refuge where one can recuperate and regain one's tranquillity and poise. Without that, one would get hopelessly exhausted.

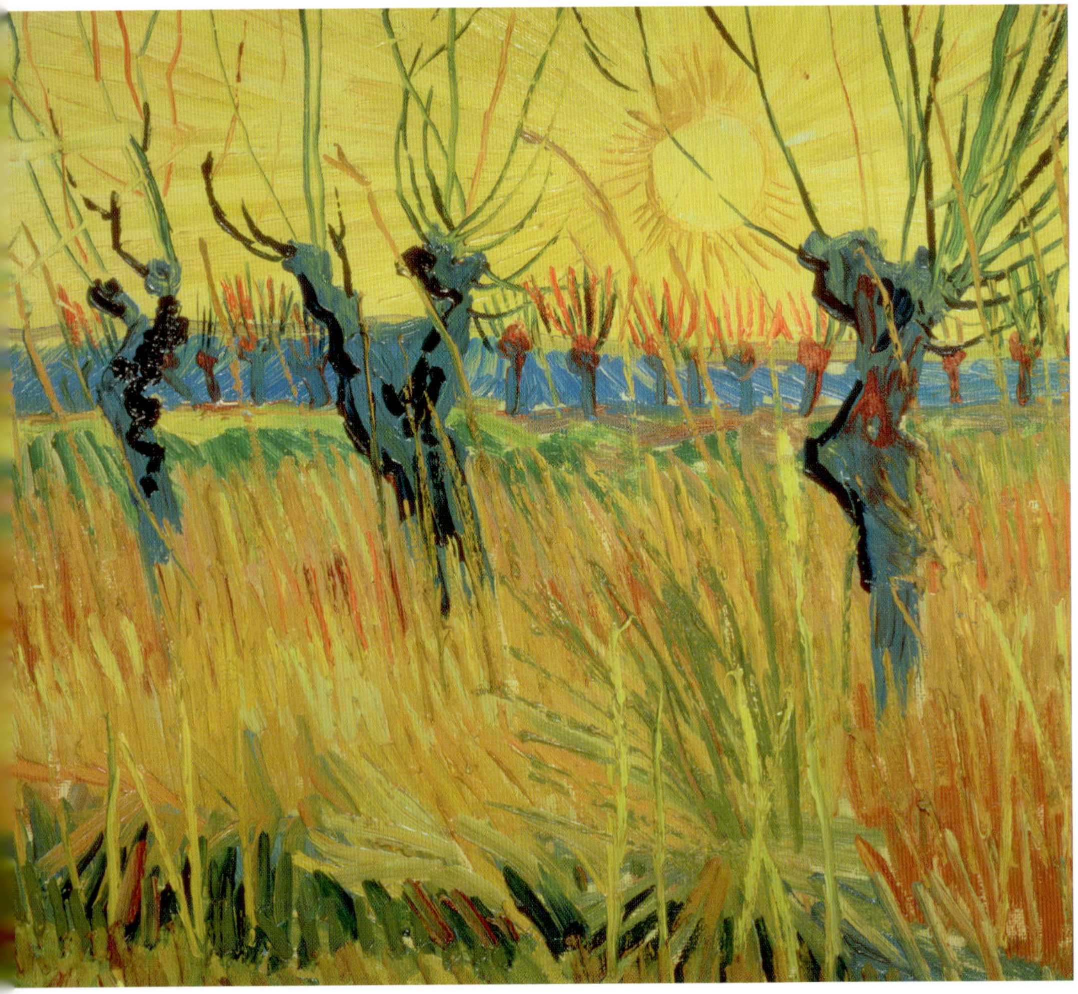

Now I'll begin by telling you that there's at least 60 centimetres of fallen snow everywhere, and it is still falling.

Arles doesn't seem any bigger than Breda or Mons.

Before arriving at Tarascon I noticed a magnificent landscape of immense yellow rocks, strangely intricate with the most imposing shapes.

In the tiny valleys between these rocks were rows of small round trees with foliage of olive-green or grey-green, which could well be lemon trees.

But here in Arles the country appears flat. I saw some magnificent red terrain planted with grapevines, with a background of mountains of the most delicate lilac. And the landscapes in the snow, with the summits white against a sky as luminous as the snow, were just like winter landscapes done by the Japanese.

Here is my address:
Restaurant Carrel,
30 Rue Cavalerie,
(Departement Bouches du Rhône) Arles."

Vincent van Gogh, tiring of his existence in Paris, where the close proximity of so many other painters had left him yearning for solitude, left the city, his brother Theo and his artist friends. Later in the year, in a letter to Paul Gauguin,

***Pollarded Willows and Setting Sun*, 1888**
MEDIUM: Oil on canvas
Courtesy of Rijksmuseum Kroller-Muller, Otterlo, Netherlands/The Bridgeman Art Library

***View of Arles*, 1889**
MEDIUM: Oil on canvas
Courtesy of Neue Pinakothek, Munich, Germany/Giraudon/The Bridgeman Art Library

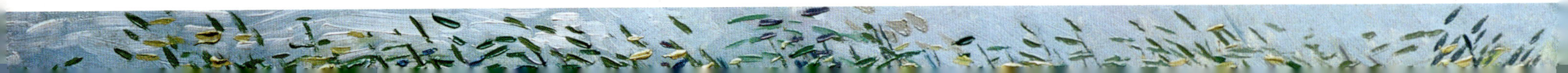

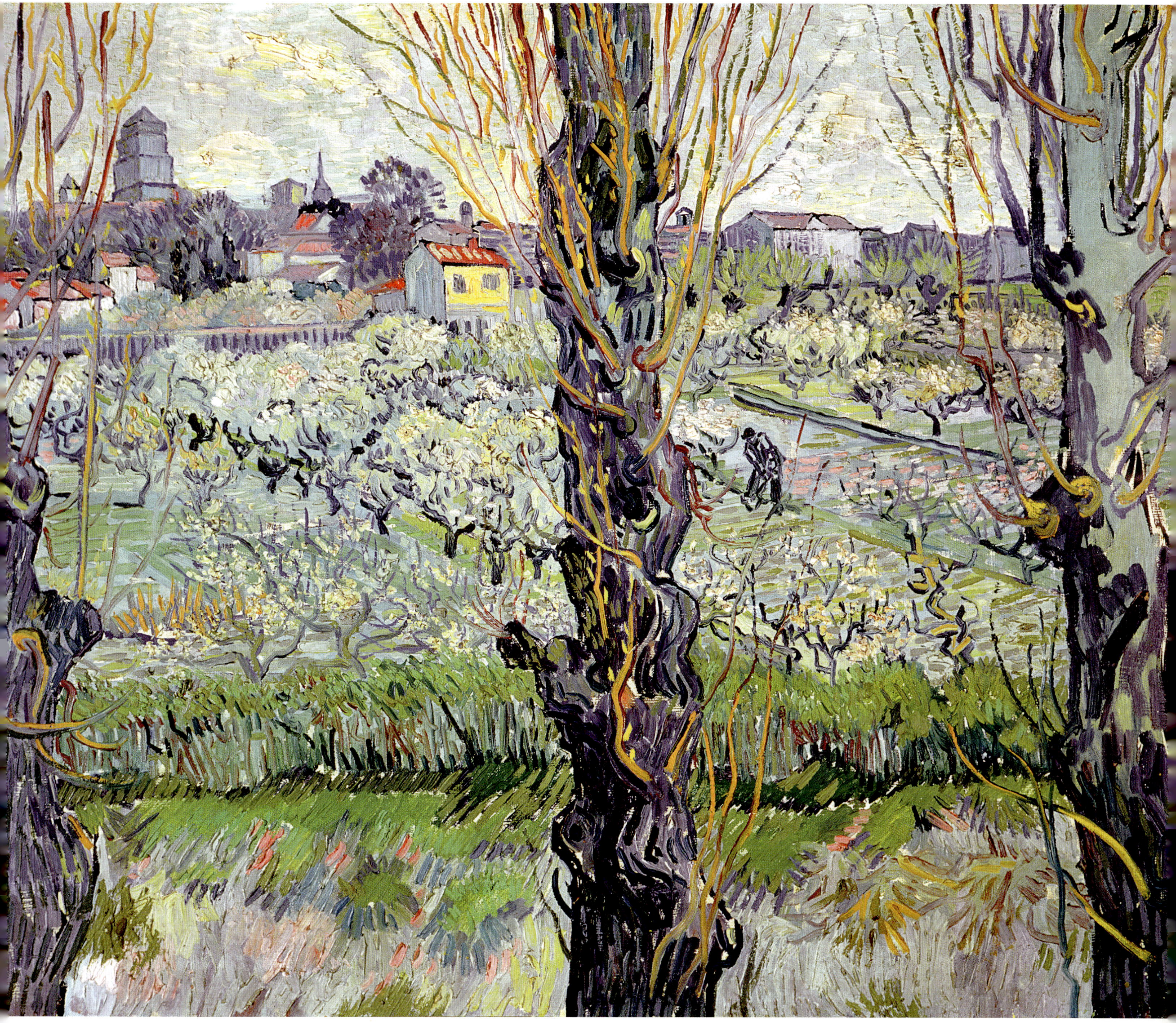

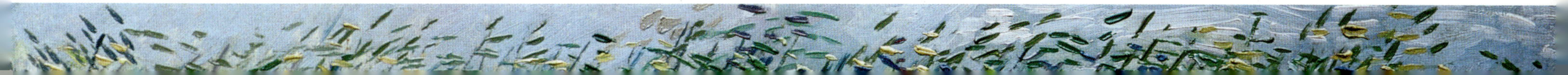

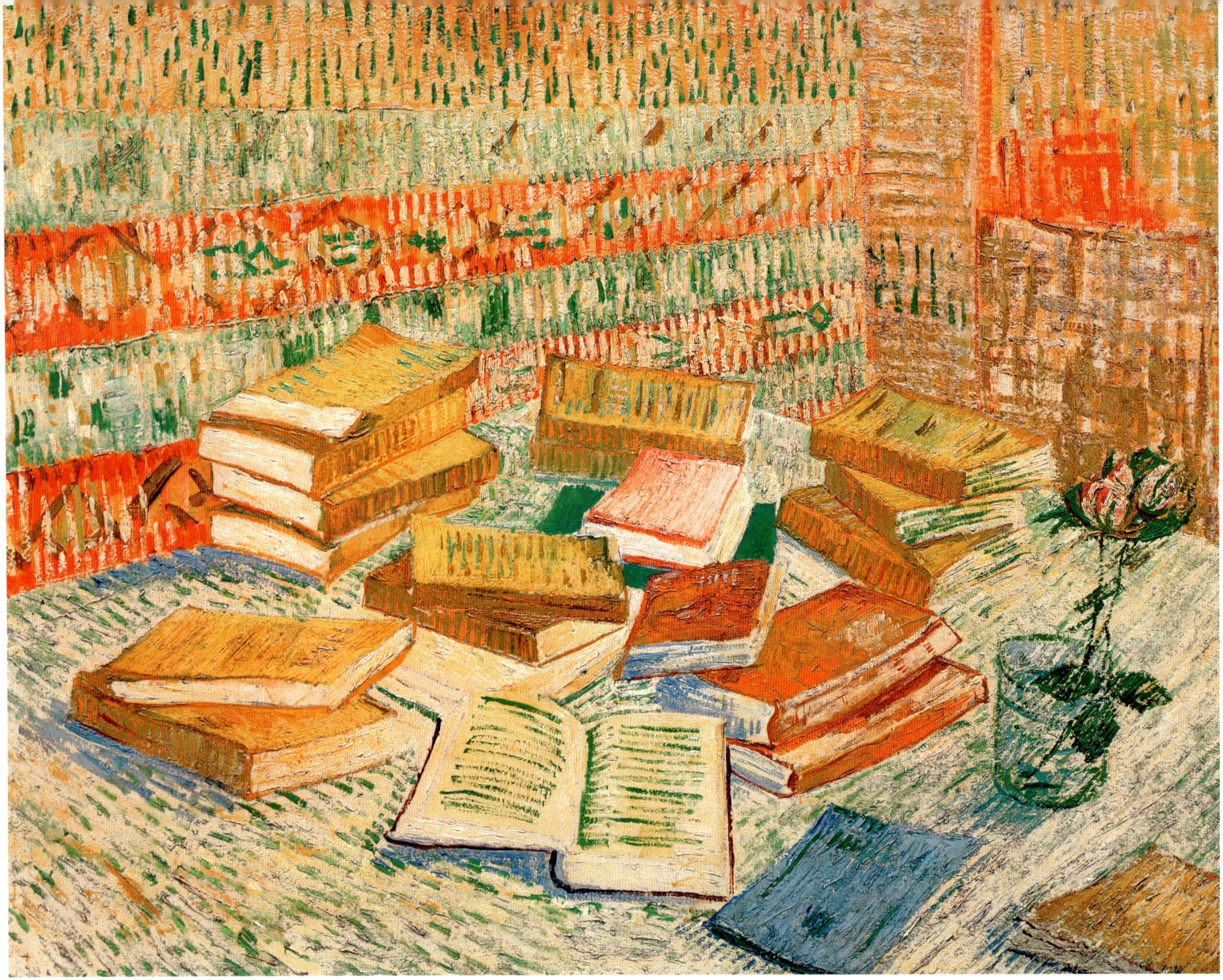

(1828–1909), he gave his reasons for leaving: 'I left Paris, seriously sick at heart and in body, and nearly an alcoholic because of my rising fury at my strength failing me'. He left Paris to take up residence in Arles, a small town between Montpelier and Marseilles. In Arles he registered to stay at Restaurant Carrel and immediately wrote to Theo to tell him the address. His letter describes the colour highlights of the journey: 'Tarascon … a magnificent landscape of immense yellow rocks'. On arrival in Arles he enthused that Japanese paintings sprang to his mind to describe the countryside.

Extract from Arles, *10 March 1888*

[…] What do you think of the news that Kaiser Wilhelm is dead? Will this precipitate events in France, and is Paris going to remain quiet? It's doubtful; and what will the effect of all this be on the trade in paintings? I read that there seems to be some question of abolishing the import duties on paintings into America; is this true?

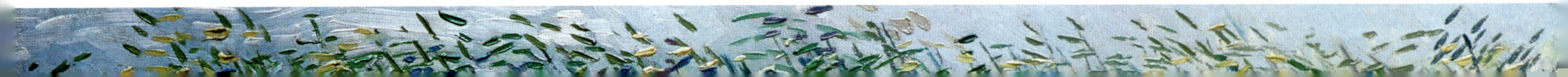

Still Life with French Novels and a Rose, 1887
MEDIUM: Oil on canvas
Courtesy of Private Collection/Giraudon/The Bridgeman Art Library

The Dance Hall at Arles, 1888, (detail)
MEDIUM: Oil on canvas
Courtesy of Musée d'Orsay, Paris, France/Giraudon/The Bridgeman Art Library

Perhaps it would be easier to get a few dealers and collectors to agree to buy the Impressionist paintings than to get the artists to agree to share the price of their paintings.

Nevertheless, the artists couldn't do better than to get together, and give over to the association, and share the proceeds of the sales, so that the society could at least guarantee its members a chance to live and to work.

If de Gas [Degas], Claude Monet, Renoir, Sisley and C. Pissarro took the initiative, saying, 'Look here, we 5 give 10 paintings each (or rather we each give to the value of 10,000 frs. to be estimated by expert members such as Tersteeg and yourself, co-opted by the society, said experts likewise to put in capital in the form of paintings) and we further undertake to hand over every year pictures to the value of …

'And we invite you others, Guillaumin, Seurat, Gauguin, etc., etc., to join with us (your paintings to undergo the same expert evaluation).'

Thus the great Impressionists of the Grand Boulevard, while giving pictures which would become general property, would keep their prestige, and the others could no longer reproach them with keeping to themselves the advantages of a reputation no doubt acquired primarily through their personal efforts and individual genius, but all the same a reputation that is growing, buttressed and actually maintained by the paintings of a whole battalion of artists who have been working in perpetual poverty. […] "

Vincent was keen to set up an artist co-operative led by his friend Tersteeg (Hermanus Gijsbertus Tersteeg (1845–1927), his former manager at Goupil & Cie), and Theo. He felt that the Impressionist painters would be interested in the idea and many other contemporary artists. On the same day in Paris, in a restaurant on the Boulevard Clichy, Theo exhibited some of Vincent's paintings with other artists – Émile Bernard (1868–1941) and Paul Gauguin. Vincent referred to their group as 'The Painters of the Petit Boulevard'. Also exhibited by Theo, in Boulevard Montmartre, were 'The Painters of the Grand Boulevard', a group of established artists including Edgar Degas (1834–1917) and Claude Monet (1840–1926).

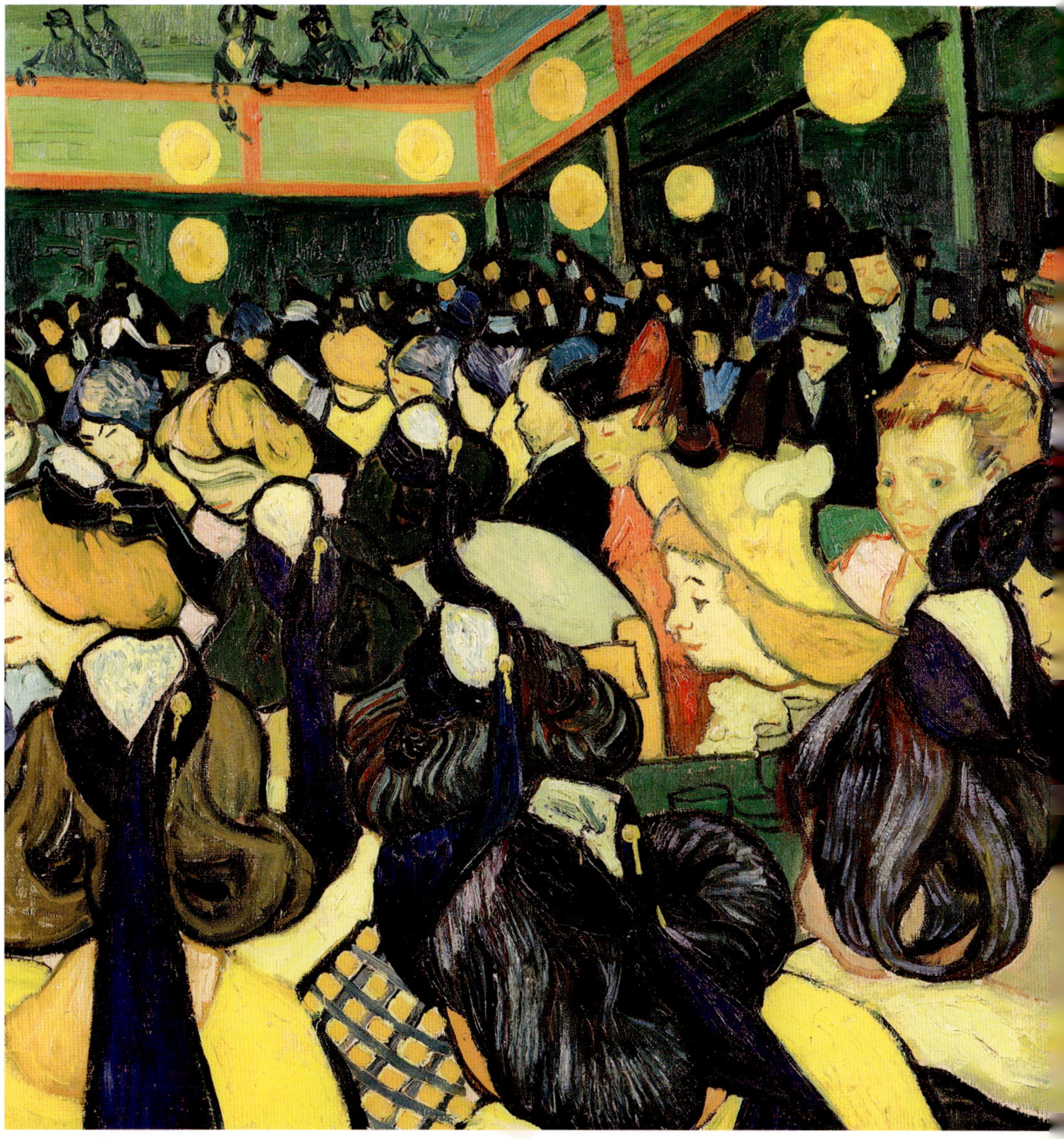

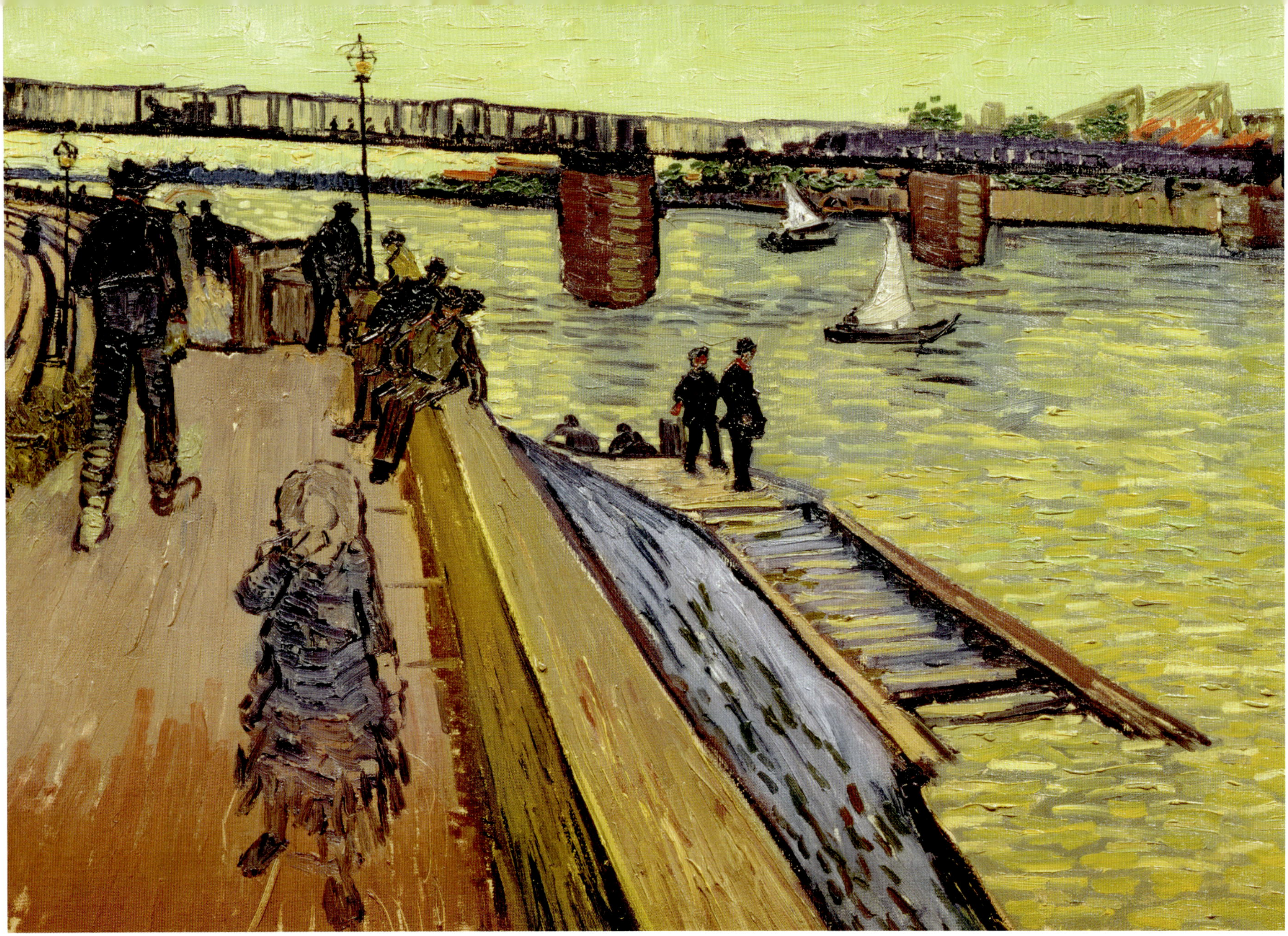

Extract from
Arles, *9 April 1888*

[…] Yesterday I saw another bull fight, where 5 men worked the bull with darts and cockades. One toreador crushed one of his balls in jumping the barricade. He was a blonde man with grey eyes and lots of sang-froid; people said he'll be ill long enough. He was dressed in sky blue and gold, just like the little horseman in our Monticelli, the 3 figures in a wood. The arenas are a fine sight when there's sunshine and a crowd.

I shall be all in when the orchards are over, for they are size 25 and 30 and 20 canvases. We should not have too many of them, even if I could knock off twice as many. It seems to me that this may really break the ice in Holland. […]

I must also have a starry night with cypresses, or perhaps above all, a field of ripe corn; there are some wonderful nights here. I am in a continual fever of work.

***Le Pont de Trinquetaille in Arles*, 1888**
MEDIUM: Oil on canvas
Courtesy of Private Collection/
Peter Willi/The Bridgeman Art Library

***Chestnut Trees in Blossom, Auvers-sur-Oise*, 1890**
MEDIUM: Oil on canvas
Courtesy of Private Collection/
The Bridgeman Art Library

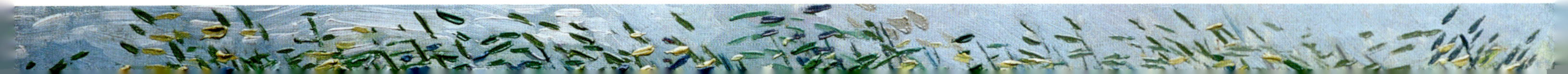

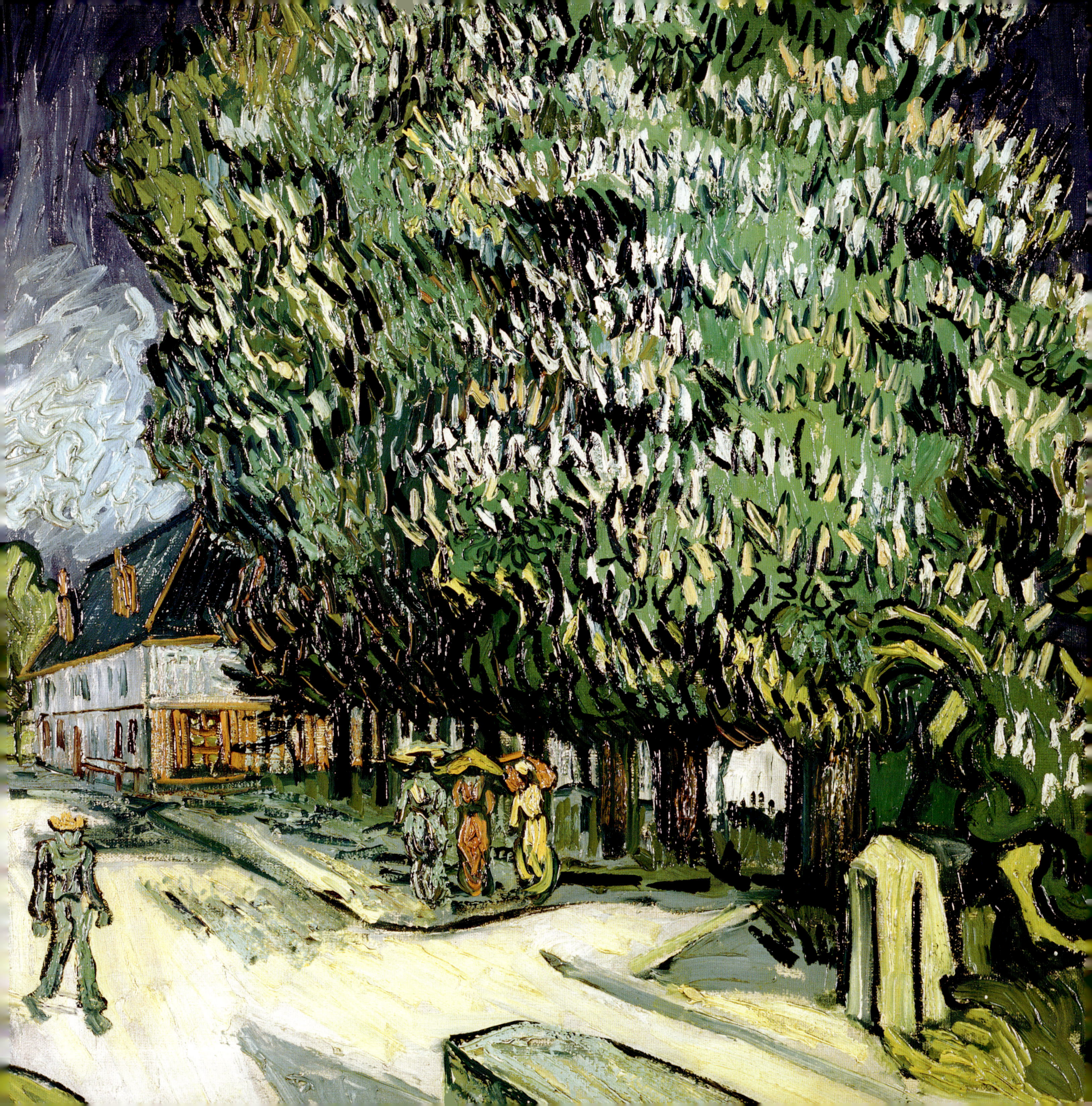

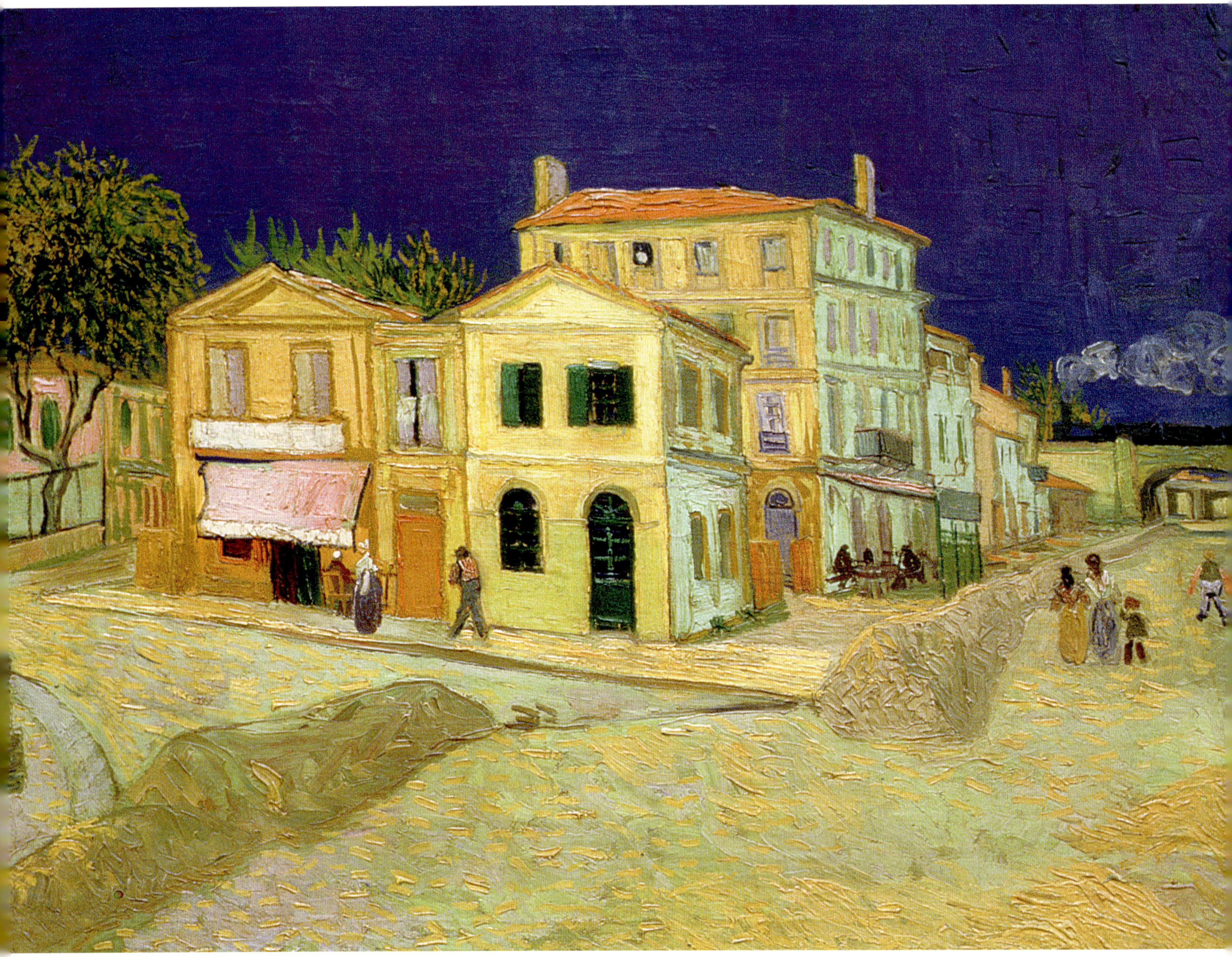

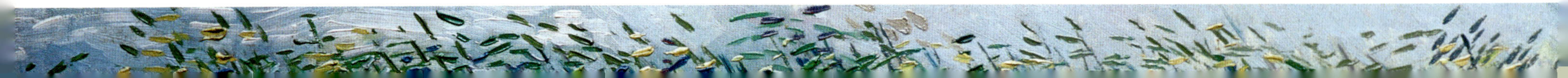

Extract from
Arles, *1 May 1888*

Many thanks for your letter and the 50 fr. note enclosed.

I don't see the whole future black, but I do see it bristling with difficulties and sometimes I ask myself if they won't be too much for me. But this is mostly in moments of physical weakness, and last week I had such a fierce toothache that much against my will I had to waste time.

Well, today I've taken the right wing of this complex, which contains 4 rooms, or rather two with two closets. It is painted yellow outside, whitewashed inside, in full sunlight. I have taken it for 15 fr. a month.

Now my idea would be to furnish one room, the one on the first floor, so as to be able to sleep there. This [house] will remain the studio and the storehouse for the whole campaign, as long as it lasts in the South, and now I am free of all the innkeepers' tricks: they're ruinous and they make me wretched. [...] I hope I have landed on my feet this time, you know – yellow outside, white inside, with all the sun, so that I shall see my canvases in a bright interior – the floor is red brick; outside, the garden of the square, of which you will find two more drawings. I think I can promise you that the drawings will get better and better.

I still have paints and brushes and several other things in stock, but one must not waste one's powder. I think, supposing you leave those worthies, I must manage to live without spending more than, say, 150 frs. a month; at present I could not do it, but you will see that in two months I shall be settled accordingly. And if by that time we are earning more, so much the better. I want to make sure of that.

[...] Meanwhile, if you approve, I shall furnish the bedroom, either hiring or buying it for cash down; I shall see about that today or tomorrow morning. I am still convinced that nature down here is just what one wants to give one colour. So that it's more than likely I shall hardly ever budge from here.

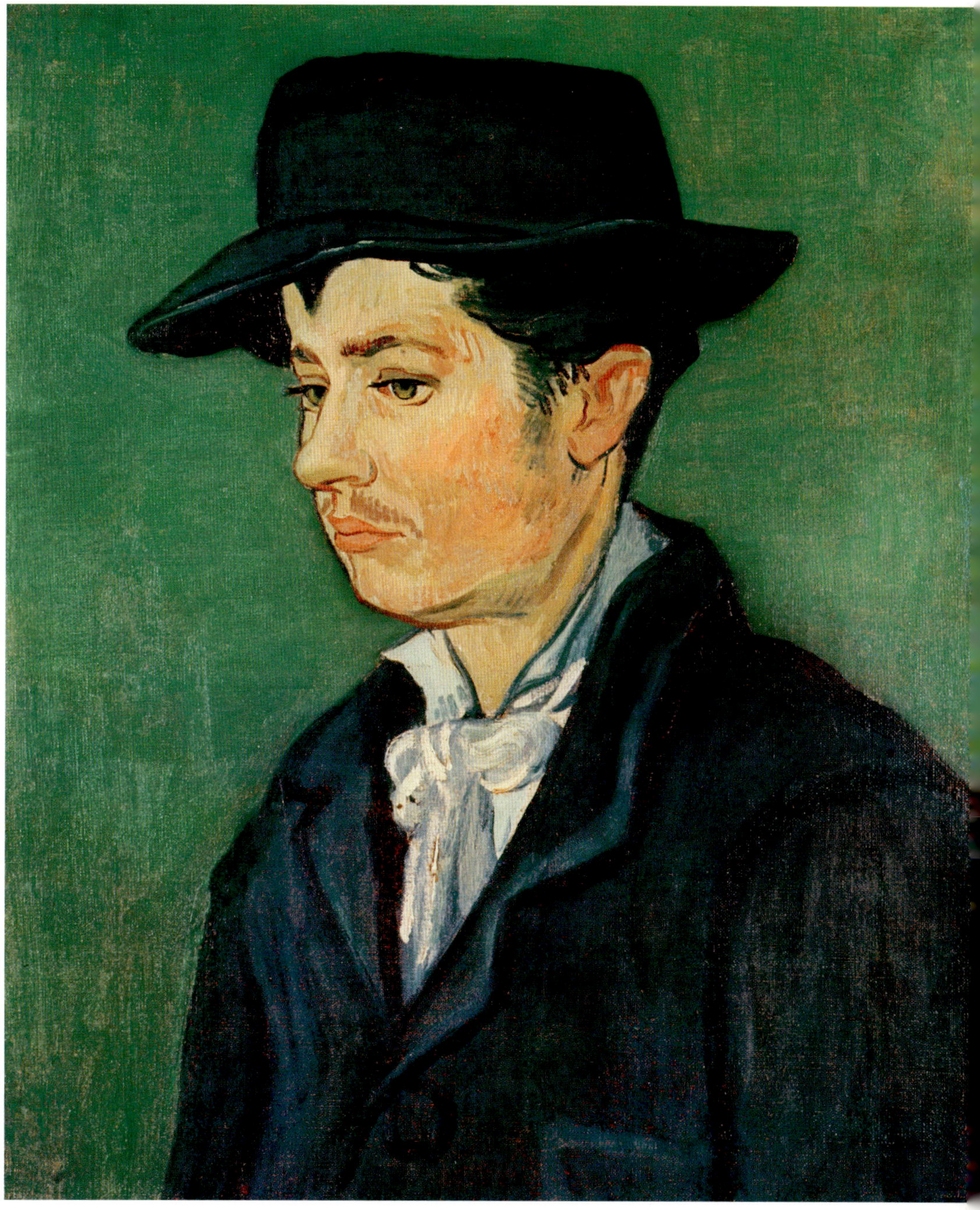

The Yellow House, 1888
MEDIUM: Oil on canvas
Courtesy of Van Gogh Museum, Amsterdam, The Netherlands/ The Bridgeman Art Library

Portrait of Armand Roulin, 1888
MEDIUM: Oil on canvas
Courtesy of Museum Boymans van Beuningen, Rotterdam, The Netherlands/Giraudon/ The Bridgeman Art Library

[…] I have one less big worry now that I have found the little white studio. […] I shall put some Japanese things up on the wall.

In May 1888, Vincent rented four rooms in the 'Yellow House', on the Place Lamartine in Arles. At first, due to impoverishment, he could only use it as his daytime studio. Gradually, over a four-month period and with the aid of Theo's allowances, Vincent paid for house furniture and some fittings for the rooms and repainting. In September 1888 he moved in and painted a picture of it, *The Yellow House*, 1888. His plan was to set up a studio for artists visiting the area.

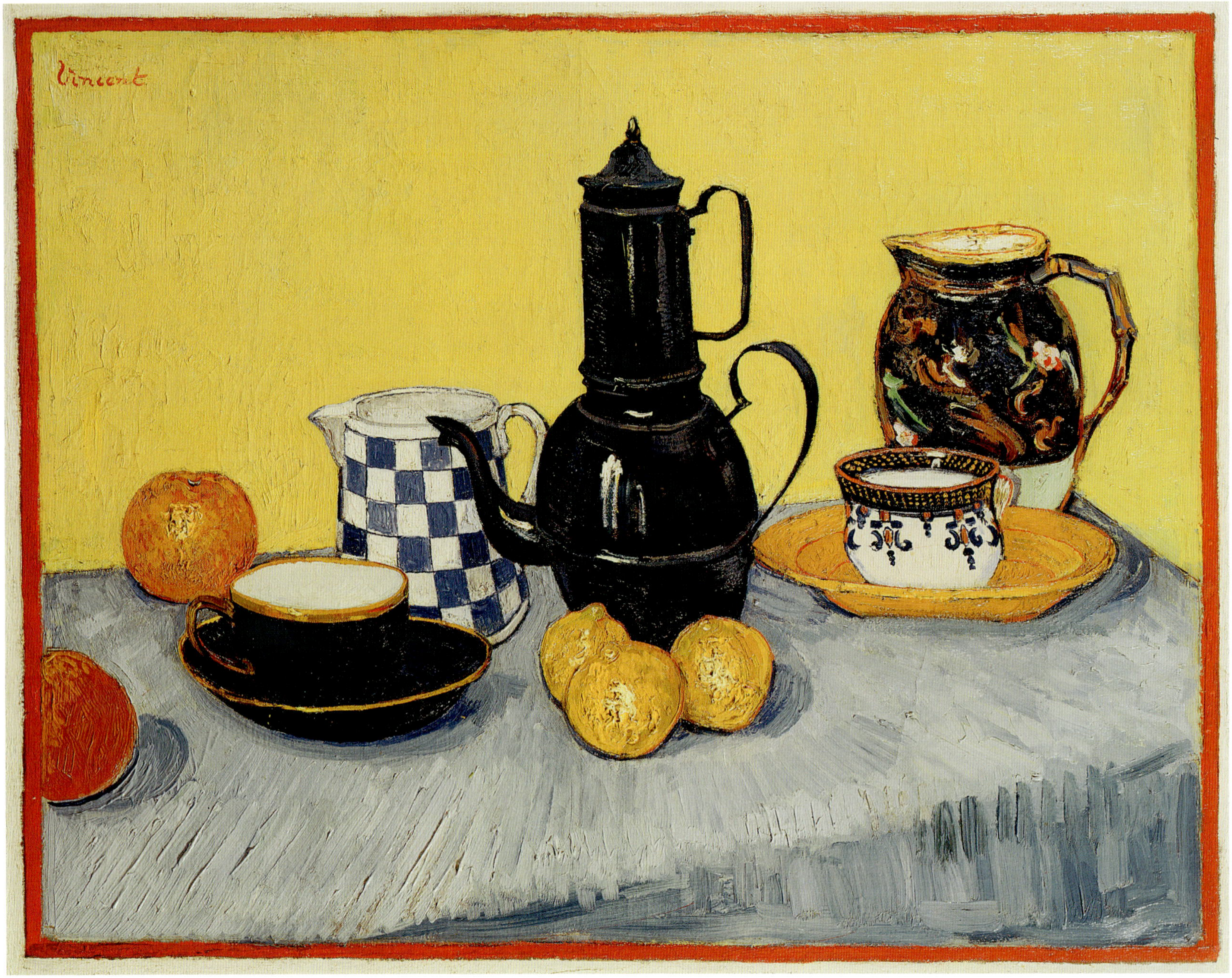

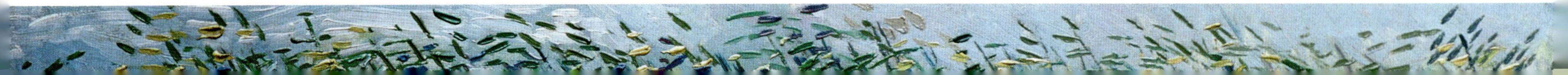

Extract from
Arles, *c. 20 May 1888*

What you write about your visits to Gruby has distressed me, but all the same I am relieved that you went. Has it occurred to you that the dazedness – the feeling of extreme lassitude – may have been caused by this weakness of the heart, and in this case the iodide of potassium would have nothing to do with the feeling of collapse? […] I often think of Gruby *here* and *now*, and I am completely well, but it is having pure air and warmth that makes it possible.

I have done two still lifes this week.

A blue enamel coffeepot, a cup (on the left), royal blue and gold, a milk jug in squares of pale blue and white, a cup – on the right – of white with a blue and orange pattern, on an earthen tray of grayish yellow, a jug in earthenware or majolica, blue with a pattern in reds, greens and browns, and lastly 2 oranges and 3 lemons; the table is covered with a blue cloth, the background is greenish-yellow, so that there are six different blues and four or five yellows and oranges.

The other still life is the majolica pot with wild flowers.

I shall not believe you if in your next letter you tell me there's nothing wrong with you. It is perhaps a more serious change, and I should not be surprised if you were a trifle low during the time it will take you to recover. In the fullness of artistic life there is, and remains, and will always come back at times, that homesick longing for the truly ideal life that can never come true.

***Still Life with Blue Enamel Coffeepot, Earthenware and Fruit*, 1888**
MEDIUM: Oil on canvas
Courtesy of Private Collection/Photo © Lefevre Fine Art Ltd, London/ The Bridgeman Art Library

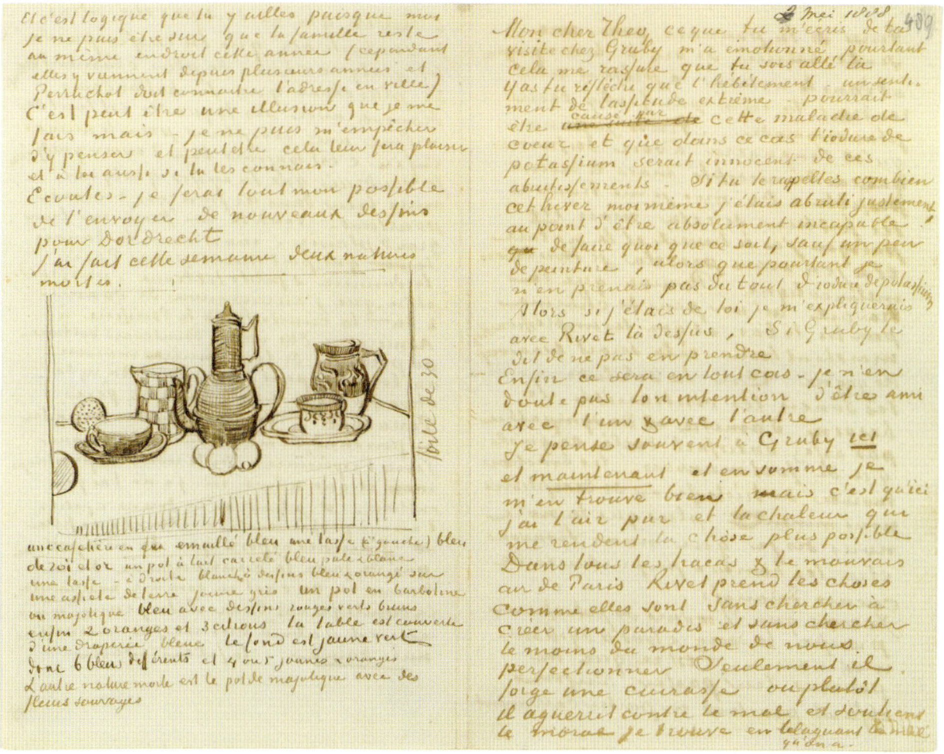

Theo's health had been suffering and Vincent advised him to seek medical help. To lighten the letter content he goes on to tell Theo about his latest paintings, two still-life works featuring vibrant blue and white hues with accent colours.

Extract from
Arles, *12 or 13 June 1888*

[…] Since the rent of the house and the painting of the doors and windows and the purchases of canvases all came at the same time, I've run out, and you would be doing me a very great kindness if you could send me the money a few days earlier.

I am working on a landscape with wheat fields which, I think, is as good as, say, the white orchard. It is in the same style as the two landscapes of the Butte Montmartre, which were at the Independents, but I think it is more robust and rather more stylish.

And I have another subject, a farm and some haystacks, which will probably be the pendant.

I am very curious to know what Gauguin plans to do. I hope he'll be able to come. You will tell me that it's pointless to think about the future, but the painting is progressing slowly and where that's concerned you do have to plan ahead. If I sold no more than a few canvases, that would be neither Gauguin's salvation nor mine. [...]

If Gauguin were willing to join us it would be, I think, a step forward for us. It would establish us squarely as the openers-up of the South, and nobody could argue with that.

From Vincent van Gogh to
Émile Bernard
Extract from
Arles, *18 June 1888*

My dear Bernard,

Forgive me for writing in haste, I'm afraid my letter will be illegible, but I did want to reply at once.

[...] It wouldn't have been such a stupid thing to do if we had all gone to Arles together, for with three of us here, we could have done our own housekeeping. And now that I have found my bearings a bit more, I am beginning to discover the advantages. [...]

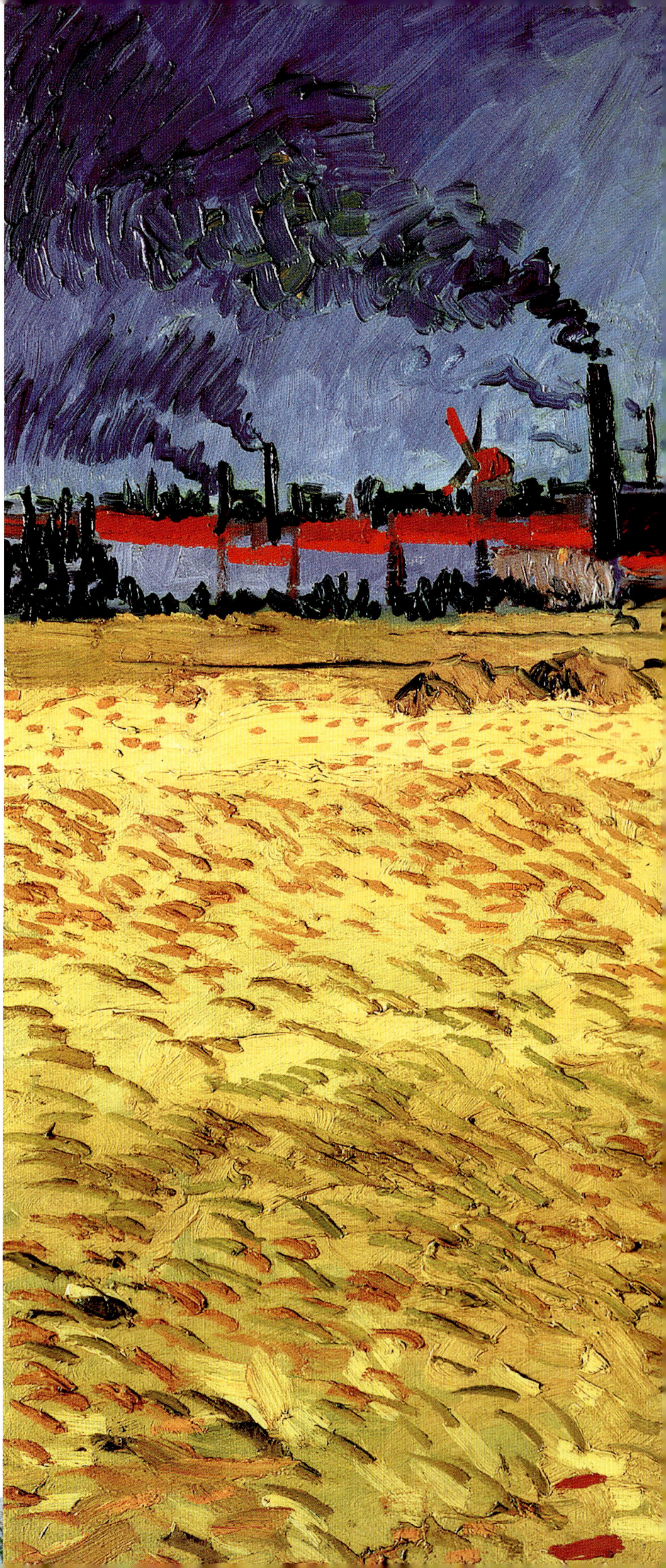

***Sunset at Wheat Field, near Arles*, 1888**
MEDIUM: Oil on canvas

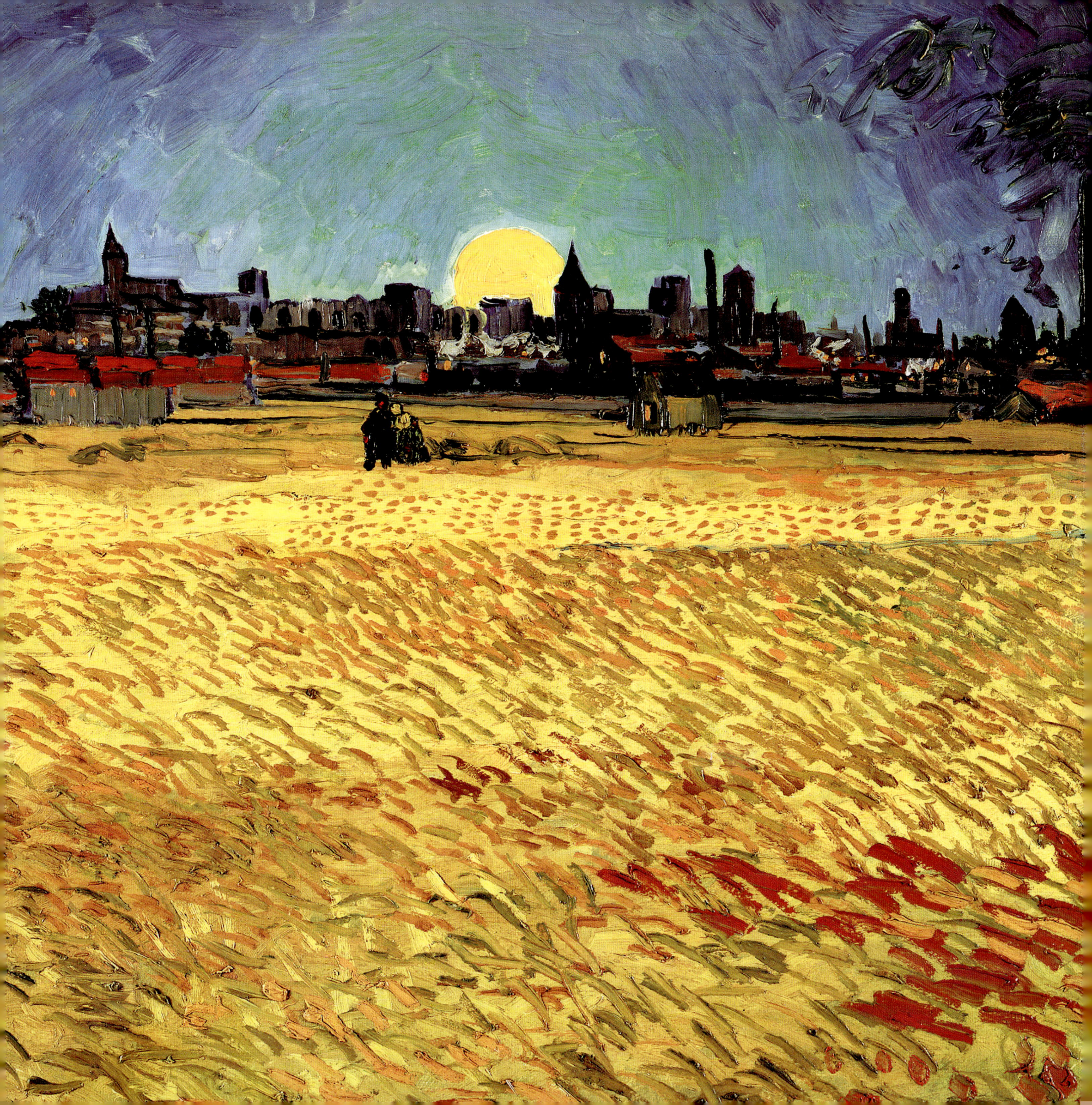

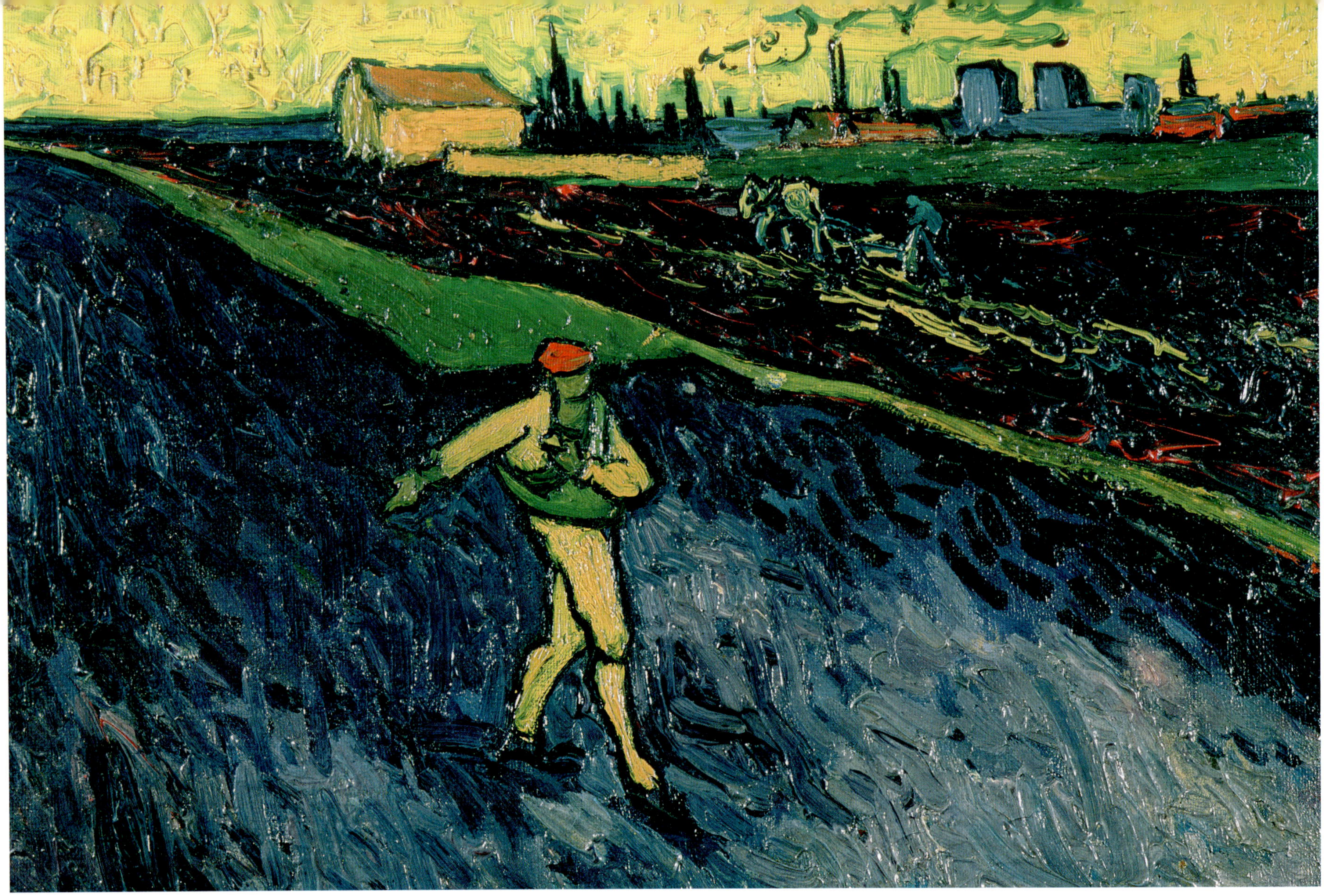

Here is a sketch of a sower: a large piece of land with clods of ploughed earth, for the most part a definite purple. A field of ripe wheat, in yellow ochre with a little carmine.

The sky chrome yellow, almost as bright as the sun itself, which is chrome yellow 1 with a little white, while the rest of the sky is chrome yellow 1 and 2 mixed. Thus very yellow.
The Sower's smock is blue and his trousers white.

Size 25 canvas, square.

There are many touches of yellow in the soil, neutral tones produced by mixing purple with the yellow, but I couldn't care less what the colours are in *reality*. I'd sooner do those naïve pictures out of old almanacs, old farmers' almanacs where hail, snow, rain or fine weather are depicted in a wholly primitive manner, like the one Anquetin used so successfully in his Moisson. To he honest with you, I have absolutely no objection to the countryside, since I grew up in it – I am still enchanted by snatches of the past, have a hankering after the eternal, of which the sower and the sheaf of corn are the symbols. But when shall I ever get round to doing the *starry sky*, that picture which is always in my mind?

Alas, alas, it is just as the excellent fellow Cyprien says in J.K. Huysman's 'En ménage': 'the most beautiful paintings are those which you dream about when you lie in bed smoking a pipe, but which you never paint'.

Herewith another landscape. Setting sun? Rising moon?

A summer evening, anyway.

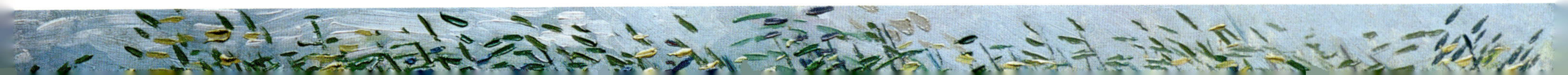

Town purple, celestial body yellow, sky green-blue. The wheat has all the hues of old gold, copper, green-gold or red-gold, yellow-gold, yellow-bronze, red-green. Size 30 canvas, square. ”

Vincent van Gogh to
Theo van Gogh
Extract from
Arles, *c. 25 July 1888*

“[…] Now if you know what a '*mousmé*' is (you will find out when you read Loti's *Madame Chrysanthème*), I have just painted one. It took me a whole week, and I haven't been able to do anything else, because I still haven't been too well. This is what annoys me – but I felt well, I would have been able to run off some more landscapes in the meantime, but to do justice to my *mousmé* I had to conserve my mental energies. A *mousmé* is a Japanese girl – Provençale in this case – 12 to 14 years old. That makes two portraits now, the Zouave and her.

[…] The portrait of the girl is against a background of white strongly tinged with malachite green, her bodice is striped blood red and violet, the skirt is royal blue, with large yellow-orange dots. The mat [sic] flesh tones are yellowish-grey; the hair tinged with violet; the eyebrows and the eyelashes are black; the eyes, orange with Prussian blue. A branch of oleander in her fingers, for the two hands are showing. ”

Vincent assures Émile Bernard that he does not need Gauguin to come to stay with him. He discusses his latest painting *La Mousmé*, 1888 (National Gallery of Art, Washington), which took him a whole week of intense concentration to paint and complete it. The title was inspired by a character in a Japanese novel, the word for a 12- to 14-year-old Japanese girl.

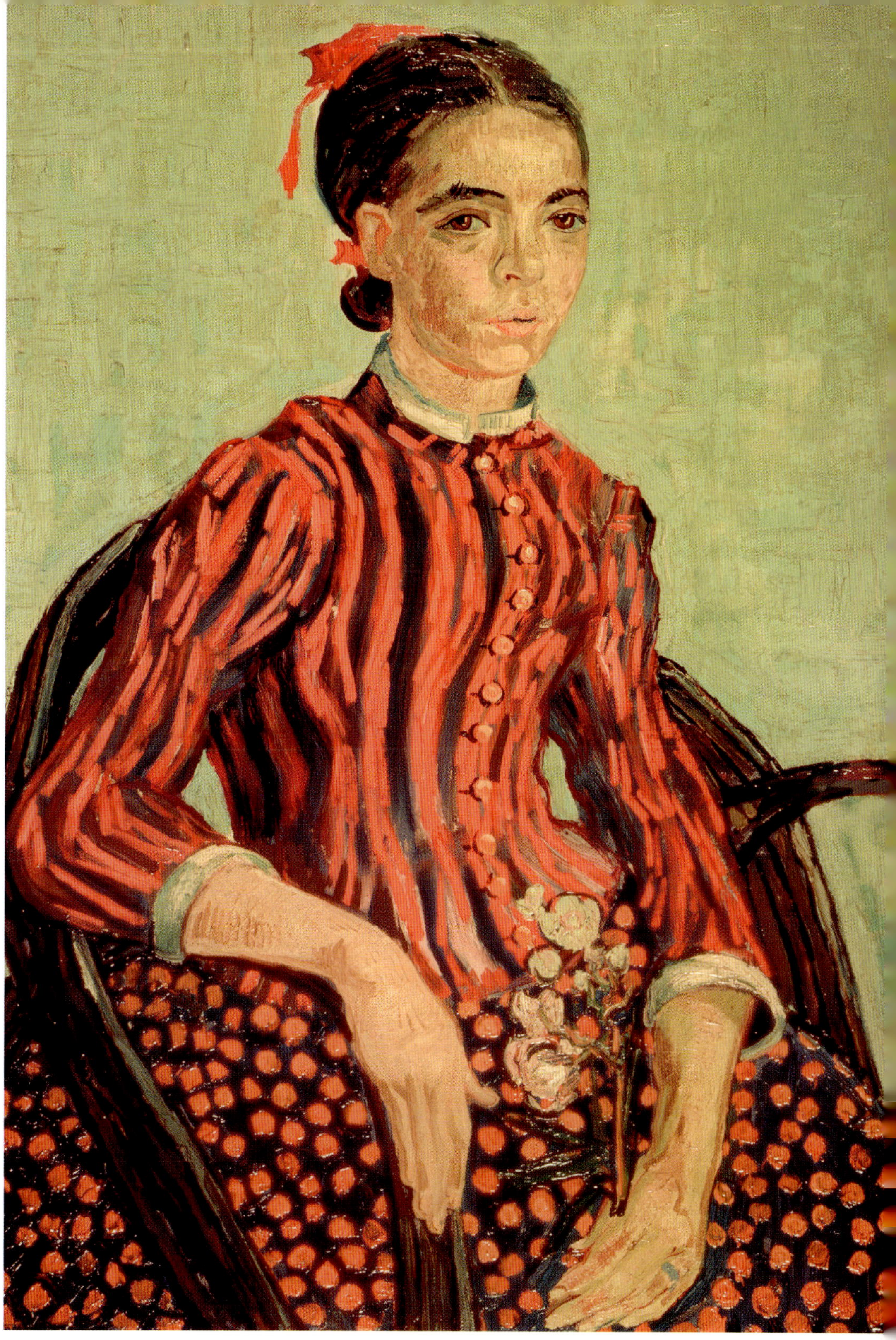

***The Sower*, 1888, (detail)**
MEDIUM: Oil on canvas
Private Collection/Photo © Christie's Images/The Bridgeman Art Library

***La Mousmé*, 1888**
MEDIUM: Oil on canvas
Courtesy of National Gallery of Art, Washington DC, USA/The Bridgeman Art Library

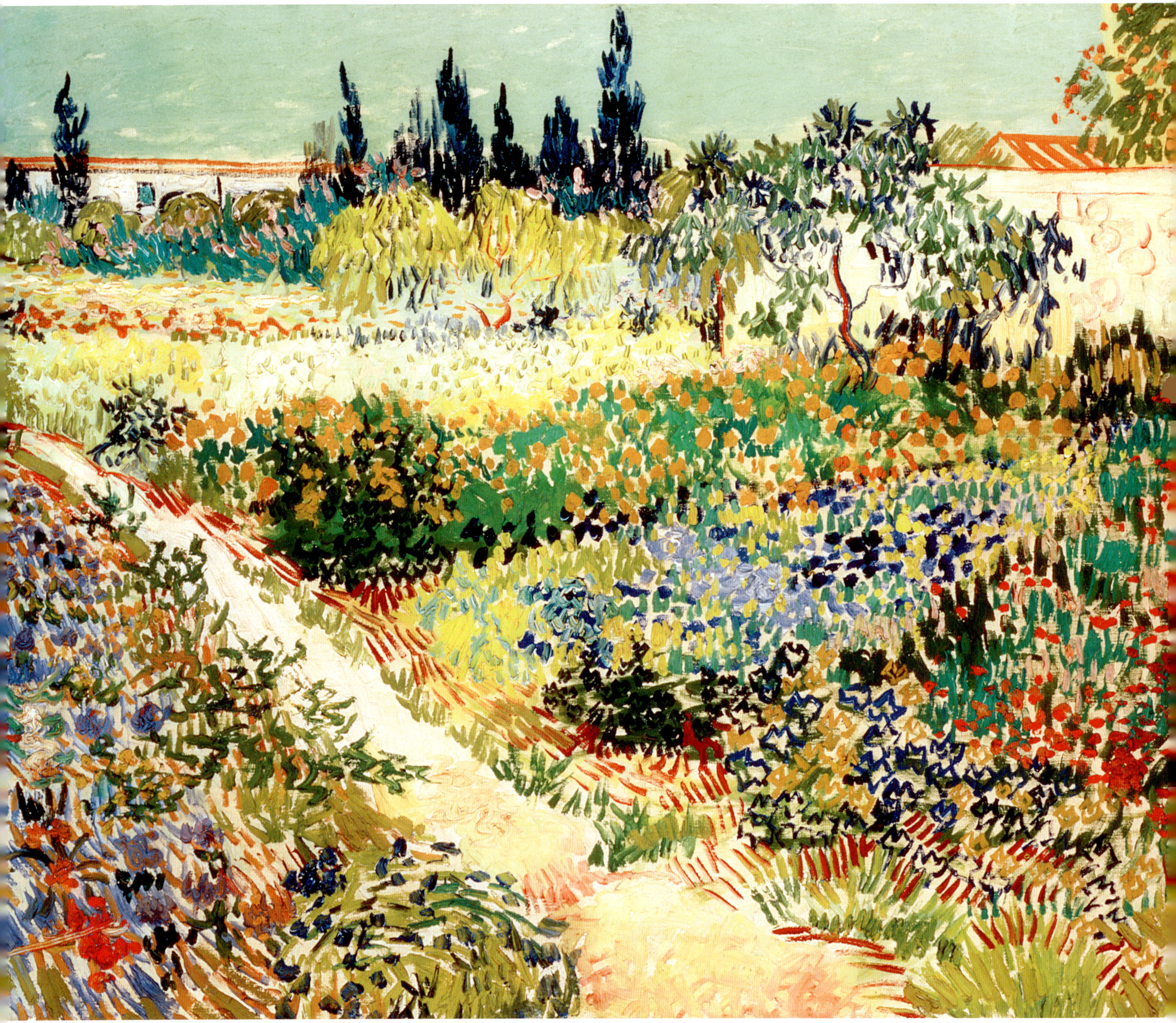
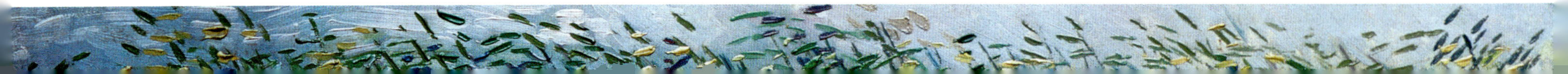

The Garden at Arles, 1888
MEDIUM: Oil on canvas
Courtesy of Haags Gemeentemuseum, The Hague, Netherlands/The Bridgeman Art Library

Wheatfield with Lark, 1887
MEDIUM: Oil on canvas
Courtesy of Van Gogh Museum, Amsterdam, The Netherlands/The Bridgeman Art Library

From Vincent van Gogh to
Willemina van Gogh
Extract from
Arles, *31 July 1888*

Dear Sister,

"I will answer your letter of this morning without delay.

[…] I am working very hard now, and I think the summer here extremely beautiful, more beautiful than I ever saw it in the North, but people here are complaining loudly that it is not the same as usual. Now and then some rain in the morning or the afternoon, but infinitely less than in our country. The harvest was gathered long ago. […]

I have a study of a garden one metre wide, poppies and other red flowers surrounded by green in the foreground, and a square of bluebells. Then a bed of orange and yellow Africans, then white and yellow flowers, and at last, in the background, pink and lilac, and also dark violet scabriosas, and red geraniums, and sunflowers, and a fig tree and an oleander and a vine. And in the distance black cypresses against low white houses with orange roofs – and a delicate green-blue streak of sky."

Vincent's subjects during this time ranged from blooming gardens to bustling nightlife. During his stay in Paris he had frequented the Montmartre bars and brothels with his friend Toulouse-Lautrec (1864–1901). The indoor nightlife, from dancers in step to lone absinthe drinkers, captured the diverse spirit of Paris at night. Vincent looked for indoor night scenes in Arles, the gaslight giving a bright, artificial colour to interiors. Vincent chose a bar he frequented, the Café de la Gare, at 30 Place Lamartine, managed by Joseph-Michel Ginoux and his wife Marie. He created two versions of its interior: *The Night Café* in oils and *The Night Café in Arles* in watercolour. Both highlight the late-night lone drinkers at tables, with which he wanted to express 'the terrible passions of human nature', perhaps a reference to his own drink problem. Work began in July 1888. He told Theo of his plan: 'Today I am probably going to start on the interior of the café where I eat, by gaslight, in the evening. It is what they call here a "cafe de nuit" […] Night prowlers can take refuge there when they have no money to pay for a lodging…'.

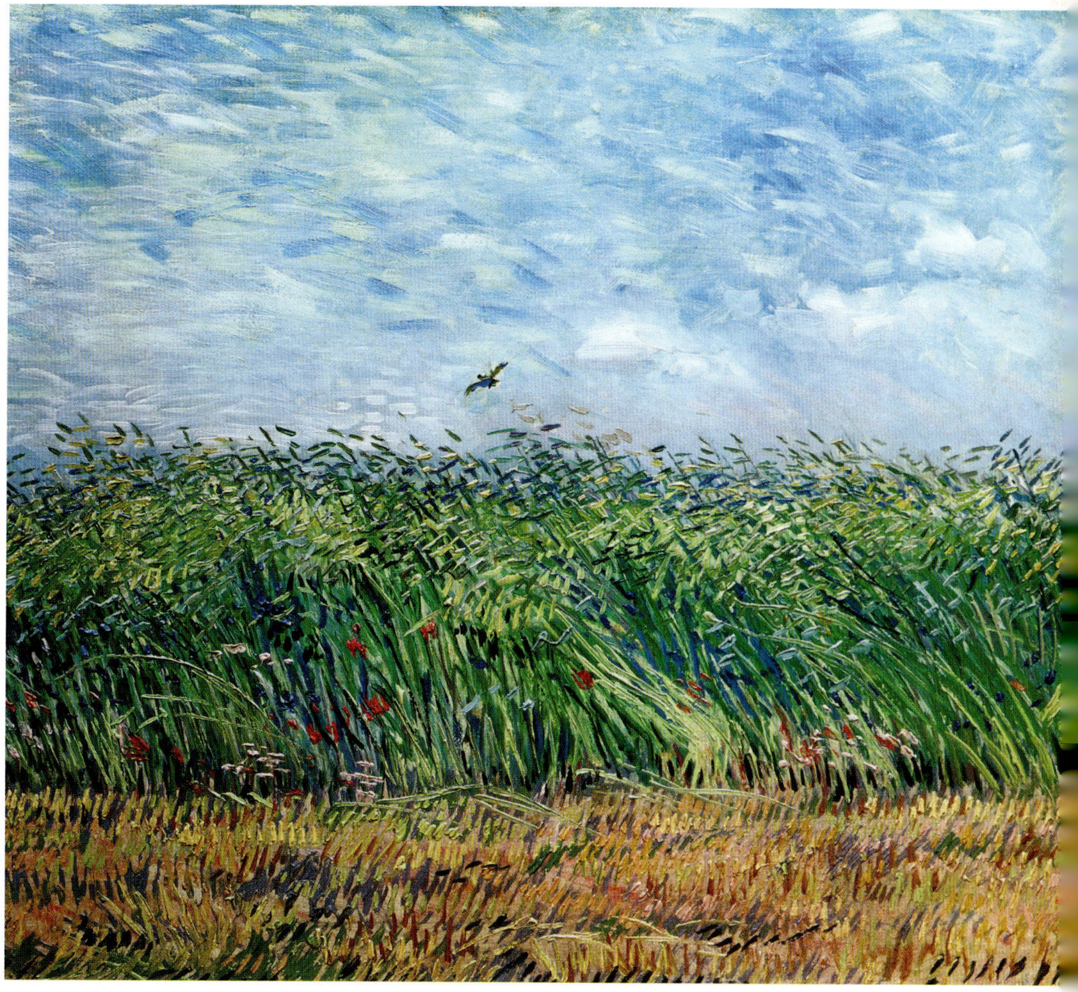

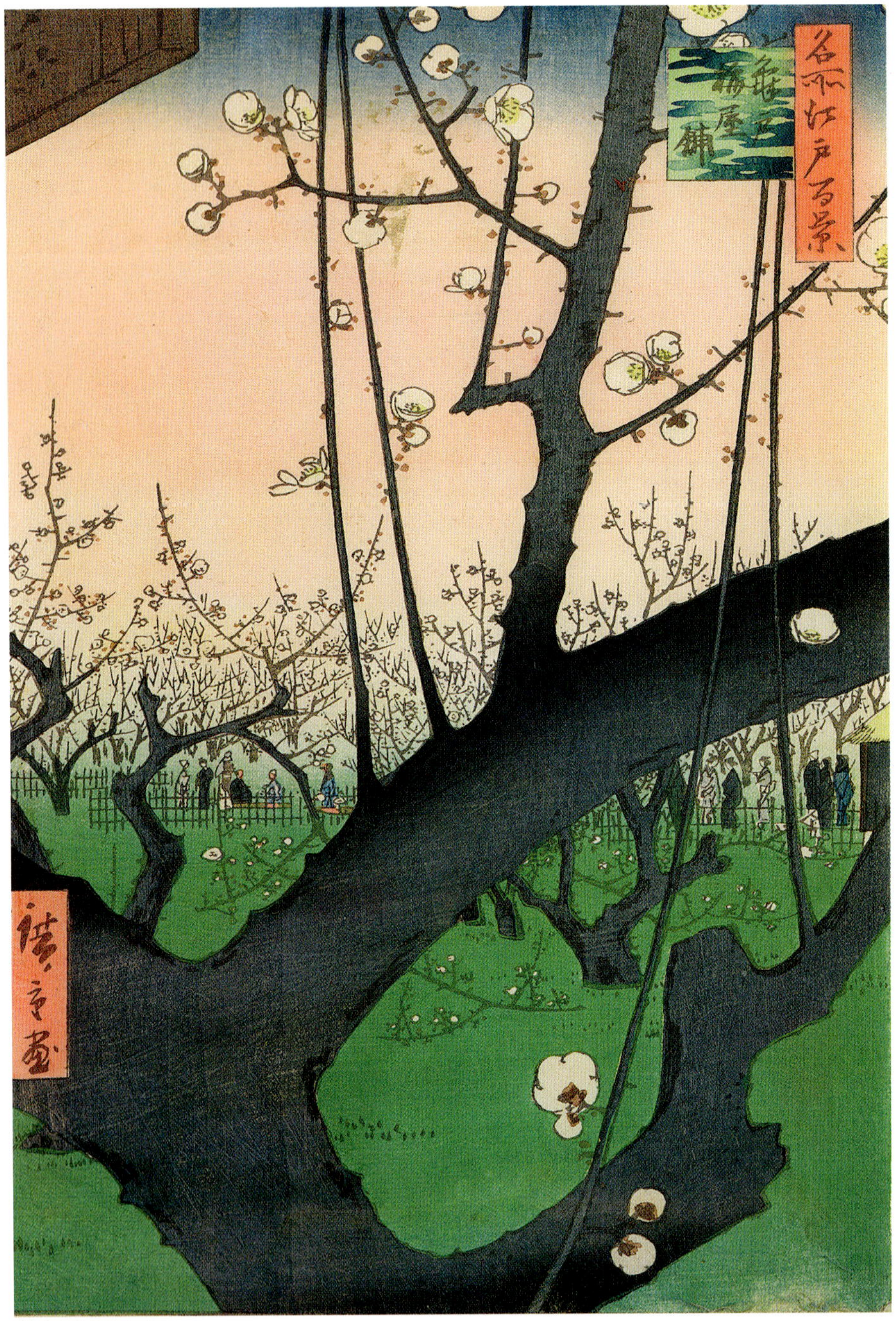

Plum Estate, Kameido, 1856–58
by Utagawa Hiroshige (1797–1858)
MEDIUM: Colour woodblock print
Courtesy of Galerie Janette Ostier, Paris, France/Giraudon/The Bridgeman Art Library

***The Green Vineyard,* 1888, (detail)**
MEDIUM: Oil on canvas
© akg-images

Vincent van Gogh to
Theo van Gogh
Extract from
Arles, *24 September 1888*

My dear Theo,

"[…] This winter I intend to do a lot of drawing. If only I could draw figures from memory, I should always have something to do. But if you take a figure by the most skilful of all the artists who sketch from life – Hokusai, or Daumier – in my opinion that figure will never compare to a figure painted from the model by those same masters or other master portrait painters. […]

I have arranged all the Japanese prints in the studio, and the Daumiers, and the Delacroixs and the Géricaults. If you come across Delacroix's 'Pieta' again, or the Géricault, I urge you to get as many of them as you can. […]

But whatever they say, the most ordinary Japanese prints, coloured in flat tones, seem admirable to me for the same reason as Rubens and Veronese. I know perfectly well that they are not primitive art. But just because the primitives are so admirable, there is absolutely no reason for me to say, as is becoming the custom, 'When I go to the Louvre, I cannot get beyond the primitives.' […]

And one cannot study Japanese art, it seems to me, without becoming merrier and happier, and we should turn back to nature in spite of our education and our work in a conventional world. […]

I envy the Japanese the extreme clarity of everything in their work. It is never dull and it never seems to be done in too much of a hurry. Their work is as simple as breathing, and they do a figure in a few sure strokes as if it were as easy as doing up your waistcoat."

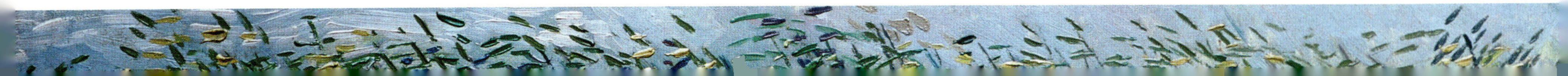

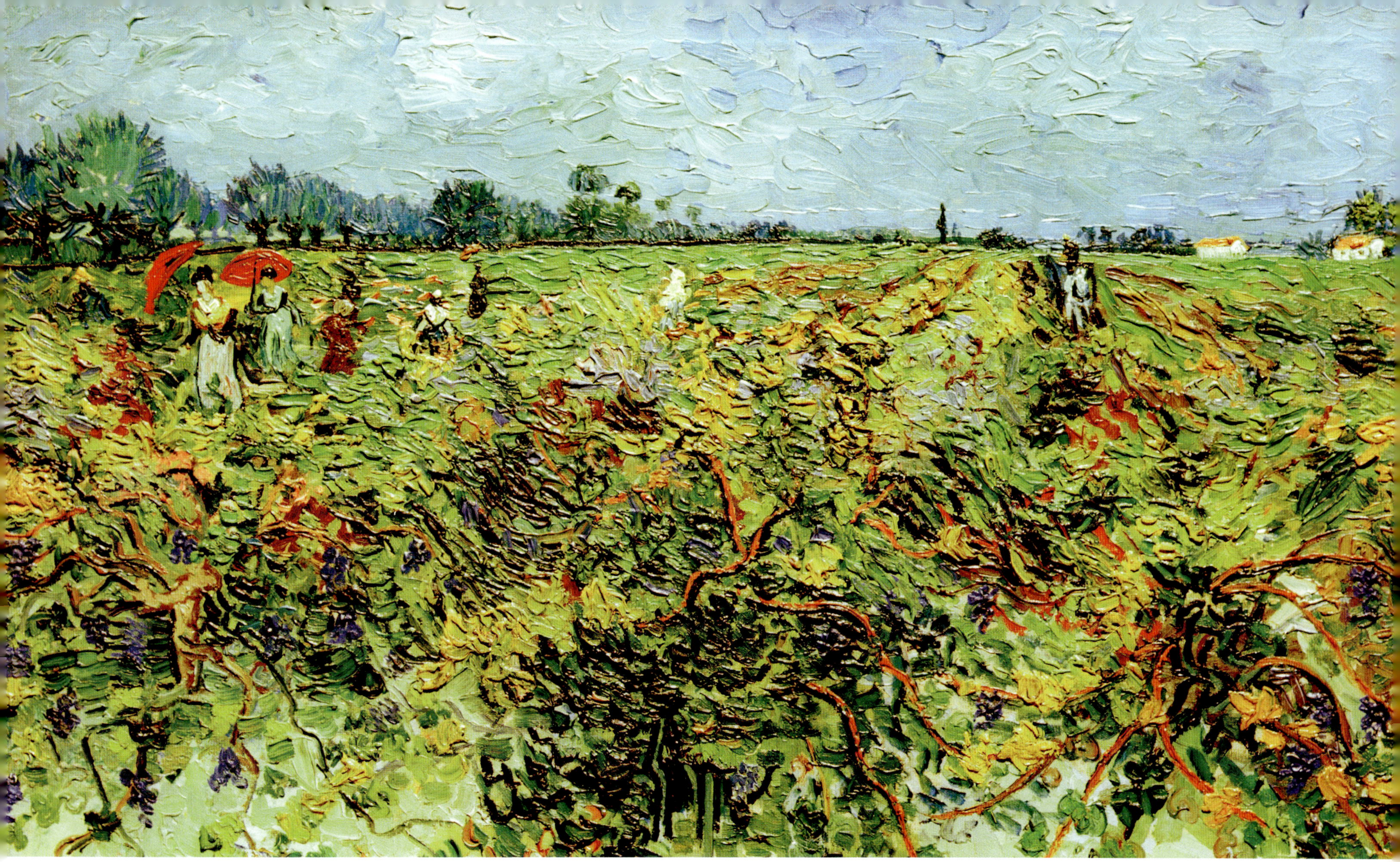

From Vincent van Gogh to

Paul Gauguin

Extract from Arles, 3 October 1888

My dear Gauguin,

"I must tell you that even while working I think continually about the plan of setting up a studio in which you and I will be permanent residents, but which both of us want to turn into a shelter and refuge for friends, against the times when they find that the struggle is getting too much for them.

[...] when I left Paris I was in a sorry state, quite ill and almost an alcoholic after driving myself on even while my strength was failing me – and then withdrawing into myself, still bereft of hope!

I am having an extraordinary spell of feverish activity these days. Right now I am tackling a landscape with a blue sky above an immense green, purple and yellow vineyard, with black and orange vines. Little figures of ladies with red parasols and little figures of grape pickers with their small cart make it even gayer. Grey sand in the foreground. Another size 30 square canvas to decorate the house.

I consider my views of art excessively ordinary compared with yours.

I have always had the coarse tastes of an animal.

[…] I feel sure that if from now on you were to consider yourself head of this studio, which we shall try to ensure will become a refuge for many – little by little, as our unremitting labour provides us with the means of completing it – I'm sure that you would then feel more or less consoled for the present ordeals of penury and ill-health, seeing that we shall probably be devoting our lives to a generation of painters that will last a long while to come. […]

I have made a special decoration, the Poet's garden, for the room you will have. The ordinary public garden contains plants and shrubs that conjure up landscapes in which one can readily imagine Botticelli, Giotto, Petrarch, Dante and Boccaccio. I have tried to distil in the decoration the essence of what constitutes the immutable character of this country.

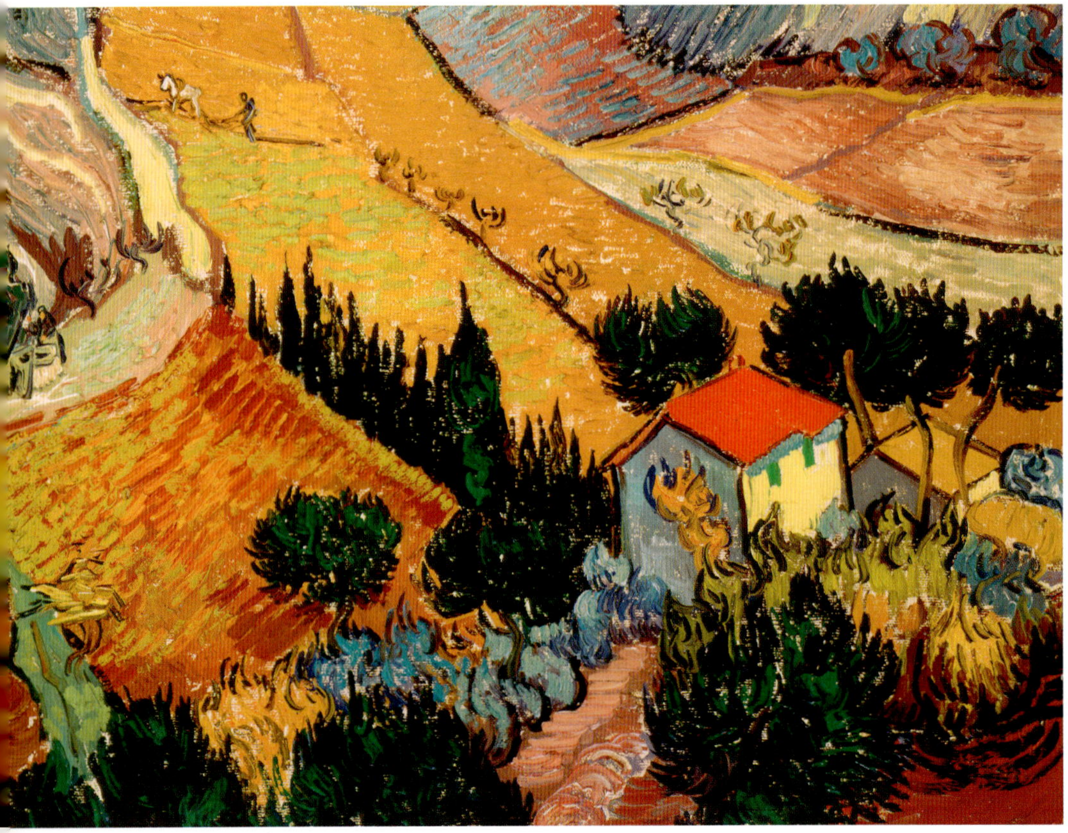

***Landscape with House and Ploughman*, 1889**
MEDIUM: Oil on canvas
Courtesy of Hermitage, St. Petersburg, Russia/The Bridgeman Art Library

***The Bedroom*, 1888**
MEDIUM: Oil on canvas
Courtesy of Van Gogh Museum, Amsterdam, The Netherlands/ The Bridgeman Art Library

And I set out to paint that garden in such a way that one is put in mind of the old poet from these parts (or rather from Avignon), Petrarch, and of the new poet from these parts – Paul Gauguin.

However clumsy this attempt may be, it may show you perhaps that I have been thinking of you with very great emotion as I prepared your studio.

Let's be of good heart about the success of our venture, and please keep thinking of this as your home, for I feel very sure that all this will last for a very long time. "

His letter to Paul Gauguin is full of the expectation and rising happiness Vincent feels at the possibility of Gauguin coming to stay in Arles. Vincent has painted and decorated and bought furniture to brighten, lighten and furnish the Yellow House and Gauguin's studio.

Vincent van Gogh to
Theo van Gogh
Extract from
Arles, 16 October 1888

My dear Theo,

" At last I can send you a little sketch […] This time it's just simply my bedroom, only here colour is to do everything, and

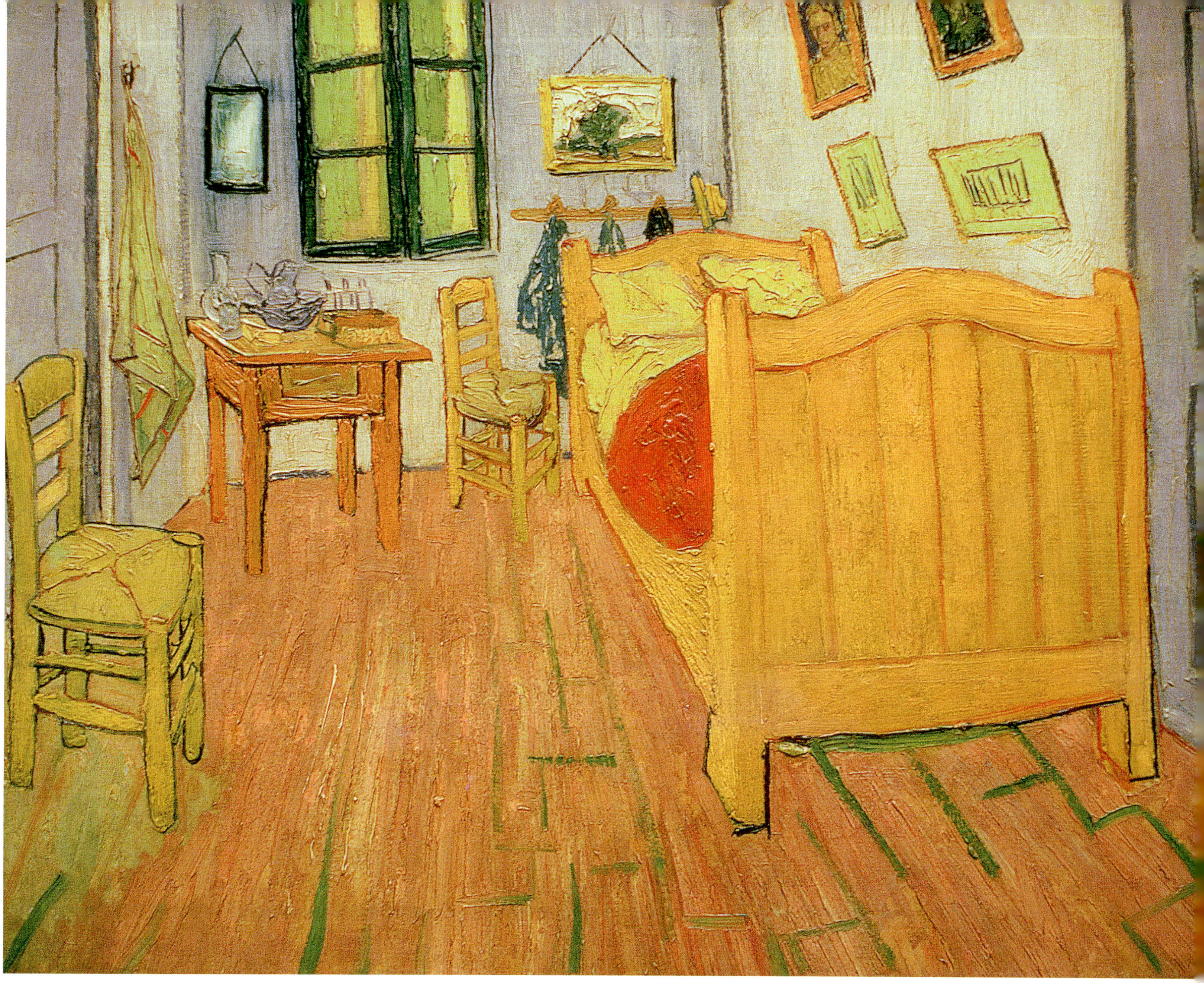

giving by its simplification a grander style to things, is to be suggestive here of *rest* or of sleep in general. In a word, looking at the picture ought to rest the brain, or rather the imagination.

The walls are pale violet. The floor is of red tiles.

The wood of the bed and chairs is the yellow of fresh butter, the sheets and pillows very light greenish-citron.

The coverlet scarlet. The window green.

The toilet table orange, the basin blue.

The doors lilac.

And that is all – there is nothing in this room with its closed shutters.

The squareness of the furniture again must express inviolable rest. Portraits on the walls, and a mirror and a towel and some clothes.

The frame – as there is no white in the picture – will be white.

This by way of revenge for the enforced rest I was obliged to take. I shall work on it again all day, but you see how simple the conception is. The shadows and the cast shadows are suppressed; it is painted in free flat tints like the Japanese prints. It is going to be a contrast to, for instance, the Tarascon diligence and the night café.

In this letter Vincent describes his painting in oils, *The Bedroom*, 1888.

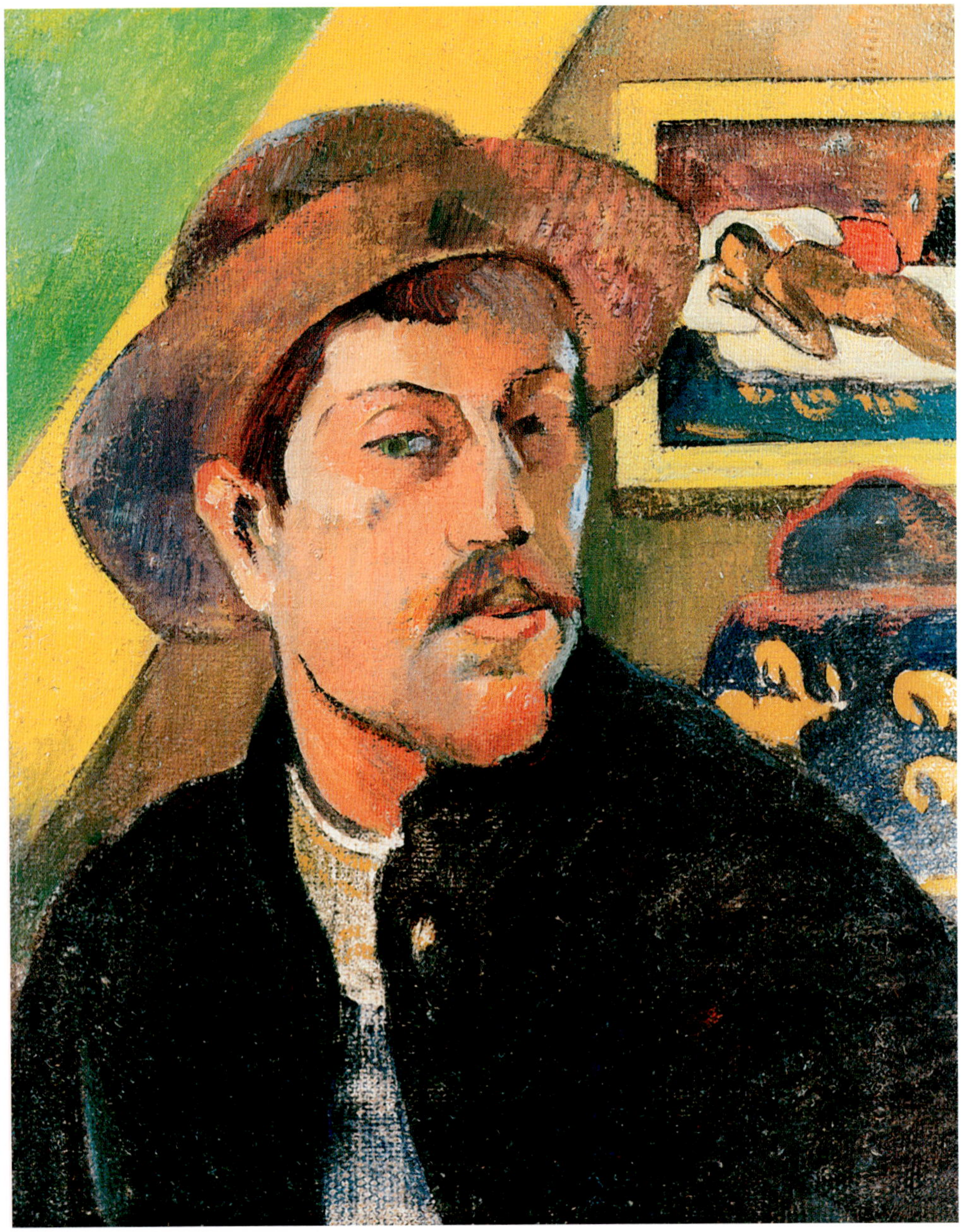

Extract from Arles, 24 October 1888

[…] As you learned from my wire, Gauguin has arrived in good health. He gives me the impression he is even better than me. […]

I cannot help it that my pictures do not sell.

The day will come when people will see that they are worth more than the price of the paint and my own living, very meager after all, that is put into them.

[…] to a large extent we are going to use cheaper colours, Gauguin as well as I. And in the same way we are going to prepare the canvas ourselves. For a while I had a feeling that I was going to be ill, but Gauguin's arrival has so taken my mind off it that I'm sure it will pass. I must not neglect my food for a time, and that is all, absolutely all there is to it.

And after a time you will have some work again.

***Self Portrait in a Hat*, 1893–94**
by Paul Gauguin (1848–1903)
MEDIUM: Oil on canvas
Courtesy of Musée d'Orsay, Paris, France/Giraudon/The Bridgeman Art Library

***The Night Café in Arles*, 1888**
MEDIUM: Watercolour on paper
Courtesy of Professor Hans R. Hahnloser Collection, Bern, Switzerland/The Bridgeman Art Library

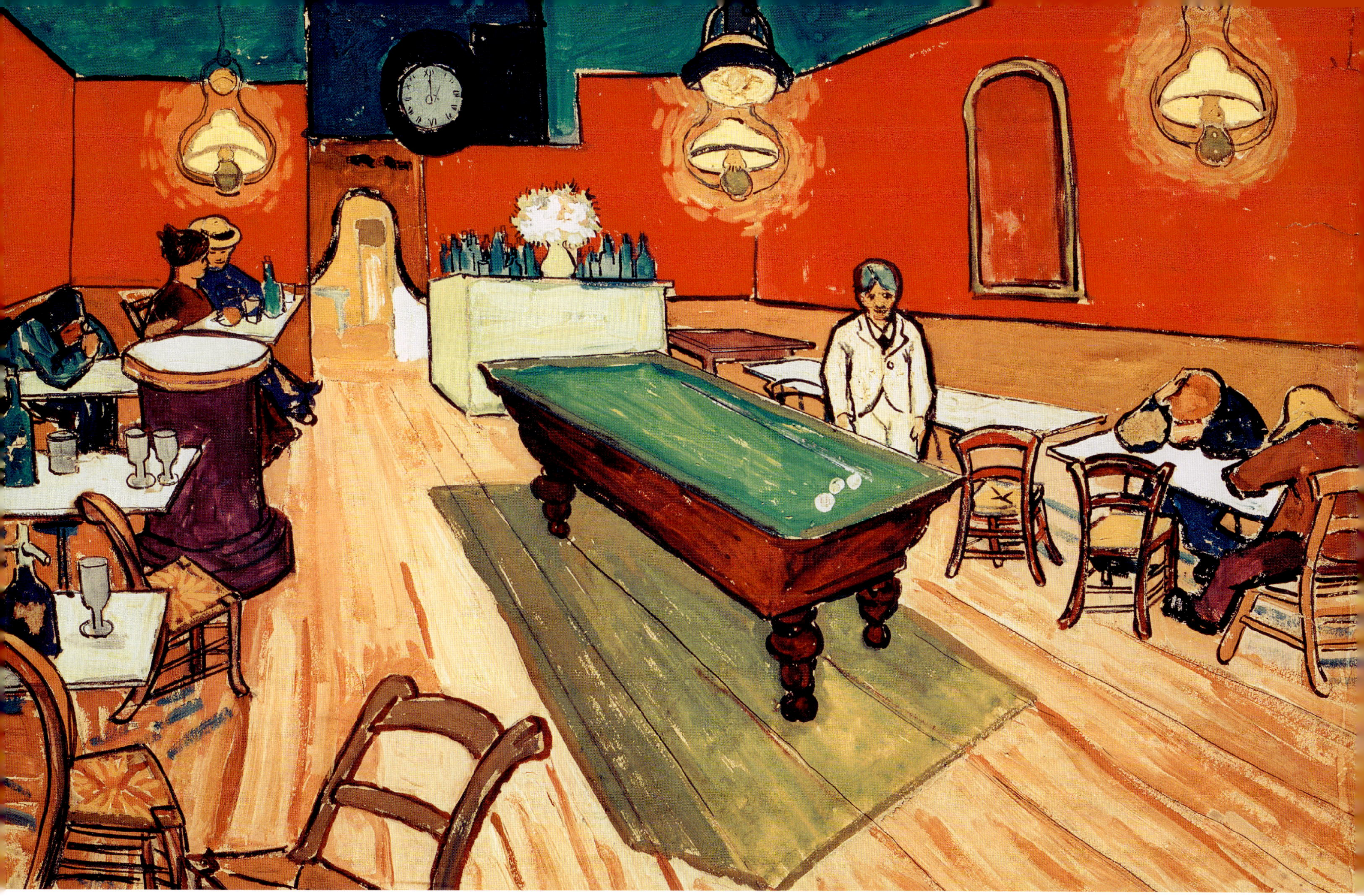

Gauguin brought a magnificent canvas, which he has exchanged with Bernard, Breton women in a green field, white, black, green, and a note of red, and the dull flesh tints. After all, we must all be of good cheer.

I believe that the time will come when I too shall sell, but I am so far behind with you, and while I go on spending, I bring nothing in. Sometimes the thought of it saddens me. ”

After months of persuasion, Paul Gauguin arrived in Arles on 23 October 1888. From his letters it is obvious that Vincent worked hard to make Gauguin as happy and comfortable as possible, but he remained nervous: 'I do not yet know what Gauguin thinks of my decorations [...] there are some studies which I know he really likes, like the sower, the sunflowers and the bedroom'. They visited the fields of La Crau (east of Arles), where Vincent created two paintings in oils *The Sower*, 1888 and *The Old Yew*, 1888. Gauguin was ready to sample the local attractions: 'He [Gauguin] and I intend to make a tour of the brothels pretty often, so as to study them'. Vincent also wanted to paint outdoor night scenes and set up his equipment in the Place du Forum. There he painted *Café Terrace, Place du Forum*, 1888 using vibrant yellow, a favourite colour, to depict the artificial

brightness of the gaslight that illuminated the outdoor tables and cobbled street. In the night sky, painted in soft blue scattered with large, twinkling stars, he captured what those who lived in the south of France knew – that the night sky when clear was never truly dark. He revisited the night sky in later paintings, such as *The Starry Night*, 1889. Having no first-hand knowledge of night painting, Vincent set to work wearing a hat with lighted candles. His odd work-wear added to the eccentricity of his character, already noted by the locals. In a letter he described his painting: 'On the terrace there are little figures of people drinking. A huge yellow lantern lights the terrace, the facade, the pavement, and even projects light over the cobblestones [...] The gables of the houses [...] are dark blue or violet. Now there's a painting of night without black. [...] and in these surroundings the lighted square is coloured pale sulphur, lemon green.'

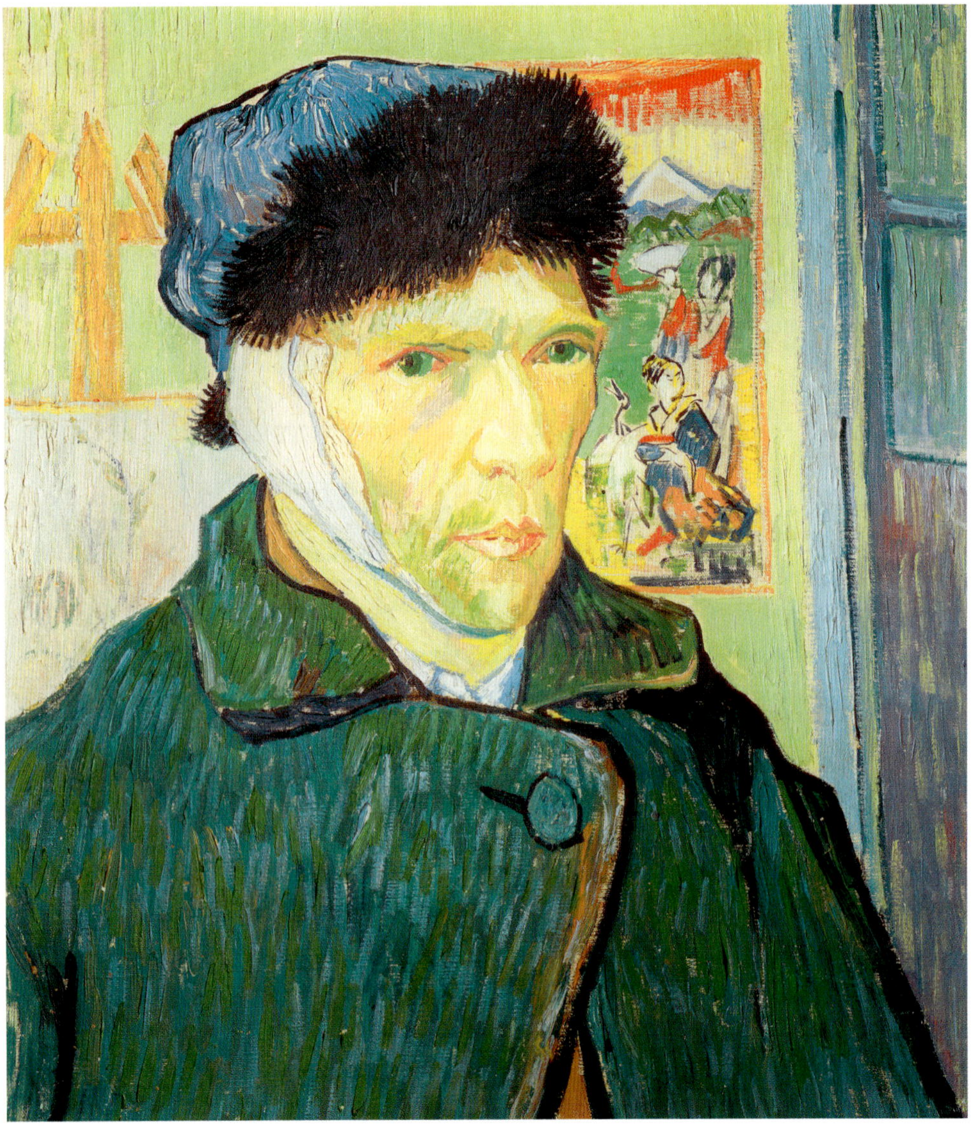

Extract from Arles, *23 December 1888*

[...] I think myself that Gauguin was a little out of sorts with the good town of Arles, the little yellow house where we work, and especially with me.

As a matter of fact there are bound to be for him as for me further grave difficulties to overcome here.

But these difficulties are rather within ourselves than outside.

Altogether I think that either he will definitely go, or else definitely stay.

Before doing anything I told him to think it over and reckon things up again.

Gauguin is very powerful, strongly creative, but just because of that he must have peace.

Will he find it anywhere if he does not find it here?

I am waiting for him to make a decision with absolute serenity.

***Self Portrait with Bandaged Ear*, 1889**
MEDIUM: Oil on canvas
© Samuel Courtauld Trust, The Courtauld Gallery, London, UK/ The Bridgeman Art Library

***The Starry Night*, over the Rhône 1888**
MEDIUM: Oil on canvas
Courtesy of Musée d'Orsay, Paris, France/Giraudon/The Bridgeman Art Library

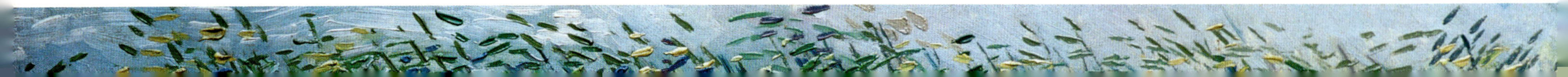

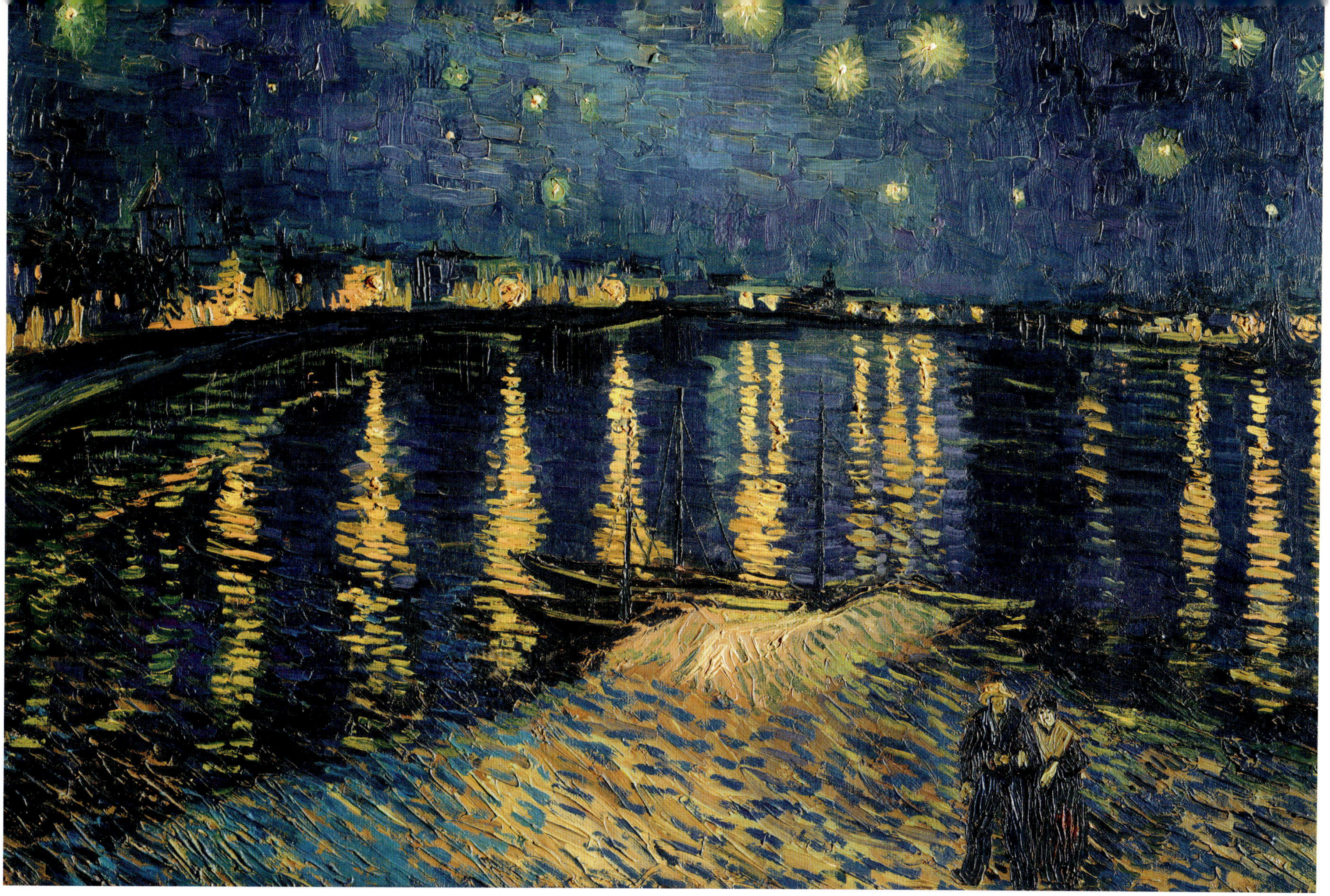

The collaboration of two volatile artists used to speaking their minds and not used to working and living together was bound to be a delicate situation. Vincent knew that he was taking a gamble when he invited his friend. After living together for nearly nine weeks and in spite of Vincent's efforts to make Gauguin welcome, their temperaments eventually led to several disagreements on many topics, from Ingres paintings to Gauguin's impression of Arles as 'the dirtiest hole in the South', an opinion completely at odds with Vincent's. Gauguin had written to Theo to say that he could not continue to live with Vincent, 'because of incompatibility of temper'. It was at this time that Vincent painted *Paul Gauguin (Man in the Red Beret)*, 1888. In his letter Vincent acknowledges, 'I think myself that Gauguin was a little out of sorts with the good town of Arles, the little yellow house where we work, and especially with me', but does not give any indication of the deterioration of his own mental state. The same evening he approached Gauguin from behind with a razor. Gauguin left the house but the next day, 24 December, he sent a telegram to Theo asking him to travel immediately to Arles. Before Theo could reach him, Vincent had cut off part of his left earlobe with the razor and taken it to a brothel to present to a woman there. A violent scene ensued. With the aid of the postman, Monsieur Roulin, Vincent returned home where the police found him unconscious. He was taken to the Hôtel-Dieu hospital, and placed under the care of Dr Félix Ray (1867–1932). Theo visited him in hospital, describing his brother as 'a poor fighter and a poor, poor sufferer'. Theo and Vincent spent Christmas together in Arles. During January and February 1889, Vincent created some of his most famous paintings.

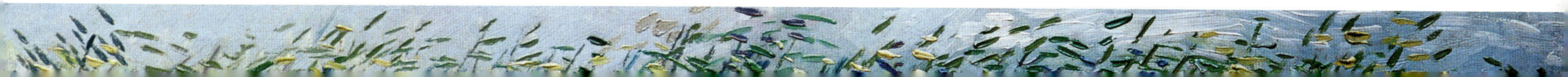

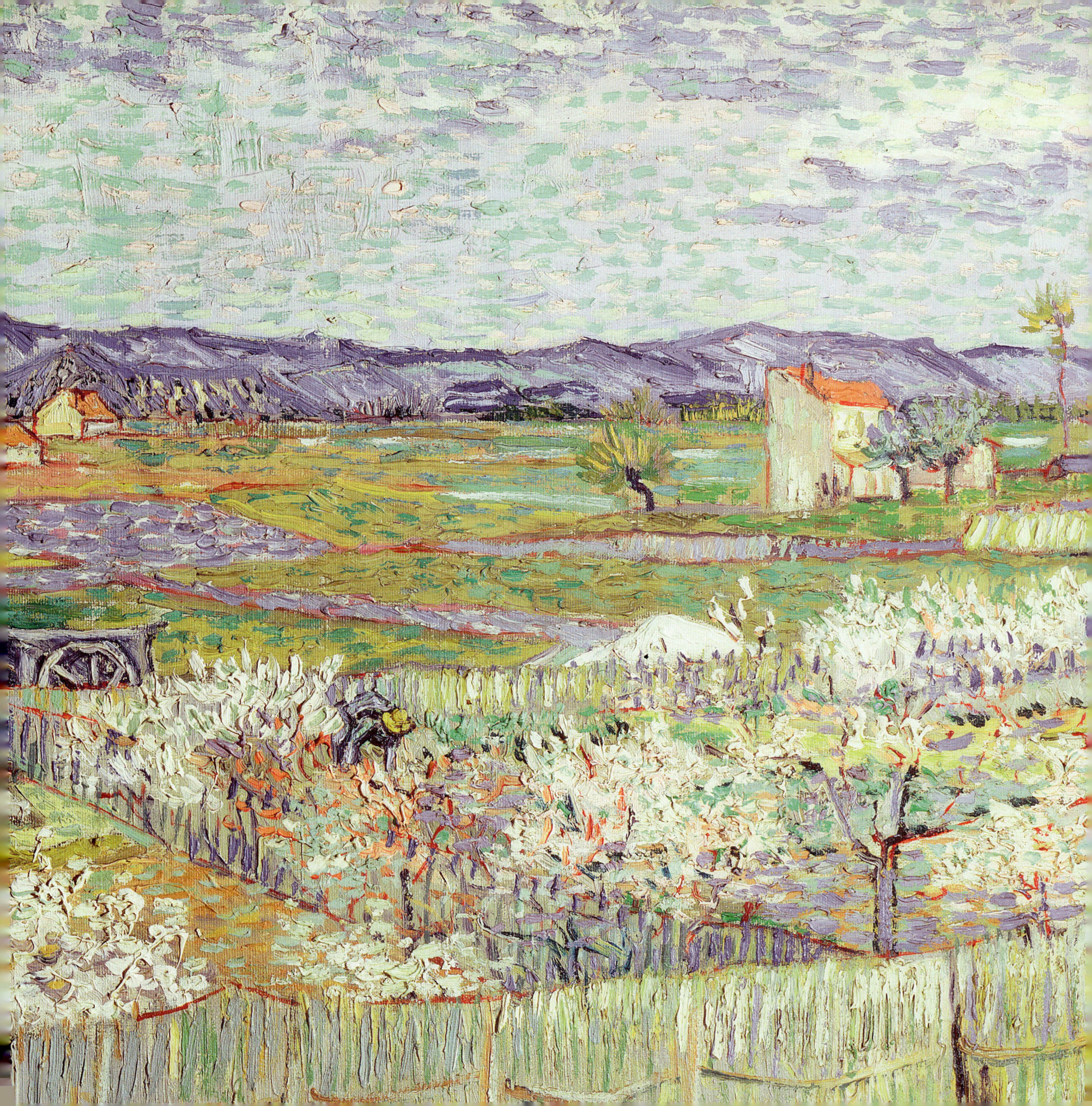

Vincent van Gogh: A Life in Letters & Art

1889–90

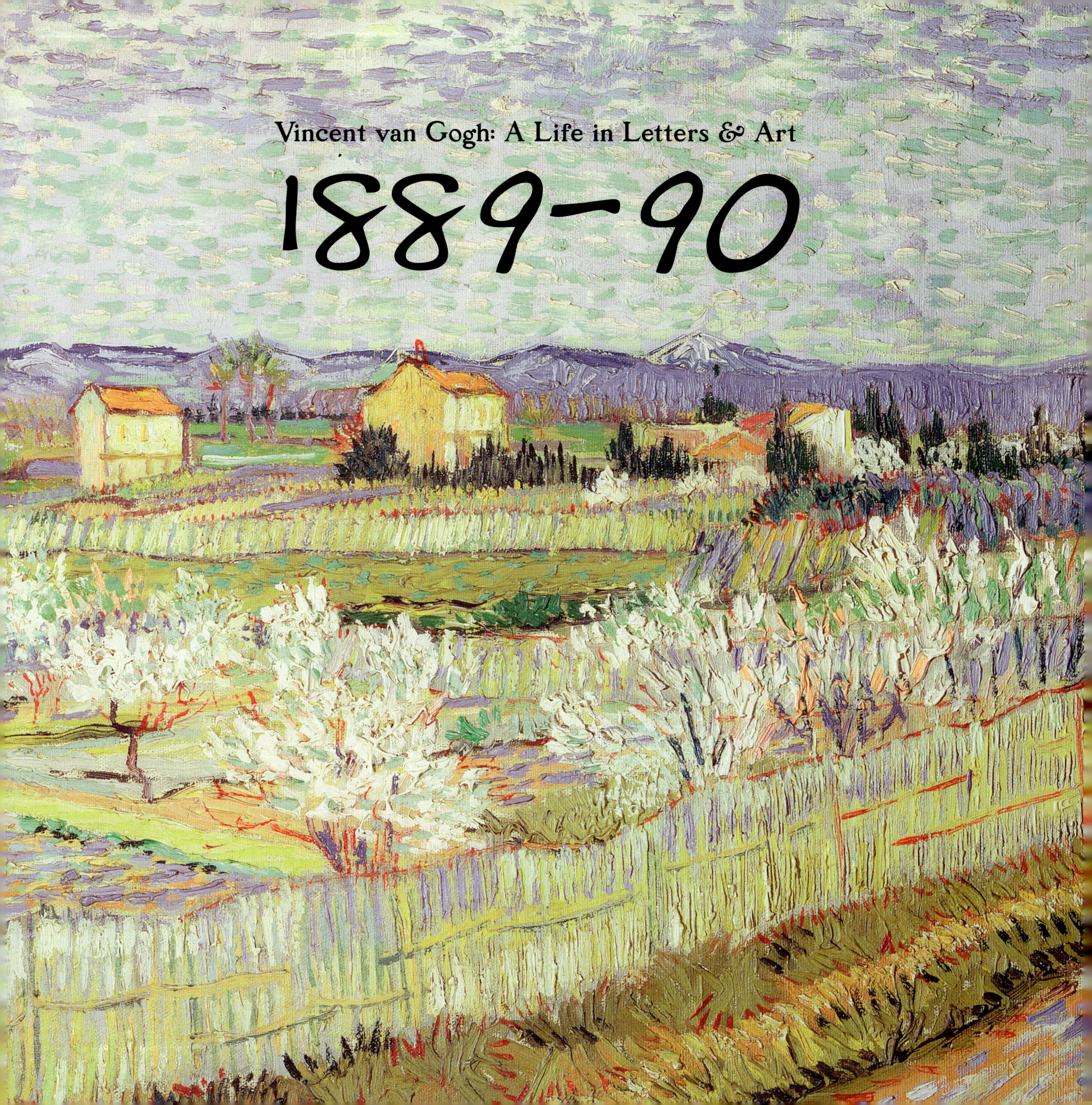

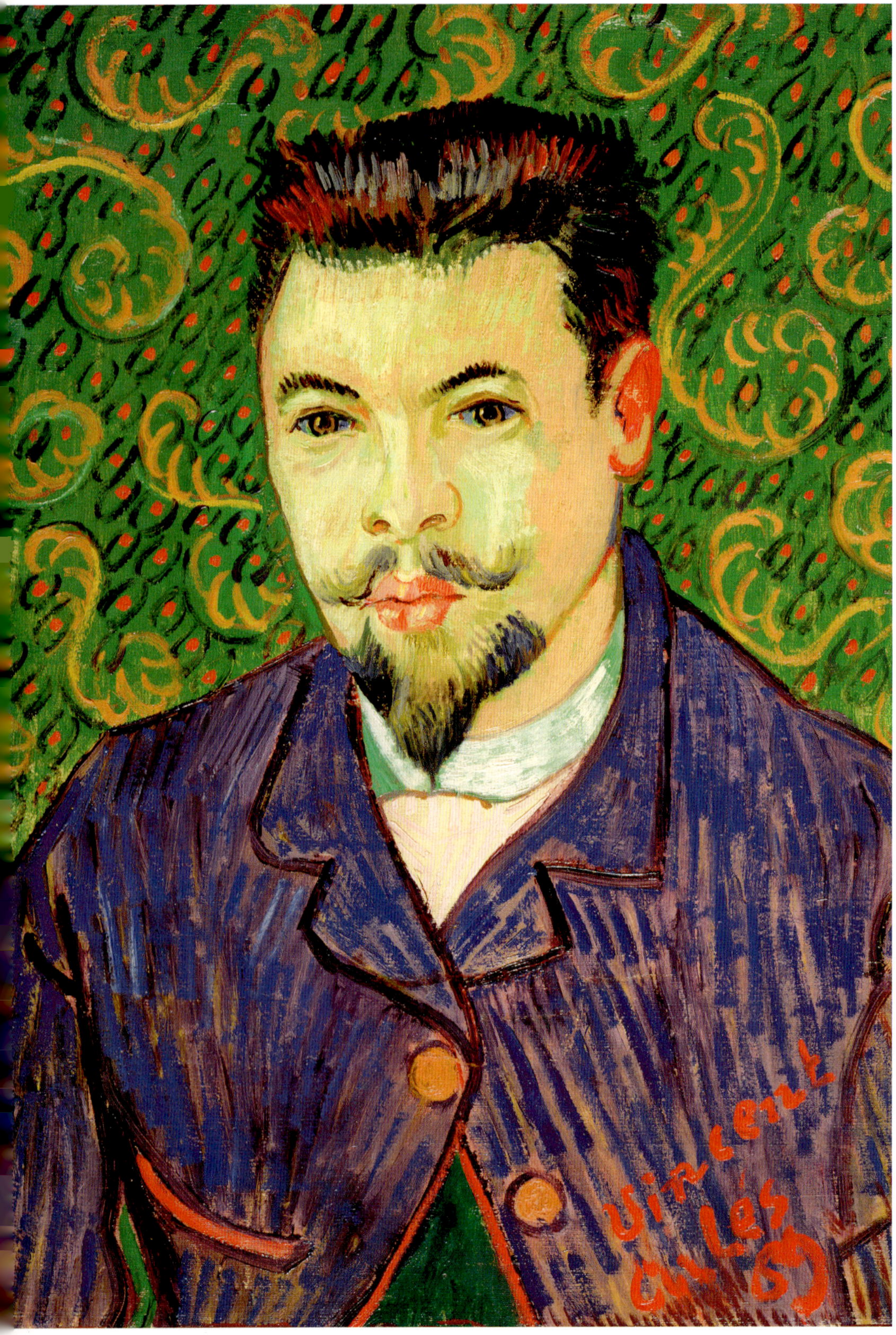

From Vincent van Gogh to
Theo van Gogh
Extract from
Arles, *9 January 1889*

My dear Theo,

"Even before receiving (this very moment) your kind letter, I had had a letter this morning from your fiancée announcing the engagement. So I have already sent her my sincere congratulations in reply, and herewith I repeat them to you.

[…] What you tell me about Gauguin gives me tremendous pleasure, that is to say that he has not given up his project of returning to the tropics. That is the right road for him. I think I see light in his plan, and I approve of it heartily. Naturally I regret it, but you understand that provided all goes well with him, that is all I want.

[…] I have had to pay quite a number of things on leaving the hospital, and though I am in no sort of a hurry for several days, it would be nice if you could send me 50 francs or so within the next few days.

I think the mistake in old Gauguin's calculations was that he is rather too much in the habit of ignoring the inevitable expenses of house rent, charwoman, and a lot of worldly things of the kind. Now all those things are weighing more on *our* shoulders, but once we have accepted them, other artists could stay with me without having those expenses.

***Portrait of Dr Félix Rey*, 1889**
MEDIUM: Oil on canvas
Courtesy of Pushkin Museum, Moscow, Russia/The Bridgeman Art Library

***Entrance to the Public Gardens in Arles*, 1888, (detail)**
MEDIUM: Oil on canvas
Courtesy of Phillips Collection, Washington DC, USA/The Bridgeman Art Library

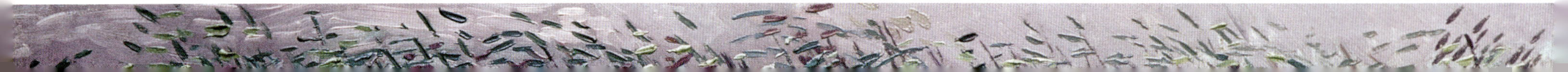

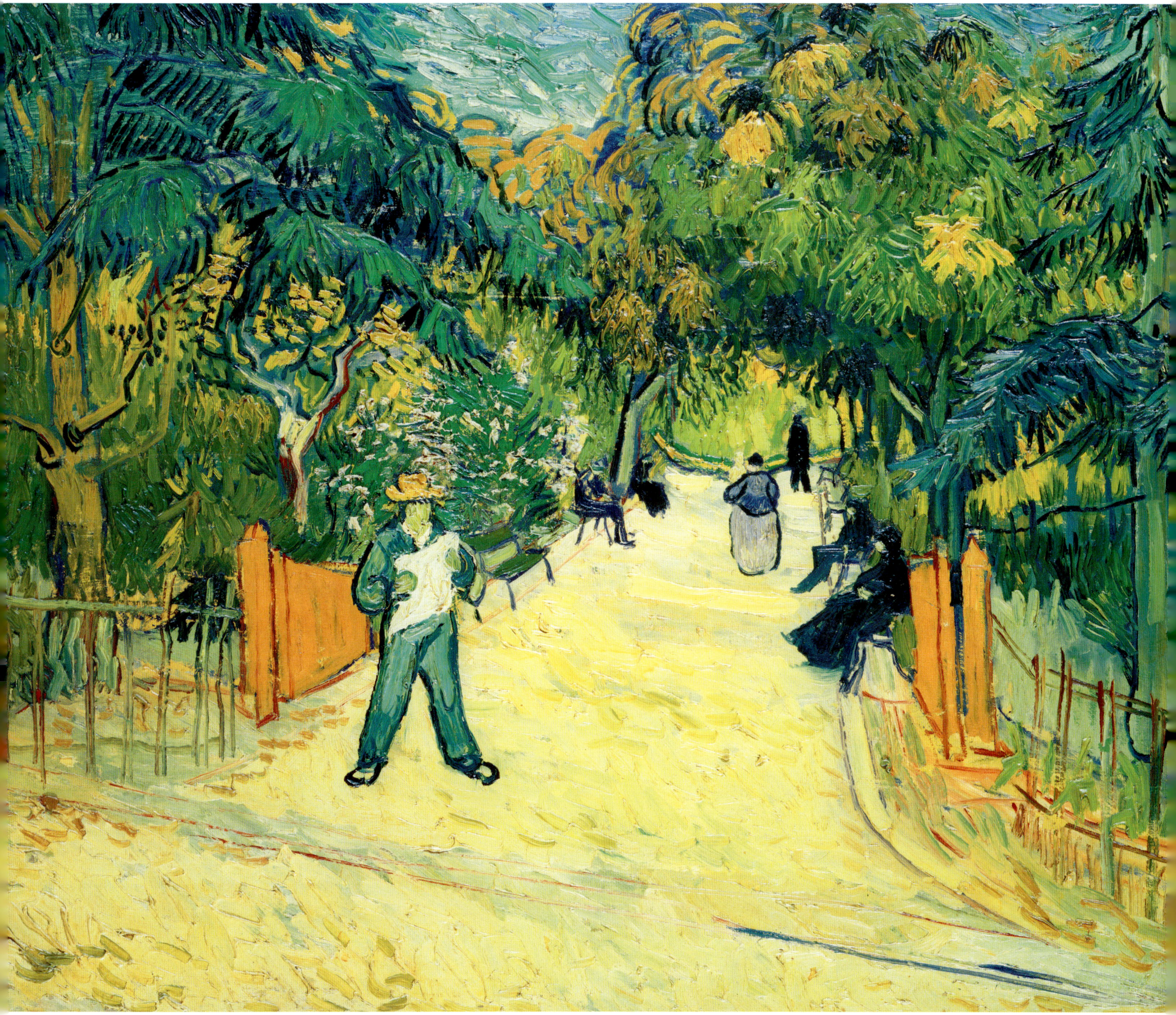
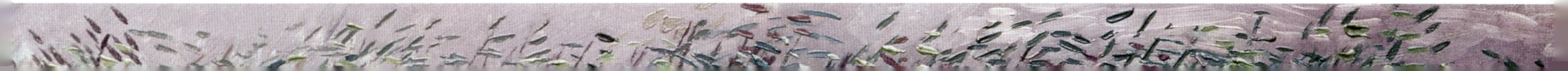

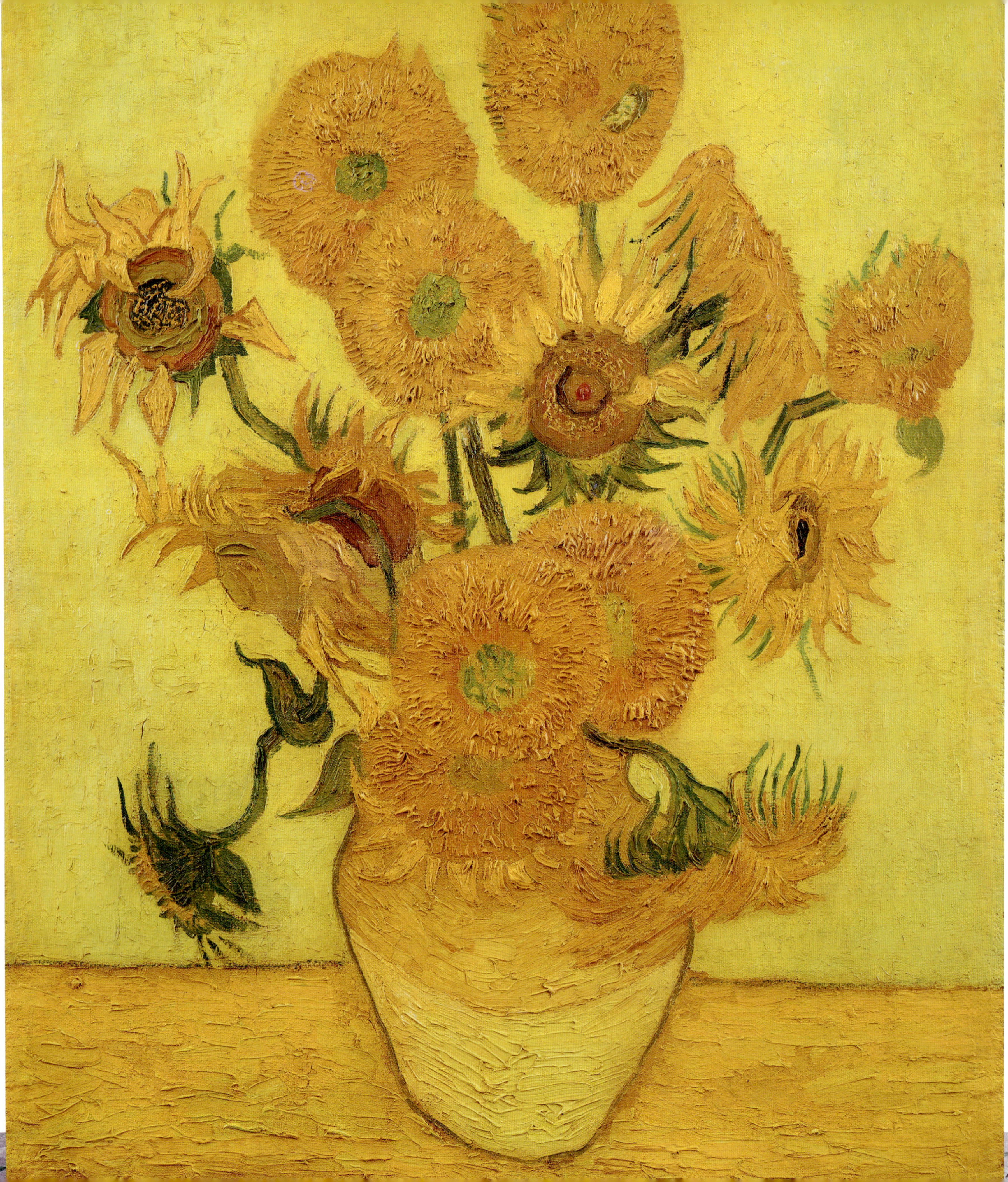

***Sunflowers in a Vase*, 1889**
MEDIUM: Oil on canvas
Courtesy of Private Collection/Photo © Christie's Images/The Bridgeman Art Library

***White House at Night*, 1890**
MEDIUM: Oil on canvas
Courtesy of Hermitage, St. Petersburg, Russia/The Bridgeman Art Library

They have just told me that during my absence the owner of my house here made an arrangement with a fellow who has a tobacco shop to turn me out and give this tobacconist the house.

This has rather upset me, for […] it was I who had it repainted inside and out, and had gas put in, etc. – in fact, who had made habitable a house which had been shut up and uninhabited for a considerable time, and which I took in a very poor condition. […]

Physically I am well, the wound is healing very well and the great loss of blood is being made up, because I eat and digest well. […]

Have you seen the portrait of me which Gauguin has, and have you seen the portrait which Gauguin did of himself during those last few days? If you compare the self-portrait Gauguin did then with the one that I still have of him, which he sent me from Brittany in exchange for mine, you will see that on the whole he himself got rested here.

[…] With a handshake, and of course you know how I wish you happy days with your fiancée. ”

Ever Yours

Vincent

Vincent had spent a few days in the asylum hospital in Arles following the incident in which he had threatened Paul Gauguin (1828–1909) with a razor before cutting off part of his earlobe and presenting it to a prostitute. He would record his bandaged face in *Self-Portrait with Bandaged Ear*, 1889. Vincent

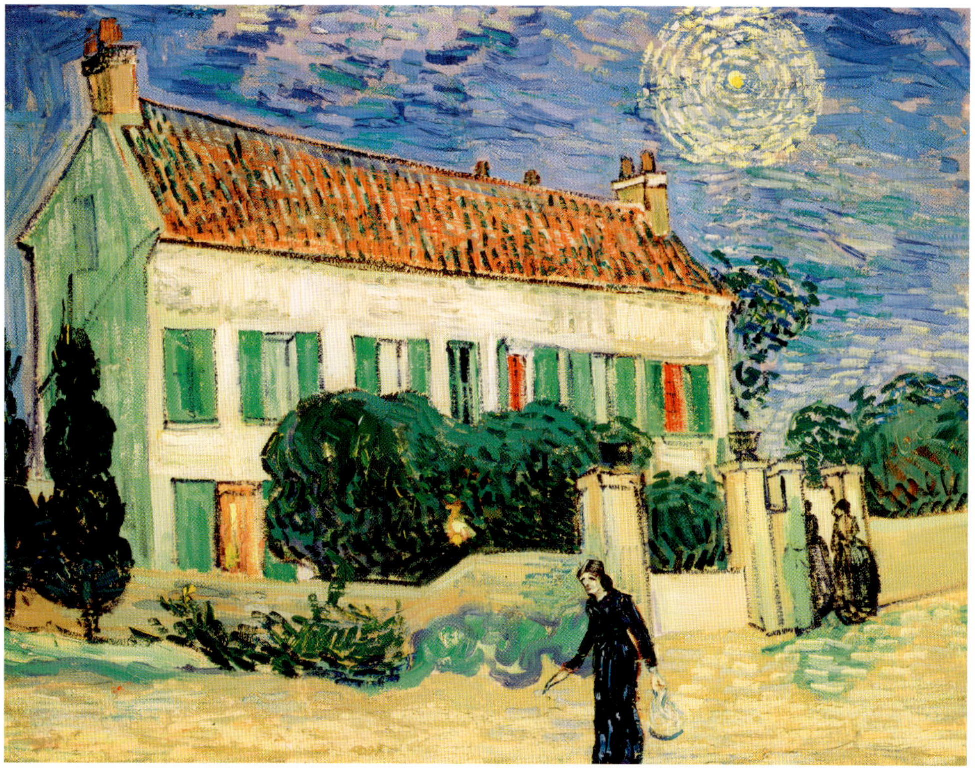

recovered from the wound and was released from hospital, but still some of his neighbours questioned his sanity. They wanted him out of the Yellow House and locked up. Vincent was astonished at local reaction but admitted, when examined by Dr Félix Rey (1865–1932), that he was not in the best of health.

From Vincent van Gogh to
Arnold Koning
Extract from
Arles, *22 or 23 January 1889*

My dear friend Koning,

“ Thanks for having wished me a happy New Year all the way from the North of our native country. I received your postcard in the hospital at Arles, where I had been quartered following

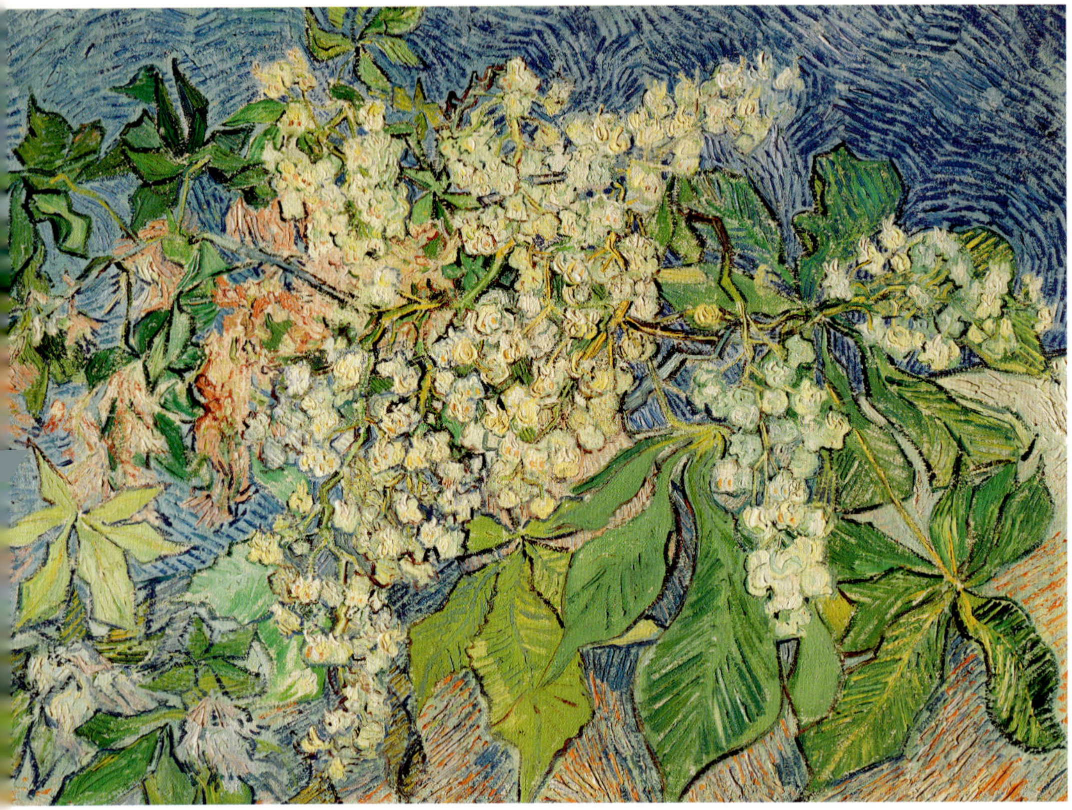

an attack of something the matter with my brains, or otherwise fever, which had nearly passed off already.

[...] At present I have in mind, or rather on my easel, the portrait of a woman. I call it 'La Berceuse' or as we say in Dutch (after van Eeden, you know, who wrote that particular book I gave you to read), or in van Eeden's Dutch, quite simply 'our lullaby or the woman rocking the cradle'. It is a woman in a green dress (the bust olive green and grey skirt pale malachite green).

The hair is quite orange and in plaits. The complexion is chrome yellow, worked up with some naturally broken tones for the purpose of modelling.

The hands holding the rope of the cradle, the same.

At the bottom the background is vermilion (simply representing a tiled floor or else a stone floor). The wall is covered with wallpaper, which of course I have calculated in conformity with the rest of the colours. This wallpaper is bluish-green with pink dahlias and spotted with orange and ultramarine.

In this I think I have run pretty well parallel with van Eeden and his style of writing, which consequently can be considered analogous to my style of painting in the matter of colours.

[...] At any rate, on leaving the hospital, I made a portrait of my own doctor. And I haven't wholly lost my equilibrium as a painter.

But of course, from that time onward I have painted quite a considerable number of studies or pictures. Among other things, last summer, two flower pieces with nothing but sunflowers in a yellow earthen pot. Painted with the three chrome yellows, yellow ochre and malachite green, and nothing else. [...]

Vincent's friend Arnold Hendrik Koning (1860–1945), a fellow artist, had sent him a postcard from Winschoten, Groningen, northern Netherlands, on 31 December 1888. Vincent had recovered sufficiently to start writing letters to friends and to start painting again. He lightly brushes off suggestions that he is mad, and mentions that his brain had suffered an attack (diagnosed as a form of epilepsy by Dr Rey). He discusses his paintings, including two still lifes of sunflowers, both entitled *Sunflowers in a Vase*, painted in 1888 and 1889 respectively. He also mentions his portraits *Félix Ray*, 1889, of his doctor at the asylum, and *La Berceuse*, 1889 of Madame Roulin. In reference to the Dutch writer Frederik Willem van Eeden (1860–1932), Vincent lightly compares Van Eeden's style of writing in *De kleine Johannes* (1887) to his own style of painting.

***Blossoming Chestnut Branches*, 1890, (detail)**
MEDIUM: Oil on canvas
Courtesy of Buhrle Collection, Zurich, Switzerland/The Bridgeman Art Library

***La Berceuse*, 1889, (detail)**
MEDIUM: Oil on canvas
Courtesy of Private Collection/ The Bridgeman Art Library

From Vincent van Gogh to
Theo van Gogh
Extract from
Arles, *3 February 1889*

My dear Theo,

"I should have preferred to reply at once to your kind letter containing the 100 francs, but since at that precise moment I was very tired and the doctor had given me strict instructions to go out for walks and make no mental exertion, I haven't written to you until today. [...]

Here, the so-called worthy town of Arles is such a peculiar sort of place that it is with good reason our friend Gauguin calls it the filthiest spot in the South. [...] Which is just to let you know that as far as I am concerned, I have no illusions about myself. Things are going very, very well, and I'll do everything the doctor says, but [...]

When I came out of hospital with good old Roulin, I fancied there'd been nothing wrong with me, it was only *afterwards* I felt I'd been ill. [...] I've already told Rey that at the first sign of a serious symptom I would come back and submit myself to the alienists in Aix, or to himself.

[...] If Gauguin, who is completely infatuated with my sunflowers, takes these two pictures, I should just like him to give your fiancée or you a couple of pictures of his, not second-rate ones but better than that. And should he take a copy of 'La Berceuse', then all the more reason for him to give a good one in return. Otherwise I wouldn't be able to complete the series I spoke to you about, which should be fit to go on show in that same little display window we have gazed at so often.

[...] As for the Indépendants, it seems to me that six pictures are too many by half. To my mind, The 'Harvest' and the 'White Orchard' are enough, with the 'Provençale Girl' or the

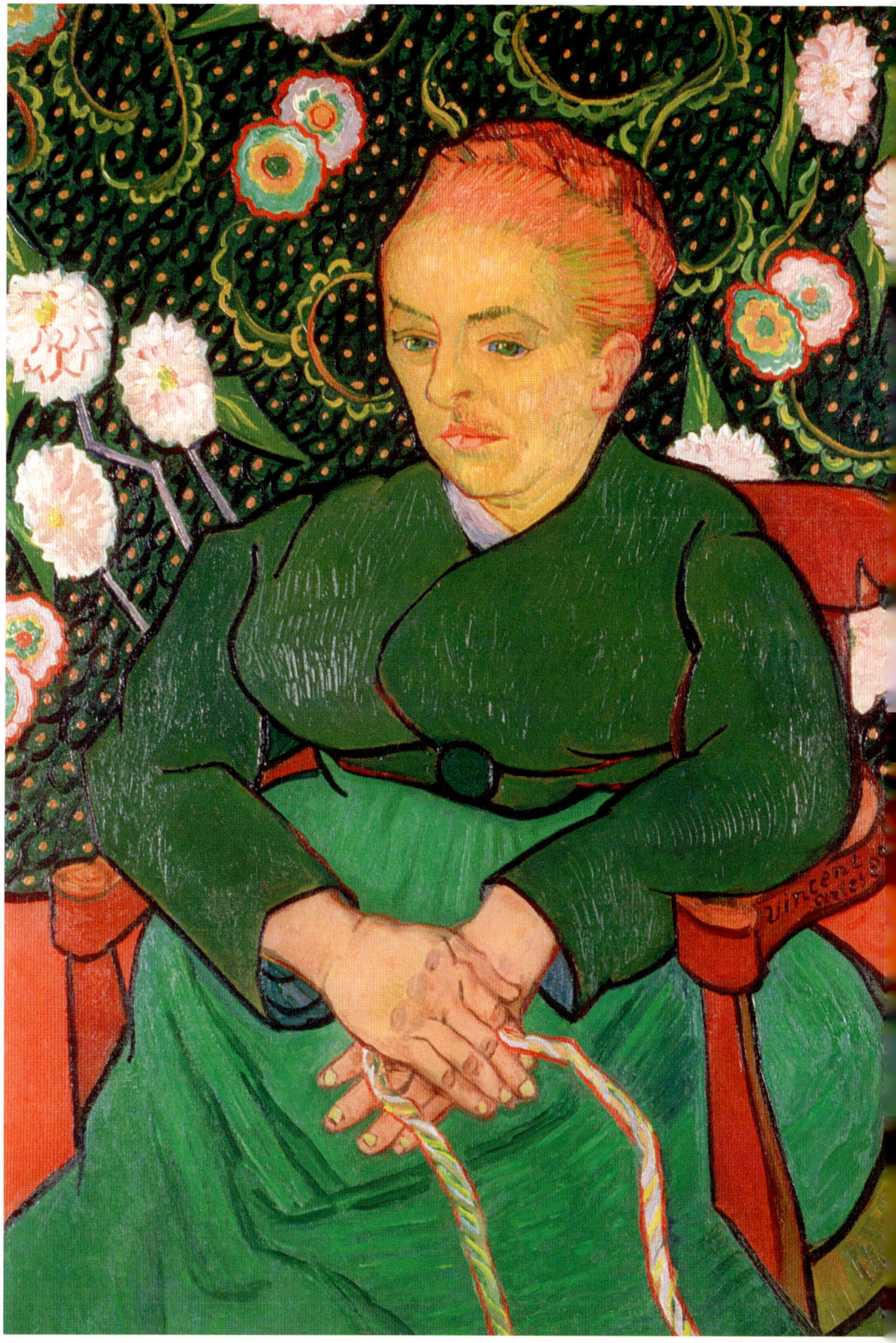

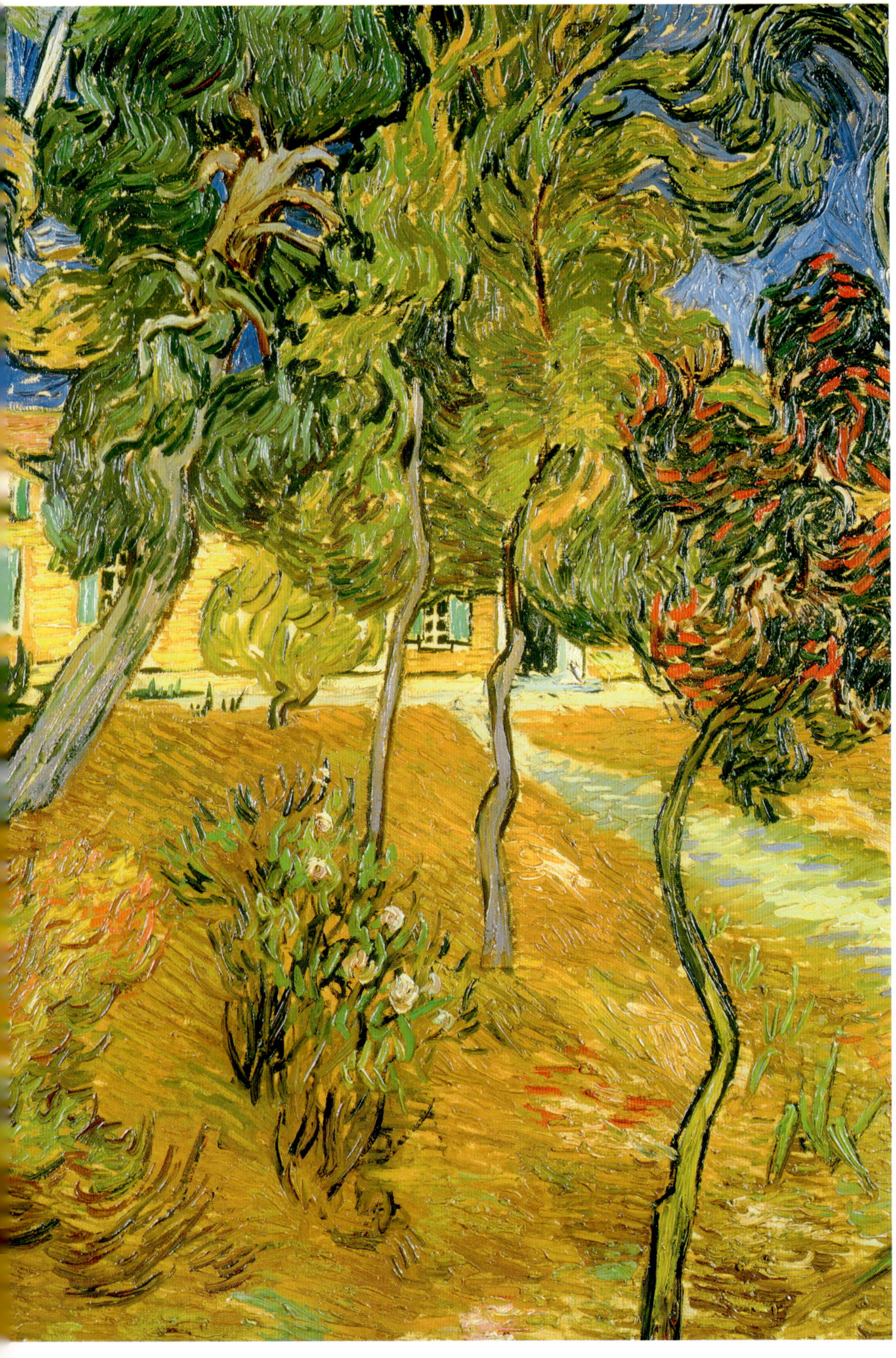

'Sower' if you like. But I really don't care. The only thing I really want to do some day is to give you a more comforting impression of this painting business of ours with a collection of about 30 more serious studies. In any case that will prove to our real friends like Gauguin, Guillaumin, Bernard, etc., that we are producing something.

As for the little yellow house, when I paid my rent the landlord's agent was very kind and behaved like an Arlésien, treating me as an equal.

So I told him that I had no need of a lease, nor of a written assurance of preference, and that in the event of my being ill payment would only be made by friendly arrangement. People here have their hearts in the right place and the spoken word is more binding than the written word.

So I shall keep the house on for the time being, as I need to feel that this is my home if I am to regain my mental health.

On 7 February 1889, Vincent was admitted to hospital again. He was in a fragile state and believed that local people were trying to poison him. On 13 February Theo contacted Dr Rey. He received the response: 'Vincent much better, hope getting better, keeping him here. Do not worry now.' Vincent returned home a few days later but by 19 March, the situation had changed dramatically. Vincent wrote to Theo: 'I write to you in the full possession of my faculties and not as a madman [...] A certain number of people here (there were more than 80 signatures) addressed a petition to the Mayor (I think his name is M. Tardieu), describing me as a man not fit to be at liberty or something like that. The commissioner of police or the chief commissioner then gave the order to shut me up again. [...] here I am, shut up in a cell all the livelong day, under lock and key with keepers [...] as far as my mental state is concerned I am greatly shaken'. On 24 March Paul Signac (1863–1935) visited Vincent at the Hôtel-Dieu and together they were allowed to visit the Yellow House, which had been closed up by the police. Signac wrote to Theo to explaining that Dr Rey felt that if

Vincent led a 'methodical life, eating and drinking normally and at regular hours' the mental crises would not be repeated. However, Signac pointed out that Vincent would need to move as his neighbours were still 'hostile' to him. What he did not mention to Theo but later revealed was that whilst in the Yellow House Vincent had wanted to drink from a bottle containing essence of turpentine. Vincent was confined to the hospital for about six weeks but was allowed out to paint under supervision. In gratitude for his visit Vincent gave Signac a painting.

Extract from
Saint-Rémy, *30 April 1889*

'...I know of no hospital where they would be willing to take me in for nothing, even supposing that I myself shouldered the painting expenses and left the whole of my work to the hospital.

And that is, I don't say a great, but still a small injustice. Even so, I should feel resigned if one took me in. If I were without your friendship, they would drive me remorselessly to suicide, and coward that I am, I should end by committing it. At this point, I hope, we are permitted to protest against society and to defend ourselves. [...]

[...] M. Salles has been to Saint-Rémy – they are not willing to give me permission to paint outside the institution, nor take me for less than 100 francs.

So this is pretty bad news.

Garden of St Paul's Hospital, 1889
MEDIUM: Oil on canvas
Courtesy of Private Collection/The Bridgeman Art Library

Mademoiselle Gachet in Her Garden at Auvers-sur-Oise, 1890
MEDIUM: Oil on canvas
Courtesy of Musée d'Orsay, Paris, France/Giraudon/The Bridgeman Art Library

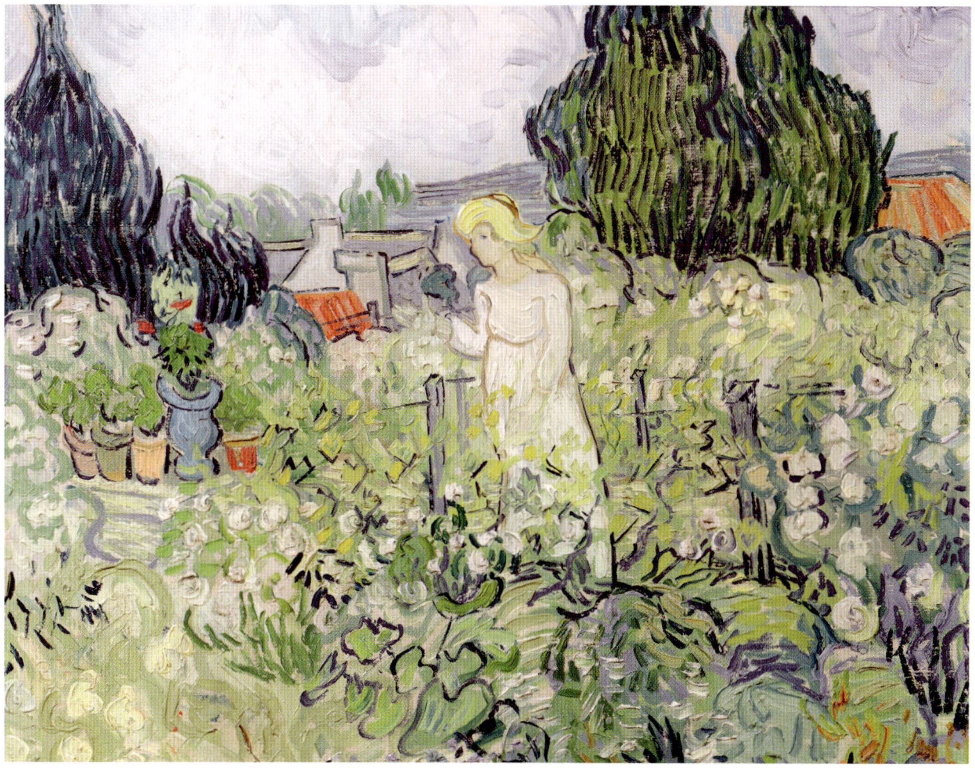

If I could get out of this mess by joining the Foreign Legion for 5 years, I think I should prefer that.

For on the one hand, being locked up and not working, I should find it hard to get better, and on the other hand, they would make us pay 100 francs a month during the whole long life of a madman.

It's a bad business, and what are we to make of it? But would they be willing to have me as a soldier?

Vincent had suggested to Theo that an alternative to paying 100 francs a month for treatment at the asylum at Saint-Rémy would be for him to join the Foreign Legion for five years. Theo replied to Vincent on 2 May, 1889, '... I entirely disapprove of... your plans to join the Foreign Legion. It is meant as an act of despair... born of an exaggerated dread of causing me expense and worry...'. Theo reminds Vincent that his despair is caused by not being able to paint at present, and he would return to it, 'How many are there who would be glad of having done the work you have accomplished...'.

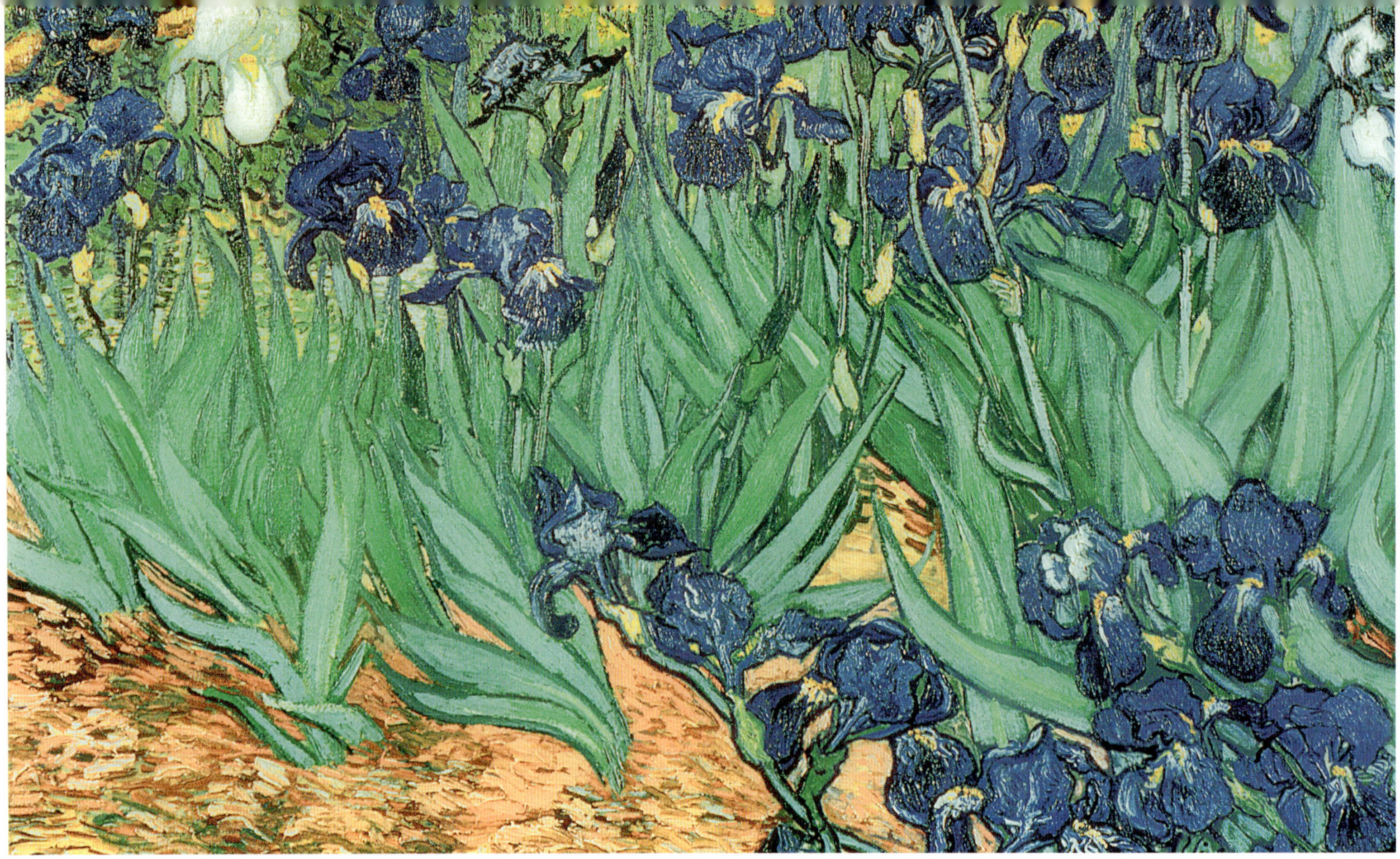

Extract from
Saint-Rémy, *c. 10–15 May 1889*

"[...] I want to tell you that I think I have done well to come here, because, by seeing the *reality* of the assorted madmen and lunatics in this menagerie, I am losing my vague dread, my fear of the thing. And bit by bit I am getting to consider that madness is just a disease like any other. Thus the change in surroundings will do me good, I think.

As far as I can tell, the doctor here is of the opinion that what I have had is some sort of epileptic attack. But I haven't asked him more about it.

Have you received the case of paintings, I am curious to know if they have suffered, yes or no?

I have two more on the go - *violet irises* and *a lilac bush*, two subjects taken from the garden.

The idea of my duty to get back to work occurs to me a lot and I believe that all my faculties for work will soon come back to me. It's just that the work often absorbs me so much that I think that for the rest of my life I will always be a bit absent-minded and awkward when shifting for myself."

Vincent left Arles and was admitted for treatment at Saint-Paul-de-Mausole Hospital, a hospital asylum in Saint-Rémy on 8 May, 1889. He wrote to Theo telling him that his doctor, Théophile Zacharie Auguste Peyron (1827–95), was inclined to think that what he had suffered was a 'sort of epileptic attack', (a diagnosis that is agreed upon today). At the hospital he was free to paint as he pleased anywhere within the asylum's walled garden. He would paint many of his most vibrant works within the walls of the asylum and on local excursions in its vicinity. During Vincent's stay in the asylum at Saint-Rémy, his brother Theo married Johanna Bonger (1862–1925).

***Irises*, 1889, (detail)**
MEDIUM: Oil on canvas
Courtesy of J. Paul Getty Museum, Los Angeles, USA/The Bridgeman Art Library

***The Exercise Yard*, 1890**
MEDIUM: Oil on canvas
Courtesy of Pushkin Museum, Moscow,

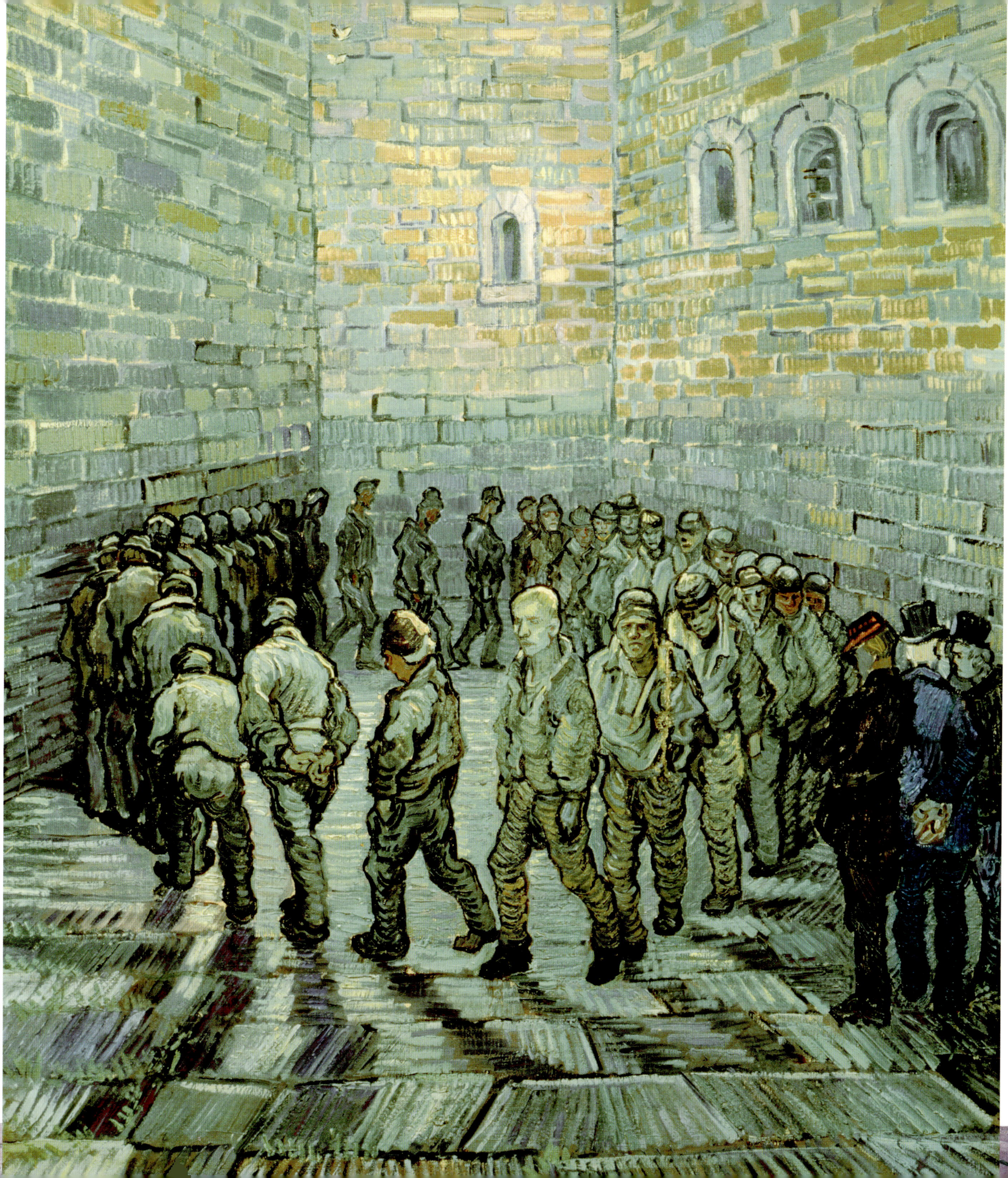

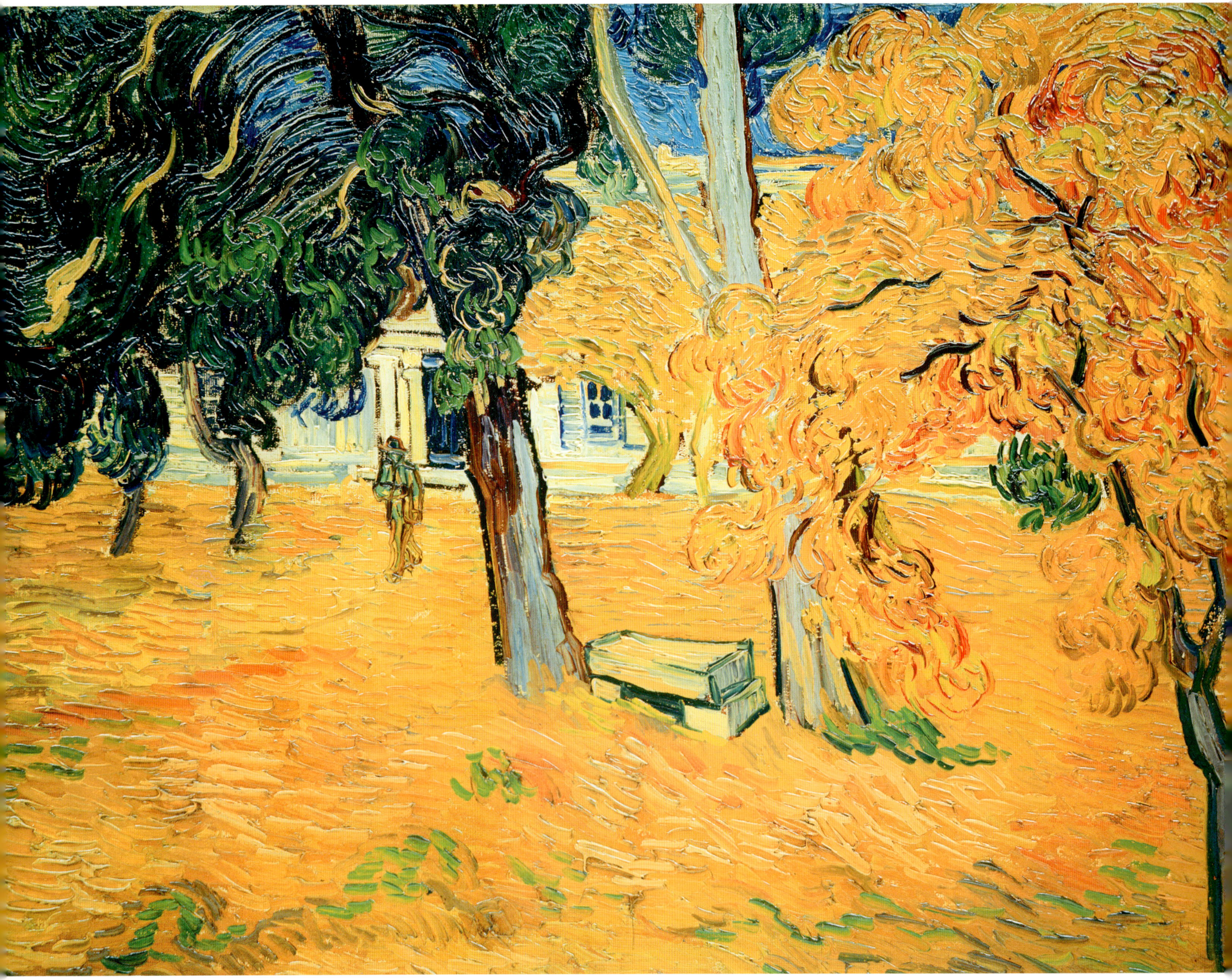

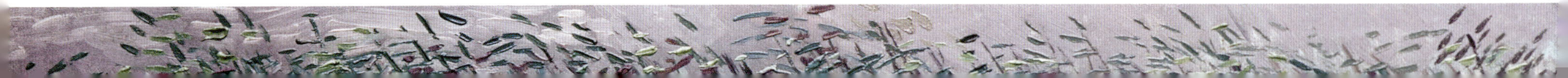

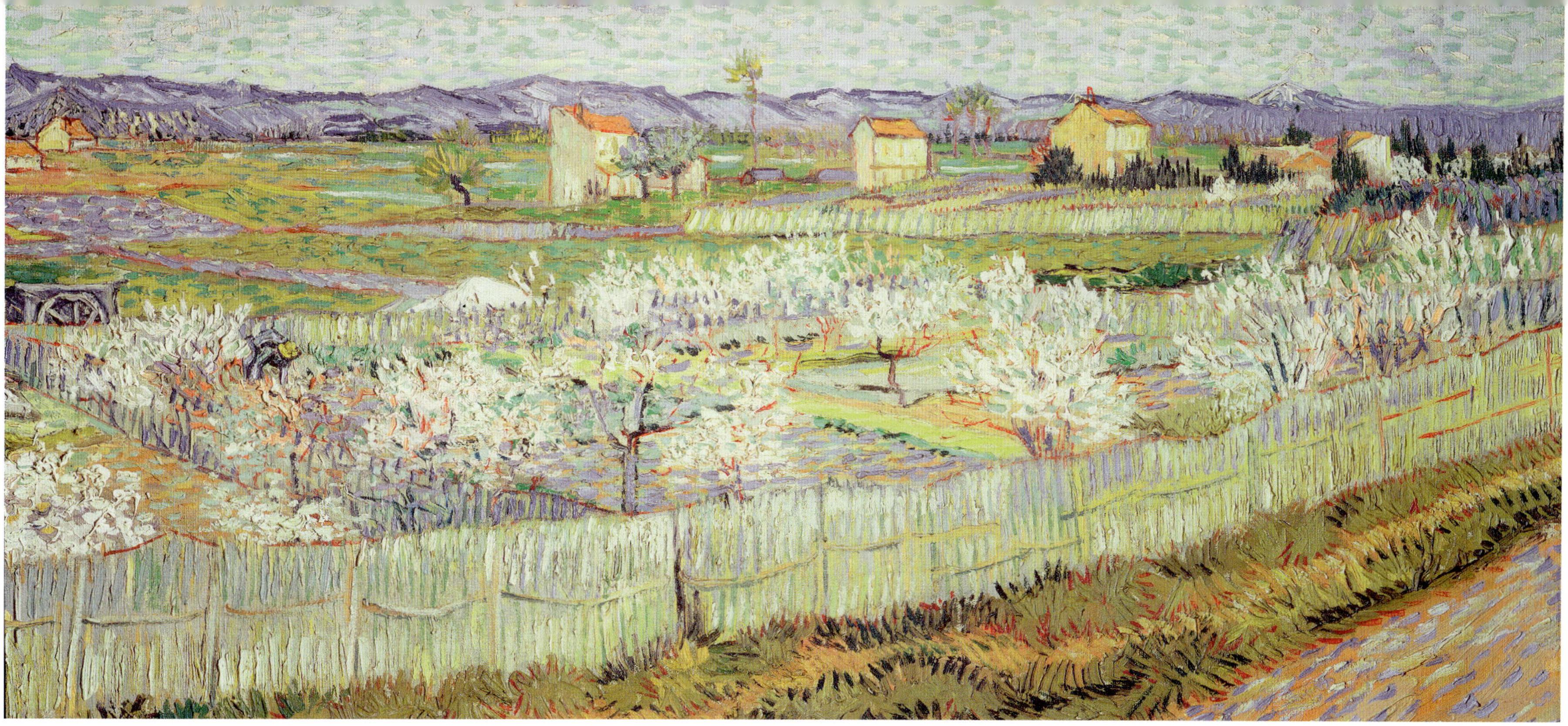

Extract from
Saint-Rémy, *22 May 1889*

[…] What you say about 'La Berceuse' pleases me; it is very true that the common people, who are content with chromos and melt when they hear a barrel organ, are in some vague way right, perhaps more sincere than certain men about town who go to the Salon.

If he will accept it, give Gauguin the copy of 'La Berceuse' that was not mounted on a stretcher, and Bernard also, as a token of friendship, but if Gauguin wants the sunflowers, it is only fair that he should give you something you like equally well in exchange.

Gauguin himself liked the sunflowers better later on when he had been looking at them for a good while.

What you also have to know is that if you arrange them this way, namely 'La Berceuse' in the middle and the two canvases of sunflowers to the right and left, it makes a sort of triptych.

[…] Since I've been here, there's been enough work for me to do, what with the neglected garden with its tall pines and long, unkempt grass mixed with all sorts of weeds, and I haven't even been outside. […]

I *assure* you that I am all right here, and that for the time being I see no reason at all to take lodgings in or around Paris. I have a small room with greenish-grey paper with two sea-green curtains with a design of very pale roses, brightened by touches of blood-red.

These curtains, probably the legacy of some deceased and ruined rich person, are very pretty in design. A very worn armchair, probably from the same source, is covered with a tapestry speckled like a Diaz or a Monticelli in brown, red, pink, white, cream, black, forget-me-not blue and bottle green. Through the iron-barred window I can see an enclosed square of wheat, a prospect like a Van Goyen, above which, in the morning, I watch the sun rise in all its glory.

[…] I take a bath twice a week now, and stay in it for two hours; my stomach is infinitely better than it was a year ago; so as far as I know, I only have to go on. Besides, I shall spend less

***The Park at St Paul's Hospital, Saint-Rémy*, 1889, (detail)**
MEDIUM: Oil on canvas
Courtesy of Private Collection/ The Bridgeman Art Library

***Peach Trees in Blossom*, 1889, (detail)**
MEDIUM: Oil on canvas
© Samuel Courtauld Trust, The Courtauld Gallery, London, UK/The Bridgeman Art Library

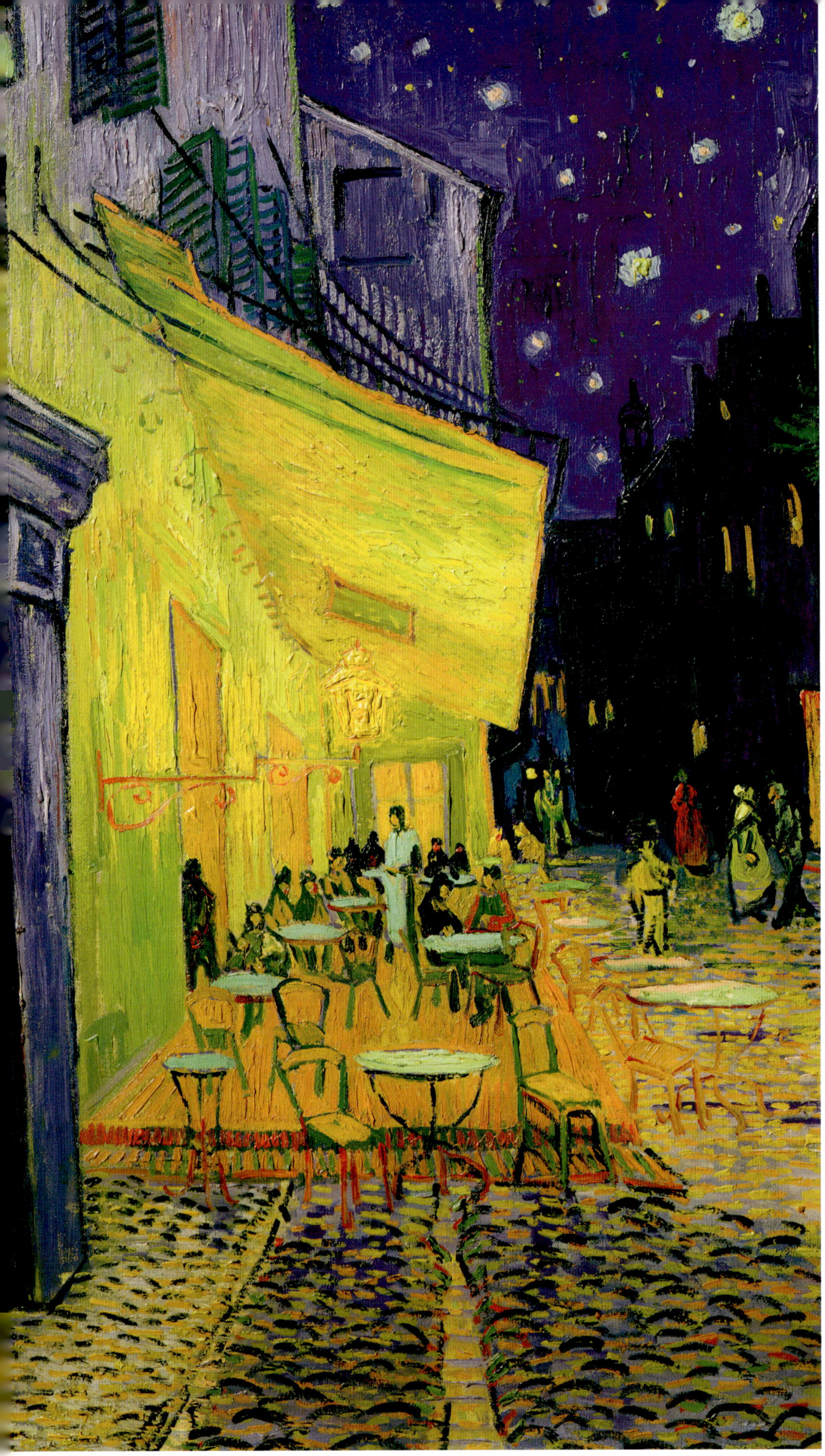

here, I think, considering that I have work in prospect again, for the scenery is lovely.

I am forced to ask you again for some paints and especially for canvas. When I sent you the four canvases of the garden I am working on, you will see that, considering my life is spent mostly in the garden, it is not so sad. […]

Again – speaking of my condition […] Most epileptics bite their tongue and injure themselves. Rey told me that he had seen a case where someone had mutilated his own ear, just as I did […] I like to think that once you know what it is, once you are conscious of your condition, and of being subject to attacks, then you can do something to prevent your being taken unawares by the anguish or the terror […] and in my case it was both sight and hearing at the same time, which is usual at the onset of epilepsy, according to what Rey said one day.

Although the pictures swallow up canvas and paint, etc., nevertheless at the end of the month I'm sure it's more profitable to spend a little more on those, making use of what I've learned, than to abandon it all, when you have to pay for my board and lodging anyway. And that's why I'm carrying on. So this month I have four size 30 canvases and two or three drawings.

But the question of money, whatever one does, is always with us, like the enemy facing the troops, and cannot be denied or ignored.

As much as anyone, I know where my duties lie in that respect. And I may yet be able to pay back everything I've spent, for I consider it to have been, if not taken from you, at least taken from the family. So that's why I've been producing pictures and shall be doing some more. […]"

***Café Terrace, Place du Forum, Arles*, 1888, (detail)**
MEDIUM: Oil on canvas
Courtesy of Rijksmuseum Kroller-Muller, Otterlo, Netherlands/The Bridgeman Art Library

***Olive Orchard, Violet Soil*, date unknown**
MEDIUM: Oil on canvas
Courtesy of Van Gogh Museum, Amsterdam, The Netherlands/The Bridgeman Art Library

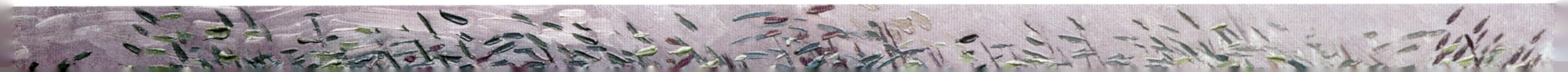

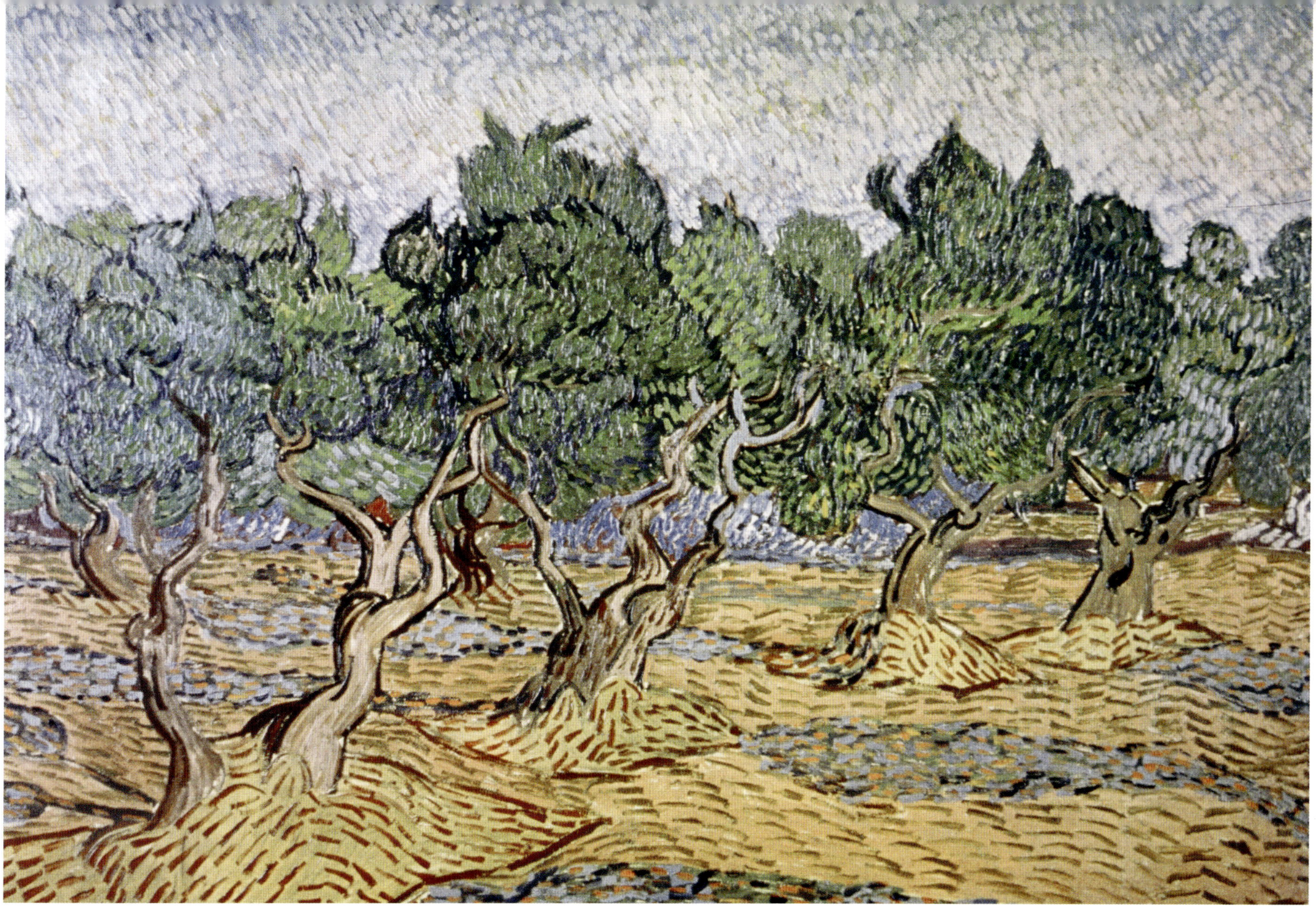

Vincent produced a large catalogue of artworks during his stay in the asylum at Saint-Rémy. He wrote to Theo that it was not such a bad life being restricted to the hospital's garden. *Irises,* May 1889 was one of the first works he produced. It was exhibited with *Starry Night over the Rhône*, 1888, at the Salon des Indépendants, Paris, in September 1889. Another early work painted soon after arriving at Saint-Rémy was *Lilacs,* May 1889, capturing the lilac blossoms in full bloom. Many paintings are of the hospital building, depicted in a vibrant yellow: *Hospital at Saint-Rémy,* 1889; *Pine trees in the Garden of the Asylum,* painted in October 1889, illustrating a deeply rich blue sky glimpsed through the tall pine trees with vibrant foliage; and *The Garden of the Asylum,* December 1889. The paintings and drawings of the gardens at Saint-Rémy are considered some of his greatest works.

From Vincent van Gogh to
Willemina van Gogh
Extract from
Saint-Rémy, *16 June 1889*

My dear sister,

"If I didn't write to you in a hurry this Sunday morning, while the canvases I have started are drying a little in the sun, I should have to wait still longer before answering your kind letter.

I hope all is well with you, and with Mother too – I think of you both very often. […]

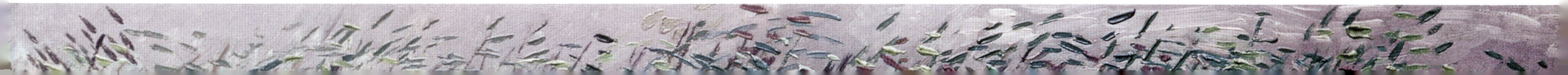

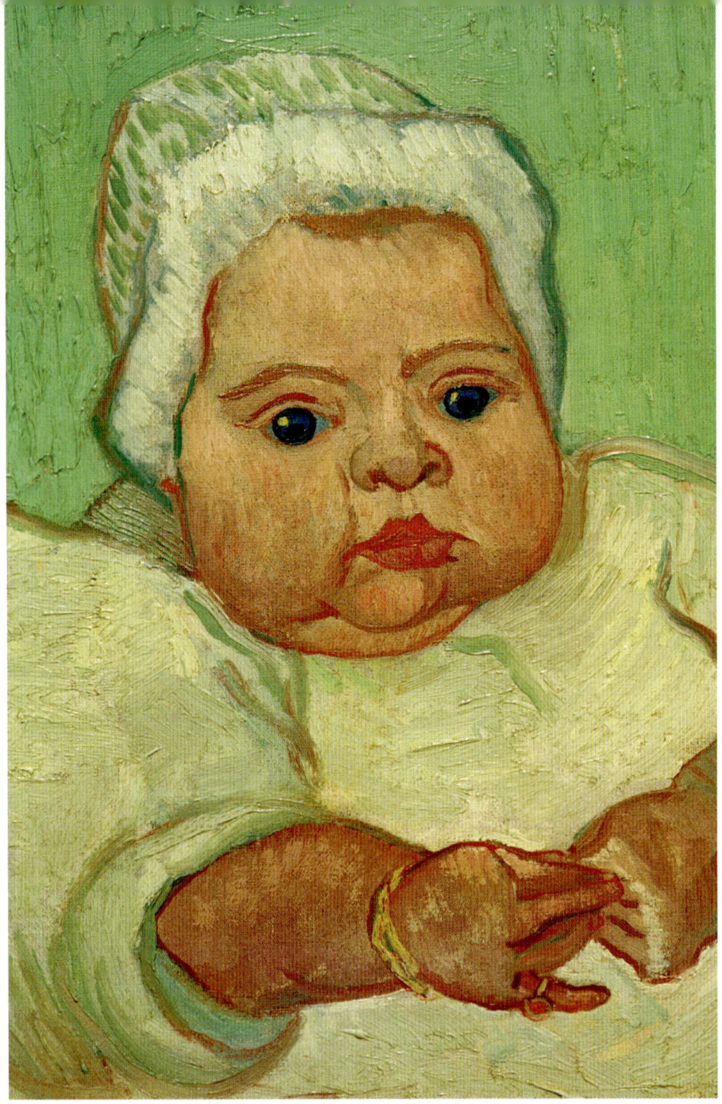

I have just finished a landscape representing an orchard of olive trees with grey leaves, somewhat like those of the willows in colour, their violet shadows lying on the sunny sand. And another one too, which represents a field of wheat turning yellow, surrounded by blackberry bushes and green shrubs. At the end of the field there is a little house with a tall somber cypress which stands out against the far-off hills with their violet-like and bluish tones, and against a sky the colour of forget-me-nots with pink streaks, whose pure hues form a contrast with the scorched ears, which are already heavy, and have the warm tones of a bread crust.

***Portrait of Marcelle Roulin*, 1888**
MEDIUM: Oil on canvas

***Portrait of Dr Gachet*, date unknown**
MEDIUM: Oil on canvas

I have still another one in which a wheat field on the slope of the hills is all devastated and smashed to earth by the pouring rain and the rushing water of a cloudburst. […]

I am sort of longing for news from Theo, who seems to be rather absorbed in his honeymoon, which is a very good thing. Last week he sent me a consignment of paints and canvases, but a month has gone by since I received a letter from him. It is a great consolation to me to know that he is no longer living alone. His wife wrote me a very good letter some time ago, which proved to me that she is a very serious young woman. […]

Now I am going out to work a little, so I wish you all prosperity and health, you and Mother too. With a kiss in thought,

Yours

Vincent

Vincent discussed his latest paintings with his mother, probably referring to *Olive Grove*, 1889 or possibly *Olive Trees with Apilles in the background*, 1889 amongst others. Following Theo's marriage on 21 April 1889 to Johanna Bonger, Theo had last written to Vincent on 21 May, probably due to ill health. Vincent is rather annoyed by the lack of correspondence but tells his sister of his respect for Jo, Theo's wife.

From Johanna van Gogh-Bonger to
Vincent van Gogh
Extract from
Saint-Rémy, *5 July, 1889*

My dear brother,

This time I shall try to write you in French; in the first place I know you like it better […]

I am now going to tell you a great piece of news, on which we have concentrated a good deal of our attention lately – it is that next winter, toward February probably, we hope to have a baby, a pretty little boy – whom we are going to call Vincent, if you will consent to be his godfather. Of course I know we must not count on it too much, and that it may well be a little girl, but Theo and I cannot help imagining that the baby will be a boy. [...]

Now I am going to say goodbye – please write us your opinion about our little boy, for a boy it must be.

Your sister

Jo

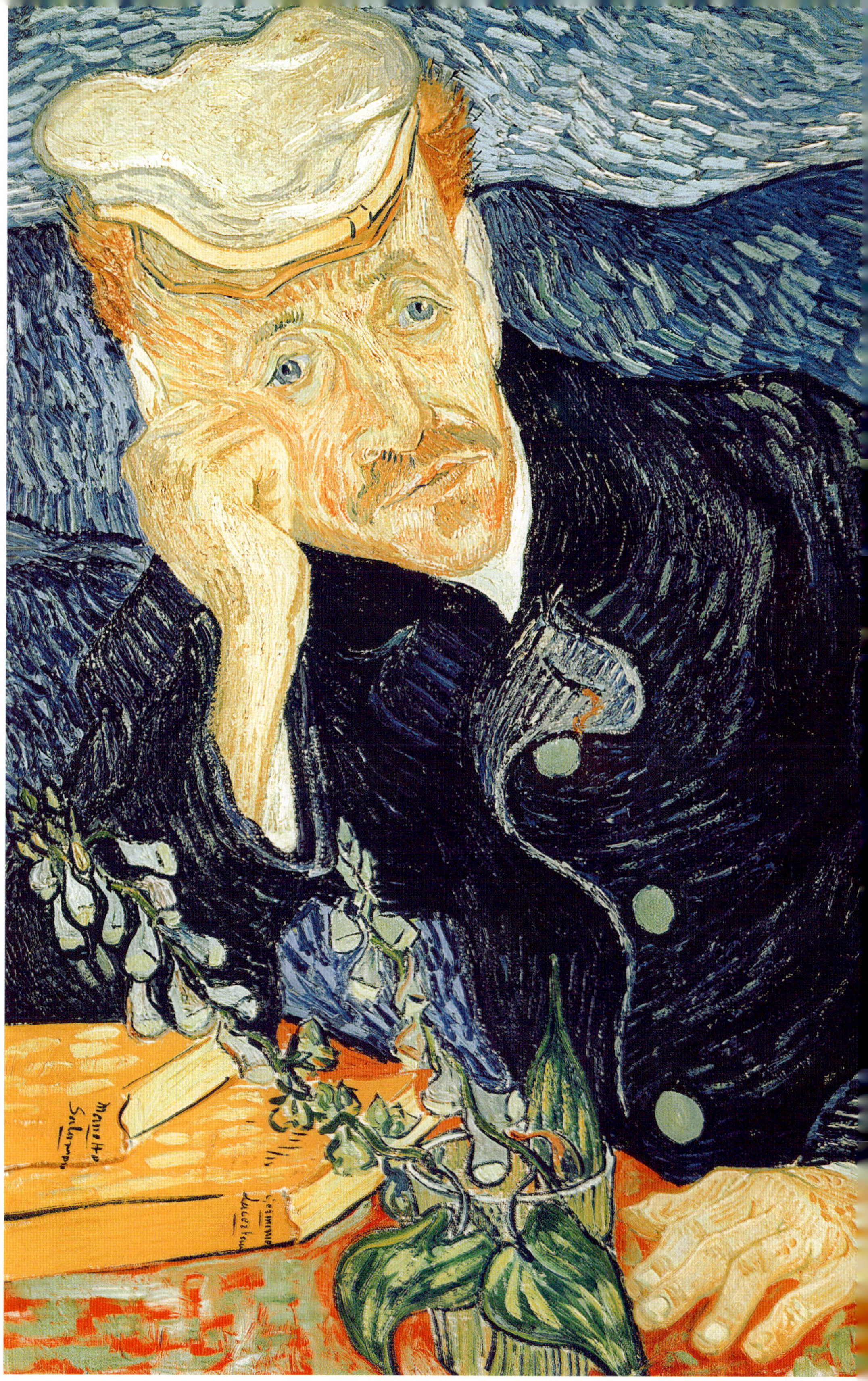

From Vincent van Gogh to

Theo van Gogh

Extract from

Saint-Rémy, *22 August 1889*

My dear Theo,

"I thank Jo very much for having written, and know that you want me to drop you a line, I must let you know that it is very difficult for me to write, my head is so deranged [...] Dr Peyron is very kind to me and very patient. [...] It would be a good thing if you perhaps wrote a word to Dr Peyron to tell him that working on my pictures is almost a necessity for my recovery, for these days without anything to do, and without being able to go to the room they have allotted me to do my painting in, are almost intolerable. [...]

I hope it is not complaining too much if I tell you these details, but I do it to prove that I am not yet in a condition to go to Paris or to Pont-Aven, unless it were to Charenton. It seems that I gather dirt and eat it, although my memory of these bad moments are vague, and it seems to me there is something shady in it. For this reason I don't know what it will mean for my painting. [...]"

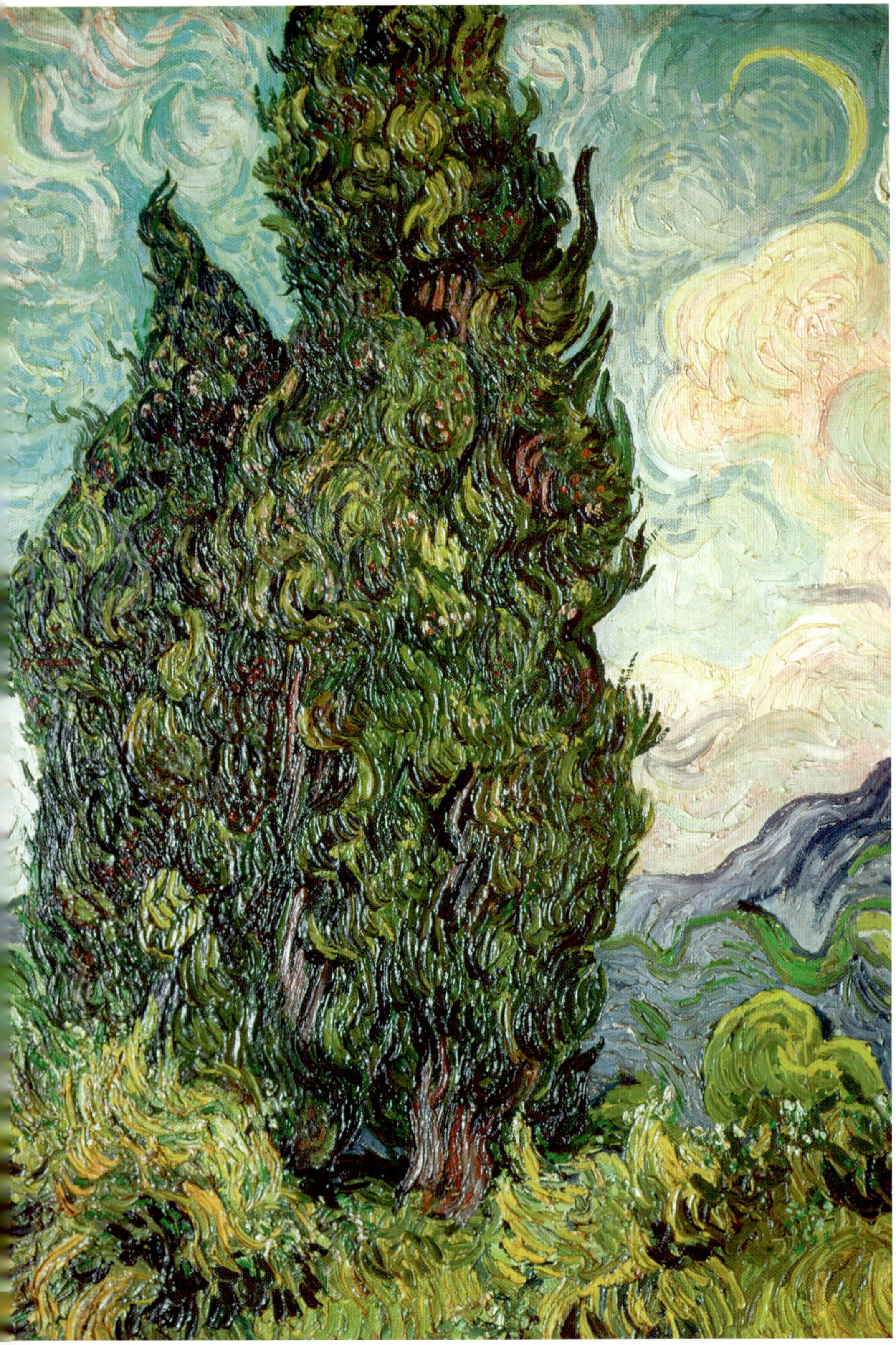

Extract from
Saint-Rémy, *5–6 September 1889*

"I have already written to you, but there are still quite a few things you said to me that I haven't answered yet.

[…] It is curious that Maus had the idea of inviting young Bernard and me for the next Vingtistes exhibition. I should like to exhibit with them very much, though I'm conscious of my inferiority by the side of so many tremendously talented Belgians.

[…] I've done the painting of the Bedroom once more. That's certainly one of my best studies – and sooner or later it must definitely be *relined*. It was painted so quickly and has dried in such a way that the turpentine evaporated straight away and the paint hasn't stuck firmly to the canvas at all. That will also have happened with other studies of mine painted very quickly and with a very full brush. Anyway, after some time this thin canvas deteriorates and cannot take a lot of impasto. You've got some excellent stretchers, damn it, if I had some like that to work with, I'd be a lot better off than with these laths you get here which warp in the sun.

They say – and I am very willing to believe it – that it is difficult to know oneself – but it isn't easy to paint oneself either. So I am working on two self-portraits at the moment – for want of another model.

Because it is high time I did a little figure work. In the one I began the first day I got up, I was thin and deathly pale. It is

***Cypresses*, 1889**
MEDIUM: Oil on canvas
Courtesy of Metropolitan Museum of Art, New York, USA/Giraudon/The Bridgeman Art Library

***Self Portrait*, 1889, (detail)**
MEDIUM: Oil on canvas
Courtesy of Musée d'Orsay, Paris, France/Giraudon/The Bridgeman Art Library

dark purple-blue, and the head whitish with yellow hair, thus with a colour effect.

But I have since started another, three-quarter profile on a light background.

Then I'm retouching this summer's studies – in fact, I am working morning, noon and night.

Are you well? – damn it, I really wish that you were 2 years further on and that these early days of your marriage, however lovely they may be at times, were behind you. I'm quite convinced that a marriage grows better with time, and that it's *then* that your constitution will recover. [...]

What you told me about Maus having been to see my canvases made me think a lot about the Belgian painters these last few days and also during my illness. As a result I was overwhelmed with memories as by an avalanche, and I tried to recall the whole of that school of modern Flemish artists until I felt as homesick as a fish out of water. [...]

I am continuing this letter again at intervals. Yesterday I began the portrait of the chief attendant, and I may do his wife as well, since he is married and lives in a little farmhouse a stone's throw from the institution.

By the end of the month I'd go so far as to say you can count on 12 size 30 canvases, but in most cases they will be the same picture twice over, a study and the final painting.

[...] In any case, what is it that we are now beginning hesitatingly to recognize as original and long-lasting? *Portraiture*. You might say that it's old stuff, but it's also quite new.

[...] My urge to do portraits is very strong these days, in fact Gauguin and I talked about this and similar matters until our nerves were strained to the point of stifling all human warmth.

I must ask for the following things for painting.

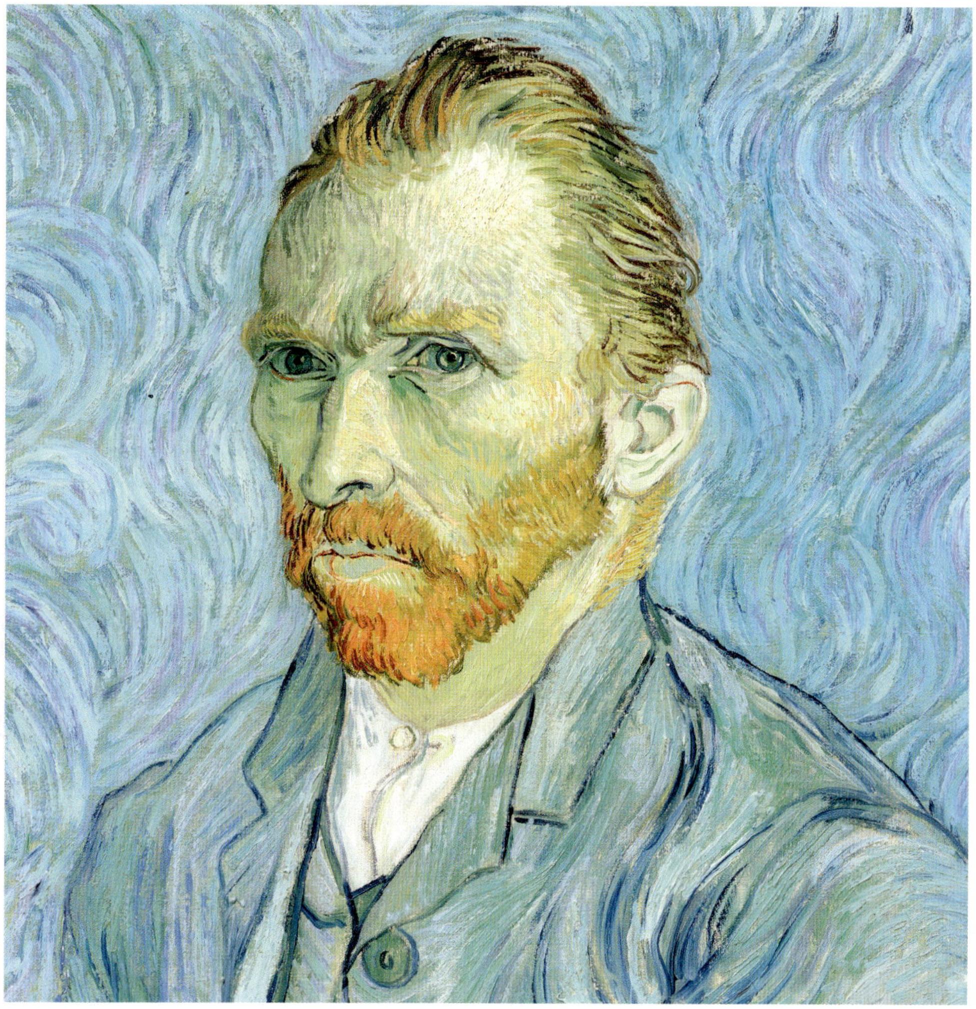

10 metres of canvas
Large tubes 6 zinc white
2 tubes emerald green
2 tubes cobalt
Small tubes 2 carmine
1 vermilion
1 large tube crimson lake
6 marten brushes, black hair

There! The reaper is finished. I think it'll be one of those you'll keep at home – it's an image of death as the great book of nature speaks of it – but the effect I've been looking for is – 'on the point of smiling'. It's all yellow, except for a line of purple hills. A pale and golden yellow. I find it odd that I saw it like that through the iron bars of a cell.

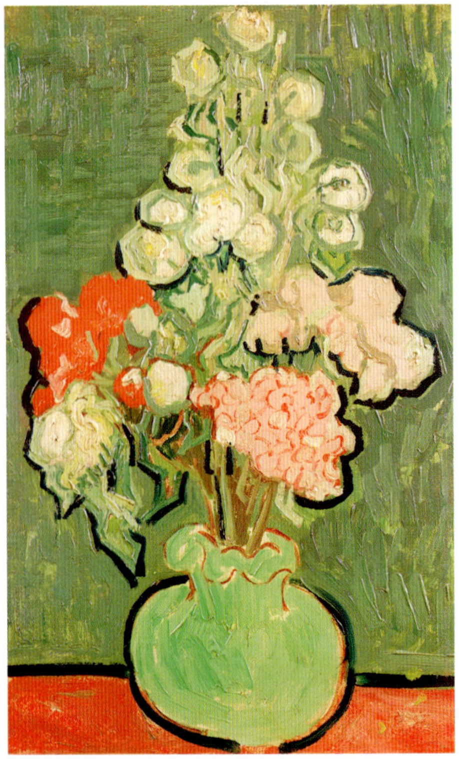

[...] I've a good mind to do the 'Reaper' over again for Mother. If not, I'll do another picture for her birthday – it will be coming later, as I'll send it on with the rest.

[...] Yes, I do think that it's a good idea to do some pictures for Holland, for Mother and our two sisters. That will make three, that is to say the Reaper, the Bedroom, the Olive trees, Wheat Field and Cypress. It will even make four, for there's somebody else I'm going to do one for as well.

I shall work at that, of course, with as much pleasure as for the Vingtistes, and more calmly. Since I feel strong, you may be sure that I shall get through a lot of work.

I am choosing the best from the 12 subjects, so that what they'll get will have been thought about a bit and specially picked. And then, it's a good thing to work for people who don't know what a picture is. [...]

The *Vingtistes* to whom Vincent refers were also known as *Les Vingt*. This group of 20 Belgian artists was formed in 1883 by entrepeneur Octave Maus (1856–93). Each year, for the annual exhibition, 20 international artists admired by the group were invited to exhibit. Vincent's paintings were exhibited in 1890. A retrospective of his work was held in 1891.

***Bouquet of Flowers*, 1890**
MEDIUM: Oil on canvas
Courtesy of Van Gogh Museum, Amsterdam, The Netherlands/Giraudon/ The Bridgeman Art Library

***The Alpilles*, 1889**
MEDIUM: Oil on canvas
Courtesy of Solomon R. Guggenheim Museum, New York, USA/Giraudon/ The Bridgeman Art Library

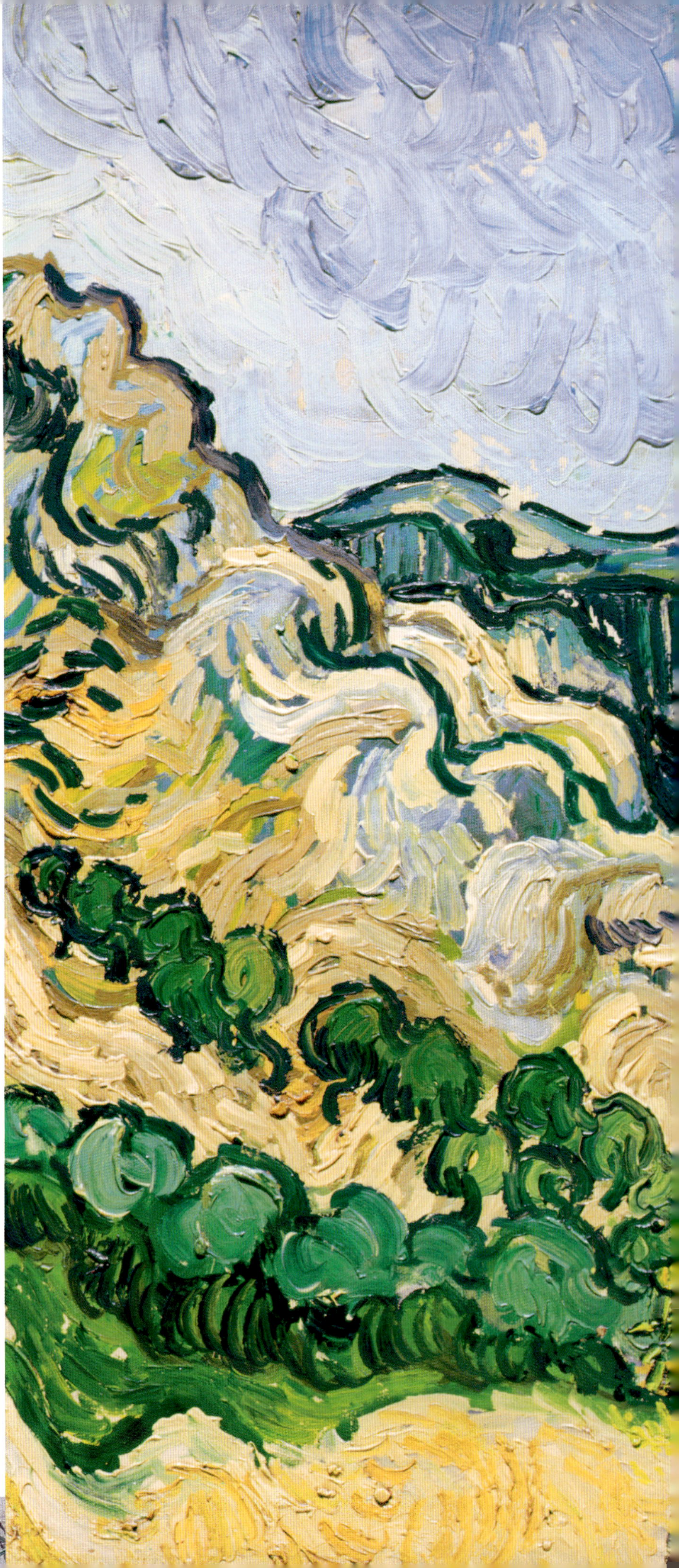

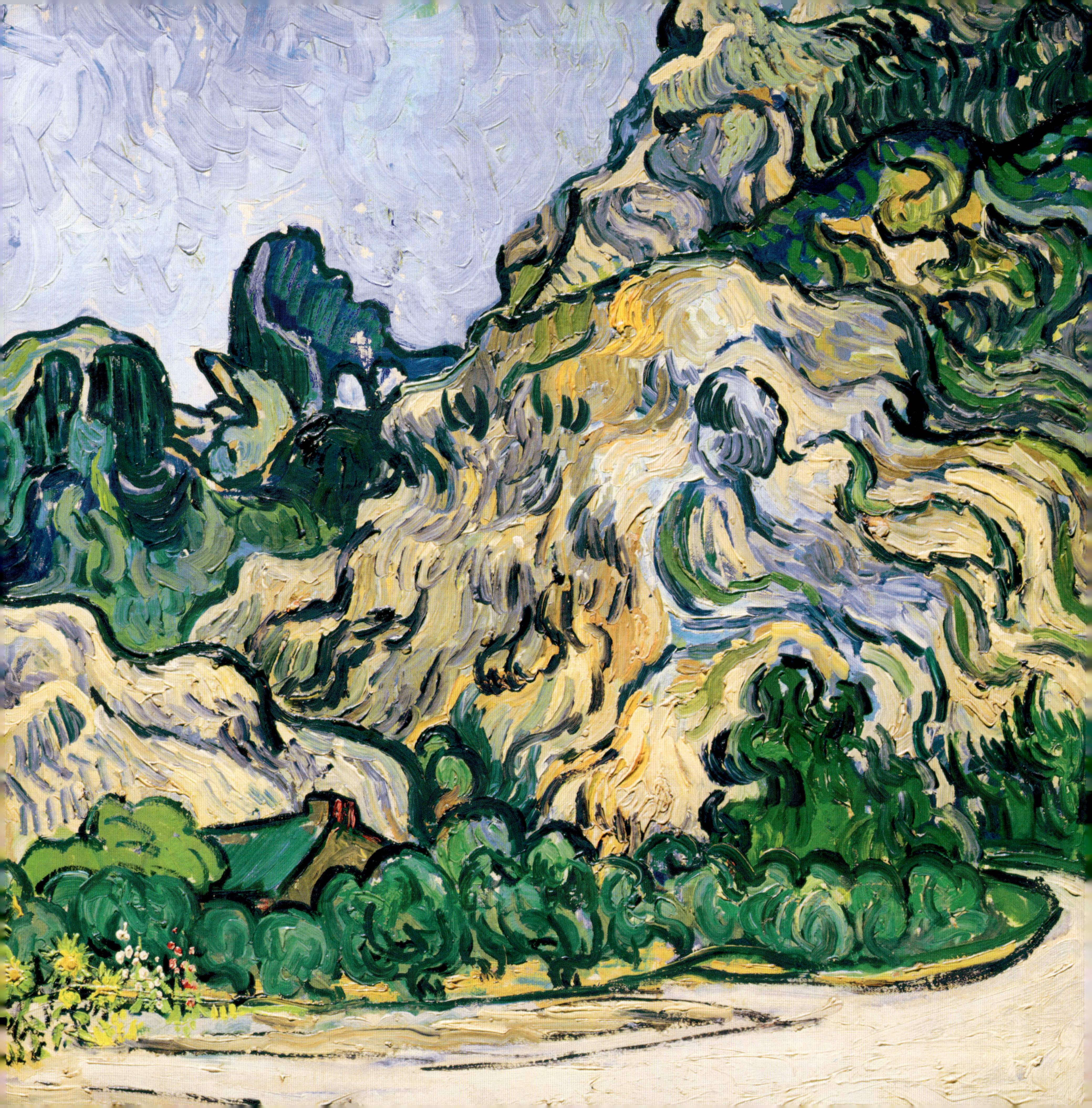

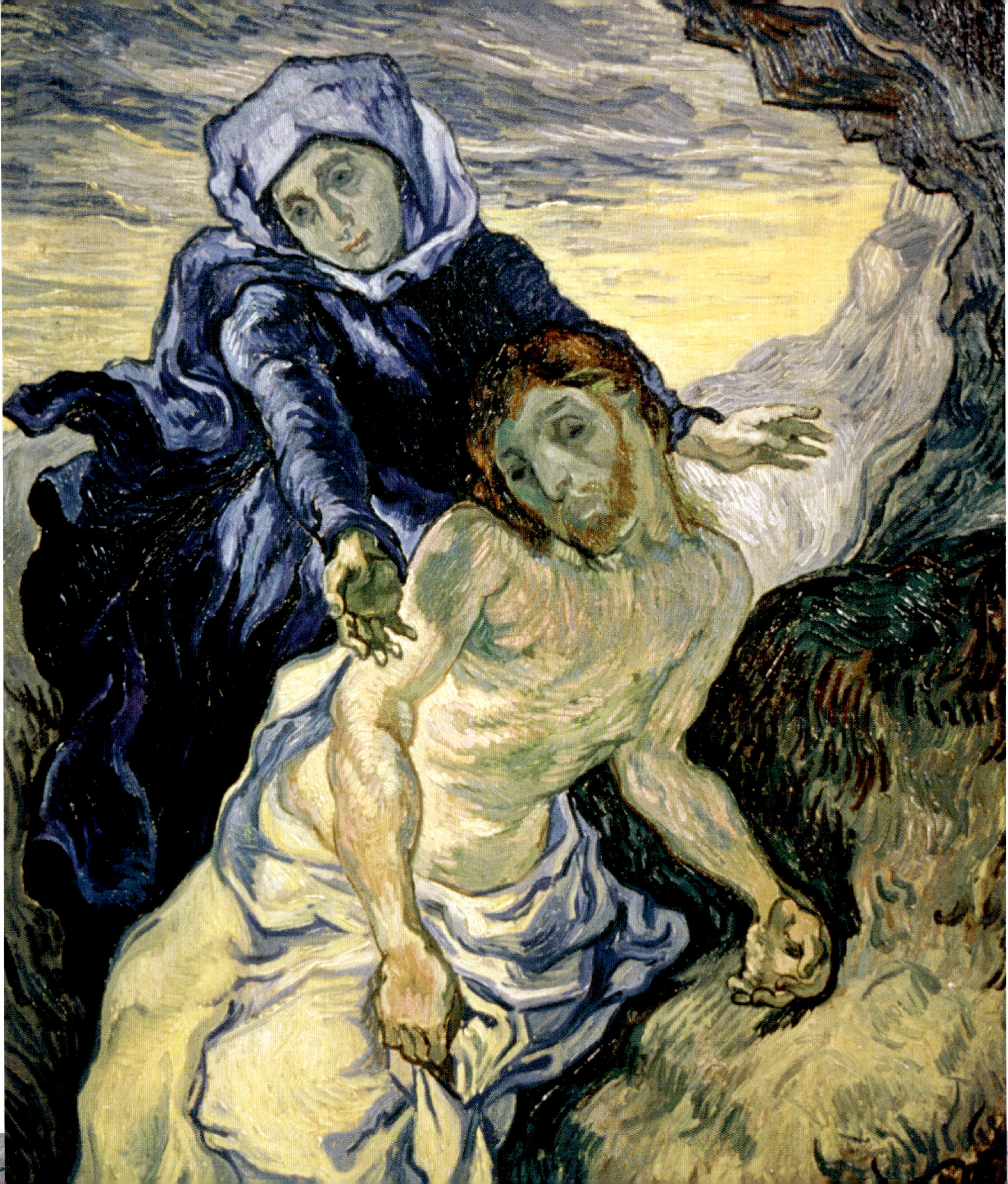

Extract from
Saint-Rémy, *8 September 1889*

[…] I am working furiously for the very reason that I know that opportunities for work do not recur. […] Especially in my case, where a more violent attack could destroy my ability to paint for good.

During the attacks I feel cowardly in the face of the pain and suffering […] in short, I am trying to recover, like someone who has meant to commit suicide, but then makes for the bank because he finds the water too cold. […]

I still tell myself that Gauguin and I will perhaps work together again. I know that G. can do even better things than he has done, but how to reassure him! I still hope to do his portrait. Have you seen that portrait he did of me painting sunflowers?

I very much wish that, when your child comes, I might be back – not with you, certainly *not*, that is impossible, but in the neighbourhood of Paris with another painter. I could mention a third alternative, my going to the Jouves, who have a lot of children and quite a household. […]

Vincent refers to feeling as though he is recovering from a failed suicide. He writes to Theo about the possibility of moving back to Paris but accommodation and finances and his health would be obstacles to a permanent move. He writes to Theo about sharing with another painter or to move in with the family of Auguste Jouve (c. 1846–1936), a French artist and a friend of Vincent.

Pieta, 1890
MEDIUM: Oil on canvas
Courtesy of Van Gogh Museum, Amsterdam, The Netherlands/ The Bridgeman Art Library

The Novel Reader, 1888
MEDIUM: Oil on canvas
Courtesy of Private Collection/Photo © Lefevre Fine Art Ltd, London/ The Bridgeman Art Library

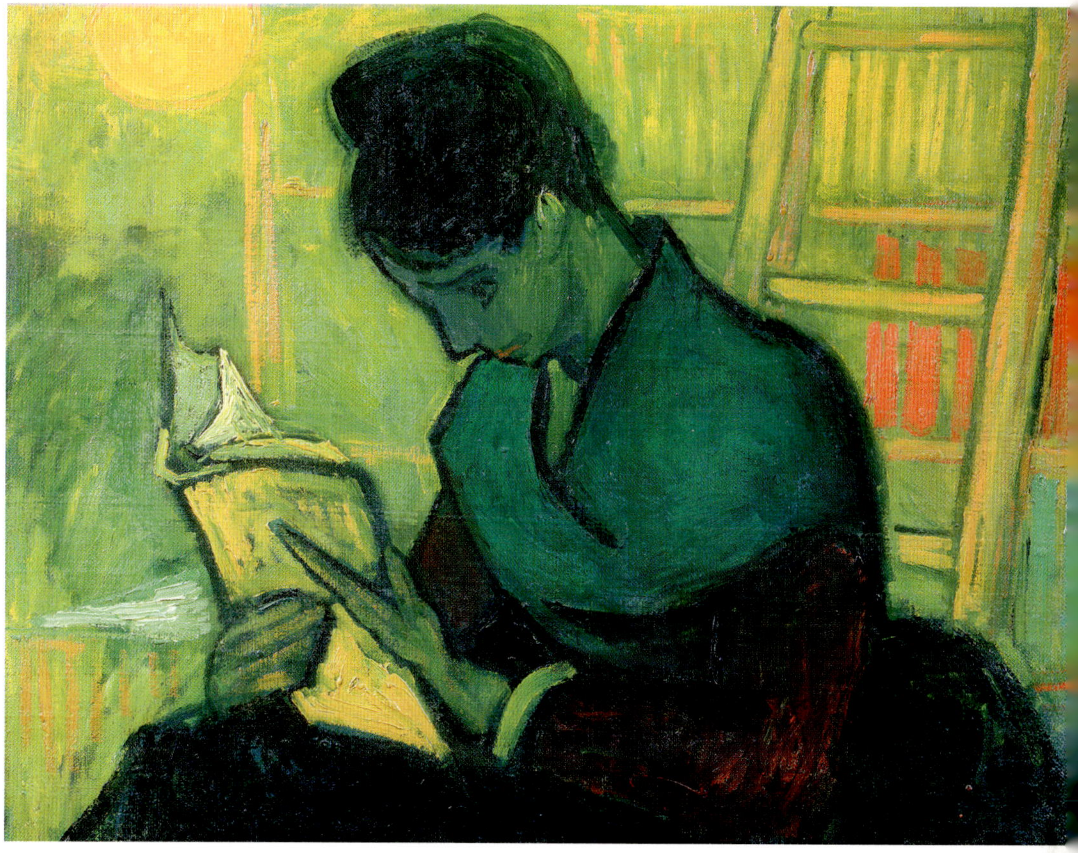

From Theo van Gogh to
Vincent van Gogh
Extract from
Saint-Rémy, *4 October 1889*

My dear Vincent,

[…]Dr. Peyron came to see me, and he seems to be well disposed toward you. … He says that for the present you are absolutely healthy, and if it weren't for the fact that it is such a short time since you had that crisis, he would already have encouraged you to leave the establishment more often. He told me that, seeing that your trip to Arles provoked a crisis, it is necessary to ascertain before you go to live elsewhere, whether you can bear a change. If you can stand these tests, he sees no objection to your leaving them.

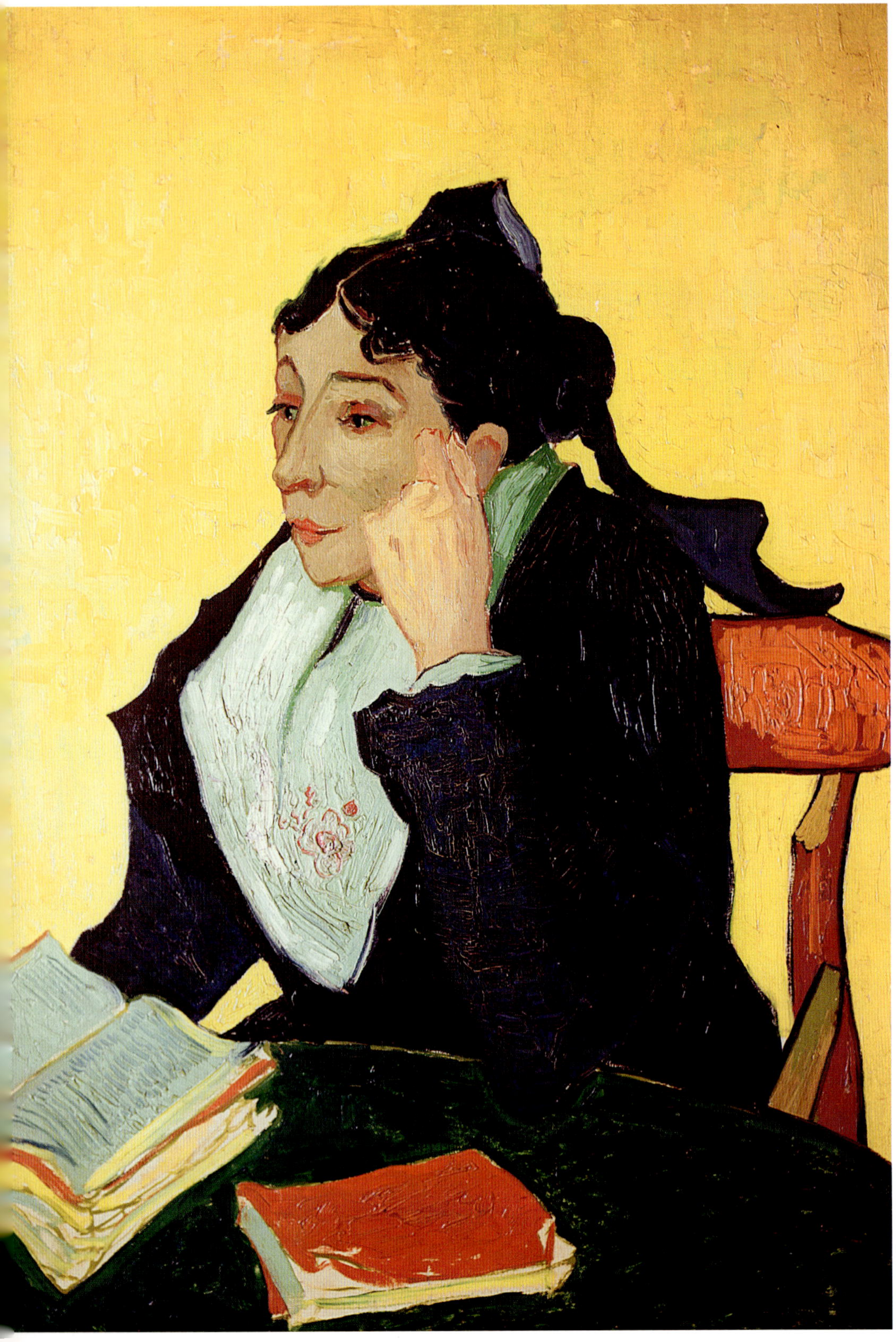

Moreover, I spoke to Pissarro, and discussed the question. I do not think he has any great authority in his own home, where his wife wears the pants. After a few days he told me that it was not possible in his own house [Vincent had asked if he could stay with Pissarro] but that he knows somebody at Auvers [Dr Paul Gachet] who is a doctor and does painting in his spare moments. He tells me the gentleman in question has been in contact with all the Impressionists. He thinks that you might possibly stay with him. He has to look him up, and will speak about the matter. If you could find something in that neighbourhood, it would be a very good thing for you...[...]

Camille Pissarro (1830–1903) had suggested to Theo that Vincent move to the north of Paris, to Auvers-sur-Oise, under the care of a therapist and psychiatrist Dr Paul-Ferdinand Gachet (1828–1909), a keen collector and patron of art, who was known to Pissarro. Vincent was keen on the plan and acknowledged that he would need to be under the doctor's care so that 'in case of an [epileptic] attack I do not fall into the hands of the police and get carried off to an asylum by force'.

From Vincent van Gogh to
Theo van Gogh
Extract from
Saint-Rémy, *2 February 1890*

My dear Theo,

I have just received your good news that you are a father at last, that Jo is over the most critical period, and finally that the little boy is doing well. That has done me more good and given me more pleasure than I can put into words. Bravo – and how pleased Mother will be! [...] No need to tell you that my thoughts have often turned to you of late, and it touched me very much that Jo had the kindness to write to me only the

***L'Arlesienne (Madame Ginoux)*, 1888**
MEDIUM: Oil on canvas
Courtesy of Metropolitan Museum of Art, New York, USA/Giraudon/ The Bridgeman Art Library

***Orchard in Blossom*, 1888, (detail)**
MEDIUM: Oil on canvas
© National Gallery of Scotland, Edinburgh, Scotland/The Bridgeman Art Library

night before. How brave and calm she was at her moment of peril, it touched me very much.

[…] I was extremely surprised by the article on my paintings you sent me. No need to tell you that I hope to keep thinking that I don't paint like that, but I do gather from it how I ought to be painting. For the article is absolutely right in the way it shows the gap to be filled, and I think that the writer really wrote it to guide, not only me, but all the other Impressionists, and even to help them make the breach in the right place. So he proposes an ideal collective ego to the others quite as much as to me. He simply tells me that here and there he can see something good, if you like, even in my work which is so imperfect, and that is the comforting part, which I appreciate and for which I hope I am grateful. […]

My illness makes me very sensitive right now, and I don't feel capable for the moment of continuing these 'translations' when such masterpieces are involved. I am stopping with the Sower on which I am working, and which is not coming on as I would wish. Being ill, however, I have thought a great deal about going on with the work. *When* I do it, I do it calmly, as you will soon see when I send you the 5 or 6 finished canvases.

[…] I'm going to stop here – I am a little anxious about a friend who, it seems, is still ill, and whom I should like to see. She is the one whose portrait I did in yellow and black, and she has changed very much. She has nervous attacks, complicated by a premature change of life, in short, very painful. She looked like an old grandfather the last time. I had promised to come back in a fortnight, but was taken ill again myself. […]

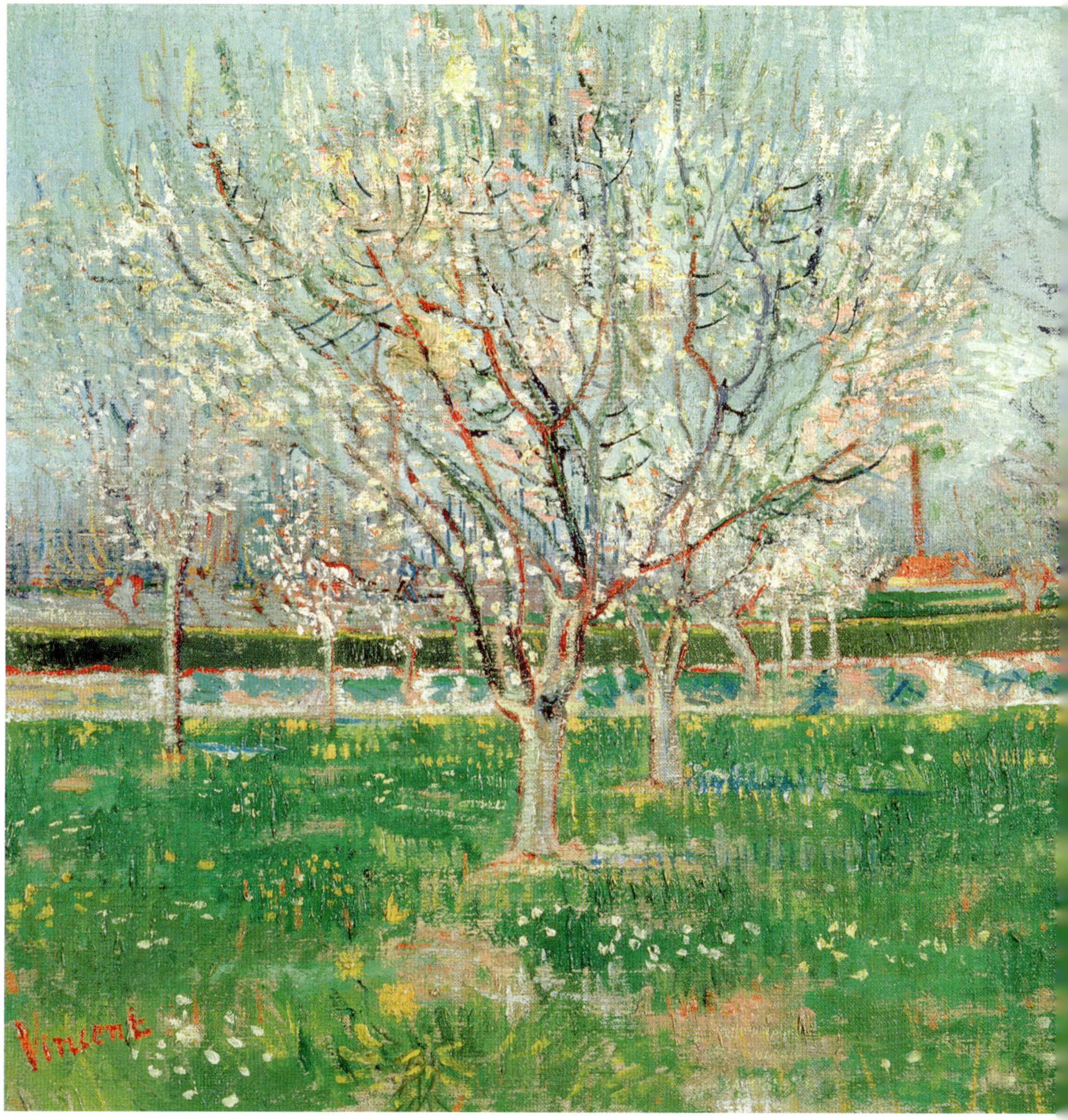

I am with you all in my thoughts, though ending my letter. May Jo long remain for us what she is now. As for the little boy, why don't you name him Theo, in memory of our Father, that would certainly give me much pleasure. ”

Theo and Johanna's son was born on 31 January 1890. Vincent wrote on 2 February with his congratulations and joy at the news, adding that it would be nice if the baby was named after their father Theodorus. However, the couple decided on Vincent Willem for their son, a name they had chosen months before.

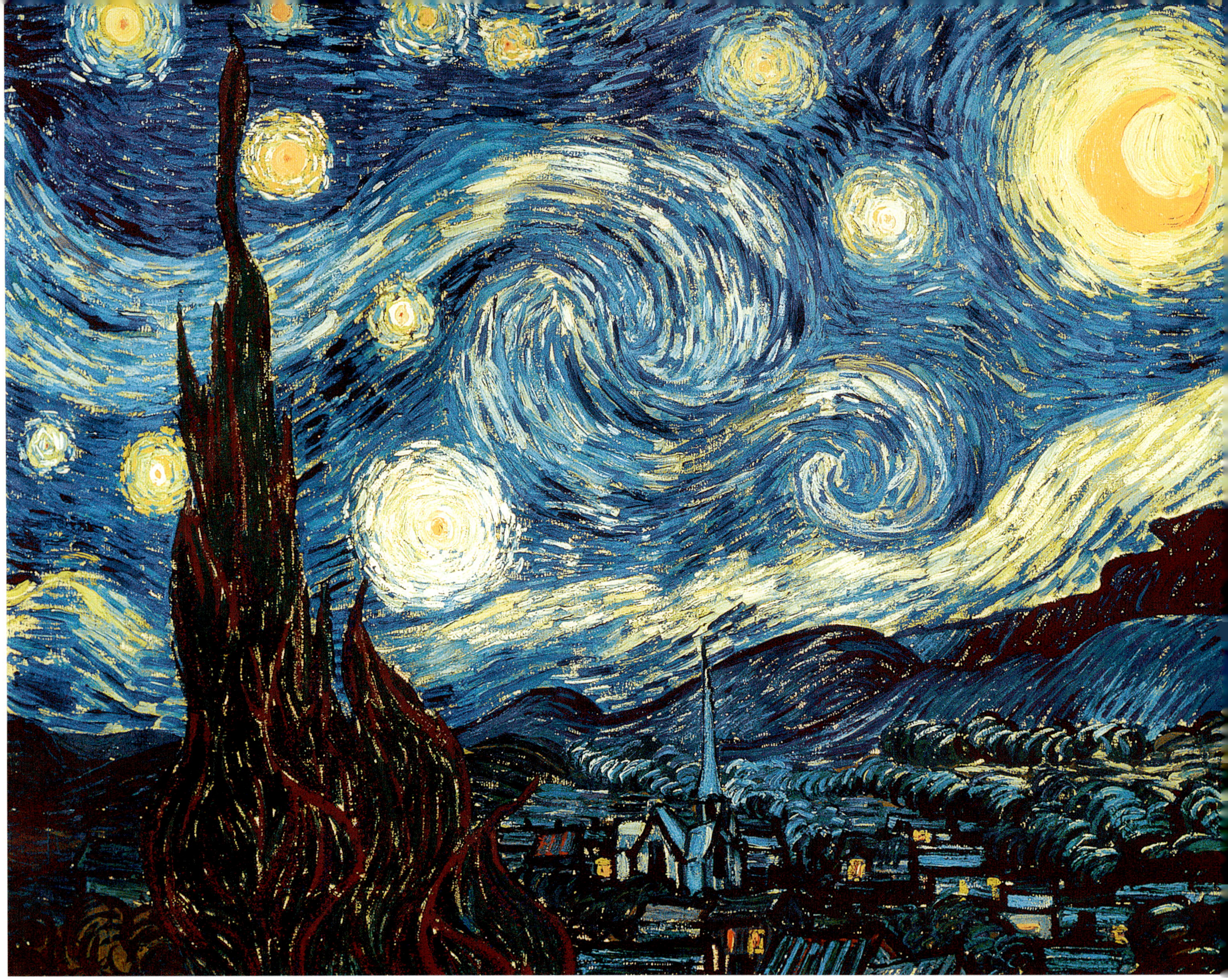

From Vincent van Gogh to

Albert Aurier

Extract from

Saint-Rémy, *9, 10 or 11 February 1890*

Dear M. Aurier

"Thank you very much for your article in the *Mercure de France*, which surprised me a good deal. I admire it very much as a work of art in itself, it seems to me that you paint with words; in fact, I encounter my canvases anew in your article, but better than they are in reality, richer, more meaningful. [...] Anyway – what I am

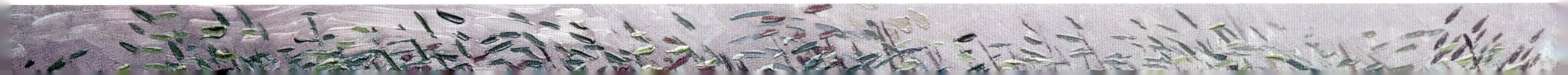

trying to say is that things seem to have mistakenly become attached to my name that you would do better to link to Monticelli [and] to Paul Gauguin, with whom I worked for several months in Arles, and whom, moreover, I already knew in Paris.

[…] A few days before we parted company, when my illness forced me to go into an asylum, I tried to paint 'his empty place'. It is a study of his wooden armchair, brown and dark red, the seat of greenish straw, and in place of the absent person, a lighted candle in a candlestick and some modern novels. Should the opportunity arise, do please take another look at this study by way of a reminder of him. It is done throughout in broken tones of green and red.

You may realize now that your article would have been fairer and – it seems to me – consequently more powerful, if, when dealing with the question of the nature of 'tropical painting' and the question of colour, you had – before speaking of me – done justice to Gauguin and Monticelli. For the role attaching to me, or that will be attached to me, will remain, I assure you, of very secondary importance.

[…] If you will do me the pleasure of accepting it, I shall include a study of cypresses for you in the next batch I send to my brother, in remembrance of your article. I am still working on it at the moment, as I want to put a small figure into it. The cypress is so characteristic of the Provence landscape. […]

The young French art critic, poet and painter, Albert Aurier (1865–92) had published an article on Vincent, 'Les Isolés: Vincent van Gogh', in *Mercure de France*, January 1890.

The Starry Night, 1889
MEDIUM: Oil on canvas
Courtesy of Museum of Modern Art, New York, USA/The Bridgeman Art Library

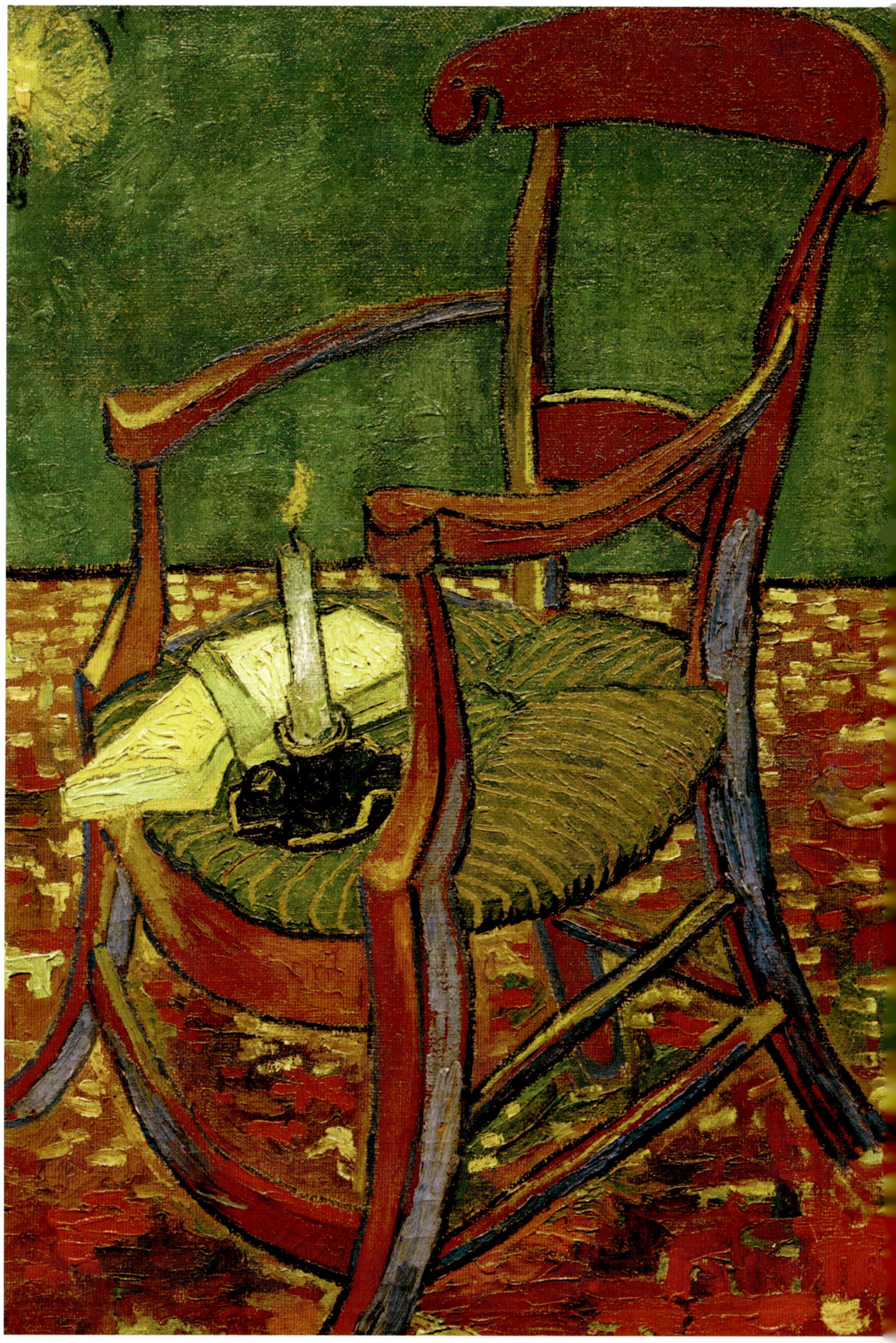

***Gauguin's Chair*, 1888, (detail)**
MEDIUM: Oil on jute
© akg-images

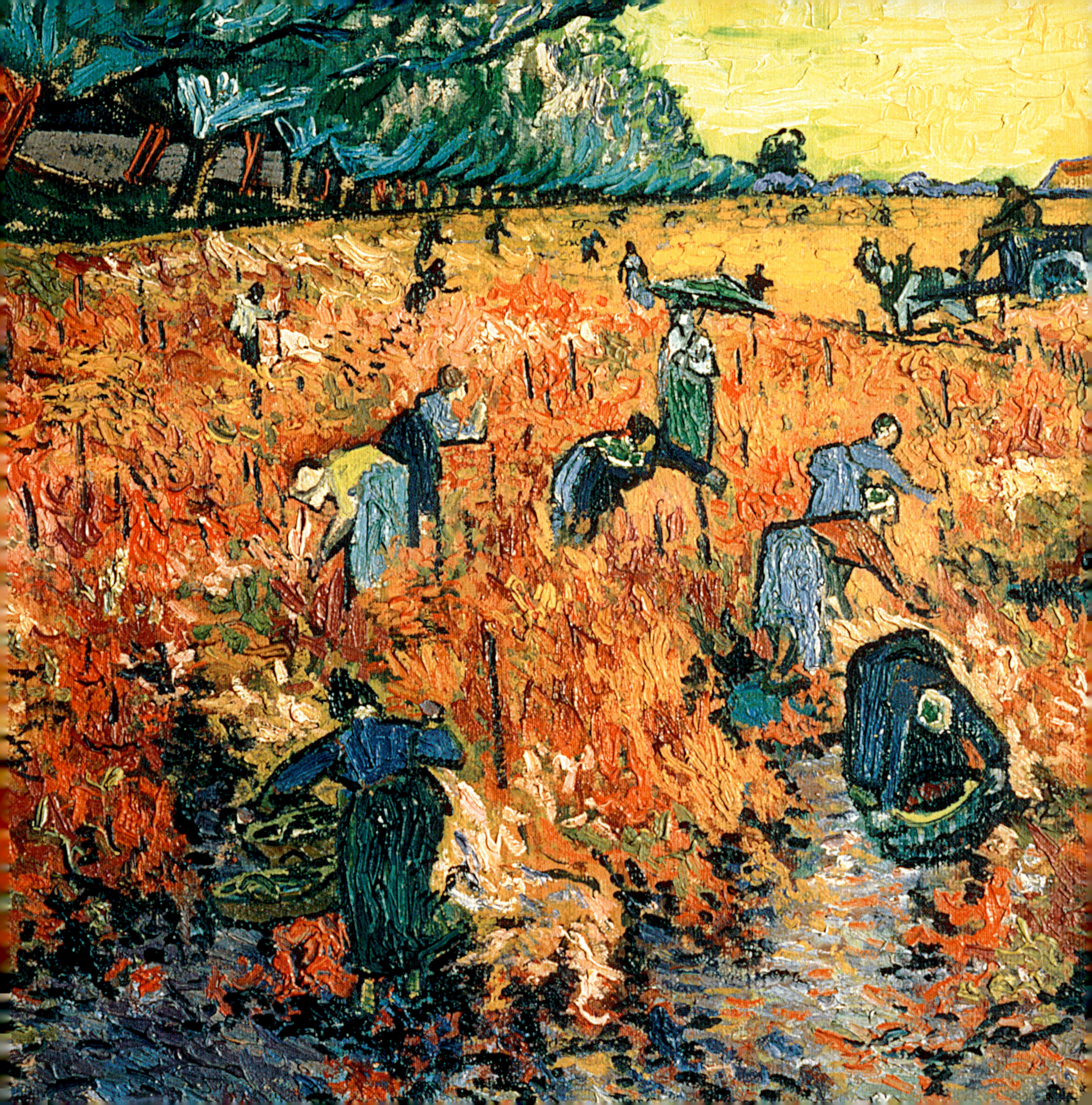

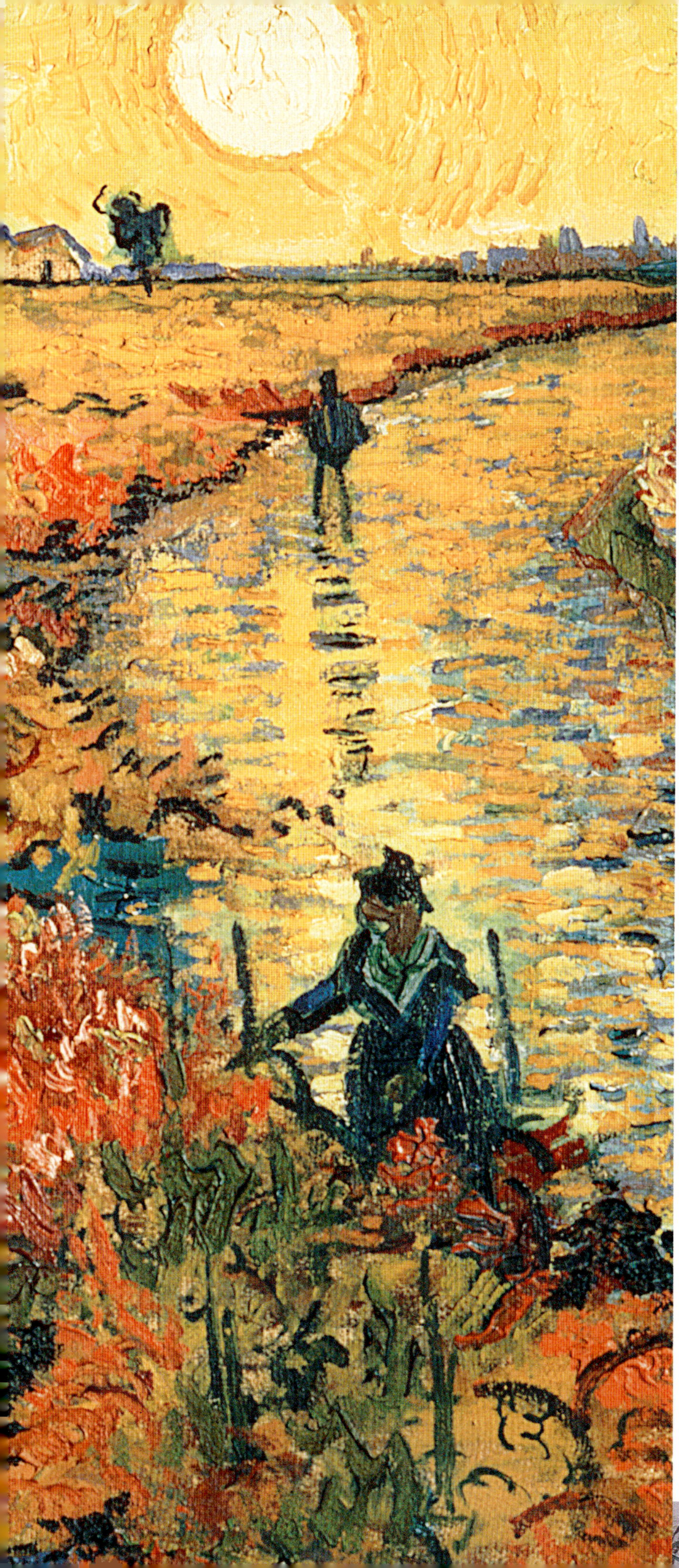

From Vincent van Gogh to his mother,

Anna van Gogh

Extract from Saint-Rémy, *c. 20 February 1890*

Dear Mother,

"I intended to answer your letter many days ago, but I could not bring myself to write, as I sat painting from morning to evening, and thus the time passed. I imagine that, like me, your thoughts are much with Jo and Theo: how glad I was when the news came that it had ended well: it was a good thing that Wil stayed on. I should have greatly preferred him to call the boy after Father, of whom I have been thinking so much these days, instead of after me; but seeing it has now been done, I started right away to make a picture for him, to hang in their bedroom, big branches of white almond blossom against a blue sky. […]

I was rather surprised at the article they wrote about me. Isaäcson wanted to do one some time ago, and I asked him not to. […] But I must admit that afterward, when my surprise had passed off a little, I felt at times very much cheered by it; moreover, yesterday Theo wrote me that they had sold one of my pictures at Brussels for 400 francs [*Red Vineyards at Arles*, 1888]. Compared with other prices, also those in Holland, this is little, but therefore I try to be productive to be able to go on working at a reasonable cost. […] Now I am strongly inclined to take advantage of my good luck in selling this picture by going to Paris to visit Theo.

***Red Vineyards at Arles*, 1888**
MEDIUM: Oil on canvas
Courtesy of Pushkin Museum, Moscow, Russia/The Bridgeman Art Library

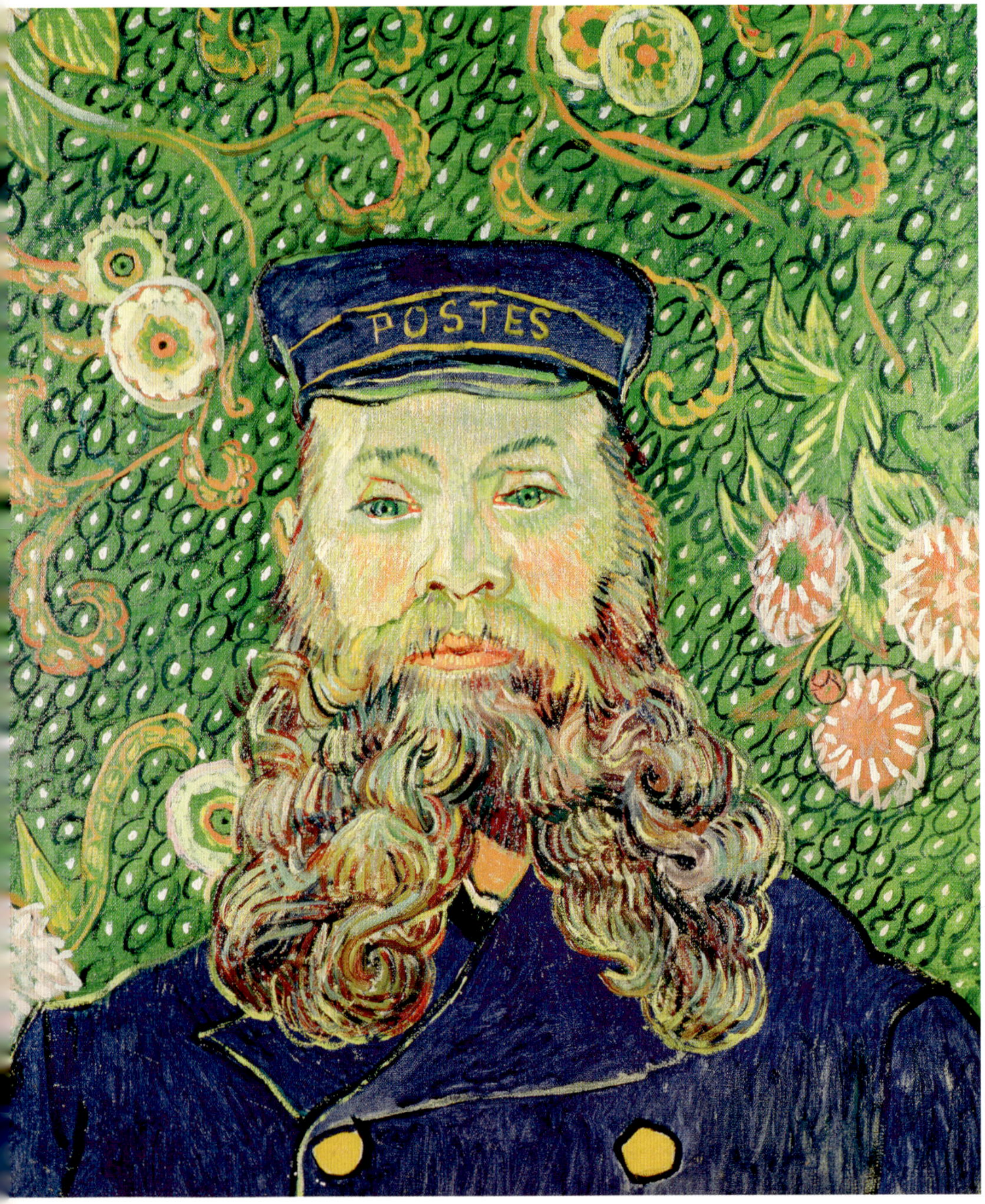

And thanks to the physician here, I shall leave feeling calmer and healthier than when I came. Trying how it goes outside a hospital is perhaps only natural."

An embrace in thought.

Your loving

Vincent

From Vincent van Gogh to Theo van Gogh
Extract from Saint-Rémy, *30 April 1890*

My dear Theo,

"Until now I have not been able to write you, but being a bit better just now, I did not wish to delay wishing you a happy year, since it's your birthday, you and your wife and child. At the same time I beg you to accept the various pictures I am sending you with my thanks for all the kindness you have shown me, for without you I should be very unhappy.

You will see that first of all there are canvases after Millet.

Not being intended for the public, perhaps you will eventually make presents of these to our sisters. But first you must keep what you like and as much as you want, it's yours absolutely. [...]

M. Peyron being away, I have not yet read my letters, but I know that some have come. He has been good enough to keep you posted on the situation, I do not know myself what to do or what to think, but I greatly wish to leave this house. That will not surprise you, I need say no more to you.

***Portrait of the Postman Joseph Roulin*, 1889**
MEDIUM: Oil on canvas
Courtesy of Museum of Modern Art, New York, USA/The Bridgeman Art Library

***The Cypresses*, c. 1889–90**
MEDIUM: Oil on canvas
Courtesy of Rijksmuseum Kroller-Muller, Otterlo, Netherlands/Giraudon/The Bridgeman Art Library

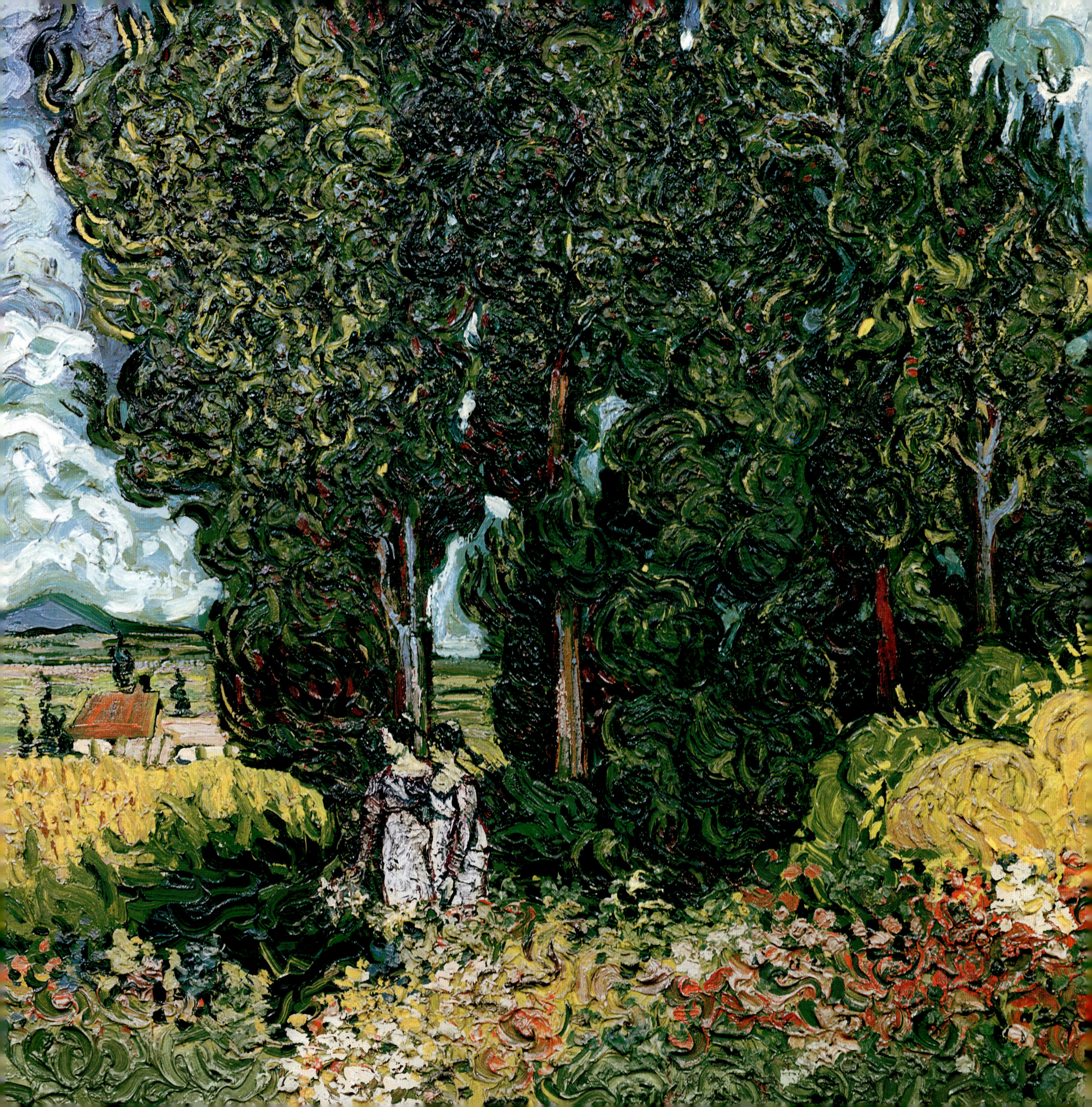

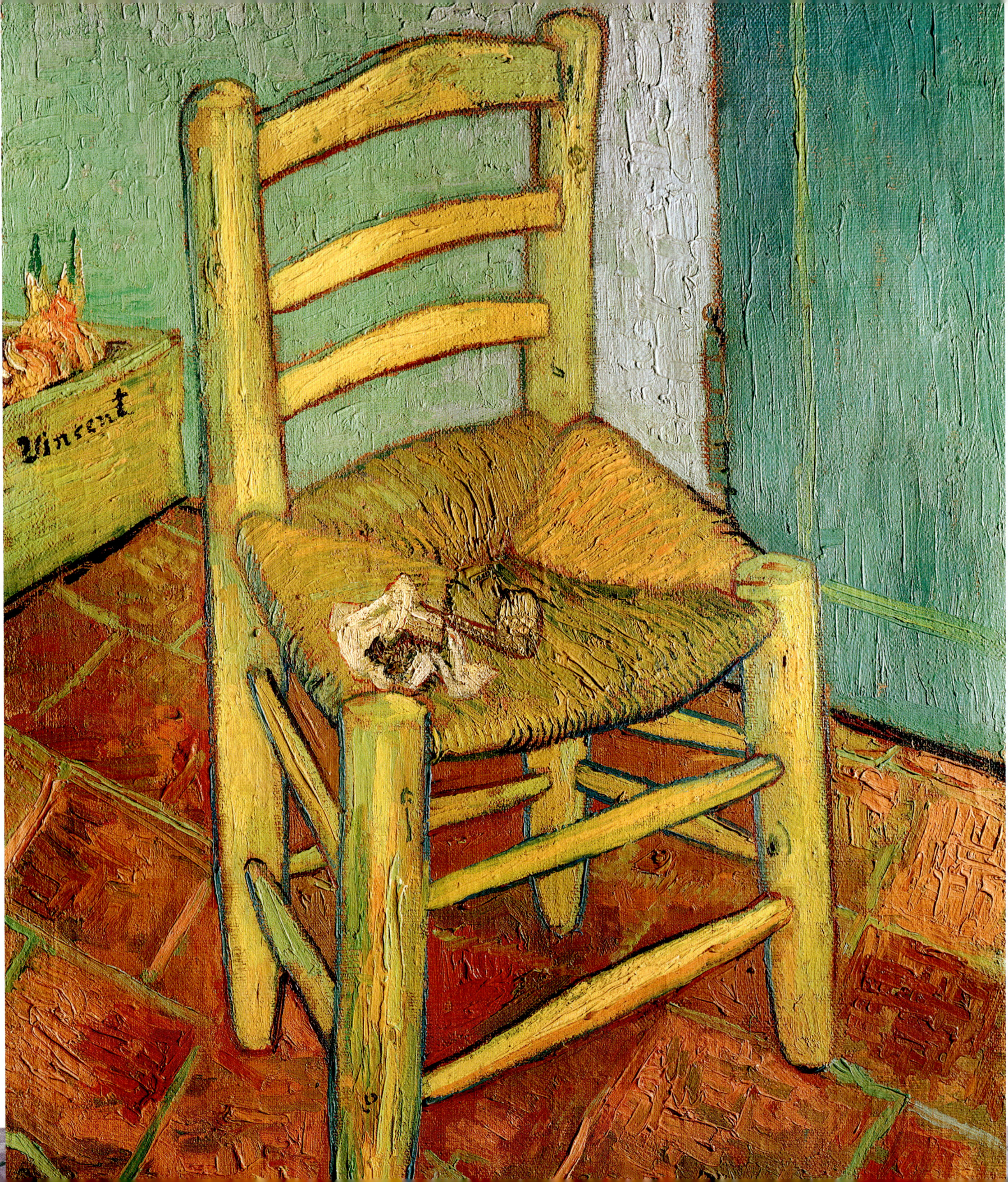
Vincent

Letters from home have come too, which I have not yet had the courage to read, I feel so melancholy. Please ask M. Aurier not to write any more articles on my painting, insist upon this, that to begin with he is mistaken about me, since I am too overwhelmed with grief to be able to face publicity. […] I felt ill at the time I was doing the almond blossoms. If I had been able to go on working, you can judge from it that I would have done others of trees in blossom. Now the trees in blossom are almost over, really I have no luck. Yes, I must try to get out of here, but where to go?"

Ever yours

Vincent

Following the critical praise that Vincent had received in Albert Aurier's article, he had experienced another mental breakdown, taking two months to recover. At a low ebb, he did not want to encourage further publicity.

Extract from Saint-Rémy, *4 May 1890*

"Thank you for your kind letter and the portrait of Jo, which is very pretty and a very successful pose. Now look, I'm going to be very straightforward in my reply and as practical as possible. First, I categorically reject what you say, that I must be accompanied the whole way. Once on the train, I will be quite safe, I am not one of those who are dangerous – and even supposing I do have an attack, there are other passengers in the carriage, aren't there, and anyway, don't they know at every station what to do in such cases?

[…] it seems to me that a fortnight at most (although I'd be happier with a week) should be enough to prepare the move. I shall have myself accompanied as far as Tarascon – even one or two stations further on, if you insist. When I arrive in Paris (I'll send a telegram on leaving here) you could come and pick me up at the Gare de Lyon.

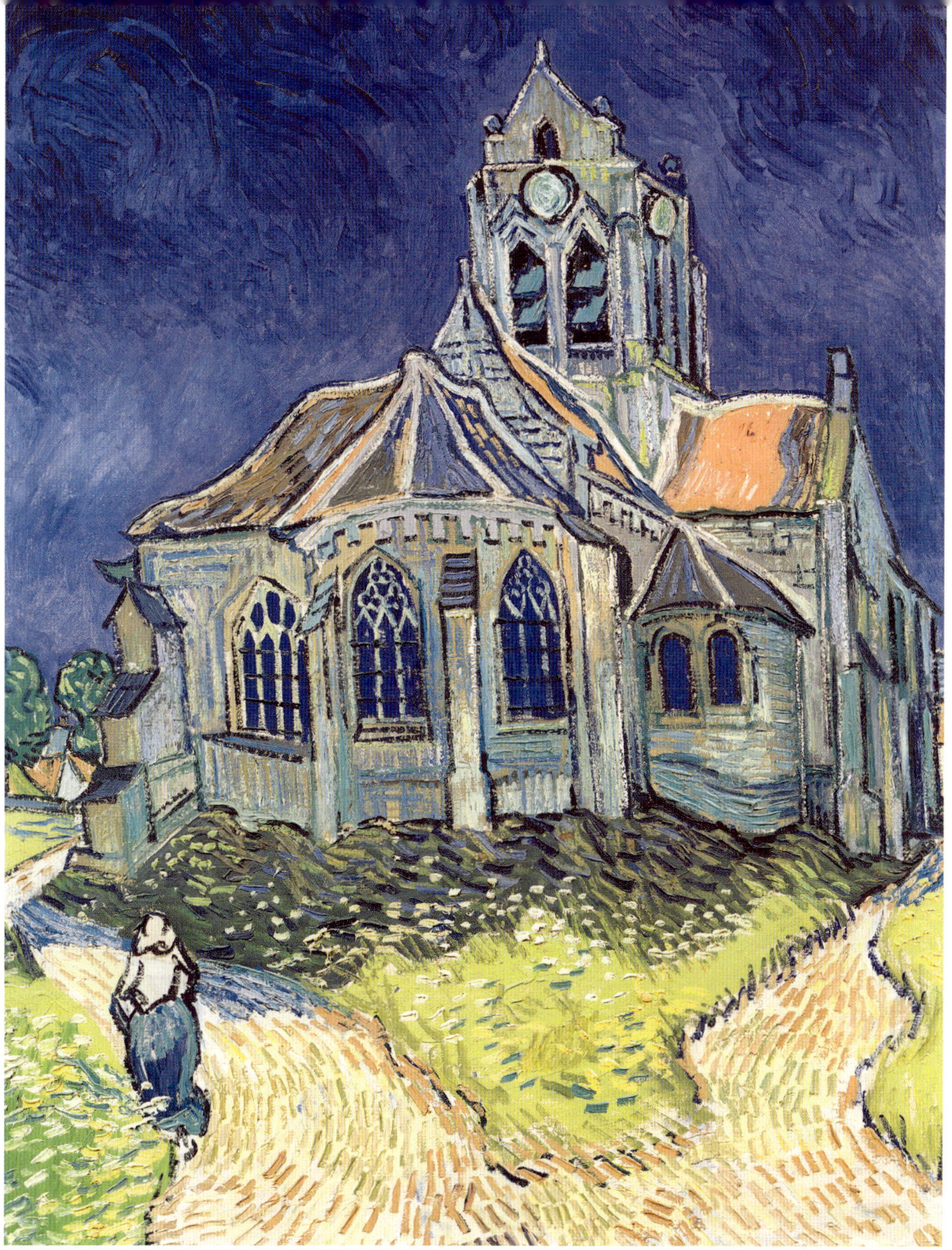

Now I should think it would be as well to go and see this doctor [Dr Gachet] in the country as soon as possible, and we could leave the luggage at the station. So I should not be staying with you for more than, let's say, 2 or 3 days. I would then leave for this village, where I could stay at the inn to begin with.

***Vincent's Chair*, 1888**
MEDIUM: Oil on canvas
Courtesy of National Gallery, London, UK/The Bridgeman Art Library

***The Church at Auvers-sur-Oise*, 1890**
MEDIUM: Oil on canvas
Courtesy of Musée d'Orsay, Paris, France/ The Bridgeman Art Library

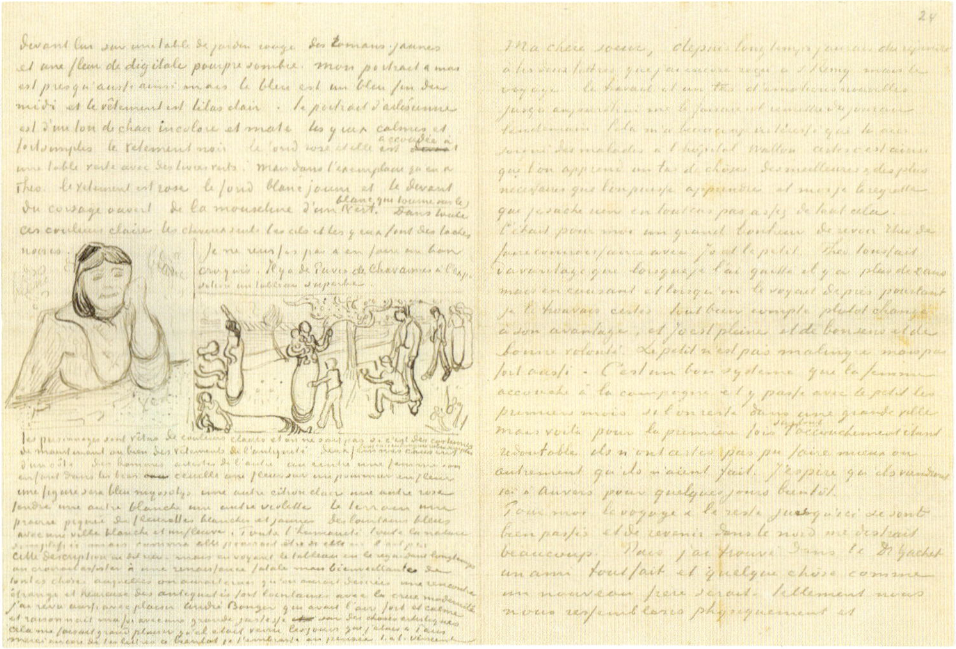

What I think you might do one of these days – without delay – is to write to our future friend, the doctor in question, 'My brother greatly desires to make your acquaintance, and preferring to consult you before prolonging his stay in Paris, hopes that you will approve of his coming and spending a few weeks in your village in order to do some studies; he has every confidence in reaching an understanding with you, believing that his illness will abate with a return to the north, whereas his condition would threaten to become more acute if he stayed any longer in the south'.

There, you write him something like that, we can send him a telegram the day after I arrive in Paris, or the day after that, and he would probably meet me at the station.

The surroundings here are beginning to weigh me down more than I can say – heavens above, I've been patient for more than a year – I need some air, I feel overwhelmed by boredom and grief.

So please ask M. Peyron to allow me to leave, let's say by the 15th at the latest… there really is a chance that the change will do me good – the work is going well, I've done 2 canvases of the newly cut grass in the grounds, one of which is extremely simple. […]

From Vincent van Gogh to
Willemina van Gogh
Extract from
Auvers-sur-Oise, *5 June 1890*

My Dear Sister,

I ought to have replied to the two letters I received when I was still at St. Rémy, but the journey, the work and a lot of new emotions caused me to postpone from day to day until this moment writing you a letter. […]

It was a great happiness to me to see Theo again, and to make the acquaintance of Jo and the little one. Theo's cough was worse than it was when I left him two years ago, but when I talked with him and saw him at close range it seemed certain to me that, all things considered, there is a change rather for the better, and Jo is full of good sense, as well as good intentions. […]

As for myself, the travelling and all the rest have come off very well so far, and coming back north has been a great distraction for me. And then I have found a true friend in Dr. Gachet, something like another brother, so much do we resemble each other physically and also mentally. He is a very nervous man himself and very queer in his behaviour […] I painted his portrait the other day, and I am also going to paint a portrait of his daughter, who is 19 years old. […]

But during the last weeks at St. Rémy I worked like a man in a frenzy, especially on bunches of flowers, roses and violet irises. I brought along a relatively large picture for Theo's and

A Vase of Roses, 1890
MEDIUM: Oil on canvas
Courtesy of Private Collection/Peter Willi/The Bridgeman Art Library

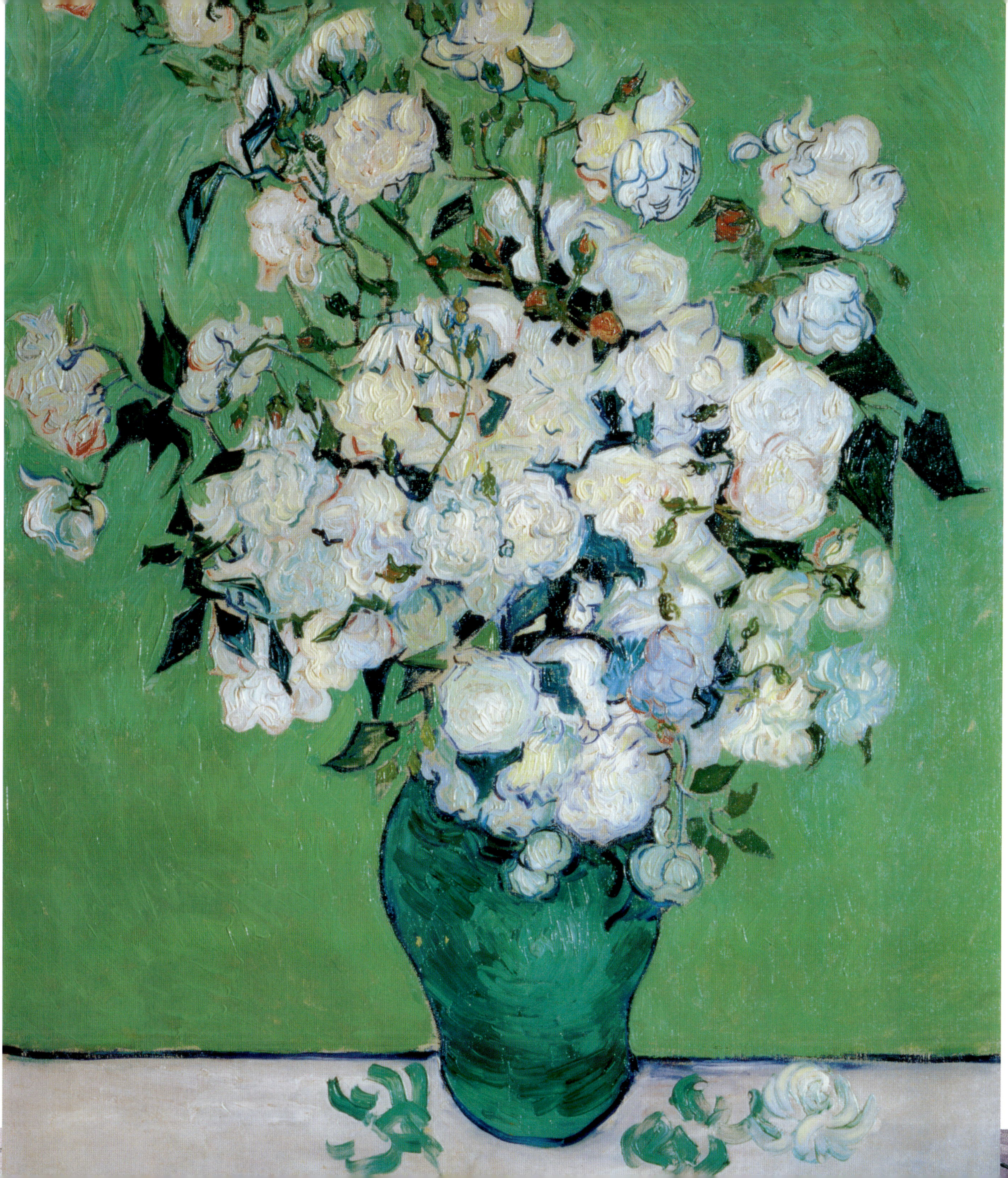

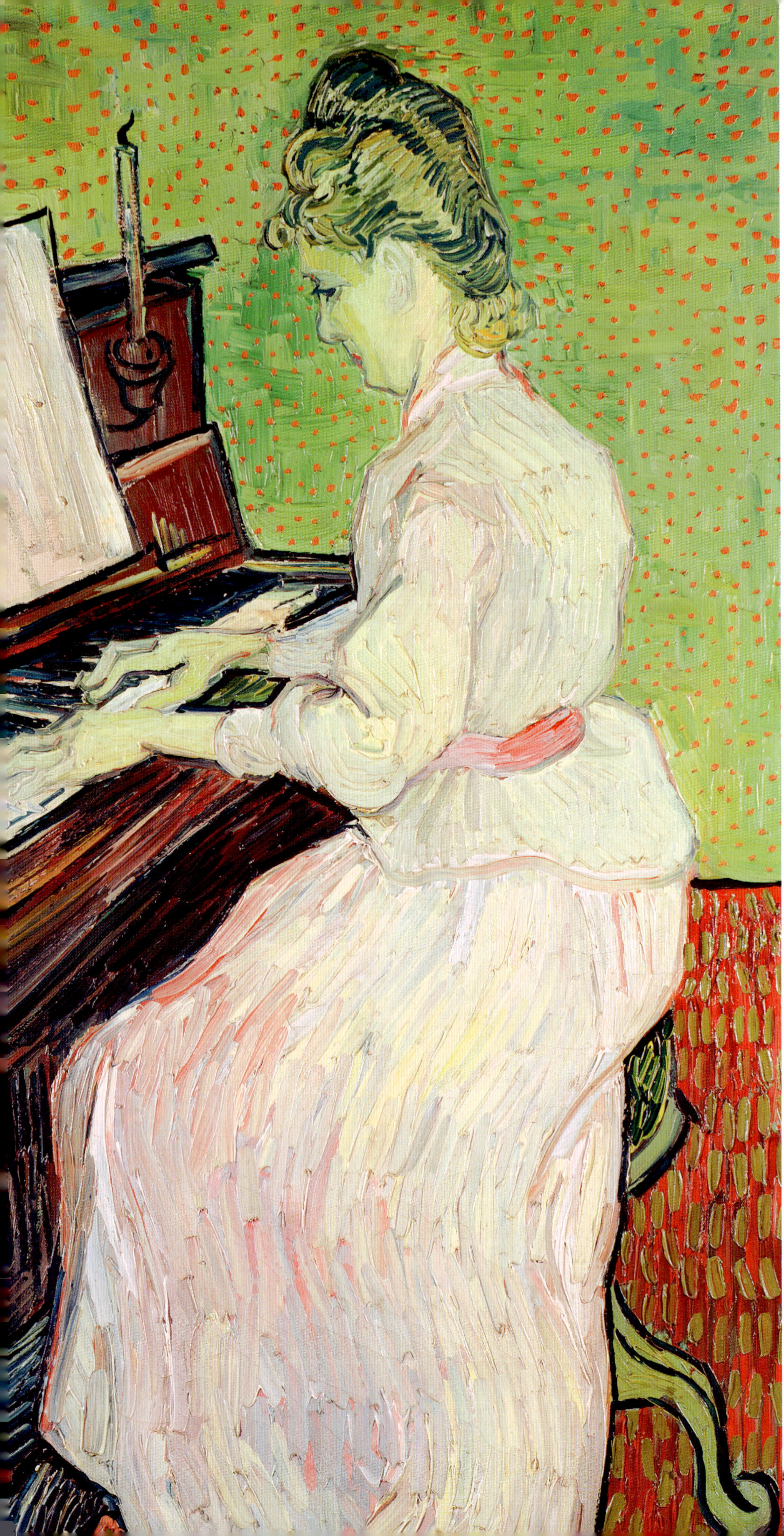

Jo's little boy – which they hung over the piano – white almond blossoms – big branches against a sky-blue background – and they also have a new portrait of the Arlésienne in their apartment.

My friend Dr Gachet is *decidedly enthusiastic* about the latter portrait of an Arlésienne, which I also have a copy of for myself – and also about a self-portrait, which I am very glad of, seeing that he will urge me to paint figures, and I hope he is going to find some interesting models for me to paint.

What impassions me most – much, much more than all the rest of my métier – is the portrait, the modern portrait. I seek it in colour, and surely I am not the only one to seek it in this direction. […] So the portrait of Dr Gachet shows you a face the colour of an overheated brick, and scorched by the sun, with reddish hair and a white cap, surrounded by a rustic scenery with a background of blue hills; his clothes are ultramarine – this brings out the face and makes it paler, notwithstanding the fact that it is brick-coloured. His hands, the hands of an obstetrician, are paler than the face. Before him, lying on a red garden table, are yellow novels and a foxglove flower of a somber purple hue.

My self-portrait is done in nearly the same way but the blue is the fine blue of the Midi, and the clothes are a light lilac. […]

Once more thanks for your letters. I hope to see you soon, I embrace you in thought. ”

Yours

Vincent

Vincent had stayed only three days with Theo and Jo and the new baby before heading for Auvers and Dr Gachet's care. Vincent found that Dr Gachet suffered from certain neuroses too, so while he did find a friend in him, Vincent questioned how Dr Gachet would cure him: 'Now when one blind man leads another blind man, don't they both fall in the ditch?'.

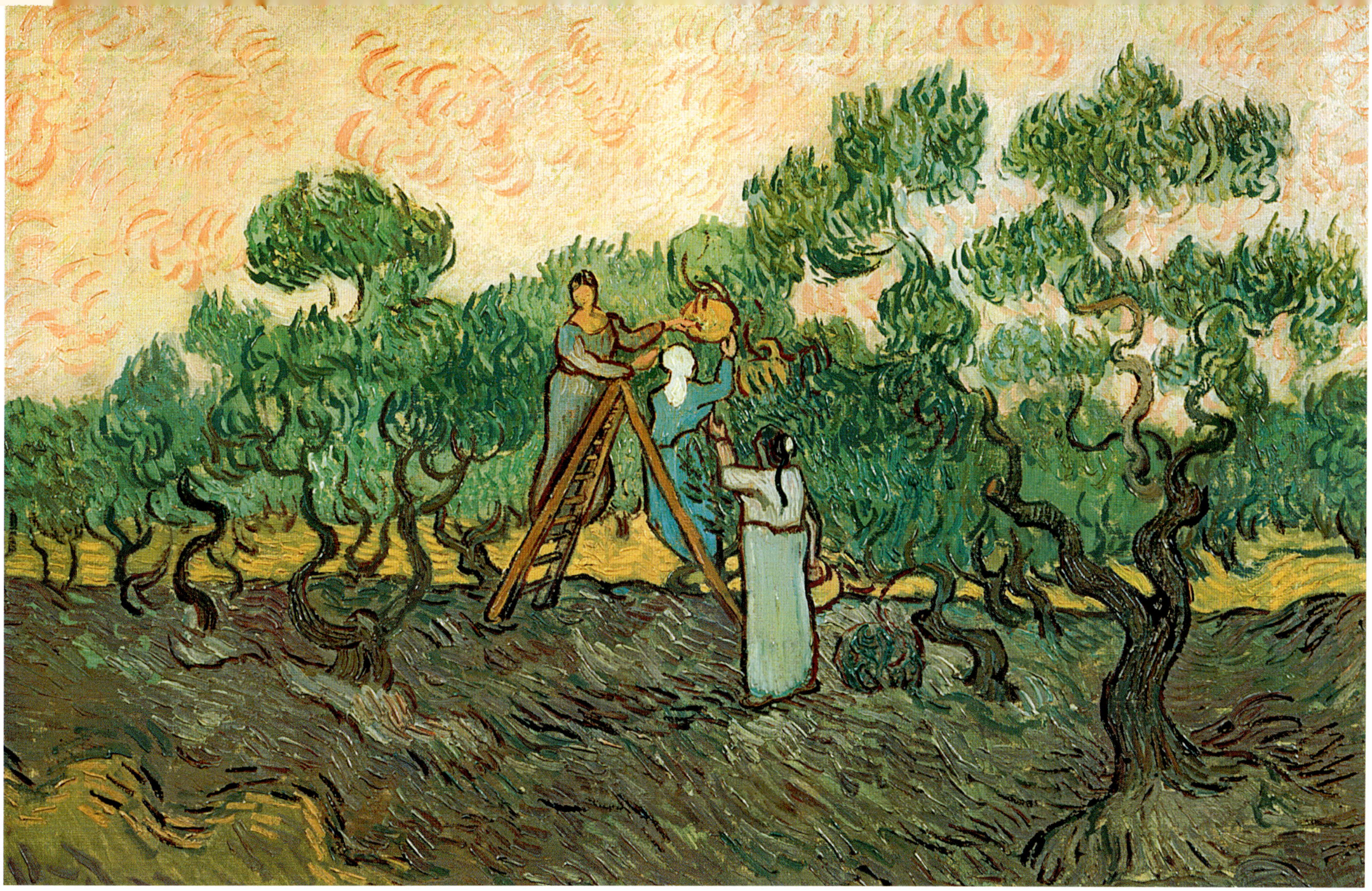

From Theo van Gogh to

Vincent van Gogh

Extract from

Paris, *30 June 1890*

My dearest brother,

"We have gone through a period of the greatest anxiety; our dear little boy has been very ill, but fortunately the doctor, who was uneasy himself, told Jo, You are not going to lose the child because of this [...]

At present we do not know what we ought to do; there are problems. [...] when I work all day long and still do not earn enough to protect that good Jo from worries over money matters, as those rats Boussod and Valadon are treating me as though I just entered their business, and are keeping me on a short allowance [...] I am going to take the plunge, and establish myself as a private dealer in my own house.

[...] Don't bother your head about me or about us, old fellow, but remember that what gives me the greatest pleasure is the knowledge that you are in good health and that you are busy with your work, which is admirable. [...]

***Marguerite Gachet at the Piano*, 1890**
MEDIUM: Oil on canvas
Courtesy of Offentliche Kunstsammlung, Basel, Switzerland/Giraudon/The Bridgeman Art Library

***The Olive Pickers, Saint-Rémy*, 1889**
MEDIUM: Oil on canvas
Courtesy of Private Collection/Peter Willi/The Bridgeman Art Library

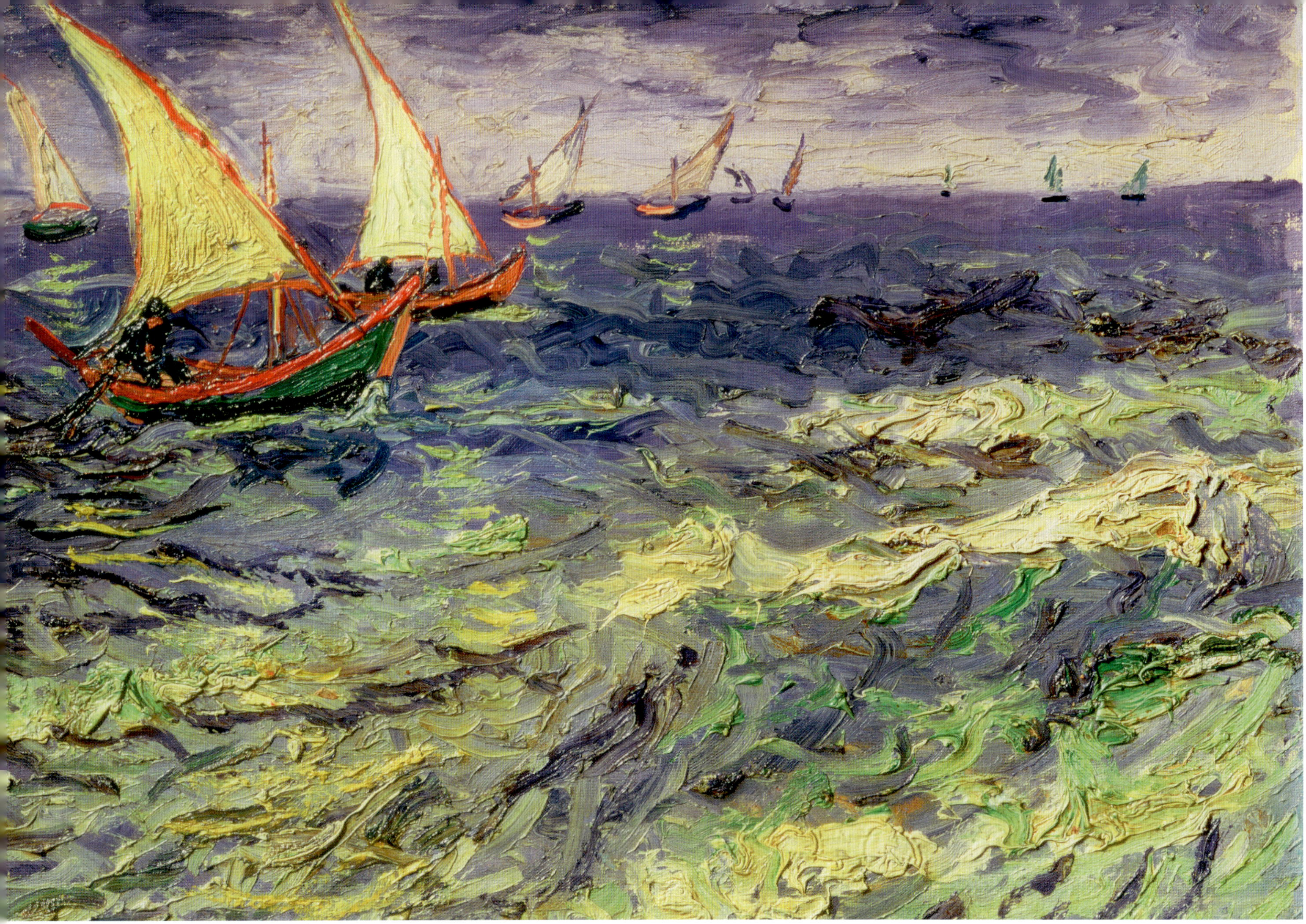

Is this enough? No – I have, and I hope from the bottom of my heart that you too will someday have, – a wife to whom you will be able to say these things. [...]

Your portrait of Miss Gachet must be admirable, and I shall be happy to see it with those spots of orange in the background. [...] Now listen, as soon as Jo is a little stronger and the little one entirely recovered, you must come and stay with us for a day or two, at least on a Sunday and some days after. [...]

In Paris Theo and Jo's baby had become sickly. They were greatly concerned and Theo wrote to Vincent to inform him. In the letter Theo also wrote of financial worries, and his idea of setting up as a private dealer. Vincent replied the same day: 'I should greatly like to come and see you'. Due to the baby's continuing ill health both Theo and Jo were exhausted. A letter on 5 July from Theo to Vincent confirmed that all was well again: 'We count on seeing you on next Sunday.'

***Seascape at Saintes-Maries*, date unknown**
MEDIUM: Oil on canvas
Courtesy of Pushkin Museum, Moscow, Russia/The Bridgeman Art Library

***The Garden of Doctor Gachet at Auvers-sur-Oise*, 1890**
MEDIUM: Oil on canvas
Courtesy of Musée d'Orsay, Paris, France/Giraudon/The Bridgeman Art Library

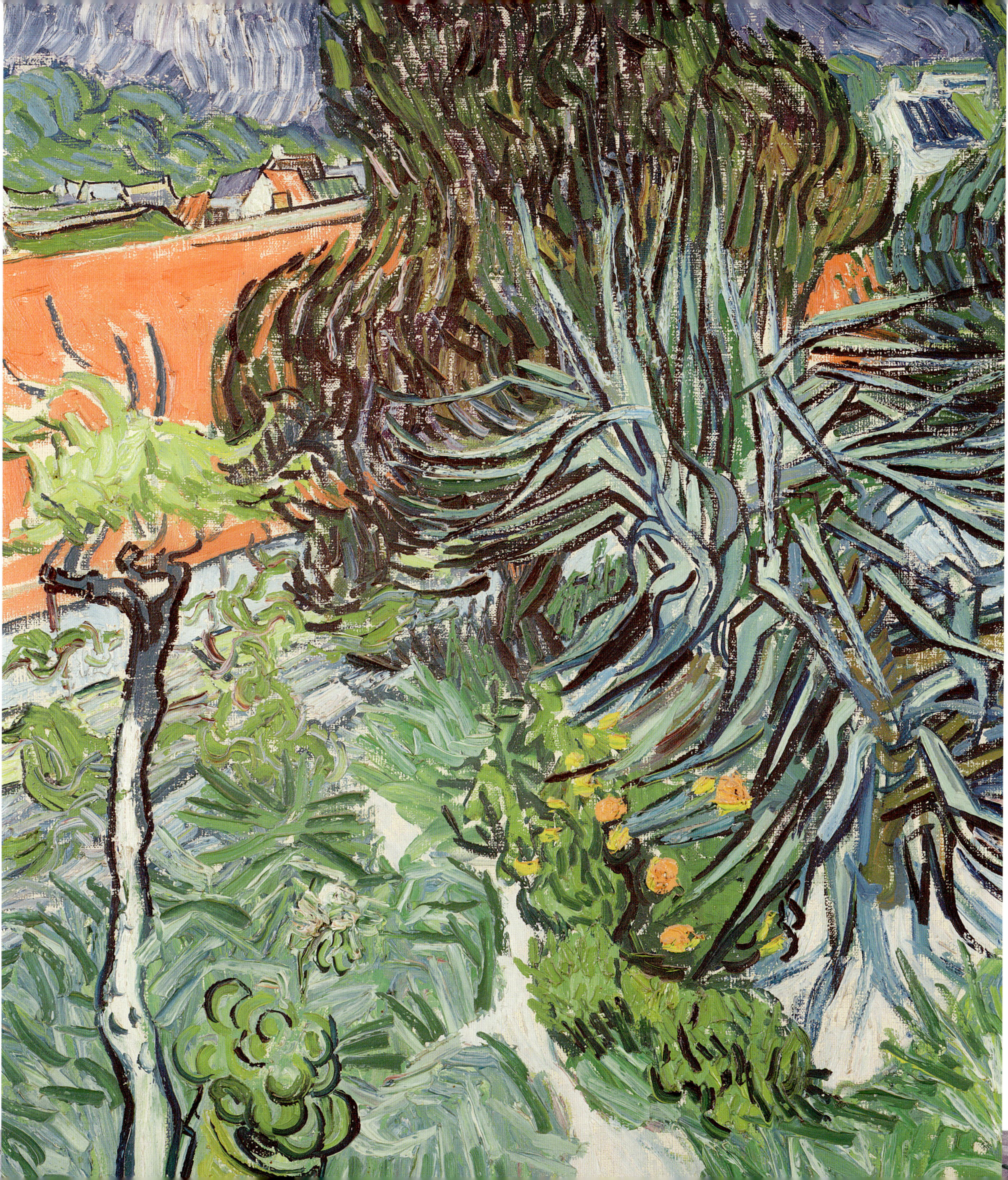

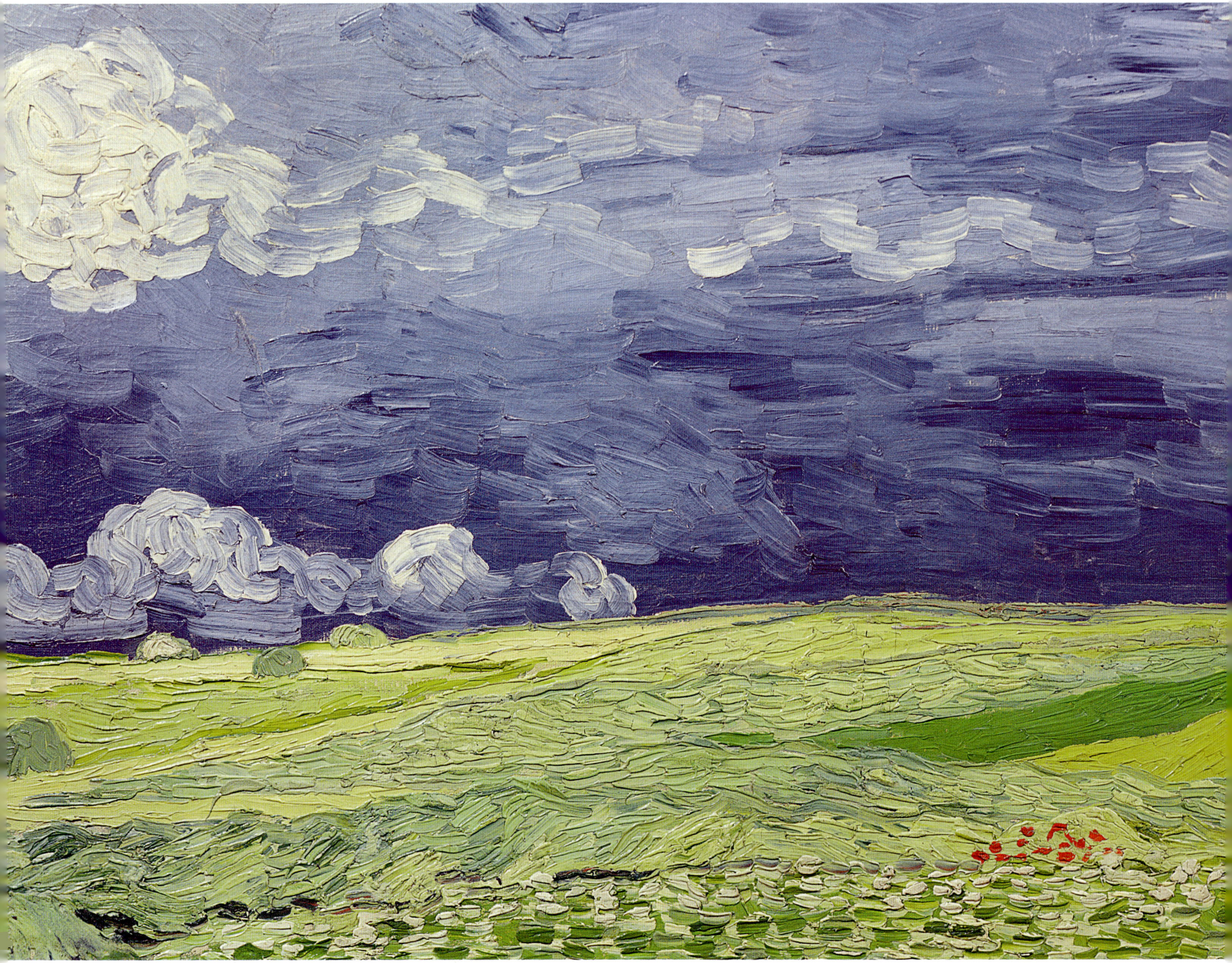

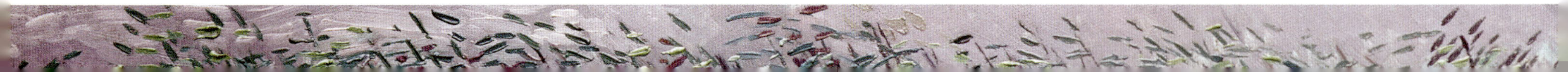

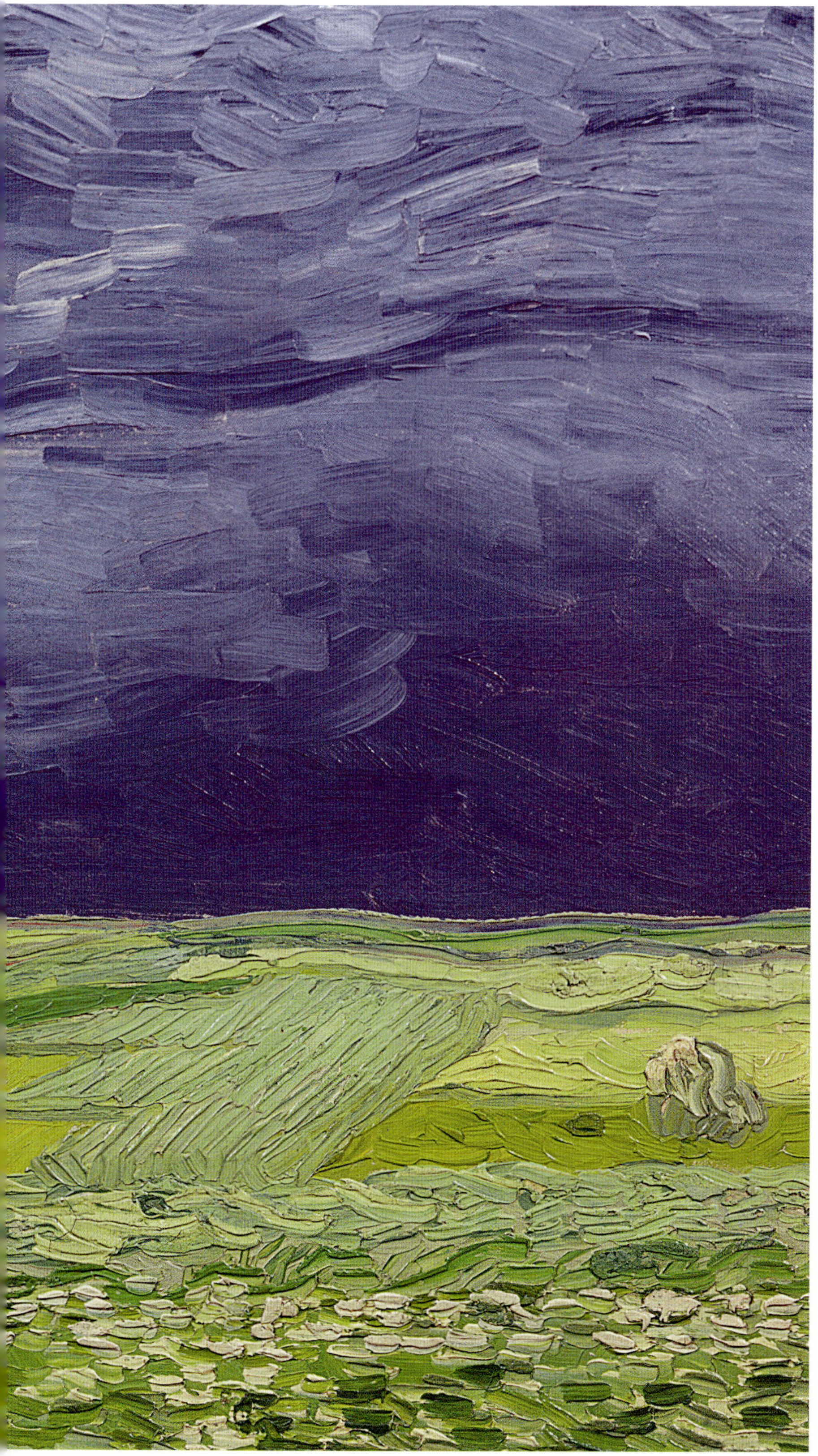

From Vincent van Gogh to

Theo and Johanna van Gogh

Extract from

Auvers-sur-Oise, *c. 10 July 1890*

Dear brother and sister,

"The letter from Jo has really been like a gospel for me, a deliverance from the distress caused by the hours I shared with you, which were a bit difficult and trying for us all. [Earlier in the month Vincent had gone on his last visit to Paris.] It is no slight matter when we are all made aware that our daily bread is at risk, no slight matter when for different reasons we are also made aware of the precariousness of our existence.

Back here, I, too, still felt very sad, and the storm which threatens you continued to weigh heavily on me as well. What is to be done? [...] I was afraid – not entirely – but nevertheless a little – that my being a burden on you was something you found intolerable – but Jo's letter proves to me clearly that you do realize that I am working and making an effort just as much as you are.

So – having arrived back here, I have set to work again [...] I have painted three more large canvases. [...] The third canvas is Daubigny's garden, a picture I have had in mind ever since I came here. [...]"

Jo had sent a letter to Vincent, which he had greatly appreciated as it had eased some of his concerns. During his visit to Paris to see Theo, Jo and baby Vincent, he had formed the impression of his being an 'intolerable' burden on his brother. His letter

***Wheatfields Under Thunderclouds*, 1890**
MEDIUM: Oil on canvas
Courtesy of Van Gogh Museum, Amsterdam, The Netherlands/Giraudon/ The Bridgeman Art Library

continues with discussion of his three current works, including *Daubigny's Garden*, 1890, and the contribution he hoped to make to Theo's income, should they be sold.

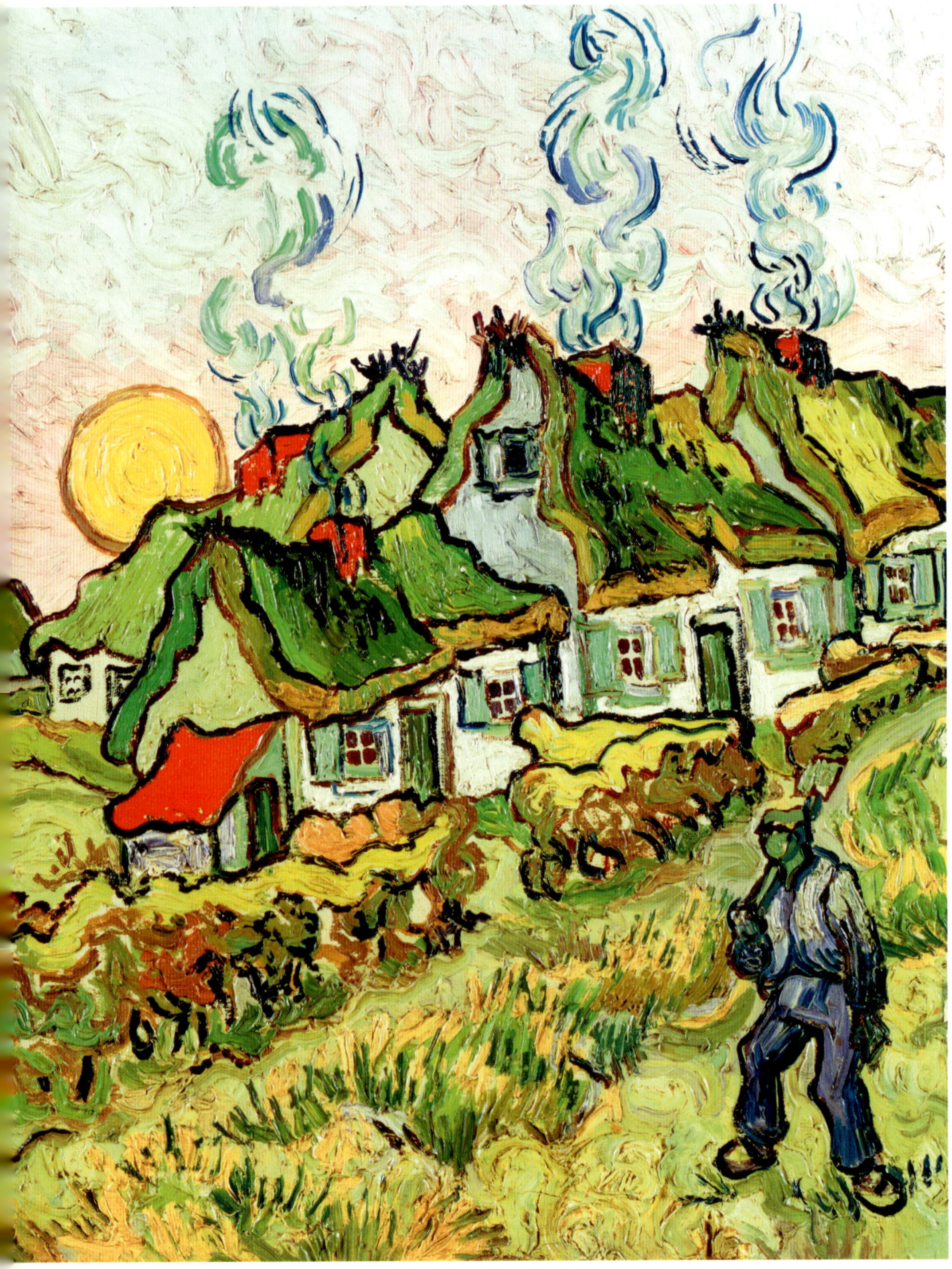

When Vincent visited Jo and Theo in Paris on 6 July 1890, he was taken aback by how ill Theo looked. Scholars argue that it was the realization that he, after many years of passing on his problems to Theo and using him to fund his life as a painter, was primarily responsible for his brother's failing health. He had stated later in July in a letter to Theo that 'As far as the peace of your household is concerned, I am as much convinced that it can be preserved as I am that it is threatened by storms'. This may have been the reason why, on 27 July 1890, he took a gun and walked into the fields near his home, shooting himself in the chest. He did not die but struggled back to the Auberge Ravoux where he was staying. Dr Gachet attended him but did not think Vincent needed to go to hospital. Theo came as soon as he received the news and stayed at his brother's bedside during the last night and day of his life.

Vincent died on 29 July 1890. The funeral was simple. Émile Bernard (1868–1941), Vincent and Theo's friend, gave an account of it: 'the walls of the room where the body lay were covered with his last canvases.... The coffin was covered with a white sheet and heaped with flowers, the sunflowers he loved so much, and yellow dahlias, yellow flowers everywhere. It was his favourite colour ... a symbol of the light he imagined in people's hearts, just as he did in his paintings.'

After the service Theo found time to give some of Vincent's paintings to those who attended, including Dr Gachet. Vincent's last paintings are some of his most powerful and expressive: *Wheatfields under Thunderclouds*, 1890, *Daubigny's Garden*, 1890, and *The Church at Auvers-sur-Ouse*, 1890.

House and Figure, 1890
MEDIUM: Oil on canvas
Courtesy of The Barnes Foundation, Merion, Pennsylvania, USA/The Bridgeman Art Library

Daubigny's Garden, 1890
MEDIUM: Oil on canvas
Courtesy of Van Gogh Museum, Amsterdam, The Netherlands/Giraudon/The Bridgeman Art Library

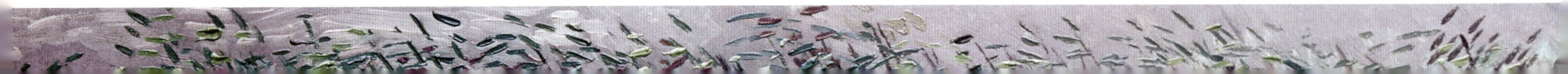

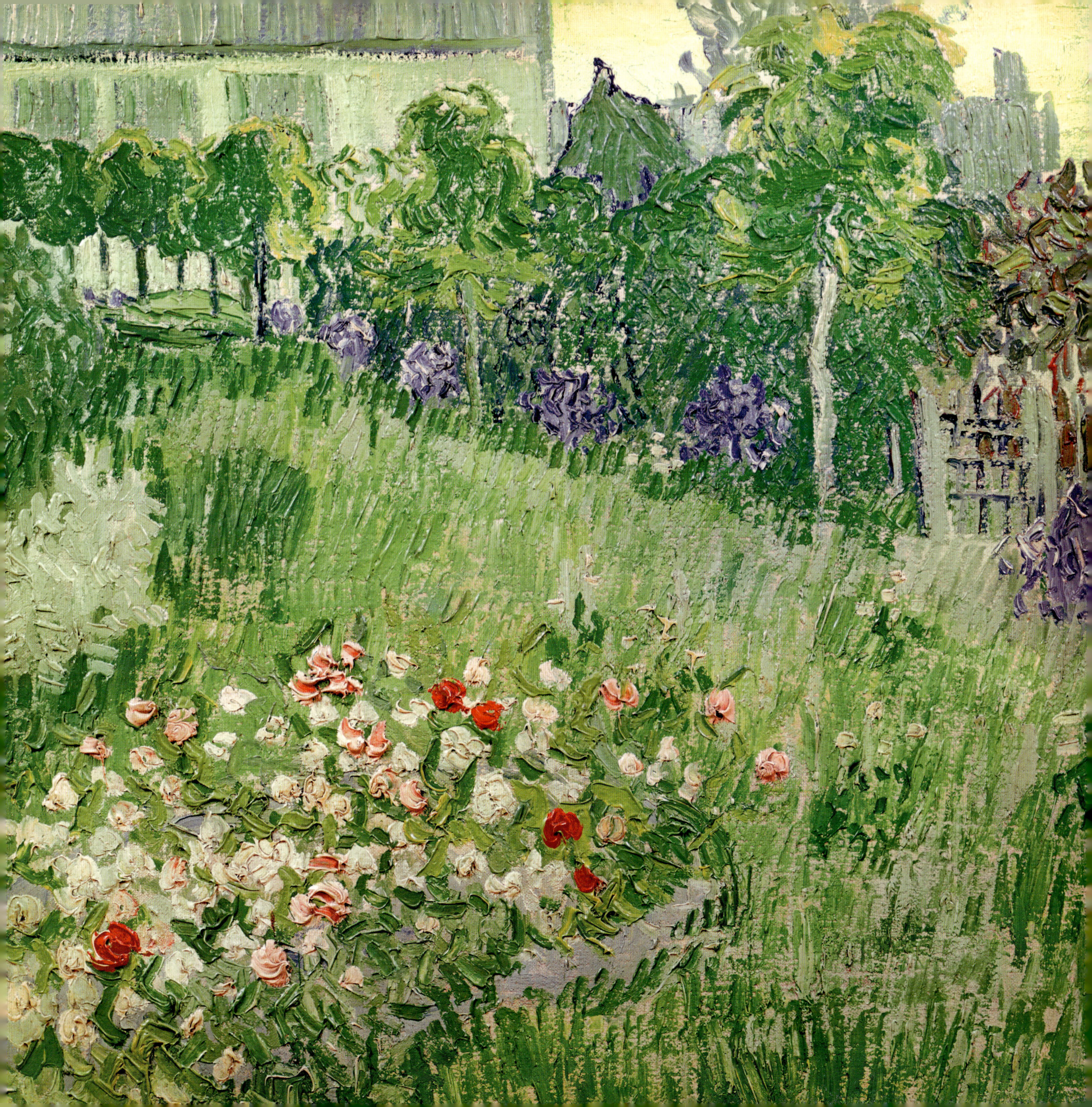

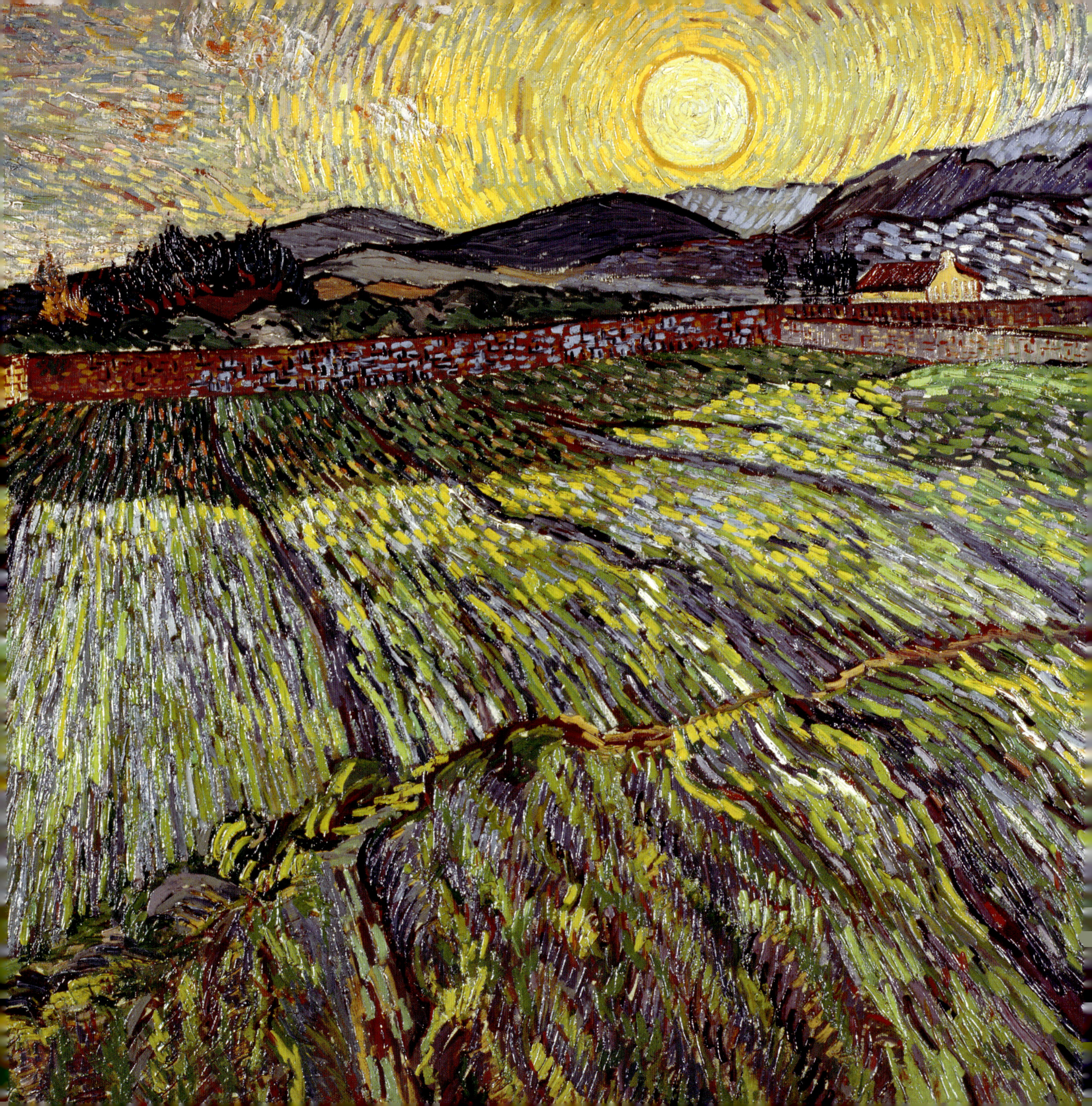

From Theo van Gogh to
His mother
Extract from
Paris, *1 August 1890*

"[…] One cannot write how sad one is, nor find solace in pouring out one's heart. May I come to you soon? I still have to make all sorts of arrangements here, but if it is possible, I would like to leave here on Sunday morning to be with you in the evening. It is a grief that will weigh on me for a long time and will certainly not leave my thoughts as long as I live, but if one should want to say anything about it, it is that he himself has found the rest he so much longed for. If he could have seen how people behaved toward me when he had left us and the sympathy of so many for himself, he would at this moment not have wanted to die.

Today I received your letter and the one from Wil, and I thank you both. I can better tell you everything than write. Dr Gachet and the other doctor were exemplary and have looked after him well, but they realized from the first moment that there was nothing one could do. Vincent said 'I would like to go like this,' and half an hour later he had his wish. Life weighed so heavily upon him, but as happens so often everyone is now full of praise, also for his talent. Maybe it was fortunate that Jo was not here, it would have been such a shock for her. May she also come once I am there? Later we will go to Amsterdam for a couple of days. Oh, Mother, I so much long to be with you. I suppose you will have written to Lies. I can't do it at this time. Tomorrow I will only know for certain whether I can leave, and if I cannot come, I will let you know. Oh, Mother, he was so very much my own brother. […]"

Six months after Vincent's death, Theo died on 25 January 1891, leaving a young wife and one-year-old son. At his death his wife Johanna van Gogh-Bonger inherited all the canvases that Vincent had painted – they were the property of Theo – and the letters that Vincent had sent.

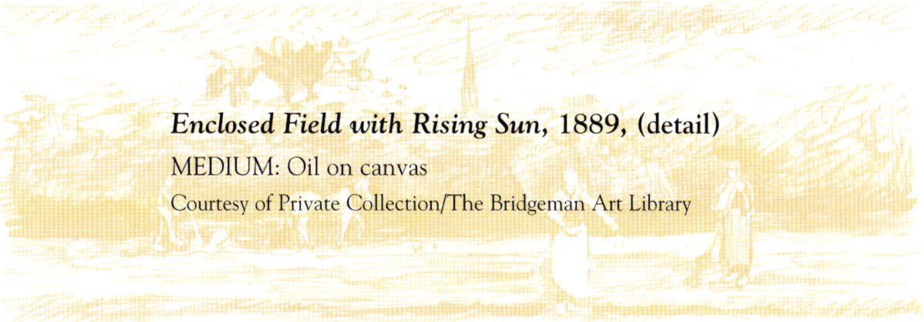

***Enclosed Field with Rising Sun*, 1889, (detail)**
MEDIUM: Oil on canvas
Courtesy of Private Collection/The Bridgeman Art Library

After Vincent's death she and Theo discussed the possibility of having the letters published. Respect for Vincent's art and his stature as a painter had grown after his death and his paintings were requested for exhibitions. The couple spoke to artist friends and to art critics such as Albert Aurier on the subject of publication, but Theo had become too ill to take the plan forward. His death in January 1891 stopped discussions. Jo moved to Bussum in Holland and devoted her time to publicizing Vincent's work. The seventh Salon des Indépendants in 1891 featured a small retrospective, and an exhibition at the Panorama Gallery, Amsterdam in 1892 included over 100 of Vincent's canvases.

Johanna van Gogh-Bonger annotated the letters. Between 1883 and 1894 Émile Bernard published extracts from Vincent's letters in *Mercure de France*. Some were published in magazines and journals in Europe. She arranged for the letters to be published in a three-volume work in 1914, 24 years after Vincent's suicide. The work was dedicated to 'the memory of Vincent and Theo', with a quotation from the Bible, 2 Samuel 1:23: 'And in their death they were not divided.' Questioned why she had waited so long to publish, she replied that her aim was to have the art of Vincent van Gogh known before the knowledge of his life. The letters were first published in the language they were written, predominantly Dutch and French. Publishing Vincent van Gogh's letters brought him to the attention of a wider audience beyond the art world, and they have been published in many languages. It is through the letters that one meets the man who painted such extraordinary works and lived such an extraordinary life.

Further Reading

Bakker, N., *The Real Van Gogh: The Artist and His Letters*, Royal Academy of Arts, 2010

Brodskaïa, N., *Post-Impressionism*, Parkstone Press, 2010

Cogeval, G. and Patry, S., *Masterpieces from Paris: Van Gogh, Gauguin, Cézanne & beyond: Post-Impressionism from The Musée D'Orsay*, The National Gallery of Australia, 2010

Druick, D.W. and Zegers, P.K., *Van Gogh and Gauguin: The Studio of the South*, Thames & Hudson, 2001

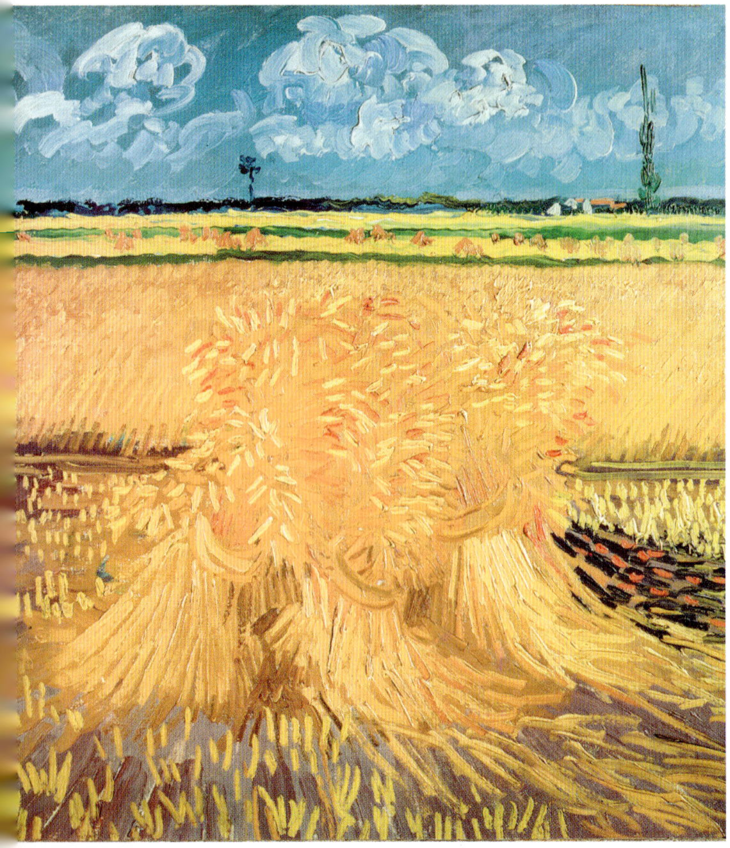

Gayford, M., *The Yellow House: Van Gogh, Gauguin, and Nine Turbulent Weeks in Arles*, Penguin, 2007

Howard, M., *Van Gogh*, Lorenz Books, 2010

Ives, C. and Stein, S. A. and Van Heugten, S., and Vellekoop, Marije., *Vincent Van Gogh: The Drawings*, Yale University Press, 2005

Jansen, L. and Luijten, H. and Bakker, N., *Vincent Van Gogh – The Letters: The Complete Illustrated and Annotated Edition*, Thames and Hudson, 2009

Kuhl, I., *Vincent van Gogh*, Prestel, 2009

Lubin, A. J., *Stranger on the Earth: A Psychological Biography of Vincent van Gogh*, Da Capo Press, 1996

McQuillan, M., *Van Gogh*, Thames & Hudson, 1989

Metzger, R., and Walther, I. F., *Van Gogh: 1853–1890*, Taschen, 2008

Metzger, R. and Walther, I. F., *Van Gogh: The Complete Paintings (25)*, Taschen, 2010

Naifeh, S., and Smith, G. W., *Vincent Van Gogh, The Life*, Profile Books, 2011

Schama, S., *The Power of Art*, Bodley Head, 2009

Sund, J., *Van Gogh (Art & Ideas)*, Phaidon Press Ltd, 2002

Thomson, B., *Van Gogh Paintings: The Masterpieces*, Thames and Hudson, 2007

Thomson, Richard., *Vincent Van Gogh: The Starry Night*, The Museum of Modern Art, 2008

Uhde, W., *Van Gogh*, Phaidon Press Ltd, 1992

Van Gogh, V., *The Complete Letters of Vincent Van Gogh*, Thames & Hudson, 1979

Van Gogh, V., *Vincent Van Gogh – The Complete Paintings*, Taschen, 1993

Van Gogh, V., and Pomerans, A., *The Letters of Vincent Van Gogh*, Penguin, 2003

Van Gogh, V., Stone, I., and Stone, J., *Dear Theo: The Autobiography of Vincent van Gogh*, New American Library, 1995

Van der Veen, Wouter., *Van Gogh in Auvers: His Last Days*, Monacelli Press, 2010

Van Huegten, S., and Pissarro, J., *Van Gogh and the Colours of the Night*, The Museum of Modern Art, 2008

Van Heugten, S. and Vellekoop, M., *Van Gogh: The Master Draughtsman*, Thames and Hudson, 2005

Wallace, C., *Leaving Van Gogh*, Spiegel & Grau, 2011

Walther, I. F., *Vincent Van Gogh*, Taschen 1992

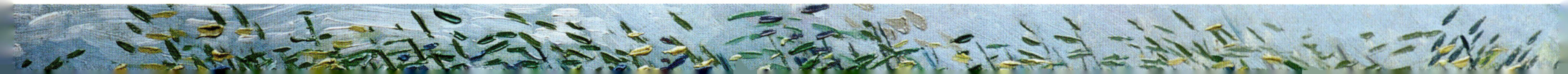

Index

Page references in *italics* refer to illustrations. Page ranges connected by hyphens take no account of intervening illustrations.

Works by Van Gogh are listed separately by title. Works by other artists are listed under the artist's name.

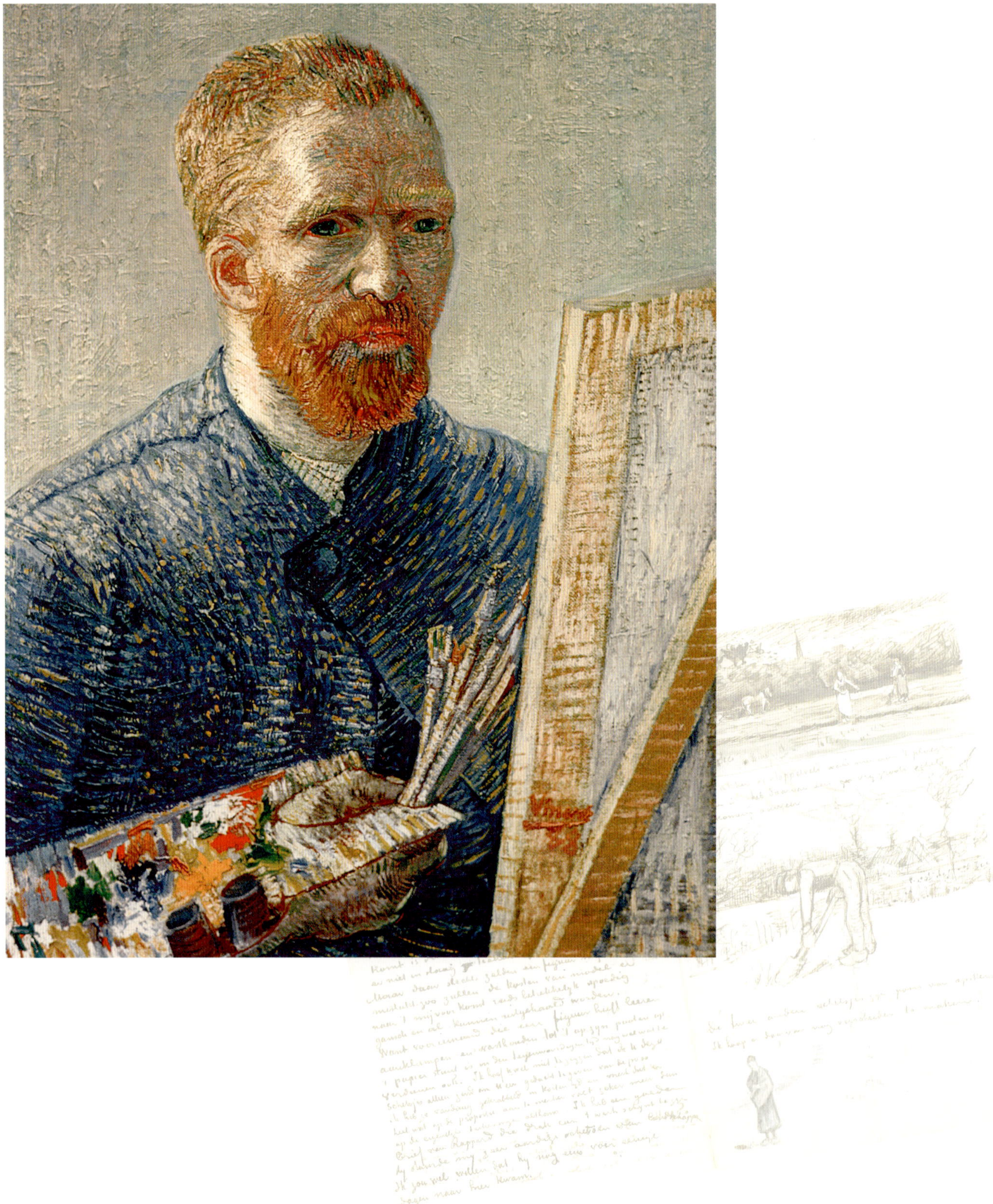